collectables

collectables

MADELEINE MARSH *GENERAL EDITOR*

2001/2
VOLUME XIII

MILLER'S COLLECTABLES PRICE GUIDE 2001/2

Created and designed by
Miller's
The Cellars, High Street
Tenterden, Kent, TN30 6BN
Tel: 01580 766411
Fax: 01580 766100

General Editor: Madeleine Marsh
Production Co-ordinator: Kari Reeves
Editorial Co-ordinator: Carol Gillings
Editorial Assistants: Rosemary Cooke, Lalage Johnstone, Frankie Leibe
Production Assistants: Caroline Bugeja, Elaine Burrell, Gillian Charles, Ethne Tragett
Advertising Executive: Jill Jackson
Advertising Co-ordinator & Administrator: Melinda Williams
Advertising Assistant: Jo Hill
Designer: Philip Hannath
Advertisement Designer: Simon Cook
Indexer: Hilary Bird
Jacket Design: Colin Goody
Production: Jessame Emms
Additional Photographers: Ian Booth, Dennis O'Reilly, Robin Saker
North American Consultants: Marilynn and Sheila Brass

First published in Great Britain in 2001
by Miller's, a division of Mitchell Beazley,
imprints of Octopus Publishing Group Ltd,
2–4 Heron Quays, London E14 4JP

© 2001 Octopus Publishing Group Ltd

A CIP catalogue record for this book is
available from the British Library

ISBN 1-84000-386-3

Illustrations by CK Litho, Whitstable, Kent
Colour origination by Pica Colour Separation Overseas Pte Ltd, Singapore
Printed and bound by Rotolito Lombarda, Italy

From left: A beaded scenic string bag, some damage, c1820–30, 9in (23cm) high. **£60–70 JPr**
A Kodak Brownie Reflex camera, in original box, c1942–52, 5in (12.5cm) high. **£20–25 BSA**
A Whitefriars Drunken Bricklayer glass vase, 1960s, 8in (20.5cm) high. **£100–120 PrB**
A Gaudy Welsh jug, decorated with oyster pattern No. 37, 1820–90, 4½in (11.5cm) high. **£90–100 CoHA**

How To Use This Book

I t is our aim to make this guide easy to use. In order to find a particular item, turn to the contents list on page 7 to find the main heading, for example, Books. Having located your area of interest, you will see that larger sections have been sub-divided by subject or maker. If you are looking for a particular factory, maker, or object, consult the index, which starts on page 486.

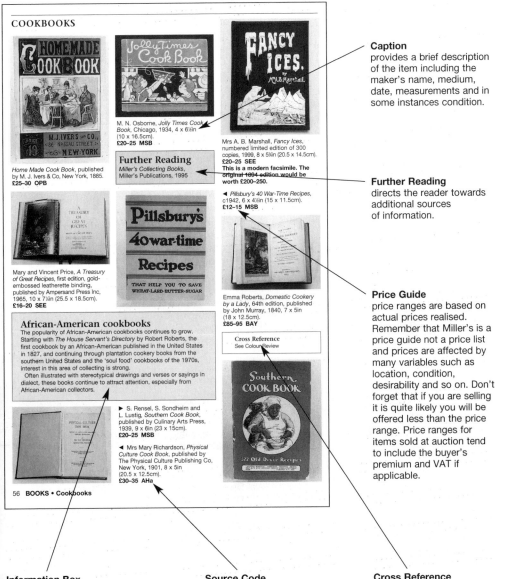

Caption
provides a brief description of the item including the maker's name, medium, date, measurements and in some instances condition.

Further Reading
directs the reader towards additional sources of information.

Price Guide
price ranges are based on actual prices realised. Remember that Miller's is a price guide not a price list and prices are affected by many variables such as location, condition, desirability and so on. Don't forget that if you are selling it is quite likely you will be offered less than the price range. Price ranges for items sold at auction tend to include the buyer's premium and VAT if applicable.

Information Box
covers relevant collecting information on factories, makers, care, restoration, fakes and alterations.

Source Code
refers to the 'Key to Illustrations' on page 476 that details where the item was photographed.

Cross Reference
directs the reader to where other related items may be found.

5

Acknowledgements

We would like to acknowledge the great assistance given by our consultants who are listed below. We would also like to extend our thanks to all the auction houses, their press offices, dealers and collectors who have assisted us in the production of this book.

ALAN BLAKEMAN
BBR Elsecar Heritage Centre
Wath Road, Elsecar, Barnsley
Yorks S74 8AF
(Advertising, Packaging, Bottles, Breweriana)

DAVID HUXTABLE
S03/05 Alfies Antique Market
13–25 Church Street
London NW8 8DT
(Advertising Tins)

ANTIQUE AMUSEMENT CO
Mill Lane, Swaffham
Bulbeck, Cambridge CB5 0NF
(Amusement & Slot Machines)

DOMINIC WINTER
The Old School
Maxwell Street, Swindon
Wiltshire SN1 5DR
(Books)

MARILYNN & SHEILA BRASS
PO Box 380503
Cambridge
USA MA 02238-0503
(Cookery)

BEVERLEY/BETH
30 Church Street
Alfie's Antique Market
Marylebone
London NW8 8EP
(Ceramics)

KEITH MARTIN
St Clere Carlton Ware
PO Box 161
Sevenoaks
Kent TN15 6GA
(Carlton Ware)

MALCOLM PHILLIPS
Comic Book Postal Auctions
40–42 Osnaburgh Street
London NW1 3ND
(Comics)

ANDREW HILTON
Special Auction Services
The Coach House, Midgham Park
Reading, Berks RG7 5UG
(Commemorative Ware)

MARTIN PACKER
41 Lyall Gardens, Birmingham
West Midlands B45 9YW
(Festival of Britain)

JIM BULLOCK
Romsey Medal Centre
5 Bell Street, Romsey
Hants SO51 8GY
(Military Medals)

PAUL MULVEY
Ink Quest
GO58 Alfies Antique Market
13–25 Church Street
London NW8 8DT
(Photographs)

KEN LAWSON
Specialized Postcard Auctions
25 Gloucester Street
Cirencester GL7 2DJ
(Postcards)

ALVIN ROSS
Oxfordshire
(Puppets)

MAUREEN SILVERMAN
Planet Bazaar, 149 Drummond Street
London NW1 2PB
(Sixties & Seventies)

DR D. DOWSON
Old Tackle Box, PO Box 55
Cranbrook, Kent TN17 3ZU
(Fishing Tackle)

GAVIN PAYNE
The Old Granary
Battlebridge Antique Centre
Nr Wickford, Essex SS11 7RF
(Telephones)

Contents

Introduction

As we at Miller's know, collecting is above all about passion. How far the most passionate collectors will go, and how much they will spend, is demonstrated by our new Record Breakers section (p. 461), devoted to collectables that have achieved world record prices at auction. These range from an empty wine bottle to a locomotive nameplate, and what is remarkable about these items is not only their value, but the fact that they were created as functional objects designed to fulfil a practical purpose and not as precious works of art.

The same is true of many collectables shown throughout this guide, from Advertising and Packaging to Writing. Take the example of Science and Technology – what would the original user of the 1930s amputation set (p. 370) think to see the grim tools of his medical trade transformed into a decorative antique? Perhaps he would need a quick swig of rescue remedy from the 19th century homeopathic medicine chest illustrated on the same page! The most surprising and certainly the most valuable item in the Science section, however, is an American construction of tubes and wires that looks as though it might have been pulled from a skip but is, in fact, a piece from ENIAC, the world's first digital computer; hence its price range of £45,000-50,000.

It's not always immediately obvious what makes an object collectable, unless of course you are in the know. To most of us the *1973 Rupert Annual* shown on p. 461, might appear virtually indistinguishable from the thousands of other Rupert annuals produced that year, though it is in fact one of only 12 whose cover shows Rupert with a brown face, which is why it fetched a record-breaking £18,315 at auction. Even the most recent books can be surprisingly valuable. How much do you think a first edition of J. K. Rowling's *Harry Potter and the Philosopher's Stone* might be worth? Turn the pages of our Books section and prepare to be amazed by some wizard prices.

Many of the objects in this book started life as children's playthings. This year we include Scandinavian trolls, Japanese robots, American children's lunch boxes – hot collectables in the United States – and comics. If your tastes run to more adult pursuits, take a peep at our Erotica section and turn to Textiles for a brief history of the swimsuit. Before you go to the bottle bank, open our feature on bottles, and don't replace the contents of your kitchen until you've read our sections on cookery books and kitchenware. Demand in these areas has been fuelled by the effect of TV chefs and a growing interest in food and drink, and collectables are undoubtedly influenced by fashion. Our current fascination with celebrity is reflected in a booming autographs market and this year's Guide includes the signatures of personalities ranging from Charles Dickens to Elvis Presley to Posh and Becks. We look at collectable cats and desirable dogs, check out vintage sewing machines and, whilst some might describe the Millennium Dome as an all too forgettable experience, we remember the Festival of Britain on its 50th birthday.

Objects shown come from across the world, with items from Europe, the United States and also for the first time, sections devoted to Scandinavian and Welsh collectables. Items span hundreds of years, dating from before Christ right up to Collectables of the Future. Prices range from thousands of pounds to under a fiver and cover every possible subject. In what other book could you find collectable shoe trees, vintage tattooing equipment and surely one of the most bizarre pieces of jewellery ever created - a pair of 19th century cufflinks, depicting a man receiving an enema?

Miller's Collectables Price Guide captures collecting in all its infinite variety, and our thanks to the collectors, dealers and auctioneers who make this book possible, and who share their passions with us. Britain is one of the leading centres for antiques and collectables in the world, which is why Miller's, in association with BBC *Homes and Antiques* magazine, has launched BACA – the annual British Antiques and Collectables Awards, to recognise excellence across the industry, and to celebrate the joy and excitement of collecting. Miller's Club members are invited to nominate candidates for every category. If you are not already a Club member, please contact us for details. Also, if you have an interesting collection yourself, or there are subjects you would like to see covered in this guide, do let us know. We are always delighted to receive your suggestions.

We look forward to hearing from you and, as ever, Happy Hunting!

Advertising & Packaging

◀ A white pottery jar, 'Indian Chutnee', c1855, 5in (12.5cm) high.
£20–25 SAS

▶ A Bryant & May matchbox, with contents, decorated in orange and white on a grey ground, c1880, 3½ x 1in (9 x 2.5cm).
£25–30 MURR

A Lorimer & Co Areca Nut Tooth Paste lid, transfer-printed with a mosque and palm trees, slight damage, late 19thC, 4¼in (11cm) diam.
£600–700 BBR
This is a rare lid both because of its unusually large size and the quality of the detailed and well-struck black transfer. High prices in the pot lid field have resulted in a sudden upsurge in fake pot lids. According to specialist auctioneers BBR, danger signs to look out for include a strong, very even, overall black transfer, a slightly creamy body colour, light weight, or incorrect crazing.

A Jacob & Co's Cream Crackers advertisement, depicting a milkmaid carrying a pail of milk and a stool, on a blue ground, framed, late 19thC, 21in (53.5cm) square.
£180–200 BBR

A Jacob & Co's Cream Crackers showcard, decorated in colours with a girl holding a tin of biscuits, framed, late 19thC, 24½ x 19½in (62 x 48.5cm).
£250–280 BBR

A James' Starch advertisement, decorated in colours on a pale blue ground, framed, late 19thC, 24¾ x 19in (63 x 48.5cm).
£160–180 BBR

▶ An Oakey's Knife Polish show-card, decorated in red and pastel colours on a pale cream ground, c1900, 18 x 12in (45.5 x 30.5cm).
£125–140 MURR

A Hudson's Dry Soap advertisement, decorated in colours with a coaching scene, framed, c1900, 9½in x 21in (24 x 53.5cm).
£90–100 BBR

A Jones's Food Warmer, ceramic, c1900, 6in (15cm) high.
£60–75 MURR

A Poulton & Noels shop counter porcelain ox tongue press, c1900, 9in (23cm) high.
£200–240 SMI

▶ A Hayden's tooth powder pot lid, in the form of an Egyptian mummy, with pale matt green glaze, early 20thC, 5½in (14cm) long.
£220–250 BBR

A Cadbury's Chocolate wooden advertising chest of drawers, modelled as a bookcase, early 20thC, 12in (30.5cm) high.
£60–70 AnS

A Zam-Buk cut-out stand-up card advertisement, decorated in red, blue, green and white, early 20thC, 20in (51cm) high.
£35–40 BBR

A Royal Doulton Golden Fleece Margarine slab, early 20thC, 15in (38cm) long.
£180–200 SMI

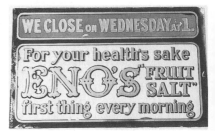

A Eno's Fruit Salt shop door glass plaque, decorated in gold on a white and blue ground, c1910, 6 x 10in (15 x 25.5cm).
£35–40 FA

A Betty Ladies' Fancy Garters cut-out stand-up card advertisement, decorated in various colours with a young woman showing her garters and stockings, 1920s, 13½ x 9in (34.5 x 23cm).
£130–140 BBR

A Swift's Corned Beef display plate, 1920s, 17in (43cm) long.
£140–150 SMI

◀ A 'Tubby Trex' advertising model, 1910–20, 16in (40.5cm) high.
£300–350 MFB

◀ A Bovril shop display board, 'To-Day's Prices', 1920s, 30 x 15in (76 x 38cm).
£50–60 SMI

▶ A Smith's Crisps shop front glass display container, c1920, 10in (25.5cm) high.
£25–30 FA

A Cadbury's chocolate box, depicting a lady with brown hair wearing a red and blue hat, c1920, 4in (10cm) long.
£12–15 YR

A Marsh's Sausage ceramic display tray, 1920s, 16in (40.5cm) wide.
£250–300 SMI

▶ A Palethorpes' Sausages cardboard box, c1930, 11in (28cm) wide.
£25–30 FA

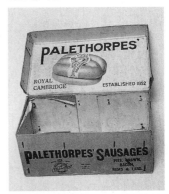

A Jacob & Co's Biscuits wooden cabinet, fitted with three long glass-fronted compartments, with marble top, 1920–30, 64in (162.5) high.
£600–700 BBR

A Wheatley's 'Stym' showcard, depicting a lion on a rock, framed, 1930s, 19 x 15in (48.5 x 38cm).
£60–70 BBR

◀ A Phillips Stick-A-Soles And Heels plastic advertising figure, 1930s, 12in (30.5cm) high.
£140–160 HUX

A J. C. & J. Field's box of candles, in pale blue and white on a dark blue ground, 1930s, 14in (35.5cm) long.
£8–10 CRN

A pair of Chocolate Wafer glass display jars, with ceramic bases, 1930s, 8in (20.5cm) high.
£180–200 each SMI

A Warlock Rich Dark Flake stand-up tobacco sign, in yellow, red and blue on a beige ground, 1930s, 10 x 8in (25.5 x 20.5cm).
£38–45 MURR

A Comptons' Gravy Salt showcard, decorated in colours on a red ground, 1930s, 14½ x 9½in (37 x 24cm).
£70–80 BBR

▶ A Wright's Biscuits tin tray, decorated in colours on a dark blue ground, 1930–40s, 16in (40.5cm) wide.
£10–12 BBR

◀ Three Graham Farish Snap Vacuum Closures boxes, containing metal clamps, lids and rubber rings, 1930–40s, 5in (12.5cm) high.
£3–5 BBR

A Marten Model resin bust, 1930–40, 16in (40.5cm) high.
£160–190 RUL

An Exide Drydex Bell Cell battery, in green, white and black on a beige ground, 1930s, 6in (15cm) high.
£3–5 YR

A pair of Drummer Dyes 'Jiffy' Dyes, 1930–50, 5in (12.5cm) wide.
£5–7 each YR

> **Cross Reference**
> See Colour Review

▶ An Insular Electric Lamp Works light bulb, in navy blue and white on an orange ground, 1940s, 6in (15cm) high.
£5–7 YR

A box of Andrew Austin 'Wash Easy' soap powder, 1942, 5in (12.5cm) long.
£5–7 YR

A Fischer photo light bulb, 1950s, 6in (15cm) high.
£8–10 RTT

12 **ADVERTISING & PACKAGING**

A Thunderbirds Bubblegum with picture card, 1965,
2 x 3in (5 x 7.5cm).
£12–15 YR

A Kellogg's Rice Krispies packet, decorated in colours, 1959, 10in (25.5cm) high.
£45–50 YR

A Standard Oil metal Rain Gauge, in red and blue on a white ground, 1960, 5in (12.5cm) high.
£20–25 RTW

▶ Three Standard Fireworks posters and a box, printed in colours, 1970–80, posters 53½in (135.9cm) high.
£45–50 BBR

COCA-COLA

The famous Coca-Cola formula was invented by Atlanta Pharmacist Dr John Pemberton in 1886. Mixed with still water, the brown syrup was initially marketed as a patent medicine and temperance beverage. With the addition of carbonated water the following year, and the rise of the soda fountain at the turn of the century, Coca-Cola soon became a favourite soft drink.

By 1910 sales had reached 11,500 gallons a day and the company was spending $850,000 a year on advertising. As more competitors entered the cola market, branding became increasingly important. From 1915 Coca-Cola began to use a standardized bottle, and in the 1920s adopted the 'hobble skirt' bottle, its fluted body named after a contemporary dress fashion. Coolers and vending machines were introduced into shops, and promotional material ranged from trays to calendars.

In the 1930s Hollywood stars promoted Coca-Cola. The nick-name Coke was first used in advertisements in 1941, and with the 1950s came the flat top can – originally designed for US servicemen overseas, and the development of television advertising. The Coke bottle was trademarked in 1960. Interest in collecting Coca-Cola memorabilia took off in the 1970s.

Today in the USA there are museums and collectors clubs, and a vast range of material for collectors to chose from. But buyer beware, many vintage items have been reproduced, so make sure that your purchase is, as the Coke slogan says, 'The Real Thing'.

A Coca-Cola enamel advertising sign, cream and white on a green and red ground, 1933, 56 x 95in (142 x 241.5cm).
£600–650 TRA

Two Coca-Cola magazine advertisements, decorated in colours, 1935, 7 x 10in (18 x 25.5cm).
£5–8 each RTT

A Coca-Cola syrup brown cardboard container box, with red and white logos, 1950s, 15in (38cm) square.
£20–25 TRA

◀ A Coca-Cola badge, with a red ground, 1960, 1in (2.5cm) diam.
£4–6 RTT

A German Coca-Cola bottle opener, 1950–60, 3in (7.5cm) high.
£10–12 RTT

A Coca-Cola wooden box, the red ground with white logo, 1960s, 18in (45.5cm) long.
£12–15 TRA

A Canadian Coca-Cola wooden box, 1960s, 18in (45.5cm) long.
£24–28 TRA

A Canadian Coca-Cola enamel sign, the red ground with yellow and white logo, 1960s, 49in (124.5cm) diam.
£275–325 TRA

A Pepsi-Cola can, with red, white and blue logo on a pale blue and white ground, mid-1960s, 5in (12.5cm) high.
£12–15 YR

◀ A Coca-Cola competition Gold Award Russell yoyo, 1970, 2¼in (5.5cm) diam.
£15–20 YO

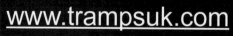

A Coca-Cola ice pick and bottle opener, c1970, 10in (25.5cm) long.
£18–20 HUX

ENAMEL SIGNS

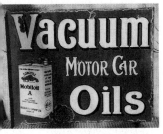

A Vacuum Motor Car Oils double-sided enamel sign, decorated in white and black on a red ground, c1912, 24in (61cm) wide.
£260–300 MURR

A Board of Agriculture and Fisheries enamel sign, in blue, gold and red on a white ground, 1915, 14in (35.5cm) high.
£65–80 WAB

◀ A Redfern enamel sign, in blue on a yellow ground, 1920s, 20 x 30in (51 x 76cm).
£170–200 JUN

A Hudson's Soap enamel sign, in green, black and white on an orange ground, 1920s, 24 x 36in (61 x 91.5cm).
£35–40 BBR

A Morris-Commercial Authorised Dealer enamel sign, in yellow and white on a blue ground, c1925, 29in (73.5cm) wide.
£375–425 JUN

A Carters Tested Seeds enamel sign, decorated with blue, orange and red Sweet Peas, 1930s, 29½ x 19½in (75 x 49.5cm).
£650–720 BBR

A Flying Service sign, in white and black on a red ground, 1940s, 72¾in (185cm) diam.
£650–750 TRA

Miller's is a price GUIDE not a price LIST

Two enamelled shop display signs, in blue and red on a yellow ground, c1930, 7in (18cm) wide.
£30–35 each SMI

ROBERTSON'S GOLLIES

In 1864 James Robertson, a former textile worker, opened a grocery shop in Paisley, Scotland. When bitter oranges proved a slow seller his wife, Marion, made them into marmalade in the family kitchen. The preserve was an instant hit, and before long the Robertsons had founded their own factory.

Marion is credited with inventing the name Golden Shred; the lemon marmalade was called Silver Shred. Printed stoneware containers were gradually replaced by glass jars and paper labels, and in 1914 a Robertson's executive,

visiting the USA, came across the golly. The black-faced golly was the hero of a series of books, written and illustrated in the 1890s by the American sisters Florence K. and Bertha Upton, and had become a popular children's character. Robertson's adopted the Golly as their trademark. From 1928 paper Gollies were stuck to jars, launching a host of Golly collectables in every medium. Today these are sought-after by collectors of black memorabilia as well as advertising and packaging enthusiasts. (*see* Books section pages 74–75).

A Robertson's Jig-saw Puzzle, decorated in colours with a village scene, 1940–50, 6 x 10in (15 x 25.5cm).
£25–30 MURR

Two Robertson's cut-out card Golly figures, one holding a jar of jam, decorated in colours, 1950s, 9in (23cm) high.
£40–45 BBR

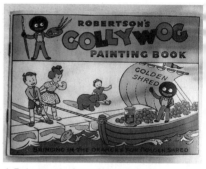

A Robertson's Golly Painting Book, decorated in orange, yellow, red, blue and black on a white ground, 1950s, 5 x 7in (12.5 x 18cm).
£25–30 MURR

► A Robertson's Golliberry Seedless Bramble jam jar, 1960s, 5in (12.5cm) high.
£3–5 YR

A Robertson's cut-out stand-up card Golly figure, decorated in colours, 1950s, 28in (71cm) high, with a Robertson's Christmas Hamper cardboard box.
£20–22 BBR

► A set of Golly figures of musicians, comprising a double bass, clarinet, drummer and two trumpet players, decorated in colours, 1970s, 3in (7.5cm) high.
£25–30 BBR

◄ A Robertson's Golly children's chair, with blue and yellow seat, 1960s, 10½in (26.5cm) high.
£65–75 BBR
This chair originally cost 19/6d, just under £1.

A Robertson's Golly collection, including two plastic Golly glove puppets, in orange, yellow and blue, 1980s, with two Robertson's Mincemeat recipes.
£3–5 BBR

TINS

The golden age of the British tin was from the 1860s–1930s. Shaped or novelty tins tend to command the highest prices. Commemorative tins (eg Royal events, Boer War) are also very collectable, as are tins with fine decoration. As good early examples become increasingly expensive, so interest is growing in post-WWII tins.

Condition is all-important when assessing value. Tins should not be battered, dented or rusted – check the hinges and the interior. Tins must be kept out of the sunlight to avoid fading and away from damp or steamy atmospheres, such as those found in the kitchen or bathroom. Shaped or novelty tins often bear the manufacturer's mark on the base, so check the bottom of containers.

Though Huntley & Palmer's are probably the most famous name in the biscuit field, there are many other companies who produced fine and decorative tins. These include, amongst others: Macfarlane Lang & Co, Jacob's, Peek Freans, Crawford of Edinburgh, Carr's of Carlisle, and in the field of confectionery: Rowntree's, Fry's and Sharps.

Tins can vary in size from large shop containers to miniatures designed either as travelling samples or Christmas stocking novelties. Each genre has its collectors.

A pair of unbranded tea tins, decorated with 'V R' and coat-of-arms in yellow on a brown ground, with red and green braiding and seals, c1890, 6in (15cm) high.
£45–50 each WAB

A Keen Robinson mustard tin, depicting Ali Baba and the 40 Thieves, decorated in colours on a pale green ground, 1890, 7in (18cm) high.
£120–150 WAB

A Brother's mustard tin, decorated with sporting scenes in black on a yellow ground, 1890s, 6in (15cm) high.
£150–180 MURR

◄ A Macfarlane Lang biscuit tin, with mirror lid, decorated with a geometric pattern in black on a yellow ground, 1900, 6in (15cm) diam.
£85–100 WAB
This was the first tin to include a mirror.

◄ A McVitie & Price tin, depicting Victoria Cross heroes, in colours on a cream ground, 1897, 5in (12.5cm) high.
£275–325 WAB

A CWS biscuit tin, decorated in colours with a Venetian scene, c1900, 6in (15cm) wide.
£70–85 WAB

A Stollwerck's Indian Pearls sweets tin, decorated in blue, orange and fawn on a white ground, German, c1900, 3in (7.5cm) high.
£20–25 RTT

A Moore Bros Teas sample tin, decorated in blue, yellow and green on a cream ground, c1900, 3in (7.5cm) wide.
£150–180 MURR

A Dalu-Kola Tea sample tin, decorated in red, green and black on a yellow ground, c1900, 1½in (4cm) wide.
£60–75 MURR

A Huntley & Palmers biscuit tin, modelled as a set of books, in brown, cream, red and green, 1903, 7in (18cm) wide.
£250–300 WAB
Many tins were designed to have a *trompe l'oeil* effect and these book tins, produced by Huntley & Palmers, were a best seller at the turn of the century. Several versions of this tin were manufactured. Spines often bear the titles of popular novels of the day, from Dicken's *Oliver Twist* to Wilkie Collin's *Moonstone*, providing a tinplate survey of middle class Edwardian reading habits.

A Huntley & Palmers purse-shaped tin, in beige simulated leather, base printed 'Huntley & Palmers Biscuits Reading & London England', early 20thC, 5½in (14cm) wide.
£12–15 BBR

A Chadwell biscuit tin, decorated with small boys, in red and green on a cream ground, with brown lid, c1920, 9in (23cm) square.
£42–50 WAB

Further reading

Miller's Advertising Tins: A Collectors Guide, Miller's Publications, 1999

A tin string box, decorated in brown and cream, with two balls of string, c1910, 7in (18cm) wide.
£25–30 WAB

A tin, the lid decorated with a dice game, in pastel colours, early 20thC, 4¾in (12cm) wide.
£1–2 BBR

An Alex Parsons Indian Cerate ointment tin, decorated with a Native American smoking a pipe, in yellow, red and green on a deep blue ground, c1920, 2in (5cm) diam.
£35–40 YR

A McVitie & Price tin, modelled as a chest of drawers, c1920, 7in (18cm) wide.
£130–160 WAB

A toffee tin, decorated with Pip, Squeak and Wilfred as musicians, in orange, red, black and cream, 1920s, 6in (15cm) diam.
£35–40 YR

A Macfarlane, Lang & Co Granola Digestive Biscuits tin, decorated in red, green and yellow on a blue ground, c1930, 12in (30.5cm) high.
£35–40 RTT

► A Tate 2lb Golden Syrup tin, 1940s, 4in (10cm) high.
£5–7 YR

A Gry-Moff cleaner tin, in blue, white and cream on a yellow ground, c1930, 6in (15cm) high.
£10–12 RTT

◄ A Jacob's 'Royal Windsor' biscuit tin, commemorating the coronation of Queen Elizabeth II, in full colour, 1953, 6in (15cm) wide.
£12–15 WAB

► A Compactoid Girl Guide's First Aid Case, decorated in red and white on a blue ground, c1930, 4in (10cm) wide.
£30–35 MURR

An Oxo postbox money box, commemorating the coronation of King George VI, decorated in gold on a crimson ground, 1936, 3in (7.5cm) high.
£20–25 WAB

A Brown & Polson's Custard Powder tin, decorated in blue, pink and black on a yellow ground, late 1940s, 4in (10cm) high.
£12–15 YR

A Cadbury's Smash Giant Size tin, 1970s, 5in (12.5cm) high.
£5–7 YR

A Peek, Frean & Co biscuit tin, depicting the Cambridge colleges, in various colours on a pale blue ground, c1960, 8in (20.5cm) diam.
£20–25 WAB

Aeronautica

A balloonists medal, 1878,
2in (5cm) diam.
£100–120 COB

A brass ash tray, depicting
a Zeppelin airship, c1910,
8in (20.5cm) wide.
£120–140 COB

An aluminium matchbox holder,
c1917, 1½in (4cm) wide.
£45–55 MURR

A De Havilland DH9 bomber
four-blade propeller, 1917,
106in (269cm) diam.
£1,600–2,000 CYA

A cardboard poster, advertising
a book on Zeppelins and
Super-Zeppelins, c1919,
10 x 14in (25.5 x 35.5cm).
£80–100 COB

A KLM Royal Dutch Air Lines
poster, 1930, 39 x 24in (99 x 61cm).
£300–350 COB

A Brooklands Flying Club German
silver shield-shaped badge,
by S. Spencer, decorated with red
enamel, 1920s, 4¾in (12cm) high.
£1,500–1,750 CARS

A framed wooden jigsaw puzzle,
depicting a Schneider Trophy
seaplane and Southampton Docks,
1931, 10 x 15in (25.5 x 38cm).
£65–80 COB

A Brazilian Zeppelin airship postal
envelope, 1932, 6in (15cm) wide.
£42–50 COB

A part of a compass from a
crashed Spitfire, 1940s.
£40–50 COB

An American wooden propeller
blade, 1930s, 72in (183cm) long.
£340–400 JUN

◀ A Spitfire aircraft wheel and tyre, 1940s, 28in (71cm) diam.
£100–120 TRA

▶ An aircraft instrument panel, 1950s, 20in (51cm) wide.
£240–280 TRA

An Air Ministry book *Silhouettes of German Aircraft*, 1940s, 7in (18cm) high.
£55–65 COB

A BEA airline ticket, 1959, 8in (20.5cm) wide.
£8–10 COB

A BOAC cup and saucer, 1950, saucer 5in (12.5cm) diam.
£16–20 HUX

A Frog Supermarine S.6B Schneider Trophy seaplane plastic construction kit, 1/72 scale, 1960s, box 7in (18cm) wide.
£12–15 COB

A BEA blue ceramic ashtray, inscribed in gold, 1960s, 5in (12.5cm) square.
£20–25 COB

A Cathay Pacific officer's cap, 1960s.
£25–30 COB

Condition

Condition is absolutely vital when assessing the value of a collectable. Damaged objects on the whole appreciate much less than perfect examples. However a rare desirable piece may command a high price even when damaged.

A pair of black BOAC in-flight socks, c1965.
£16–20 HUX

A metal half-propeller blade, 1970s, 37in (94cm) long.
£60–70 TRA

Amusement & Slot Machines

► A J. Mason & Co Medical Battery slot machine, c1890, 12in (30.5cm) wide.
£1,800–2,200 HAK

A Victorian Mechanical Trading Co bronzed cast-iron 'Test your Grip', 19in (48.5cm) high.
£1,000–1,200 CAm

► A Fair-O-Graph coin-operated stereoscopic viewer, with electric motor, coin mechanism and cast viewing hood, in oak case with marquee, c1900, 19½in (49.5cm) wide.
£500–600 SK(B)

An Imperial cast-iron electric shock machine, with the slogan 'Electricity Is Life', c1900, 20in (51cm) high.
£700–800 CAm

A J. Mason & Co automatic Medical Electric machine, c1895, 54in (137cm) high.
£2,000–2,500 HAK

An Allwin gaming machine, with coin mechanism, in painted wooden case, c1900, 24in (61cm) high. **£200–240 SK(B)**

A Caille Commercial double gaming machine, 1920s, 26in (66cm) high. **£1,000–1,200 CAm**

A cast-iron grip tester, painted in red and gold, c1910, 59in (150cm) high. **£600–700 CAm**

▶ A Handni wall-mounted ball bearing game, 1917, 24in (61cm) high. **£400–480 CAm**

◀ A German Waren Automat Art Nouveau-style chocolate vending machine, c1910, 36¼in (92cm) high. **£2,000–2,400 KOLN Besides the chocolate, this machine awards every fifth user a prize, such as a cigarette lighter, a pair of scissors, a knife and fork or a brush. Every second user receives a certificate for a variety of merchandise.**

A German chocolate vending machine, with a cast-iron hen on an embossed tin nest, c1920, 22¾in (58cm) high.
£2,500–2,750 KOLN

A Samson Fivewin ball game machine, 1920s, 26in (66cm) high.
£500–550 JUN

◄ An Allwin ball game machine, in painted wooden case, c1930, 25in (63.5cm) high.
£140–160 SK(B)

► A Jennings Sun Chief one-armed bandit gaming machine, c1950, 28in (71cm) high.
£500–600 CAm

A Mills Horsehead Bonus one-armed bandit gaming machine, restored, 1937, 26in (66cm) high.
£600–750 AMc

◄ An American postage stamp vending machine, 1960s, 15in (38cm) high.
£30–35 TRA

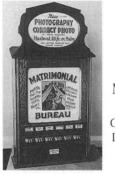

Antiquities

An Aegean marble chalice, with stem and foot, late 2nd millennium BC, 3½in (9cm) high.
£500–600 HEL

An Egyptian granite stele, inscribed with various figures and hieroglyphs, New Kingdom, XIXth–XXth Dynasty, 14th–11th century BC, 10in (25.5cm) wide.
£2,500–3,000 HEL

◄ A faïence ushabti fragment depicting Princess Mehit-En-Weshet, 3rd Intermediate Period, 11th–10th century BC, 3½in (9cm) high.
£1,000–1,200 HEL

Three Egyptian ushabti fragments, 6th–4th century BC, tallest 4in (10cm) high.
£40–50 each HEL

► Two Scottish carved stone heads, 15thC, tallest 9in (23cm) high.
l. king   **£300–350**
r. boy   **£200–240 CYA**

A Greek terracotta female figure, repaired, 4th century BC, 9in (23cm) high.
£600–700 HEL

An Egyptian alabaster alabastron-shaped flask, with lug handles, New Kingdom, 14th–11th century BC, 5½in (14cm) long.
£400–500 HEL

An Egyptian painted cartonnage fragment, with a figure of Isis and various other figures, 3rd Intermediate Period, 11th–10th century BC, 24in (61cm) long.
£1,600–2,000 HEL

A pair of Roman gold earrings, inset with glass and with Heraklean Club finials, 2nd–3rdC, 1in (2.5cm) long.
£700–800 HEL

A wooden sarcophagus fragment, painted with hieroglyphics, Roman Period, 1st–3rdC, 21in (53.5cm) long.
£450–550 HEL

GLASS

A Roman green opaque mould-blown and twisted glass pitcher, from Italy, 1stC, 5in (12.5cm) high.
£250–275 Sama

A Roman glass swizzle stick, from southern Italy, 2ndC, 6in (15cm) long.
£145–165 Sama

A Roman green glass vessel, from Palestine, rim repaired, 2nd–3rdC, 5in (12.5cm) high.
£225–275 Sama

A Roman moss green glass flask, from Palestine, 2nd–3rdC, 6in (15cm) high.
£225–275 Sama

A Roman olive green glass jug, from Palestine, repaired, 3rdC, 9in (23cm) high.
£350–400 Sama

◀ A Roman pale green glass balsamarium, with applied twin handles and spiral decoration, from the Holy Land, 3rd–4thC, 4in (10cm) high.
£225–275 Sama

A Roman unguentarium perfume bottle, from Syria, 3rd–4thC, 6in (15cm) high.
£95–105 OTT

METALWARE

A Celtic-type Bronze Age axe head, 5in (12.5cm) long.
£75–85 BSA

A Romano Egyptian bronze model of a hound, 1st–2ndC, 2in (5cm) long.
£500–600 HEL

◀ A pair of Roman bronze casket feet, found near Colchester, Essex, 3rd–4thC, 1in (2.5cm) high.
£50–60 Sama

A horse and rider shaped brooch, enamelled in red and blue, with hinge lugs and catchplate, pin missing, 1st–2ndC, 1in (2.5cm) long.
£85–95 ANG

A Roman brooch, in the shape of an eagle, 3rd–4thC, 1in (2.5cm) long.
£65–80 BSA

◀ A bronze bust of Mars, wearing a Corinthian helmet, found in Norfolk, 1st–3rdC, 1½in (4cm) long.
£60–70 ANG

▶ A Roman bronze chariot fitting, in the shape of a horse's head, 4thC, 6½in (16.5cm) high.
£2,000–2,500 HEL

A late Roman supporting-arm brooch, with arched bow and linear decoration, complete with catch, found in Cambridgeshire, pin and spring missing, slight damage, mid-5thC, 1¼in (3cm) long.
£35–40 ANG

An early Christian bronze finger ring, the bezel with a cross surrounded by incised patterns, found near Rome, 5thC.
£275–325 Sama

A medieval caltrop, 2in (5cm) long.
£35–45 BSA
A caltrop is a barbed weapon that was employed against cavalry.

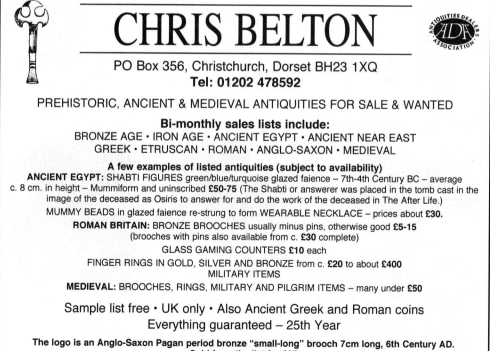

POTTERY

A Greek Mycenaean jug, with banded decoration, 12th century BC, 7in (18cm) high.
£300–360 HEL

Cross Reference
See Ceramics

An Iron Age *amphora*, with geometric decoration, from Cyprus, 10th–8th century BC, 12in (30.5cm) high.
£425–500 HEL

A Greek terracotta jug, with trefoil rim and single strap handle, the main body incised with vertical lines, 6th century BC, 5in (12.5cm) high.
£200–220 Sama

A Greek Athenaen white-ground *lekythos*, base restored, 5th century BC, 8½in (21.5cm) high.
£800–1,000 HEL
Ex-Lord Elgin collection.

A Greek black-glazed *kylix* or drinking vessel, with impressed design of palmettes, 4th century BC, 6in (15cm) diam.
£220–250 Sama

A Greek Apulian ware black-glazed *oinochoe* or pouring jug, with trefoil rim and slip decoration, 4th century BC, 5½in (14cm) high.
£300–350 Sama

A Romano-British wheel-made jar, with ridged decoration, damaged, 1st–2ndC, 7in (18cm) high.
£200–220 Sama

A Roman buff ware oil lamp, decorated with a jaguar in discus, the reverse with a tortoise, 2ndC, 4in (10cm) wide.
£200–240 OTT

A medieval jug, 13thC, 9in (23cm) high.
£1,300–1,500 JHo

◄ A Roman red ware oil lamp, decorated with a fox in discus, from Tunisia, 3rdC, 5in (12.5cm) wide.
£65–80 OTT

A green glazed double lamp, c1600, 6in (15cm) high.
£85–95 BSA
This lamp was found in a wall in Kent.

Architectural Salvage

A French Gothic tracery wooden panel, 15thC, 14in (35.5cm) wide.
£100–120 AnSh

A pair of carved oak lion masks, mounted in later frames, early 17thC, 9in (23cm) high.
£250–300 AnSh

▶ A Georgian brass door handle, 18thC, 10in (25.5cm) wide.
£150–170 BWA

A pair of carved wooden panels, 16th–17thC, 29in (73.5cm) long.
£350–400 OCH

An English carved oak panel, c1650, 23in (58.5cm) long.
£85–95 AnSh

A pair of carved oak lion masks, early 18thC, 7in (18cm) high.
£270–320 AnSh

An elm planked door, 18thC, 69in (175.5cm) high.
£275–325 WEL

A carved oak swag, 18thC, 31in (78.5cm) long.
£75–85 OCH

A Victorian cast-iron rainwater hopper, 19thC, 11in (28cm) high.
£25–30 BYG

◀ A lead well-head hopper, dated '1807', 12in (30.5cm) wide.
£180–200 DOR

A Victorian Tudor rose terracotta tile, 19thC, 7in (18cm) square.
£20–25 RECL

◀ A Victorian terracotta chimney pot, 19thC, 24in (61cm) high.
£35–45 RECL

A Victorian buff vented chimney pot, 19thC, 36in (91.5cm) high.
£60–70 RECL

A Hayward Bros cast-iron manhole cover, c1860, 12in (30.5cm) diam.
£35–40 WAB

Two Tamar decorative terracotta wall tiles, in red and buff, marked 'Tamar Works, Wallington, near Plymouth, Patent No. 20H', early 1900s, 6in (15cm) square.
£8–10 each DOR

► A wrought-iron fence panel, c1900, 72in (183cm) wide.
£240–300 A&H

◄ A wrought-iron garden gate, c1900, 38in (96.5cm) wide.
£80–100 A&H

► A cast-iron downpipe bracket, 1920s, 14in (35.5cm) wide.
£20–25 A&H

BATHROOM FITTINGS

A late Victorian blue and white transfer-printed lavatory pan, 'The Burrator', 17in (43cm) high.
£400–500 NOST

A Victorian Sanitas wash-down lavatory pan, 16in (40.5cm) high.
£350–400 DOR

A Royal Doulton Art Deco-style lavatory pan, 1930s, 16in (40.5cm) high.
£400–500 WRe

◄ An Art Deco washbasin, with reconditioned nickel-plated taps and waste, 1930s, 23in (58.5cm) wide.
£350–400 WRe

A chrome-plated perfume dispensing lavatory pull, c1950, 32in (81.5cm) long.
£25–30 WAB

◄ A nickel-plated wall-mounted shower and taps, 1930s, 24in (61cm) high.
£280–330 DOR

A pair of chrome-plated Art Deco bath taps, restored, 1930s.
£120–150 ACT

DOOR STOPS & BOOT SCRAPERS

A wall-mounted boot scraper, with original fixing nails, late 18thC, 18in (45.5cm) wide.
£80–90 OCH

A Georgian cast-iron boot scraper, 14in (35.5cm) wide.
£75–85 HCJ

◄ A cast-iron door stop, in the form of Rev Joshua Brooks from the Victorian novel *The Manchester Man*, 19thC, 6in (15cm) high.
£70–80 MFB

A cast-iron door stop, in the form of a woodcutter, 19thC, 15in (38cm) high.
£135–155 MFB

A cast-iron door stop, in the form of Bacchus the Greek god of wine, 19thC, 10in (25.5cm) high.
£150–180 MFB

▶ A combination cast-iron boot scraper and brush, on a cast-iron stand, c1909, 8in (20.5cm) wide.
£100–120 SMI

Innovative cast-iron wares

Cast-iron door stops, or door porters, were produced in vast numbers in the Victorian period, stimulated by the development of the rising hinge in the late 18th century, which caused doors to swing closed automatically. Subjects ranged from animals to figures, and major manufacturers included Coalbrookdale and Kenricks.

Another popular item produced by the same companies was the cast-iron boot scraper. Dirty streets in town, and sporting life in the country made these objects a necessity and, by 1871, Kenrick and Sons was offering 157 different varieties of boot scraper. Some were designed to be fixed to the ground, others were freestanding and could be used inside or out. Combination scrapers and brushes were also available. However, with the advent of cleaner streets and motorized transport, demand for boot scrapers lessened.

Art Deco

CERAMICS

A Susie Cooper pottery Studio jug, decorated in green with Rams pattern, 1930s, 8½in (21.5cm) high.
£170–200 SWO

A Limoges coffee set, decorated with alternate bands of yellow with gold highlights and black insects, milk jug and one lid missing, 1928, 10in (25.5cm) high.
£175–225 MD

A Losol ware ginger jar, decorated with Magnolia pattern, 1920s, 7in (18cm) high.
£225–250 BEV

A John Mackee Brocksford ware yellow plate, stamped with a black lion with 'Mackee' above and 'Brocksford ware' below, 1900–20, 10in (25.5cm) diam.
£10–12 ES

A Myott bowl, decorated with an orange, black and green pattern on a blue ground, 1930s, 9in (23cm) diam.
£70–90 PrB

A Myott jug, decorated with an orange and brown pattern on a yellow ground, 1930s, 8in (20.5cm) high.
£80–90 DBo

A Royal Dux tazza, the bowl supported by a chinoiserie figure, 1930s, 12in (30.5cm) high.
£450–550 MD

An Arthur Wood pitcher, with grey and turquoise pineapple-effect stripes and light brown rim and handle, pattern No. 794, marked on base 'A. Wood Ltd, Burslem, England', 1930–35, 9½in (24cm) high.
£25–30 ES

A Royal Venton cake plate, decorated with a yellow and green pattern, 1930s, 9in (23cm) wide.
£65–75 PrB

FURNISHING

A walnut-veneered circular display cabinet, with leaded glass door panels, labelled 'Superlative', Leeds, 1930s, 42in (106.5cm) diam.
£500–600 BDA

A pedestal coffee table, with walnut decorative inlay, 1930s, 21in (53.5cm) square.
£180–200 BTB

A Waring and Gillow walnut-veneered bedroom suite, comprising dressing table, stool and wardrobe, 1930s, dressing table 30in (76cm) wide.
£800–900 BDA

GLASS

A French *pâte de verre* glass hanging lamp, with original gilded brass fittings, c1920, 32in (81.5cm) high.
£250–300 JW

A wrythen-moulded flint glass tumbler, 1920s, 4in (10cm) high.
£110–130 RUSK

A Jobling glass celery vase, 1930s, 8in (20.5cm) high.
£65–75 PIL

A Jobling bird and panel vase, 1930s, 8in (20.5cm) high.
£55–65 PIL

A Czechoslovakian Art Deco pink glass decanter and six shot glasses on a tray, 1930s, tray 15in (38cm) wide.
£140–160 JEZ

◄ A Venetian Barovier pink glass two-handled vase, c1930, 7in (18cm) high.
£150–180 BRU

A glass lemonade set, decorated with silver stars and handles, 1930s, jug 8in (20.5cm) high.
£80–100 BEV

STATUETTES & FIGURES

A Royal Dux figure of a female Spanish dancer, wearing a blue shawl and light blue dress, c1920, 15in (38cm) high.
£700–850 TWr

A M. Guiraud pair of stoneware crackle glaze bookends, French, c1920, 6in (15cm) wide.
£340–380 ANO

▶ A ceramic figure of a clown musician, wearing a blue jacket and brown trousers, 1920–30, 12¼in (31cm) high.
£320–380 ASA

A Katshütte porcelain figure of a dancer, painted in colours, standing on an oval base, printed marks, 1930s, 13½in (34cm) high.
£180–220 L&T

A bronze and ivory figure of a female dancer, on a green marble base, 1930s, 5½in (14cm) high.
£500–600 P(B)

An F. Iffland bronze figure of a naked Egyptian female hornblower, on a marble base, signed, 1930s, 13½in (34.5cm) high.
£300–350 P(B)

A painted plaster figural lamp, in the form of a naked woman holding a frosted glass orb, on an ebonized and chromium plinth base, c1930, 28¼in (72cm) high.
£450–500 L&T

A bronze and ivory figure of a dancing girl, wearing a green skirt and red and gilt jacket, on a marble base, c1925, 9½in (24cm) high.
£900–1,000 P(B)

A spelter figure of a female dancer, on a turned onyx base, c1930, 11in (28cm) high.
£170–200 L&T

A French spelter figure of Diana, signed 'Limousin', 1930s, 19in (48.5cm) high.
£600–700 MD

An H. Moreau pair of silvered bronze leaping gazelle bookends, on marble bases, signed, c1924, 5in (13cm) high.
£230–260 P(B)

Two Lorenzl bronze figures of female dancers, signed, 1930s, 9in (23cm) high.
£900–1,100 each MD

◀ A black enamel and chrome figure of a female dancer, 1930s, 8½in (21.5cm) high.
£120–140 SWO

▶ A G. Deihle bronze figure of a standing man, on a marble base, signed on base, 1930s, 11¾in (30cm) high.
£240–280 P(B)

WALL MASKS

A wall mask, depicting a woman wearing green earings, c1930, 6in (15cm) high.
£80–100 OTT

A James Cope wall mask, depicting a woman with yellow hair and a red and black hat, signed, c1934, 7in (18cm) high.
£65–75 BEV

A James Cope wall mask, depicting a woman with an orange hat, 1930s, 7in (18cm) high.
£100–120 CoCo

A Goebels Babe bee wall mask, c1930, 5in (12.5cm) high.
£180–220 FA

A Leonardi green wall mask, depicting a woman c1937, 9in (23cm) high.
£145–165 MD

◀ A Goebels wall mask, depicting a woman with yellow hair, wearing a rose, with a black and green checked hat, 1930s, 9in (23cm) high.
£220–250 BEV

Art Nouveau

An Emile Gallé faïence jug, in the form of a jester seated on a drum, decorated with gilt on a cream ground, hand-painted mark to base 'E. Gallé Nancy', c1900, 15¾in (40cm) high.
£230–260 P(B)

A Minton Secessionist bottle vase, No. 33, restored, c1900, 8in (20.5cm) high.
£150–170 OTT

A Bretby two-handled vase, No. 1669, the body cased in a lustrous copper skin mounted with polychrome pottery jewels, marked, late 19thC, 13in (33cm) high.
£100–120 BR

A Liberty & Co oak bookcase, c1900, 33in (84cm) high.
£700–800 PVD

Cross Reference
See Colour Review

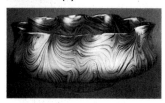

An iridescent glass bowl, with a meandering rim and swirls of peacock blue, mauve and green, c1900, 10½in (26.5cm) diam.
£375–425 RTo

A pair of Royal Doulton vases, the green swirl grounds decorated with blue and white flowers and cream leaves, c1918, 12in (30.5cm) high.
£300–350 SWO

A Daum cameo glass bowl, decorated with leaf and berry pattern in pink on an opaque ground, marked 'Moda' to side, c1900, 6in (15cm) diam.
£220–250 P(B)

A Ruskin copper brooch, early 20thC, 2½in (6.5cm) diam.
£40–50 WAC

► A 15ct gold foliate pendant, set with blue topaz and seed pearls, 1½in (4cm) long, with chain.
£220–250 SWO

An oak jardinière, banded and studded with copper, made for Liberty, 1900, 36in (91.5cm) high.
£120–160 P(B)

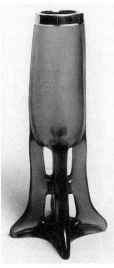

A silver-mounted green glass vase, London 1903, 6½in (16.5cm) high.
£100–120 WAC

A wrought-iron tea stand with copper trays, early 20thC, 32in (81.5cm) high.
£100–120 WAC

▶ A silver-plated comport, the circular base with floral bracket supports, carrying a gilt and pink glass bowl decorated with medallions and female portraits, early 20thC, 11in (28cm) high.
£160–180 P(B)

An Archibald Knox pewter three-piece tea set, No. 231, c1900, teapot 4½in (11.5cm) high.
£800–900 PVD

An American silver belt, probably by Unger Brothers, the central motif of two confronting high relief female heads framed by sinuous drifting hair, connected to similar graduated profiles, marked 'Sterling 1331', early 20thC, 25¾in (65.5cm) long.
£550–650 P(B)

A Joseph Rodgers & Sons silver-plated three-piece tea set, c1900, teapot 5in (12.5cm) high.
£60–70 WAC

An oak armchair, with upholstered panel and seat, the shaped side panels and seat rail pierced with yin/yang roundels, c1910.
£550–650 L&T

An oak hall settle, the panelled back pierced with stylized plant shapes, the arms surmounted by orb finials, the lidded seat with a compartment below, c1910, 48in (122cm) wide.
£550–660 L&T

A Liberty & Co Tudric pewter vase, applied with heart-shaped Ruskin enamels, c1920, 7¾in (19.5cm) high.
£400–500 PVD

Arts & Crafts

An Ault yellow anthemion jardinière, attributed to Dr Christopher Dresser, c1890, 6in (15cm) high.
£375–425 HUN

A pair of Ault yellow pottery flower shells, c1890, 6in (15cm) high.
£440–480 HUN

An Ault flower arranger, by Dr Christopher Dresser, signed, c1893, 3in (7.5cm) high.
£120–140 NCA

A Burmantoft art pottery yellow-glazed vase, the slender neck with piecrust rim, c1890, 8in (20.5cm) high.
£200–240 HUN

A Dunmore gourd vase, with dark green and black glaze, 1870–1900, 8¾in (22cm) high.
£160–180 SQA

A Dunmore Grecian-style two-handled vase, with green, brown and ochre glaze, 1870–1900, 5¼in (13.5cm) high.
£85–95 SQA

An Elton ware flown-glaze jug, moulded with alpine flowers, c1900, 5in (12.5cm) high.
£200–240 HUN

A Baron Pottery red five-piece chocolate set, c1900, pot 7in (18cm) high.
£40–50 BSA

LOCATE THE SOURCE
The source of each illustration in Miller's can be found by checking the code letters below each caption with the Key to Illustrations, pages 476–484.

▶ A Longpark udder vase, decorated with a butterfly in orange and blue on a brown ground, 1920–30, 3¾in (9.5cm) high.
£20–25 Law

An Aller Vale waisted cylindrical vase, with twin handles, decorated in coloured slips with foliate branches, minor damage, 1900–10, 7½in (19cm) high.
£20–25 DSG

METALWARE

A pair of Scottish silver-plated comports, the shaped circular bowls inset with oval Arts and Crafts-style cabochons, raised on a collared stem and circular base, maker's mark 'J R of Glasgow', c1900, 10in (25.5cm) wide.
£220–250 Hal

An Aesthetic movement hammered copper coal bin, the hinged lid opening to reveal a lined interior, the front and lid repoussé-decorated with stylized sunflowers, on curved wrought-iron feet, c1890, 19¼in (49cm) wide.
£450–500 L&T

A pair of hammered copper chamber sticks, c1900, 7in (18cm) high.
£125–145 WAC

A Keswick School of Industrial Art copper tray, embossed with a stylized leaf and rose pattern, c1900, 11½in (29cm) diam.
£200–225 WAC

A silver scrolling pendant, decorated with blue, green and turquoise enamel, some damage, Birmingham 1908, 2in (5cm) long.
£100–120 SWO

A silver octagonal covered salt cellar, by Peter Frederick Alexander, in the form of a capstan, with punch-beaded, hammered and riveted design, the plain loose cover with a ball finial concealing a blue glass liner, London 1906, 4¾in (12cm) diam.
£250–280 CGC

A copper table coaster, c1910, 6in (15cm) diam.
£60–70 WAC

Condition

The condition is absolutely vital when assessing the value of a collectable. Damaged pieces on the whole appreciate much less than perfect examples. However a rare desirable piece may command a high price even when damaged.

An Elkington & Co Arts & Crafts-style silver tea set, Birmingham 1929, teapot 5in (12.5cm) high.
£340–380 CGC

Asian Works of Art

A Chinese elmwood chest, the front panel carved with the dogs of Fo, late 19thC, 38in (96.5cm) wide.
£370–£420 OE

A Chinese leather trunk, from Shanghai, late 19thC, 33in (84cm) wide.
£350–420 K

Two Chinese leather hat boxes, one double-stacked, 1860–90, tallest 18in (45.5cm) high.
l. £100–120
r. £200–240 SOO

A Chinese lacquered elm grain barrel, with gilt design, late 19thC, 18in (45.5cm) high.
£270–300 SOO

◄ A fuchi and kahira set, decorated with mixed metal inlay of warriors, signed 'Sei Ryu Ken Hamano Naotoki', 18thC, 1¼in (3cm) wide.
£450–500 SK

A Chinese carved ivory ten-piece devil's ball, c1900, 9in (23cm) high.
£210–240 FA

► A Japanese purse, embossed and painted with dragons, suspended from a circular ivory toggle with embossed silver mount, early 20thC, 5¼in (13.5cm) wide.
£110–130 CGC

A Japanese Satsuma box and cover, with chrysanthemum knop, two sides decorated with figures and two with butterflies, signed 'Kyozan', Meiji period, 1868–1912, 3¼in (8.5cm) wide.
£2,500–2,800 WW

BASKETS

A Chinese rattan salt pan, late 19thC, 28in (71cm) long.
£500–550 HGh

Items in the Asian Works of Art section have been arranged in date order within each sub-section.

A northern Thai Akha tribe basket, early 20thC, 24in (61cm) high.
£150–180 K

A Japanese bamboo *ikebana* flower basket, signed 'Chikuunsai', early 20thC, 20in (51cm) high.
£2,600–3,000 KJ

◀ A pair of Chinese salt-water-reed baskets, from Shantung Province, 19thC, 15½in (39.5cm) high.
£540–600 GHC

FIGURES & SCULPTURES

A pair of Chinese red earthenware horses' heads, Han Dynasty, 7in (18cm) high.
£600–700 Sama
The Tianma Heavenly Horse was credited in official records with being capable of running 1000 li (310 miles) a day and of sweating blood. To illustrate the legend of the Tianma, red pigment was used. The desire of the Han ruling class to own Tianma led to their enthusiasm for horse models to furnish their graves.

A Chinese carved wood shrine figure, Ming Dynasty, 17thC, 10in (25.5cm) high.
£200–220 Sama

◀ A Japanese bronze tiger, with buffed and matt stripes, glass eyes and dark brown patina, Meiji period, 1868–1911, 13in (33cm) long.
£500–550 SK

A Japanese Satsuma figure of the Bodhisattva Sho-Kannon, Deity of Compassion, decorated in turquoise enamels, Meiji period, 1868–1911, 12½in (32cm) high.
£1,000–1,200 Bon(C)

NETSUKE

An ivory *netsuke*,
Issun-Boshi, 19thC,
2in (5cm) high.
£220–250 JaG

An ivory *netsuke*,
depicting a boy wearing
a lion mask, signed
'Tomo-Chika', c1860,
2¼in (5.5cm) high.
£1,800–2,000 KIE

An ivory *netsuke*, depicting
a snake, frog and skull,
19thC, 1¼in (3cm) high.
£750–850 HUR

Netsuke development

Kimonos, the traditional Japanese costume, had
no pockets, so personal possessions, such as
the *inro* (medicine or seal case) and the *yatate*
(writing case), were hung from the belt, or *obi*,
by cords. These cords were tightened by a small
slip bead called the *ojime*, and secured by a
toggle known as the *netsuke*, the word coming
from *ne* 'a root', and *tsuke* 'to fasten'. In use
from the late 16th century, *netsuke* were initially
formed from natural objects, such as pieces of
root and small gourds. However, they gradually
evolved into masterpieces of miniature
craftsmanship, carved in every material from
wood to stone, and covering every subject from
animals, to plants, to mythological figures.
Netsuke were often made to complement, both
decoratively and symbolically, the imagery
displayed on the *ojime* and the *inro*, but as well
as being complex and allusive works of art, they
were also practical objects, the design of which
had to be smooth enough not to snag the fine
embroidered silk of the kimono. By the 18th
century, specialist *netsuke* artists were signing
their creations, and the first half of the 19th
century was a golden age of production, as
designs became increasingly naturalistic and
intricate. By the 1860s, however, the Japanese
had begun to adopt European dress. Need for
the *netsuke* gradually declined, inferior products
were manufactured for the Western collectors'
market and craftsmanship deteriorated.

◀ A fruitwood *shashi netsuke*, depicting Daruma,
with carved tobacco and pipe case, c1880,
3in (7.5cm) high.
£170–200 KIE

PRINTS & PICTURES

A Japanese *oban* triptych woodcut print,
by Chikanobu, entitled 'Noble Ladies of
the Tokugawa Period', 1890s, 14 x 28in
(35.5 x 71cm).
£165–185 JaG

◀ A Japanese woodcut print of the moon
and plum blossoms, by Koson, 1900–1910,
14½ x 7½in (37 x 19cm).
£180–200 JaG

A Japanese painting
of a mounted warrior
with retinue, signed
with three characters
and one seal, framed
and glazed, late 19thC,
24 x 18in (61 x 45.5cm).
£100–120 SK

POTTERY & PORCELAIN

A Chinese Sichuan black pottery amphora, each side carved with two spiralling motifs, Han Dynasty, 7in (18cm) high.
£350–400 Sama

A Chinese bowl and cover, from the *Jung Tau* cargo, c1690, 3½in (9cm) diam.
£400–450 SPU

A pair of Chinese export covered vegetable dishes, with fruit knop finials to the domed covers, painted in underglaze blue with a fenced lakeland scene within diaper borders, one damaged, late 18thC, 11¾in (30cm) wide.
£450–500 CGC

A Chinese green pottery pricket stick, Yuan Dynasty, 10in (25.5cm) high.
£145–165 Sama

A Japanese blue and white *kendi*, c1660, 8½in (21.5cm) high.
£1,800–2,200 GeW

A Chinese *famille rose* jardinière, decorated with figures on a terrace, early 19thC, 7½in (19cm) wide.
£450–500 AH

◀ A blue and white glazed bowl, from the *Diana* cargo, c1816, 5½in (14cm) diam.
£60–75 RBA

A Chinese gilded *famille rose* tea bowl and saucer, Yongzheng period, 1723–35, saucer, 3½in (9cm) diam.
£230–280 GLD

A Chinese blue and white tea bowl and saucer, with café-au-lait exterior, Qianlong period, 1736–95, saucer 4in (10cm) diam.
£190–230 GLD

A Batavian-style blue and white tea bowl and saucer, decorated with bamboo and a peony, from the *Nanking* cargo, c1750, saucer 4½in (11.5cm) diam.
£225–250 RBA

A Chinese double-ogee bowl, decorated with a continuous landscape of pavilions, trees and buildings with a castellated wall in the background, marked, Daoguang period, 1821–51, 5½in (14cm) diam.
£180–220 Hal(C)

NORITAKE

A Noritake trio, decorated with sweet peas on a cream ground, 1920s, plate 6½in (16.5cm) wide.
£35–40 DgC

A Noritake lady's ashtray, decorated with gold on a cream ground, 1920, 4½in (11.5cm) wide.
£25–30 DgC

A Noritake plate, hand-painted with a lakeside scene within a crimson and gold border, c1925, 9½in (24cm) wide.
£100–120 RIA

A Noritake tureen, decorated in gold and blue, marked 'The Ceylon Noritake Nipon', c1930, 12in (30.5cm) wide.
£35–40 EAS

▶ A Noritake seven-piece cake set, decorated with stylized lustre fruit in orange, purple, cream and brown, 1925, plate 6½in (16.5cm) diam.
£85–100 DgC

A Noritake 11-piece coffee set, decorated in gold and cream, 1920s, pot 7½in (19cm) high.
£150–180 DgC

A Noritake jug, bowl and five plates, decorated with roses in green, brown and orange, 1920, plate 6½in (16.5cm) diam.
£45–50 DgC

TEXTILES

A Chinese Canton black silk shawl, with a macramé fringe, hand-embroidered in orange and cream, c1880, 50in (127cm) square.
£250–280 JPr

A pair of Chinese silk cuffs, hand-embroidered in cream, green, yellow and gold on a blue ground, 19thC, 27in (68.5cm) wide.
£120–140 JPr

▶ A pair of Chinese sleeve panels, embroidered with water fowl and lotus in blue, cream and pink on a white ground, framed, late 19thC, each 18 x 3½in (45.5 x 9cm).
£250–300 PBr

A Japanese purple silk kimono, the hem decorated with white flowers and green foliage, 1920s.
£335–375 ASG
Every kimono depicts a season, and flowers in bloom, this example represents spring.

Automobilia

A Joseph Lucas self-contained Autolite acetylene gas lamp, c1906, 11in (28cm) high.
£130–150 BKS

A sterling silver model of the Napier-Campbell World Land Speed Record car Bluebird, by The Goldsmiths & Silversmiths Co, with a barometer and eight-day clock set in the offside wheels, on a marble base, assayed in London 1930, 24¾in (63cm) long.
£60,000–66,000 BKS
This trophy was presented to Captain Sir Malcolm Campbell by Napier & Son Ltd to commemorate his record-breaking run in the car at Daytona, USA in 1931.

▶ A charcoal drawing, 'Record Attempt 1930', by John Oxford, with label 'Lent for exhibition by the proprietors of *The Autocar*', framed and glazed, signed and dated 1930, 9¾ x 21in (25 x 63.5cm).
£2,100–2,400 BKS

A Russian silver cigarette case, impressed with a vintage car, the catch decorated with a single ruby, marked, c1927, 3½in (9cm) wide.
£600–700 BKS

▶ A pen and ink picture, 'Christmas 1947, The Dingbat Drivers Club', by Russell Bockbank, the reverse dated '24/12/47', 16½ x 11in (42 x 28cm).
£330–370 BKS

◀ A Fairey Aviation Motor Cycle and Car Club wooden wall plaque, 1930s, 20in (51cm) diam.
£250–300 COB

An American aluminium street sign, 1950s, 25in (63.5cm) wide.
£30–35 TRA

A Castrol pennant, 'Isle of Man TT week 1955', 7in (18cm) wide.
£25–30 COB

A Harris Tweed flat cap, worn by Colin Chapman, with label marked 'A. C. B. Chapman' and letter of authenticity, 1969.
£530–590 BKS
This cap was worn by Chapman up to and during the 1969 American Grand Prix. Jochen Rindt won the race for Lotus and Chapman threw his cap into the air in celebration as the car passed the chequered flag. It was caught by the chief mechanic, who subsequently was told to keep the cap as a memento.

A Griffin Clubman Formula One racing helmet, worn by Graham Hill, 1974.
£3,200–3,600 BKS

An Ascot Races enamel and leather key fob, 1960, 2in (5cm) long.
£6–7 RTT

A Ferrari piston and con-rod, used by Michael Schumacher in the engine of his 1997 Formula One Ferrari when it won the Monaco Grand Prix, signed by the driver.
£475–550 BKS

An Esso game, 'Instant Insanity', 1967, 11 x 8in (28 x 20.5cm).
£30–35 MURR

A Formula One racing car steering wheel, used by Niki Lauda, signed by the driver in white pen, dated '8.82'.
£900–1,000 BKS

► A Triumph Bonneville commemorative plate, limited edition of 1000, 1990, 9in (23cm) diam.
£35–40 COB

Bicycles

The increasing popularity of cycling has helped fuel demand for vintage bicycle memorabilia. A record £99,000 was paid recently for an unusual 1890s bicycle, and this section includes a tricycle by the Starley brothers (suppliers of tricycles to Queen Victoria) that fetched over £25,000 at auction.

Bonhams & Brooks are now holding regular cycling ephemera sales. Late 19th and early 20th century examples tend to command the highest prices, as do cycling posters from the same period. Enthusiasts are also showing interest in material from later decades, particularly racing bikes.

A transitional Vélocipède, with iron-tyred wooden wheels, shaped backbone, turned fork separators, twisting handlebars and rear brake mechanism, 1870, driving wheel 37in (94cm) diam.
£1,800–2,000 BKS

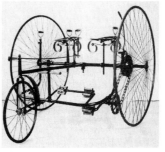

A Starley Brothers Sociable tricycle, The Royal Salvo, with rack-and-pinion steering, the differential driving both rear wheels, with hand-operated band-brake to differential housing, 1882, rear wheels 46in (117cm) diam.
£25,000–30,000 BKS
The Salvo name was originally applied to a patented tricycle by James Starley and was granted Royal approval after Queen Victoria purchased two tricycles in 1880.

A Juvenile Ordinary, possibly by Hillman, Herbert and Cooper, frame No. 8792, 1883, front wheel 43in (109cm) diam.
£1,400–1,600 BKS

A Quadrant Tricycle Co agent's advertising poster, depicting riders on machines in a country setting, framed, c1888, 30 x 35in (76 x 89cm).
£475–525 BKS

A Peugeot cross-frame Safety Bicycle, with pivot steering and tangent spokes, frame No. 18919, 1889.
£2,400–2,700 BKS

A French Humber advertising poster, 'Premiere Marque du Monde', laid to linen and board-mounted, c1893, 51 x 39in (129.5 x 99cm).
£200–250 BKS

A French tricycle, with original tyres and saddle, repainted, late 19thC.
£300–350 YEST

◄ A Vanity Fair supplement lithographic print, 'Cycling in Hyde Park', depicting members of London society with their cycles in the park, framed and glazed, 1896, 13 x 19in (33 x 48.5cm).
£400–450 BKS

A Gladiator Triplet Racing bicycle, as used in the Simpson Chain competitions and advertisement, 1896, wheels 28in (71cm) diam.
£2,900–3,200 BKS

An Edwardian studio photograph of cyclists, by G. B. Esam, 6 x 7in (15 x 18cm).
£8–10 RTT

A leather bicycle repair kit pouch, with contents, c1920, 7in (18cm) long.
£20–25 WAB

◄ A French Michelin lithographic poster, 'Le Meilleur le Moins Cher', depicting Mr Bibbendum riding a bicycle, licence stamp in lower corner, framed and glazed, c1910, 41 x 32in (104 x 81.5cm).
£250–300 BKS

A lithographic advertising poster, 'Triumph Cycles', in the style of Misti, in cream, orange and black on a green ground, dated 1907, 46 x 30in (117 x 76cm).
£260–300 BKS

> Miller's is a price GUIDE not a price LIST

A Raleigh advertising card, 'The All-Steel Bicycle', depicting a lion chasing a rider on a bicycle, framed, 1920s, 22 x 30in (56 x 76cm).
£300–350 JUN

◄ An Alcyon Path racer, frame No. 191000, with Alcyon chain set, headstock and nickel-plated drop bars, 1920, frame 22in (56cm).
£260–300 BKS

A Thapex Apex Inflator Co bicycle pump, c1930, 16in (40.5cm) long.
£10–12 WA

The Thoroughbred Sunbeam Bicycles brochure, 2nd edition, 1934, 8in (20.5cm) square.
£18–22 RTT

► A Schwinn Black Phantom boy's bicycle, with original paintwork, tyres and fittings, 1950s.
£700–800 BKS

Books

CHILDREN'S BOOKS

Without question, the children's publishing phenomenon at the turn of the new millenium has been J. K. Rowling's Harry Potter books. Using only her initials (publishers feared that a female name might alienate boy readers), Joanne Rowling produced her first novel, *Harry Potter and the Philosopher's Stone*, in 1997. A sequel has followed every year and eventually the complete series will comprise seven books, charting Harry's entire career at Hogwart's School of Witchcraft and Wizardry. The Harry Potter books might have sold millions of copies across the globe, but a first edition, first issue of that first book is as rare as the philosopher's stone itself. The print run of the first edition of *Harry Potter and the Philosopher's Stone* was limited to only 500 copies, 200 of which apparently were paperback proof copies while, of the remaining 300 hardbacks, a large proportion went to libraries. Thus, a first edition is a real rarity. The copy shown in the Colour Review on page 74 is valued at £8–10,000. *The Antiques Trade Gazette* has also reported a first edition offered for £15,000. First editions of other Harry Potter books are also desirable. *Harry Potter and the Chamber of Secrets* had an initial print run of 1–2,000 copies, and the example illustrated on page 52 fetched over £2,000 at auction. *Harry Potter and the Prisoner of Azkaban* can be worth around £150. The fourth book, however, *Harry Potter and the Goblet of Fire*, was issued in an apparently unprecedented print run of one million copies, delighting readers everywhere, but providing less scope for the rarity-loving book collector.

A wooden horn book dolly, probably made of oak, the arms and legs jointed with string, crudely carved facial features, inset ivory or bone panel to the body with polka-dot alphabet, with initials 'J. E.', dated '1810', 7in (18cm) high.
£900–1,100 DW

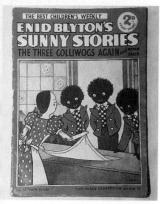

Hans Andersen's Fairy Stories, with pop-up pictures, 1930, 8 x 7in (20.5 x 18cm).
£35–40 A&J

◄ *Enid Blyton's Sunny Stories*, No. 54, 1938, 7 x 5in (18 x 12.5cm).
£8–10 OCB

► Elinor Brent-Dyer, *Beechy of the Harbour School*, first edition, 1955, 6 x 5in (15 x 12.5cm).
£80–90 OCB

Enid Blyton, *Playing at Home*, devised and illustrated by Sabine Schweitzer, published by Methuen, 1955, 6 x 9in (15 x 23cm).
£40–50 J&J

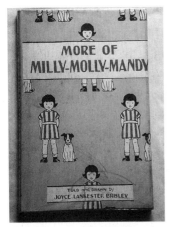

Joyce Lankester Brisley, *More of Milly-Molly-Mandy*, reprint, 1971, 8 x 5in (20.5 x 12.5cm).
£8–10 OCB

Dorita F. Bruce, *Dimsie Head Girl*, Oxford Books for Girls, reprint, 1945, 7½ x 5in (19 x 12.5cm).
£12–15 OCB

Lewis Carroll, *Through the Looking-Glass, and What Alice Found There*, illustrated by John Tenniel, first edition, first issue with 'wade' not 'wabe' on p.21, presentation copy from the author to Mary Burnett with his inscription in purple ink on half-title, 1872, 8vo.
£8,250–9,250 BBA

Lewis Carroll, *The Hunting of the Snark, an Agony in Eight Fits*, illustrated by Henry Holiday, first edition, published by Macmillan and Co, grey printed dust jacket with advertisement for *Alice* in its 49,000th issue and *Looking-Glass* in its 38,000th issue, 1876, 8vo.
£6,250–7,000 BBA

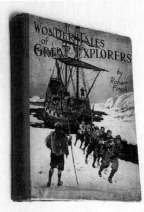

Robert Finch, *Wonder Tales of Great Explorers*, c1950, 10 x 8in (25.5 x 20.5cm).
£8–10 AnS

Kenneth Grahame, *The Wind in the Willows*, frontispiece by Graham Robertson, first edition, first issue, with dust jacket, 1908, 8vo.
£15,500–17,000 BBA

> **Cross Reference**
> See Colour Review

Howard R. Garis, *Uncle Wiggily's Silk Hat*, *Uncle Wiggily and the Pirates*, *Uncle Wiggily's Make Believe Tarts*, 1940s, 7 x 6½in (18 x 16.5cm).
£12–15 each OPB

◀ Kate Greenaway, M. H. Spielmann and G. S. Layard, *Kate Greenaway* with an original pencil sketch by Kate Greenaway, No. 82 of 500 edition of de luxe copies, signed by John Greenaway, published by A. & C. Black, 1905, 4to.
£520–600 BBA

Alfred Judd, *The Track of Danger*,
published by Sheldon Press, 1928.
£7–8 AnS

Lothar Meggendorfer, *Bubenstreiche,
Ein Verwandlungs Bilderbuch*,
published by J. F. Schreiber,
Esslingen & Munich, with movable
colour pictures and black and
white illustrations, c1900, folio.
£500–600 DW

George Lowther, *The Adventures
of Superman*, illustrated by Joe
Shuster, first edition, published
by Random House, New York,
inscribed 'Feb 6th 1943 Grand
Central Station NYC', 1942.
£175–200 CBP

The Old Nursery Rhymes,
illustrated by Lawson Wood,
published by Thomas Nelson &
Sons, c1930, 11 x 9in (28 x 23cm).
£30–35 J&J

▶ Beatrix Potter, *The Tale of Peter
Rabbit*, first edition, second issue,
limited to 200 copies, 1902, 16mo.
£6,000–6,600 DW

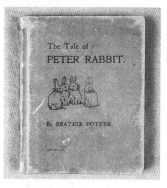

Frank Richards, *Billy Bunter and the Blue Mauritius*, first edition, 1952, 8 x 5in (20.5 x 12.5cm).
£45–55 OCB

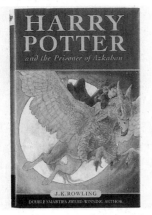

J. K. Rowling, *Harry Potter and the Prisoner of Azkaban*, first edition, 1999, 8vo.
£150–180 BBA

Transforming Performers with Surprise Pictures, with six colour lithographic plates with lift-up flaps, published by Dean & Son, broken spine, one flap missing, inscribed 1875, small 4to.
£200–250 DW

► J. K. Rowling, *Harry Potter and the Prisoner of Azkaban, Harry Potter and the Chamber of Secrets, Harry Potter and the Philospher's Stone*, Collectors' Edition set, first editions, 1997, each 10 x 7in (25.5 x 18cm).
£340–400 AHa

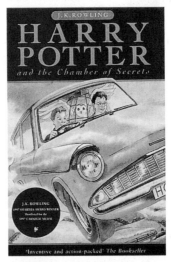

J. R. R. Tolkien, *The Hobbit*, with ten plates and pictorial endpapers illustrated by the author, first edition, first issue with 'Dodgeson' corrected in ink on inside lower flap of jacket, published by George Allen and Unwin, 1937, 8vo.
£21,000–23,000 S
The presence and excellent condition of the dust jacket make this book particularly desirable. Without the jacket the value would be less than half that quoted.

◄ J. K. Rowling, *Harry Potter and the Chamber of Secrets*, first edition, published by Bloomsbury, signed by the author, 1998, 8vo.
£2,400–2,800 S

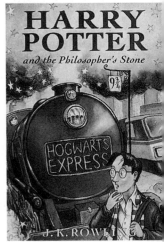

J. K. Rowling, *Harry Potter and the Philosopher's Stone*, proof copy, published by Bloomsbury, 1997, 8vo.
£1,800–2,000 S
The uncorrected proof copy of the first Harry Potter story, with publication and price details on the lower cover. The pictorial design on the glazed wrappers by Thomas Taylor is the same as that on the boards of the published edition, Harry and the Hogwarts Express at platform 9¾ and Professor Dumbledore on the lower cover, but with a few variations. The spine and lower cover of the proof are cream, as opposed to purple, and the design is fully bled on the proof, whereas the pictorial design on the upper cover of the published edition is set in a central panel, the title, author's name and single-line review in red and black panels above and below. These uncorrected proof copies are more common in the marketplace than the hardback first edition.

COOKBOOKS

The market for cookery, wine and food books continues to grow stronger because of increasing interest in gastronomy and oenology. Collectors are concentrating on building cookbook libraries and wine cellars. More and more restaurants are catering to a clientele that is becoming increasingly sophisticated when it comes to fusion cookery methods and the use of exotic foods.

People will always be interested in what they eat and how it is prepared. Old cookery and wine books are interesting to read, and collectors are joining culinary historical societies to learn about the history of food.

During the last year, collectors have been surfing the Internet with increased frequency, searching for books they would like to acquire for their libraries. It has become increasingly easy to price and purchase books on the Internet. Fears have been voiced that this new approach to buying and selling cookbooks may signal the demise of many of the delightful shops that welcomed browsers. Also, with the use of the Internet, greater numbers of cookbooks are coming to light as sellers find that they can reach a larger public and realize higher prices with the increased demand for these items. Prices for old and rare cookbooks, especially those from the 1600s to the mid-1900s, have continued to spiral upwards. The auction by Sotheby's of the Tore Wretman Collection, and the Poulain & LeFur cookbook auction recently have added to the strength of an already strong market. Antiquarian book shows and fairs continue to attract healthy numbers of attendees.

As with any other antiques or collectables, condition and rarity continue to drive the market. Rigid guidelines for the condition of a book, as established by professional societies, have helped to make purchases by collectors more stable. Collectors continue to buy through catalogues from established dealers, and these catalogues, many of them well-illustrated and well-researched, are becoming collectable themselves.

As demand for rare and collectable cookbooks continues to grow, prices will probably continue to rise and collectors will become more discerning in what they choose to add to their libraries. **Marilyn Brass**

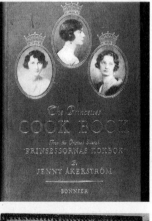

◄ Jenny Akerström, *The Princesses Cook Book*, 1936, 8¾ x 6in (22 x 15cm). **£40–45 MSB**

Fredrick Accum, *Culinary Chemistry*, first edition, published by R. Ackermann, cased, 1821, 7¾ x 4¾in (19.5 x 12cm). **£750–900 OPB**

► Martha Lee Anderson, *Good Things to Eat*, edition 124, 1939, 4½ x 6in (11.5 x 15cm). **£12–15 MSB**

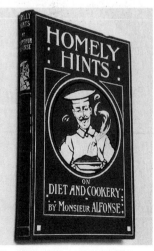

Monsieur Alfonse, *Homely Hints on Diet and Cookery*, worn, 1902, 6¾ x 4½in (17.5 x 11.5cm). **£12–15 SEE**

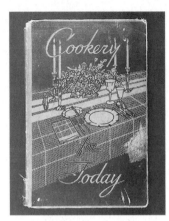

Ann Batchelder, *Cookery for Today*, 1932, 9¼ x 6¼in (23.5 x 16cm).
£12–15 MSB

A. Beauvilliers, *L'Art du Cuisinier*, 2 volumes, incomplete, 1814–16, 8 x 4½in (20.5 x 11.5cm).
£85–95 SEE
Beauvilliers was a great rival of Careme and was described by Brillat Savarin as 'for more than 15 years the most famous restaurateur in Paris'.
In complete and perfect condition this book could fetch as much as £1,500.

◄ Pilaff Bey, *Venus in the Kitchen*, first edition, illustrated by Bruce Roberts, introduction by Graham Greene, published by Heinemann, 1952, 8½ x 5½in (21.5 x 14cm).
£16–20 SEE

Mrs Beeton's Book of Household Management, revised edition, with 12 colour plates, original decorative cloth, 1869, 7 x 5in (18 x 12.5cm),
£150–180 BAY

Mrs Beeton's Household Management, published by Ward, Lock & Co, c1920, 8 x 6½in (20.5 x 16.5cm)
£40–45 SMI

◄ *Mrs Beeton's All About Cookery*, original decorative cloth, published by Ward, Lock & Co, 1901, 8 x 5½in (20.5 x 14cm).
£50–60 BAY

Margaret M. Bridwell, *Kentucky Fare*, 1953, 8½ x 5½in (21.5 x 14cm).
£20–25 MSB

◄ *The Candy-Maker*, published by Jesse Haney & Co, New York, 1878.
£65–75 OPB

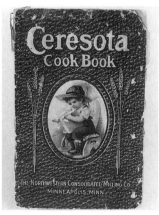

Ceresota Cook Book, published by The Northwestern Consolidated Milling Co, Minneapolis, 1912, 8¾ x 6in (22 x 15cm).
£25–30 MSB

Richard Briggs, *The English Art of Cookery*, second edition, 12 copper plates, printed for G. G. J. & J. Robinson, rebound in cloth, 1791, 8 x 4¾in (20.5 x 12cm). **£500–550 SEE**

Hannah Glasse, *The Art of Cookery Made Plain and Easy*, c1790, 8¼ x 5in (21 x 12.5cm). **£200–250 SEE**
Hannah Glasse (1708–70) wrote the most famous English cookery book of the time, yet her identity remained obscure until, in the 20thC, a local historian traced her to Northumberland and her half-brother, Sir Lancelot Allgood. She did not write, as is often said, 'First catch your hare…', but rather 'Take your hare when it is cas'd and make a pudding…'

Winifred S. Gibbs, *Economical Cooking*, 1912, 7 x 5in (18 x 12.5cm). **£20–25 MSB**

Elizabeth David, *French Country Cooking*, first edition, illustrated by John Minton, published by John Lehmann, 1951, 8 x 5in (20 x 12.5cm). **£20–25 SEE**
With its dust jacket, this book would be worth twice as much.

Olive Green, *One Thousand Simple Soups*, 1907, 6½ x 4½in (16.5 x 11.5cm). **£45–50 MSB**

Jules Gouffe, *Le Livre de Cuisine*, published by Hachette, Paris, 1902, 11 x 7in (28 x 18cm). **£180–220 AHa**

Home Made Cook Book, published by M. J. Ivers & Co, New York, 1885.
£25–30 OPB

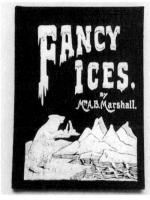

Mrs A. B. Marshall, Fancy Ices, numbered limited edition of 300 copies, 1999, 8 x 5¾in (20.5 x 14.5cm).
£20–25 SEE
This is a modern facsimile. The original 1894 edition would be worth £200–250.

M. N. Osborne, Jolly Times Cook Book, Chicago, 1934, 4 x 6½in (10 x 16.5cm).
£20–25 MSB

Pillsbury's 40 War-Time Recipes, c1942, 6 x 4½in (15 x 11.5cm).
£12–15 MSB

Mary and Vincent Price, A Treasury of Great Recipes, first edition, gold-embossed leatherette binding, published by Ampersand Press Inc, 1965, 10 x 7¼in (25.5 x 18.5cm).
£16–20 SEE

Elizabeth Raffald, The Experienced English Housekeeper, 1801, 8 x 5in (20.5 x 12.5cm).
£125–150 AHa

Emma Roberts, Domestic Cookery by a Lady, 64th edition, published by John Murray, 1840, 7 x 5in (18 x 12.5cm).
£85–95 BAY

African-American cookbooks

The popularity of African-American cookbooks continues to grow. Starting with The House Servant's Directory by Robert Roberts, the first cookbook by an African-American published in the United States in 1827, and continuing through plantation cookery books from the southern United States and the 'soul food' cookbooks of the 1970s, interest in this area of collecting is strong.

Often illustrated with stereotypical drawings and verses or sayings in dialect, these books continue to attract attention, especially from African-American collectors.

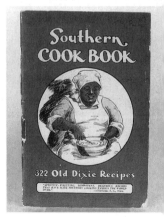

▶ S. Rensel, S. Sondheim and L. Lustig, Southern Cook Book, published by Culinary Arts Press, 1939, 9 x 6in (23 x 15cm).
£20–25 MSB

◀ Mrs Mary Richardson, Physical Culture Cook Book, published by The Physical Culture Publishing Co, New York, 1901, 8 x 5in (20.5 x 12.5cm).
£30–35 AHa

Mrs Rundell, *A New System of Domestic Cookery*, published by Johnson, Chapman and Bell, slight damage, rebacked, 1852, 5 x 3in (12.5 x 7.5cm).
£42–50 SEE

Annette Rosen, *The Advocate Cookbook*, supplement to *The Jewish Advocate*, 1929, 10¾ x 7¾in (27.5 x 19.5cm).
£17–20 MSB

Kate Smith's Favorite Recipes, second anniversary edition, published by General Foods Corporation, 1940, 9½ x 7¾in (24 x 19.5cm).
£18–20 MSB

Cross Reference
See Colour Review

◀ Louis Eustache Ude, *The French Cook*, third edition, 1815, 8¼ x 5in (21 x 12.5cm).
£275–325 SEE

Soups Savouries Sweets, by a Practical Housewife, published by Richard Bentley & Son, 1889, 7 x 5½in (18 x 14cm).
£50–60 AHa

▶ *Table Treats*, published by The C. F. Sauer Company, Richmond, Virginia, c1925, 8½ x 5½in (21.5 x 14cm).
£10–12 MSB

Warne's Model Cookery and Housekeeping Book, edited and compiled by Mary Jewry, early 20thC, 7 x 5in (18 x 12.5cm).
£30–35 SMI

H. J. Wehman, *Confectioner's Guide and Assistant*, 1939, 7½ x 5½in (19 x 14cm).
£12–15 MSB

LITERATURE

Raymond Chandler, *The Long Goodbye*, first English edition, slight damage, 1953, 8vo.
£90–100 DW
This edition pre-dates the first American publication.

Thomas Hardy, *Tess of the D'Urbervilles*, first edition published by Osgood, McIlvaine and Co, original cloth, 1895, 8 x 6in (20.5 x 15cm).
£50–60 BAY

Wyndham Lewis, *Apes of God*, No. 298 of 750 copies signed by the author, illustrations by the author, original cloth, dust jacket, published by The Arthur Press, 1930, 4to.
£320–360 WilP

Sir Arthur Conan Doyle, *The Hound of the Baskervilles*, first edition, 16 plates by Sidney Paget, original gilt and black pictorial cloth, published by George Newnes, slight damage, 1902, 8vo.
£350–400 BBA

James Joyce, *The Mime of Mick, Nick and the Maggies*, first edition, paperback limited edition of 1,000 numbered copies, 1933, 9½ x 6½in (24 x 16.5cm).
£300–350 CATH

Anthony Trollope, *The American Senator*, first edition, three volumes, original cloth, 1877, 8 x 5in (20.5 x 12.5cm).
£200–240 BAY

H. Rider Haggard, *King Solomon's Mines*, original decorated cloth, 1899, 8 x 6in (20.5 x 15cm).
£65–75 BAY

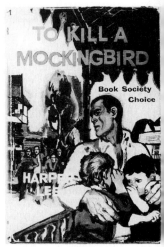

Harper Lee, *To Kill a Mockingbird*, first English edition, slight damage, 1960, 8vo.
£200–220 DW

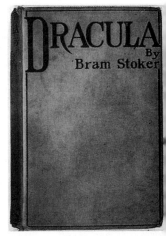

Bram Stoker, *Dracula*, first edition, first issue, original yellow cloth lettered in red, slight wear, 1897, 8vo.
£4,300–4,800 DW

NATURAL HISTORY

W. F. Kirby, *Butterflies and Moths of Europe*, with 54 coloured plates, printed by Cassell & Co, 1907, 11 x 9in (28 x 23cm).
£120–150 AHa

Francis Bacon, *Sylva Sylvarum or a Natural History in Ten Centuries*, published by W. Rawley, 1676, 12 x 8in (30.5 x 20.5cm).
£300–350 AHa

John Blackwall, *A History of the Spiders of Great Britain and Ireland*, two volumes, with 29 hand-coloured plates, published by Ray Society, 1861–64, large 4to.
£330–360 DW

B. Maund, *The Book of Hardy Flowers*, with approximately fifty coloured copper-plates of flowers and 190 wood engravings, published by Groombridge, 1851–52, 8 x 7in (20.5 x 18cm).
£200–250 AHa

Dr Walter Nicol, *The Forcing, Fruit & Kitchen Gardener*, fourth edition, with six copper-plates, printed for William Creech, Edinburgh, Longman & Co, J. Harding and T. Hamilton, London, 1809, 9 x 6¼in (23 x 16cm).
£350–390 OPB

▶ Mary E. Unger, *The Favorite Flowers of Japan*, with coloured illustrations by T. Hasegawa, bound concertina-style in original pictorial boards, with folding card case, 1901, small 4to.
£450–500 BBA

A Universal System of Natural History, Birds, five volumes, with 165 hand-coloured copper-plates, 1790, 9 x 6in (23 x 15cm).
£1,800–2,000 AHa

PRAYER BOOKS & BIBLES

The Book of Common Prayer, bound with *The Holy Bible*, in contemporary calf, with brass clasps, 1634, 9 x 7in (23 x 18cm).
£520–560 BAY

The Book of Common Prayer, bound in blue morocco with gilt and red oval inlay, 1781–84, 8 x 6in (20.5 x 15cm).
£400–450 BAY

A German Bible, with ivorine cover, mother-of-pearl cross and gilt-metal mounts, c1890, 4 x 3in (10 x 7.5cm).
£30–35 DP

TRAVEL & TOPOGRAPHY

William Harrison Ainsworth, *The Tower of London*, illustrated, 1840, 9 x 6in (23 x 15cm).
£12–15 DW

Aeneas Anderson, *Narrative of the British Embassy to China, in the Years 1792, 1793, and 1794*, first edition, in contemporary mottled calf, heavily worn, 1795, 4to.
£90–110 DW

W. E. D. Allen and Paul Muratoff, *Caucasian Battlefields, a History of the Wars on the Turco-Caucasian Border 1828–1921*, first edition, with eight black-and-white illustrations and 39 maps, published by Cambridge University Press, 1953, 8vo.
£110–130 DW

John Auldjo, *Ascent of Mont Blanc*, with six hand-coloured plates, in full maroon straight-grained morocco, rebacked, 1828, 12 x 10in (30.5 x 25.5cm).
£500–575 BAY

Philippe Avril, *Travels into Divers Parts of Europe and Asia, Undertaken by the French King's Order to Discover a New Way by Land into China*, first English edition, in contemporary speckled calf, the title printed in red and black, slight damage, 1693, 12mo.
£300–350 DW
Philippe Avril (1654–98), Jesuit traveller, set out in 1685 to find an overland route to the Far East. He went via Cyprus, Syria, Asia Minor and Persia, but was turned back on reaching Astrakhan on the northern shores of the Caspian Sea; subsequently he returned to Constantinople, then to France via Poland and Moldavia, arriving home in 1690.

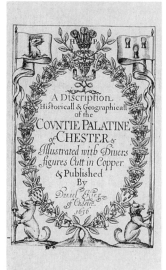

The Vale-Royall of England or, The County Palatine of Chester, first edition, with two double-page maps of Cheshire and the Isle of Man, one plan and 18 plates, 17thC ink signatures of John Jackson on front free endpaper and dedication leaf, published by Daniel King, 1656, folio.
£750–850 BBA

W. H. Bartlett, *Gleanings, Pictorial and Antiquarian, on the Overland Route*, first edition, with two maps, a folding panorama of Alexandria and 23 steel-engraved views, in contemporary calf, 1851, 8vo.
£100–120 DW

Sir Richard Colt Hoare, *A Collection of Forty Views in North and South Wales*, in full green straight-grain morocco, 1804, 11 x 9in (28 x 23cm).
£430–480 BAY

Bottles

Although the Romans imported glass to Britain, it was not until the 16th century that a native glass-making industry was established in England, and not until the 17th century that glass bottles were much used for wines and spirits. Pottery containers were more common, such as the Bellarmine flask, its bearded mask said to represent Cardinal Bellarmino (1542–1621), Italian priest and scourge of the Protestants. Ceramics remained a popular medium, and this section includes Reform flasks, made to celebrate the passing of the Reform Act of 1832, and stoneware ginger beer bottles. The value of the latter depends on the attraction and quality of the transfer-printing, and the rarity of the bottle's maker and location, since many collectors focus on specific geographical areas. Early glass wine bottles can command exceptionally high prices (see Record Breakers, p.461).

In addition to alcohol, a wide variety of bottles were developed for the fizzy drinks industry. The torpedo-shaped Hamilton bottle (introduced by William Hamilton, c1814) was designed to lie on its side so that the cork would stay wet and swollen, and not pop out. In the 1870s, Hiram Codd invented the Codd bottle with its marble stopper, hence the expression 'a load of old codd's wallop'. Clear and aqua Codd bottles can still be picked up very cheaply, but rare coloured examples and more unusual designs can make three-figure sums and more.

This section concludes with poison and medicine bottles. Because people were predominantly illiterate, these were often made in coloured glass and were shaped so that they could be identified by touch. Here again, the rarest designs can fetch hundreds or even thousands of pounds, and recent records include £11,000 paid for a mid-19th century medicine bottle in the USA, a true bottle bank.

Rhenish Bellarmine stoneware jug, the ovoid body moulded and incised with a bearded mask over an oval armorial panel, 17thC, 13¼in (33.5cm) high.
£500–550 HYD

► A Dutch dark olive-green glass onion bottle, with pontilled kick-up base and tapered neck with applied string rim, c1710, 6½in (16.5cm) high.
£85–100 BBR

A dark olive-green glass shaft-and-globe bottle, with fleur-de-lys seal, 1670–80, 7in (18cm) high.
£2,000–2,200 BBR

A dark olive-green glass mallet bottle, with applied string rim and kick-up pontil base, 1720–30, 6¾in (17cm) high.
£180–200 BBR

A shell-encrusted port bottle, from the *Diana* cargo, c1816, 9¾in (25cm) high.
£125–150 RBA

An Old Fulham Pottery 'Adaptable Hot Water Bottle', for muff or pocket, 19thC, 4in (10cm) diam.
£130–150 ALA

A red earthenware harvest bottle, with brown-green glaze, the shoulder impressed 'Jacob Pratt 1824', 5½in (14cm) high.
£180–200 BBR

◄ A dark olive-green glass squat cylinder bottle, with double collar lip, kick-up pontil base, chip to base, 1780–90, 8in (20.5cm) high.
£35–40 BBR

A Bellarmine-style grey saltglaze flagon, incised 'Iron Peartree Water Near Godstone Surrey', with two raised medallions below the neck, probably 18thC, 14¾in (37.5cm) high.
£1,400–1,600 BBR

A Bourne Potteries two-tone saltglaze stoneware spirit flask, moulded as a male figure seated on a barrel, impressed 'Success to Reform', c1832, 8in (20.5cm) high.
£130–150 Hal

◄ A Shaws Patent skittle aqua glass Codd bottle, embossed 'Goldberg & Zefferitt Johannesburg & Boksburg, Shaws Patent Wm Barnard & Sons London', 1890–1910, 7½in (19cm) high.
£38–45 BBR

A dark olive-green glass Alloa-type onion bottle, with white enamelled flecks, c1800, 5in (12.5cm) high.
£550–610 BBR

A brown saltglaze Reform flask, in the form of Queen Victoria, impressed mark, restored 1837, 8¼in (21cm) high.
£85–100 BBR

LOCATE THE SOURCE

The source of each illustration in Miller's can be found by checking the code letters below each caption with the Key to Illustrations, pages 476–484.

An amber glass dumpy Codd bottle, embossed 'Codds Patent 4 Rylands & Codd Makers Stairfoot Barnsley', 1890–1910, 7½in (19cm) high.
£200–220 BBR

A cobalt-blue glass flask, possibly Barrons Glassworks, with clear glass stopper, embossed with grapes and vines, 1890–1910, 9¼in (23.5cm) high.
£180–220 BBR

A cobalt-blue glass Harden Grenade Sprinkler Fire Extinguisher, vertically ribbed and with star trademark, sealed and with contents, 1900–10, 17in (43cm) long.
£600–700 BBR

An Oakhill Brewery olive-green glass beer bottle, c1900, 10in (25.5cm) high
£8–10 BSA

A Mason's mallet bottle, with raised Masonic symbols, impressed scroll 'Janet Jackson', 1900–10, 7⅜in (19.5cm) high.
£550–610 BBR

A blue glass Hardens Hand Grenade Fire Extinguisher, vertically ribbed and with star trademark, marked, sealed and with contents, 1900–10, 6¼in (16cm) high.
£75–85 BBR

Two Denby saltglaze bottles, with impressed oval marks, c1912, tallest 6½in (16.5cm) high.
l. £7–8
r. £10–12 KES

Cross Reference
See Colour Review

▶ A rubber hot water bottle, in the form of a child wearing a space helmet and holding a crescent moon, 1950–60, 12in (30.5cm) long.
£20–25 JUN

POISON & MEDICINE BOTTLES

A pontilled glass medicine bottle, embossed 'Warren & Rosser Skinner Street London', 1860–70, 6½in (16.5cm) high.
£480–530 BBR

A set of four clear pharmacy bottles, with blown stoppers, 1860–70, 11in (28cm) high.
£200–240 BWA

A set of four green poison bottles, with glass stoppers, c1890, 8in (20.5cm) high.
£230–270 BWA

A Handyside's dark olive-green glass medicine bottle, embossed 'Handyside's Consumption Cure', 1890–1910, 10¾in (27.5cm) high.
£170–190 BBR

A Wilsons emerald-green glass poison bottle, embossed 'Miriams Embrocation Not to be Taken Caution Patent', 1899, 4¼in (11cm) high.
£280–320 BBR

A Warner's two pint amber glass medicine bottle, embossed 'Warners Safe Cure London Eng Toronto Canada Rochester N.Y. U.S.A.', 1900–10, 11¼in (28.5cm) high.
£375–425 BBR

Two cobalt-blue glass poison bottles, embossed vertically 'Poisonous Not To Be Taken', 1900–10, tallest 8¾in (22cm) high.
£40–50 BBR

▶ A Warner's amber glass medicine bottle, embossed 'Warner's Safe Compound', with original label and contents, 1900–10, 5½in (14cm) high.
£450–500 BBR
This is the extremely rare version with flat side panels, and the only recorded example with contents and label.

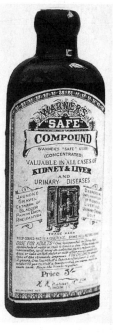

A concrete butcher's shop advertising figure, in the shape of a pig, late 19thC, 23in (58.5cm) high.
£550–650 MFB

A Sunlight Soap cardboard advertisement, c1900, 14in (35.5cm) high.
£45–50 COB

▶ A Milkmaid Brand Milk enamel sign, framed, c1910, 47in (119.5cm) high.
£250–300 JUN

A Zebra Paste Grate Polish wooden display box, c1910, 15in (38cm) wide.
£45–55 SMI

A John Bull tin advertising figure, c1910, 4in (10cm) high.
£110–125 HUX

A Weetabix cereal packet, 1950s, 10in (25.5cm) wide.
£35–40 YR

A Walt Disney Video Days cardboard advertising stand, 1970s, 35in (89cm) high.
£18–22 TRA

A Robertson's plaster Golly figure, with illuminating jar of Golden Shred, on circular plinth, 27½in (70cm) high.
£700–770 BBR

A papier mâché display figure, in the shape of a pig, c1920, 20in (51cm) high.
£220–250 SMI

A Coca Cola refrigerator, 1950–60s, 37in (94cm) high.
£600–660 EDO

◀ A Coca Cola enamel advertising sign, 1950s, 36in (91.5cm) diam.
£250–300 EDO

◀ A PG Tips toy monkey, 1970s, 14in (35.5cm) high.
£18–20 HUX

A Le Pelican Rouge Belgian coffee tin, depicting Queen Victoria with Heads of State, c1900, 15½in (39.5cm) high.
£500–550 **HUX**

A Christie's biscuit tin, in the shape of a windmill, c1925, 11in (28cm) high.
£500–550 **HUX**

A Butlin's sweet tin, c1960, 5in (12.5cm) wide.
£12–15 **WAB**

A set of Huntley & Palmer book tins, 1901, 7in (18cm) wide.
£220–265 **WAB**

A Parkinson's Original Tit-Bits tin, 1920s, 6in (15cm) high.
£38–45 **MURR**

A Rayline Wonder Polish tin, 1930, 4in (10cm) diam.
£12–15 **YR**

A Player's Navy Cut Cigarettes tin, 1950s, 3in (7.5cm) wide.
£15–20 **WAB**

▶ A Mars Bar tin, in the shape of a safe, 1970s, 7in (18cm) high.
£12–15 **PLB**

A Muratti's Cigarettes tin, c1920, 3in (7.5cm) wide.
£30–35 **WAB**

A Macfarlane Lang & Co biscuit tin, 'The House that Jack Built', c1930, 6in (15cm) wide.
£165–200 **WAB**

A Fulcreem tin money box, in the shape of a house, with lockable side window, 1920–30s, 5½in (14cm) high.
£50–60 **BBR**

A walnut-veneered circular display cabinet, 1930s, 45in (114.5cm) diam.
£600–660 BDA

◀ A silk screen print of the *Normandie*, c1975, 26in (66cm) square.
£40–50 COB

A wooden dumb waiter, c1925, 38in (96.5cm) high.
£45–50 FA

A pair of Henri Bergé & Alméric Walter *pâte de verre* bookends, in the shape of squirrels, signed, c1930, 5in (12.5cm) wide.
£1,800–2,000 TWr

A pair of Continental ceramic bookends, in the form of a lady, 1930s, 4½in (11.5cm) high.
£65–80 CoCo

A pair of Venetian blue glass tazzas, probably Venini & Cappellin, Murano, c1925, 9¾in (25cm) high.
£250–300 BRU

A Rowntree chocolate box, 1929, 11in (28cm) long.
£18–20 YR

◀ A Crown Corona Lizard jug, c1943, 7in (18cm) high.
£75–85 CoCo

An Art Deco French spelter and ivoreen figure of a female dancer, on an onyx base, 1930s, 12in (30.5cm) high.
£425–500 JEZ

▶ An Art Deco table lamp, with a metal and ivorine figure of a fashionable lady seated on an alabaster base, 1930s, 12¼in (30cm) high.
£400–500 P(B)

An Eugène Wave for Women advertising figure, 1930s, 12in (30.5cm) high.
£140–160 HUX

A Czechslovaki-Karami terracotta figure, 1930s, 18in (45.5cm) high.
£120–150 BTB

An Empire ware Black Marguerite pattern chintz smoker's set, with six ashtrays, 1930s, 5in (12.5cm) wide.
£100–120 BEV

A Gibson's Sheila teapot, 1930s, 6in (15cm) high.
£80–95 CoCo

A Grimwade Rubian ware Flames pattern plate, designed by Ike Mattison, 1930, 6½in (16.5cm) diam.
£42–50 CoCo

A Japanese toucan cruet set, 1930s, 4in (10cm) high.
£50–60 JEZ

A Goldscheider Heuzeg figure of a dancing girl, signed, Austrian, 1930s, 15in (38cm) high.
£1,200–1,400 MD

▶ A Royal Dux wall mask, in the form of a lady's head, a flower brooch attached to her collar, 1930s, 8in (20.5cm) high.
£180–220 BEV

A Gray's hand-painted jug, signed 'Dora', 1930s, 4½in (11.5cm) high.
£150–165 PrB

A Hancock Ivoryware hand-painted vase, 1930s, 6in (15cm) high.
£75–90 BEV

◀ A Royal Dux figure of a woman, pink triangle mark, 1920–30, 7in (18cm) high.
£220–250 JEZ

▶ A Losol ware vase, decorated with flowers and birds, 1920s, 9in (23cm) high.
£180–200 BEV

An American Crescent
Cycles lithographic poster,
after F. W. Ramsdell, linen-
mounted and wrapped,
on board, some surface
damage, 1899, 80 x 40in
(203 x 101.5cm).
£350–400 BKS

A Limoges enamel miniature plaque,
1910–20, 5in (12.5cm) high.
£420–500 JEZ

A Frueruth powder bowl, the lid
surmounted by a butterfly,
German, 1900, 8in (20.5cm) high.
£400–450 MD

A pair of twisted tear
glass vases, c1900,
10in (25.5cm) high.
£400–500 ALiN

Two wall lanterns, with
coloured glass panels
and cut and pierced
brasswork and bevellers,
c1880, 18in (45.5cm) high.
£320–360 ASH

A pair of lustre glass
vases, in pewter mounts,
c1900, 8in (20.5cm) high.
£320–380 WAC

A silver brooch, in the
form of a woman's
head, marked, c1901,
1in (2.5cm) high.
£40–50 TB

A wooden picture frame,
12in (30.5cm) high.
£150–175 TWr

A lacquered copper lantern,
c1900,16in (40.5cm) high.
£700–800 WAC

A copper jardinière, the
tapering body composed
of rivetted panels
decorated with four
applied brass celtic motifs,
each centred with a
Ruskin-like ceramic boss,
c1900, 9in (23cm) high.
£180–200 P(B)

◄ A WMF sugar basket,
with cranberry glass liner,
c1900, 4¾in (12cm) high.
£160–190 WAC

A copper-framed mirror, c1910, 18in (45.5cm) diam.
£250–300 WAC

A pair of brass lanterns, lacquered, 12in (30.5cm) high.
£600–675 WAC

A Newlyn copper candlestick, c1910, 5½in (14cm) wide.
£160–190 WAC

A Burmantofts two-handled pottery vase, c1890, 5in (12.5cm) high.
£250–300 HUN

An Ault pottery humorous double fish face vase, by Dr Christopher Dresser, c1892, 7in (18cm) high.
£800–900 HUN

◀ A pair of Brannam pottery vases, by James Drawery, 1887, 8in (20.5cm) high.
£250–300 HUN

A provincial-style blue and white porcelain bowl, from the Nanking cargo, freely painted with flowers and patterns, c1750, 5in (12.5cm) diam.
£100–125 RBA

A soup dish, from the Nanking cargo, decorated with Three Pavilion pattern, c1750, 9in (23cm) diam.
£325–375 RBA

A Chinese Celadon dessert service, comprising four serving dishes and ten plates, each piece brightly painted with insects, birds and flowers, late 19thC.
£350–400 Bea(E)

A Japanese Noritake cup and saucer, c1905, cup 2½in (6.5cm) high.
£100–125 RIA

A Japanese Imari porcelain bowl, 19thC, 9in (23cm) diam.
£400–450 BRU

◄ A Chinese silk panelled and hand-embroidered skirt, late 19thC, 28in (71cm) long.
£150–180 JPr

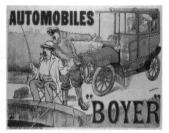

An Automobiles Boyer poster, after P. Chapellier, trimmed, laid on linen and stretched on a wooden frame, c1904, 46 x 62in (117 x 157.5cm).
£550–650 BKS

A G. Borel & Cie poster, advertising Blériot aeroplanes, c1910, 30 x 86in (76 x 218.5cm).
£1,250–1,500 COB

A Hutchinson Tyres cardboard poster, c1912, 18 x 14in (45.5 x 35.5cm), framed.
£200–250 COB

A silver-painted metal pedal Pursuit Plane, 'Juvenile Delinquents', with wooden propeller and rubber tyres, fully restored, c1920.
£2,000–2,200 S(Cg)

A Frederick Gordon Crosby picture 'Line Painting', in pen, ink and watercolour, signed and dated '1937', 15½ x 13in (40 x 33cm).
£1,900–2,300 BKS

A BOAC clothes pegs and line kit, in leather pouch, c1960, 5in (12.5cm) wide .
£10–12 HUX

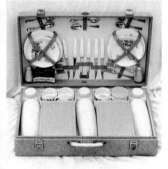

A Brexton picnic hamper, unused, 1960s, 23in (58.5cm) wide.
£150–175 PPH

A wooden wall plaque of a 1954 Ferrari Le Mans car, c1960, 45in (114.5cm) long.
£500–550 BKS

▶ A Rheos Formula 1 racing helmet, belonging to Ayrton Senna when driving for McLaren, sponsors' logos include Honda, Marlboro, Nacional and Boss, dark-tinted visor, radio and wiring fitted, 1990.
£12,500–14,000 BKS

A pair of Sparco racing gloves, belonging to Damon Hill when driving for his last season with Jordan in 1999, Benson & Hedges logo, signed in black, mounted and framed, 12 x 18in (30.5 x 45.5cm).
£650–750 BKS

E. M. Brent-Dyer, *The Chalet School Reunion*, first edition, 1963, 8 x 5in (20.5 x 12.5cm).
£100–120 OCB

Enid Blyton, *Noddy And Big Ears Have A Picnic,* Tiny Noddy Book 6, 1950s, 3in (7.5cm) square.
£8–10 OCB

Jean de Brunhoff, *Babar And Father Christmas,* first edition, published by Methuen, 1940, 14 x 10in (35.5 x 25.5cm).
£60–70 OCB

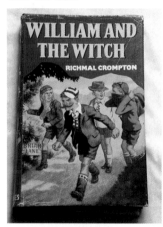

Richmal Crompton, *William And The Witch,* first edition, 1964, 7½ x 5in (19 x 12.5cm).
£80–90 OCB

Captain W. E. Johns, *Biggles Fails To Return,* published by Hodder & Stoughton, 1950, 7½ x 5in (19 x 12.5cm).
£10–12 OCB

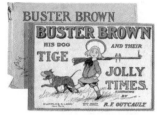

Cupples & Leon, New York Herald, *Buster Brown His Dog Tige And Their Jolly Times,* illustrated by Richard F Outcault, No. 1 card cover comic book in colour with rare printed dust wrapper by Dean & Son for UK import, *Buster And Tige Go Shooting, Fishing And Play Cowboys,* first issue, some wear, 1906, 11 x 16in (28 x 40.5cm).
£170–200 CBP

Peyo, *The Smurfette*, a Smurf adventure book, 1976, 11 x 9in (28 x 23cm).
£8–10 GAZE

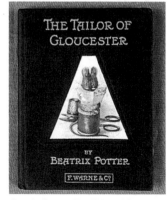

Beatrix Potter, *The Tailor of Gloucester,* published by F. Warne & Co, first edition, slight wear, 1903, 16mo.
£550–650 DW

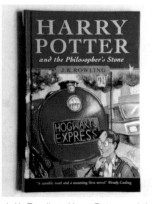

J. K. Rowling, *Harry Potter and the Philosopher's Stone,* first edition, signed by the author, 1997, 8 x 5½in (20.5 x 14cm).
£8,500–10,000 AHa

Cassell's Dictionary of Cookery, published by Cassell, Petter & Galpin, rebound in cloth, c1877, 9¼ x 6in (23.5 x 15cm).
£75–85 SEE

Housekeepers' Friend, published by A. Wheeler & Co, 1881, 11½in (29cm) high.
£35–40 OPB

Mrs Isabella Beeton, *The Book of Household Management*, published by Ward Lock & Co, entirely new edition revised and corrected, rebound in cloth, some pages repaired, 1880, 6½ x 4½in (17 x 11.5cm).
£130–150 SEE

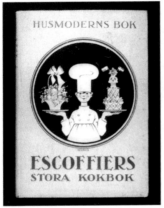

Mrs M. Lincoln et al, *Home Helps, A Pure Food Cook Book*, published by The N. K. Fairbank Co, Chicago, USA, 1910, 7⅛ x 4¾in (18.5 x 12cm).
£15–20 MSB

Escoffiers Stora Kokbok, Volume 1, Husmoderns Bok, Stockholm, 1927, 9½ x 7in (24 x 18cm).
£25–30 MSB

Blanche Caramel, *Le Nouveau Livre de Cuisine*, published by Gautier-Languereau, Paris, 1927, 7½ x 4¾in (19 x 12cm).
£35–40 MSB

Elizabeth O. Hiller, *The Calendar of Sandwiches & Beverages*, booklet and box, 1920s.
£45–50 OPB

Elizabeth O. Hiller, *New Calendar of Salads*, booklet, 1920s.
£20–25 OPB

Ambrose Heath, *Good Savouries*, frontispiece by E. Bawden, published by Faber, 1950, 7½ x 5in (19 x 12.5cm).
£5–7 SEE

Brown & Polson, *Light Fare Recipes*, 1920–30, 8½ x 4½in (21.5 x 11.5cm).
£20–25 SMI

A pair of green glass poison bottles, with stoppers, c1890, 10in (25.5cm) high.
£160–180 BWA

A glass Hasu-No-Hana perfume bottle, by J. Grossmith & Son, with original contents and box, c1900, 5in (12.5cm) high.
£120–140 BAO

An aqua glass bottle, embossed 'Spes Bona Aerated Water Works, Johannesburg' to front, 'Acme Patent, 4 Sole, Makers Dan Rylands Ltd, Barnsley' to rear, some surface dullness, c1900, 9⅞in (25cm) long.
£140–160 BBR

A Doulton Lambeth Bellarmine jug, decorated with a tan salt-glazed bearded face below silver rim, impressed mark 'Doulton Lambeth' to base, marked to rim, 1895–6, 5in (12.5cm) high.
£200–240 BBR

A Hardens Blue Star glass fire grenade, c1910, 6in (15cm) high.
£45–50 WAB

A Fryco Cloudy Lemon Squash bottle, with contents, 1920s, 6in (15cm) high.
£15–18 RTT

An Icilma green glass bottle of skin toner, c1920, 7in (18cm) high.
£15–18 RTT

An MGM Jerry rubber hot water bottle, 1986, 12in (30.5cm) high.
£10–12 HarC

▶ A clear glass bottle of Corona Orangeade, 1950s, 12½in (32cm) high.
£12–15 SVB

A box of six sample bottles of Mason's O.K Sauce, 1950s, 4in (10cm) high.
£50–60 HUX

A George III satin harewood twin tea caddy, with shell inlay, c1790, 7in (18cm) wide.
£820–900 BBo

A Victorian tortoiseshell playing card box, 1840s, 3½in (9cm) wide.
£350–400 SWO

A Victorian papier mâché fitted sewing box, 1860s, 11in (28cm) wide.
£350–400 SWO

A walnut tea caddy, with brass-banded lid, c1850, 8in (20.5cm) wide.
£250–300 MB

A pair of Mauchline ware jewellery boxes, c1860, 8in (20.5cm) wide.
£900–1,200 TWr

A Victorian shell shoe, 6in (15cm) long.
£35–40 BSA

A Victorian burr walnut double decker writing/jewellery box, inlaid with mother-of-pearl, c1870, 12in (30.5cm) wide.
£300–350 MB

A Victorian figured walnut lady's dressing box, fitted with various containers and glass bottles with silver-plated tops, 12in (30.5cm) wide.
£450–500 OTT

A Mauchline ware sycamore box, depicting Maidstone New Bridge, c1880, 3in (7.5cm) wide.
£35–40 MB

A brass 'Mary Box' tobacco tin, dated Christmas 1914, 5in (12.5cm) wide.
£25–30 WAB

▶ A mother-of-pearl and abalone card case, 19thC, 4in (10cm) long.
£220–250 BBo

A Mocha ware pint ale tankard, c1860, 5in (12.5cm) high.
£100–120 WeA

◀ A Barlow Thomason-style copper corkscrew, with bone handle, 19thC, 7in (18cm) long.
£250–300 TSV

▶ A Doulton stoneware Thorne's Whisky jug, 1880–90, 7¾in (19.5cm) high.
£170–200 BBR

A Doulton Kingsware flask, decorated with black transfer-printed scene commemorating a flight over Sydney Harbour, the reverse with 'Dewar's', 1914, 6½in (16.5cm) high.
£275–300 BBR

A Royal Doulton Artware whiskey jug, decorated with applied grapes and vines, 20thC, 6¼in (16cm) high.
£220–250 BBR

A Bullards' Beers enamel advertising sign, 1920, 18 x 10in (45.5 x 25.5cm).
£275–325 RTT

A wooden cocktail and smoking bar piece, to store and light cigarettes, 1930s, 12in (30.5cm) wide.
£150–170 BEV

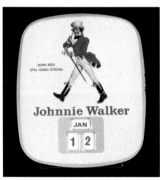

A Johnnie Walker calendar, 1950–60s, 11 x 9¼in (28 x 23.5cm).
£35–45 HUX

◀ A Ridlers Cider tin tray, 1930s, 12in (30.5cm) diam.
£12–15 RTT

A resin and cork bottle stopper, in the form of Winston Churchill, 1940–50s, 3½in (9cm) high.
£50–60 TSV

▶ A Guinness
tin tray, 1950s,
13 x 16½in
(33 x 42cm).
£40–50 HUX

A Dewar's Scotch Whisky
advertising figure, c1950,
10in (25.5cm) high.
£45–55 HUX

A glass cocktail shaker,
with pewter top, 1950s,
7½in (19cm) high.
£8–10 SCM

A set of Carlton Ware Guinness toucans, handpainted,
restored, c1960, largest 10in (25.5cm) long.
£400–450 BSA

A Mirro aluminium shaker
and Wonder Bar Instant
Cocktail Mixers, 1950s–60s,
shaker 4¼in (11cm) high.
£25–30 SpM

▶ A bottle of 1961
Macallan Scotch Whisky,
commemorating the 35 year
anniversary of *Private Eye*
magazine, No. 2810 of 5,000
bottles, 12in (30.5cm) high.
£80–100 P(Sc)

A bottle of 1964 Moet &
Chandon champagne,
12in (30.5cm) high.
£200–250 P(B)

A corkscrew, in the
shape of a seal and ball,
possibly Wade, 1960s,
2½in (6.5cm) high.
£25–30 TSV

A cased cocktail set, containing beakers and
corkscrew with space for bottles, late 1960s–70s,
13 x 8in (33 x 20.5cm).
£40–50 PPH

A Baby Cham melamine
ashtray, made by
Praesidium, 1970s,
10in (25.5cm) long.
£12–15 BSA

An anodised aluminium
corkscrew, 1960s–70s,
7in (18cm) long.
£18–22 TSV

Fun and Frolic, with illustrations by Louis Wain, published by Collins' Clear Type Press, London & Glasgow, 1908, 10 x 8in (25.5 x 20.5cm).
£60–70 MRW

A Louis Wain (1860–1939) picture of a cat, The Early Italian, in watercolour, bodycolour and crayon, inscribed with title on reverse, 7¼in x 5in (18.5 x 12.5cm).
£4,000–4,500 C

A Carlton Ware novelty napkin ring, modelled as a hump-back cat, 1930s, 3in (7.5cm) high.
£90–100 BEV

A Wood's Pussyfoot series yellow teapot, modelled as a cat, 1930s, 8in (20.5cm) high.
£95–115 BEV

Two Wade Disney cats, Si and Am, 1960s, largest 5¾in (14.5cm) high.
£280–300 PC

A West German jug, modelled as a cat, 1950s, 8in (20.5cm) high.
£25–30 BEV

Kathleen Hale, *Orlando the Judge*, 1970, 7 x 9in (18 x 23cm).
£25–30 OCB

► A Royal Crown Derby paperweight, modelled as a cat, 1997, 3in (7.5cm) wide.
£40–50 WAC

A Carlton Ware teapot, modelled as a cat, 1980s, 9in (23cm) wide.
£70–90 JEZ

A Beswick Beatrix Potter model of Ginger, 1976–82, 3¾in (9.5cm) high.
£275–300 SAS

Boxes

A George III mahogany tea caddy, with decorative inlay, 4in (10cm) square.
£450–500 OTT

An oak and mahogany sarcophagus jewel box, with brass fittings, 1815, 10in (25.5cm) wide.
£250–300 MB

A William IV rosewood sewing box, with pewter stringing and mother-of-pearl inlay, c1820, 12in (30.5cm) wide.
£325–375 OTT

A burr walnut single tea caddy, 1840, 7in (18cm) high.
£350–400 MB

A Sheraton inlaid mahogany tea caddy, 1795–1810, 9in (23cm) wide.
£300–350 MB

A yew wood tea caddy, c1820, 7in (18cm) wide.
£400–480 TWr

A Victorian trinket box, inlaid with light and dark squares of mother-of-pearl, mid-19thC, 4in (10cm) wide.
£250–300 BBo

A Tunbridge Ware tea caddy, inlaid with rosewood, c1850, 8in (20.5cm) wide.
£450–500 MB

A tortoiseshell card case, inlaid with a mother-of-pearl floral design, 19thC, 4in (10cm) high.
£250–300 BBo

A Victorian mahogany-cased domestic medicine chest, the hinged lid opening to reveal six bottles with stoppers, some with labels, the drawer below with a balance, 6½in (16.5cm) wide.
£800–900 TRM

A Mauchline ware sycamore tumbler box, decorated with a view of Hunstanton beach, 1860, 3in (7.5cm) high.
£35–40 MB

▶ An Edwardian japanned brass-mounted tin cash box, c1910, 5in (12.5cm) wide.
£20–25 WAB

An olive wood tea caddy, with brass bandings, 1860, 9in (23cm) wide.
£300–350 MB

A walnut veneered table chest, with brass Gothic-style mounts and carrying handles to the sides, the interior veneered with rosewood, 19thC, 15¼in (38.5cm) long.
£800–900 Mit

A Mauchline ware miniature trunk, decorated with a view of Dover, c1870, 3in (7.5cm) wide.
£50–60 ALA

A Victorian burr walnut writing box, with military brass work and green leather interior, 14in (35.5cm) wide.
£250–300 OTT

A Tunbridge Ware tea caddy, 19thC, 4in (10cm) wide.
£250–300 TWr

A porcupine and ebony box, 19thC, 8in (20.5cm) wide.
£85–100 TMi

A Victorian honey oak stationery box, with dovetail drawer, 12in (30.5cm) high.
£225–250 AMR

Breweriana

A White Horse Whisky advertising wooden coat hanger, 1930s, 4in (10cm) high.
£7–8 FA

A Black & White Whisky advertising penknife, c1930, 3in (7.5cm) long.
£10–12 WAB

Cross Reference
See Colour Review

A silver-plated ice bucket, 1930s, 6in (15cm) high.
£100–115 BEV

An Art Deco silver-plated and frosted glass cocktail shaker, decorated with various cocktail recipes, 1930s, 11in (28cm) high.
£40–50 SCM

A silver-plated cocktail shaker, 1930s, 8in (20.5cm) high.
£50–60 BEV

▶ A red Bakelite and silver-plated soda syphon, 1945–50, 11in (28cm) high.
£10–12 SCM

A white-banded clear glass cocktail decanter, 1950s, 8½in (21.5cm) high.
£16–20 SCM

A Showerings Champagne Cider metal tray, decorated in green, red and yellow on a cream ground, with khaki rim, 1950s, 12in (30.5cm) diam.
£20–25 MURR

▶ A set of six plastic cocktail coasters, decorated in colours with wine glasses and cocktail snacks, 1960s, 3½in (9cm) diam.
£8–10 SpM

◀ A Coracle red and white drinks set, fitted for five bottles and six glasses, 1950s, 20in (51cm) wide.
£75–85 PPH

A Brexton cased drinks set, 1960s, 13in (33cm) high.
£55–65 PPH

▶ A musical plastic and chrome decanter, modelled as a boat, 1960s, 16in (40.5cm) long.
£60–70 FA

A set of 96 champagne caps, mounted in a red velvet-lined frame, 1970s, 19in (48.5cm) wide.
£60–70 BBR

A pair of Babycham glasses, with gilt rims, decorated in colours, 1970s, 5½in (14cm) high.
£2–3 each BSA

A Daily Mirror Andy Capp double-sided beer mat, decorated in red, white and blue, 1960, 4½in (11.5cm) diam.
£3–5 BSA

Miller's is a price GUIDE not a price LIST

A Babycham melamine wall plaque, by Praesidium, decorated in colours, with a blue and yellow rim, 1970s, 12in (30.5cm) diam.
£10–12 BSA

A Linney Products Coronation Street Rovers Return cocktail shaker, 1997, 9in (23cm) high, with green and yellow mat and box.
£15–18 KEN

A Lively and Bagley Gins advertising rain gauge, with a glass phial on a metal base, American, 1980s, 4¼in (11cm) high.
£5–7 RTW

▶ A Coronation Street Rover's Return green and yellow plastic ice bucket, 1997, 6in (15cm) high.
£15–20 KEN

ASHTRAYS & MATCH STRIKERS

A Schweppes Soda Seltzer ceramic ashtray, commemorating Queen Victoria's Golden Jubilee, 1897, 6in (15cm) high.
£90–110 MURR

A Schweppes ceramic ashtray, decorated in blue, red and brown and dedicated to 'H.M. The King and H.R.H. The Prince of Wales', 1900–10, 6in (15cm) high.
£55–65 MURR

A Green & Smith's match striker, 1910, 4½in (11.5cm) diam.
£50–60 BBR

A Robertons's Scotch Whisky enamel ashtray, 1910–20, 6in (15cm) diam.
£42–50 MURR

A Coates' Original Plymouth Gin blue and white match striker, by Shelley, c1911, 5in (12.5cm) diam.
£90–100 FA

A Barclay's Beers copper ashtray, 1930s, 5in (14cm) square.
£12–15 RTT

A Possil Pottery Glasgow Tennent's Lager Beer ashtray, 1940s, 4in (10cm) diam.
£12–15 PC

A White Horse Whisky ceramic ashtray, modelled as a horse's hoof, in cream and grey glaze with red and black lettering and with silver horseshoe base, 1930s, 2½in (5cm) high.
£80–90 BBR

A Black & White Scotch Whisky ceramic ashtray, 1930s, 5in (12.5cm) square.
£20–25 HUX

► A Carlsberg ceramic ashtray, by Wade, decorated with a view of Copenhagen, 1980s, 6in (15cm) diam.
£6–8 BSA

FIGURES

A White Horse Scotch Whisky coloured pottery Toby-style bust, 1920s, 9¼in (23.5cm) high.
£130–150 BBR

A Captain Morgan Rum rubberoid figure, decorated in red, green, yellow, black and red, 1930s, 13in (33cm) high.
£100–110 BBR

▶ A Beswick Double Diamond coloured figure of a striding man, with a briefcase in one hand and a bottle of Double Diamond in the other, 1930s, 7¾in (19.5cm) high.
£50–60 BBR

◀ A Black & White Whisky metal advertising group of terrier dogs, 1940s, 8in (20.5cm) high.
£140–150 DBr

A Churtons Scotch Whisky rubberoid figure, wearing a black coat, grey trousers and white shirt, on a wooden plinth, 1930s, 10¼in (26cm) high.
£190–220 BBR

A Canadian Club Whisky multicoloured plastic figure of an ice hockey player, 1940s, 9in (23cm) high.
£80–90 BBR

A Mackinlay's Scotch Whisky composition figure, with green and yellow tartan kilt, 1950s, 7in (18cm) high.
£120–130 DBr

An Old Grand Dad gold-coloured rubberoid bust, 1950s, 11½in (29cm) high.
£35–45 BBR

◀ A Lamb's Navy Rum plastic figure of a sailor, with a blue coat and black hat, 1960s, 10in (25.5cm) high.
£80–100 DBr

▶ A Queen Anne Scotch Whisky plastic figure, with a crimson robe, 1960s, 9in (23cm) high.
£90–100 DBr

A Beswick Worthington E coloured pottery group, 1960s, 9in (23cm) high.
£130–150 BBR

GUINNESS

Guinness advertising first began in 1928. The advertising agency S. H. Benson Ltd came up with the famous slogan 'Guinness is good for you'. Artist John Gilroy (1898–1985) produced a series of classic designs, including the 'Guinness for Strength' girder poster in 1934 and, from the following year, the toucan character, launching a whole menagerie of Guinness animals.

Initially, Gilroy had intended to use a pelican, and it was copywriter and crime novelist Dorothy L. Sayers who changed the bird and provided the slogan 'How grand to be a Toucan, just think what Toucan do'. In addition to Gilroy, Guinness employed many major illustrators, among them Ronald Searle, Ardizzone and Giles.

In the 1950s the company commissioned Carlton Ware to produce advertising ceramics, and over the years Guinness has produced a vast amount of memorabilia. In 1996 Christies South Kensington held a Guinness sale, which totalled nearly £85,000, and demand for Guinness ceramics resulted in a series of Carlton Ware fakes (see *Miller's Collectables Price Guide* 1998/99). As Alan Blakeman from BBR notes, 'Guinness remains one of the most buoyant and consistent specialist areas in the advertising world!'

A set of six boxed Guinness waistcoat buttons, on a yellow ground, 1950s.
£65–75 P(B)

A Guinness Huntley & Palmers biscuit tin, 1950s, 10in (25.5cm) wide.
£130–150 HUX

A Guinness beer mat, decorated in orange, black and blue, late 1950s, 4½in (11.5cm) diam.
£2–3 BSA

A set of five Guinness booklets, 'Alice, where art thou?', 'Untopical Songs', 'Can This be Beeton?', 'Game Pie', 'What Will They Think of Next?', 1950s, 9 x 7in (23 x 18cm).
£40–45 each HUX

A Guinness plate, decorated with blue and white willow pattern depicting two Chinamen chasing each other, late 1950s, 7in (18cm) diam.
£35–40 BBR

A Carlton Ware Guinness lustre plate, decorated in black and white with a pink surround, 1950s, 10in (25.5cm) diam.
£75–100 MURR

A Guinness plastic-covered tin on card advertisement, late 1950s, 12 x 8in (30.5 x 20.5cm).
£100–110 BBR

A Guinness Toucan ceramic model, decorated in black, yellow and orange with red lettering around the base, late 1950s, 3½in (9cm) high.
£240–280 BBR

A Carlton Ware Guinness ceramic kangaroo model, printed mark to base, late 1950s, 4in (10cm) high.
£85–95 BBR

A Guinness plastic condiment set, decorated in red and black on a cream ground, late 1950s–60s, tallest 5in (12.5cm) high.
£35–40 BBR

A Guinness barometer, with 'Lovely Day for a Guinness' in silver lettering on the wooden surround, late 1950s, 8in (20.5cm) diam.
£50–60 BBR

A set of Guinness laminated calendars, decorated in colours, 1955–60, 4in (10cm) high.
£15–20 each HUX

A Guinness advertising tin tray, decorated in brown, red and black on a white ground, 1960s, 16½in (42cm) wide.
£20–25 HUX

▶ A Guinness electric clock, decorated in black, cream and white on a red ground, 1970s, 12in (30.5cm) wide.
£50–60 MURR

A Guinness ceramic group of Tweedledum and Tweedledee, with green trousers and brown jackets, probably Wade, with 'Compliments of Guinness' card, late 1950s, 3in (7.5cm) high.
£65–80 BBR

A Carlton Ware Guinness condiment set, decorated with coloured toucans, late 1950s, tallest 3¾in (9.5cm) high.
£65–75 BBR

A Guinness advertising tray, decorated in red, black and cream on a white ground, 1970s, 12in (30.5cm) wide.
£35–40 MURR

JUGS & FLASKS

▶ A Glenlivet Whisky stoneware jug with a green top, transfer-printed in black, 1900–1910, 6½in (16.5cm) high.
£430–480 BBR

A White Horse Whisky jug, with dark blue body and silver-coloured rim and handle, 1900–10, 9in (23cm) high.
£120–140 MURR

A Royal Doulton Greenlees Brothers Claymore Scotch Whisky salt-glazed jug, with brown and tan body, marked, 1900–10, 6¾in (17cm) high.
£1,300–1,500 BBR

A Gilbey's Old Strathmill Highland Whisky stoneware jug, with brown rim and green glazed body, 1910, 5¾in (14.5cm) high.
£260–300 BBR

An Old Scottish Dew jug, decorated with black transfer-print, with brown top and tan salt-glazed body, 1900–10, 7¼in (18.5cm) high.
£330–360 BBR

A Charles Wilkinson & Co Whisky jug, black transfer-printed with a woman dousing a drunken Scotsman beneath a hand pump, 1900–10, 8¼in (21cm) high.
£600–700 BBR
This particular shape is exceptionally rare, and probably only the second or third of this type to come on the UK market in over 20 years.

A Doulton Kingsware flask, for Dewars, decorated in colours with a bust of Ben Jonson, on a dark brown ground, c1910, 10in (25.5cm) high.
£140–160 MURR

▶ A Doulton globular flask for Greenlees Brothers Claymore Whisky Distillers, decorated with Tam O'Shanter pursued by witches, marked, 1911, 6¾in (17cm) high.
£550–650 BBR

A ceramic quart jug, transfer-decorated with cobalt-blue hop design, 1919, 7in (18cm) high.
£42–50 WAB

A John Jameson Whisky ceramic jug, decorated in black on a yellow ground, c1920, 9in (23cm) high.
£140–160 MURR

An A. & A. Crawford's Scotch Whisky ceramic jug, decorated with blue and white willow pattern, 1930s, 6in (15cm) high.
£70–85 MURR

Items in the Jugs & Flasks section have been arranged in date order.

▶ An Old Smuggler Scotch Whisky white glazed ceramic character jug, with gold rim, 1960s, 6¾in (17cm) high.
£65–75 BBR

A Jamie Stuart Liqueur Scotch ceramic jug, transfer-printed with blue and white willow pattern, 1920, 5½in (14cm) high.
£160–180 BBR

A Johnnie Walker square ceramic jug, decorated in red, yellow and black on a white ground, 1920s, 6in (15cm) high.
£120–140 MURR

A McNish Special Scotch Whisky ceramic jug, with pale green body and tartan bands to top and bottom, 1930s, 3¾in (9.5cm) high.
£190–210 BBR

▶ A Buchanan's Black & White Whisky ceramic jug, decorated with black and white design, 1920s, 5in (12.5cm) high.
£130–150 BBR

A Dewar's White Label Whisky yellow ceramic jug, with black inscription, 1930, 3½in (9cm) high.
£30–35 BBR

A Doulton Kingsware full figural flask, decorated in colours with detachable head stopper, 1932, 10in (25.5cm) high.
£400–450 BBR

▶ A Bell's Scotch Whisky ceramic water jug, 1970s, 5in (12.5cm) high.
£20–25 HarC

A Doulton Kingsware ceramic Crown jug, for Dewars Whisky, issued to commemorate the coronation of King George VI, marked, 1937, 6in (15cm) high.
£100–220 BBR

A Ballantine's Scotch Whisky dark green ceramic jug, in the shape of a knight's helmet, 1950s, 7in (18cm) high.
£50–60 BBR

WINES & SPIRITS

Star of this section is the bottle of 50-year-old Macallan Whisky. Macallan is an exceptionally desirable distillery because since the 1930s it has produced bottles of single malt, in an environment where 98 per cent of Scottish malt whisky goes into blends such as Johnnie Walker. The whisky was distilled in 1928 and bottled in 1983, the bottle labelled 006 of 500.

Despite the fact that the alcohol volume had dropped from 63.8 per cent strength to 38.5 per cent, as the *Antiques Trade Gazette* noted, this rare Scotch was of interest to three categories of collector: the consumer, the investor and the museum curator. When sold at auction by Philips, Edinburgh, it was contested to a final hammer price of £4,000.

A bottle of Hooper's Rare Port, with wicker-covered body and handle, black and yellow paper labels, with cork and contents, c1876.
£1,000–1,200 ES

A bottle of Macallan 50-year-old Anniversary Malt, No. 006 of 500, distilled in 1928, with a letter of authenticity signed by Allan G. Shiach, Chairman, and a leather-bound wooden presentation case, 75cl @ 38.6%, at cask strength.
£4,000–5,000 P(Sc)

A bottle of Dow's 1945 Vintage Port, with embossed wax seal.
£180–200 P(B)

A bottle of Tomatin 10 Years Old Scotch Whisky, with khaki label, bottled 1960s, 26⅔fl oz @ 70° proof.
£80–100 P(Sc)

◄ A bottle of Glenfarclas 18 Year Old Single Malt Scotch Whisky, the label depicting a Morgan car and inscribed 'Distilled & Bottled for The Morgan Sports Car Club by Glenfarclas Distillery for the Scottish International Morgan Gathering 23–25 June 1989', 75cl @ 40%.
£150–180 P(Sc)

◄ A Linlithgow 600 black ceramic decanter, filled in 1989 to commemorate the 600th anniversary of the granting of the Royal Charter to the Burgh of Linlithgow, containing a 10 year old blend specially produced by Morrison Bowmore Distillers, bottle No. 061 of 600, in red tartan-lined presentation case, 75cl @ 43%.
£120–150 P(Sc)

Buttons

An Ice Age button, made from a slice of Baculum or fossilized walrus bone, 2in (5cm) diam.
£20–25 JBB
This button was found in northern Canada.

A Ton bac button, etched with a horserider, c1750, 1½in (4cm) diam.
£250–300 JBB
Ton bac is an early type of mixed metal.

An octagonal gilt and copper button, engraved and chased with geometric design, late 18thC, 1½in (4cm) diam.
£90–100 TB

◄ A Matthew Boulton cut-steel button, mounted with a Wedgwood porcelain centre, c1780, 2in (5cm) diam.
£800–900 JBB

A French porcelain button, decorated in colours with a robin on a branch, early 19thC, 1in (2.5cm) diam.
£40–45 TB

A mother-of-pearl button, etched with black, c1820, 3in (7.5cm) diam.
£250–300 JBB
This was known as a coaching button and worn on a gentleman's overcoat.

A Victorian ivory wheatsheaf button, 1½in (4cm) diam.
£22–25 JBB

A copper button, enamel-decorated in colours with Little Bo Peep, c1880, 2in (5cm) diam.
£110–130 JBB

► A shell button, with applied carved crescent moon, 1880–90, 1½in (4cm) diam.
£125–150 TB

A button, with a stamped brass oak tree surrounded by a leafy border, applied to a white metal background of buildings and a windmill, 1880–1890, 1½in (4cm) diam.
£12–15 TB

A set of six French Art Nouveau silver-plated buttons, in original case, c1900, 1½in (4cm) diam.
£190–200 JBB

Two French enamel buttons, depicting card suits, set in brass borders, c1930, ¾in (2cm) diam.
£8–10 each TB

A plastic button, moulded with an 18thC-style lady's head, c1920, 3in (7.5cm) diam.
£25–28 JBB

A set of six carved vegetable ivory buttons, 1935–40, ⅞in (22mm) diam.
£25–28 TB

An American Bakelite button, in the shape of a Black-Eyed Susan, 1930–40, 2in (5cm) diam.
£12–15 TB

A Japanese Arita porcelain button, in the shape of a carp, c1930–40, 1¼in (3cm) wide.
£45–50 TB

A set of three glass buttons, with platinum trim, 1950s, ½in (12.5mm) diam.
£3–5 BQ

▶ A set of 24 French gilt-brass buttons, 1940s, 1in (2.5cm) diam.
£4–5 each SLL

◀ A pair of heart-shaped casein buttons, decorated with a portrait of Diana, Princess of Wales, 1982, 2in (5cm) wide.
£7–8 each JBB

Cameras

An Agfa Optima 35mm compact camera, 1950s, 5in (12.5cm) wide.
£20–25 VCL

An Ensign Simplex-Auto plate camera, c1900, 4in (10cm) wide.
£40–50 SWO

A Balda Baldina camera, with a compur shutter, f2.9 50mm lens, and a coupled rangefinder, 1940, 4¾in (12cm) long.
£100–120 VCL

> Miller's is a price GUIDE not a price LIST

► An Imperial Savoy Snap Shot camera, 620 film size, American, c1956, 6in (15cm) wide.
£10–12 BSA

Three Coronet Camera Co Midget cameras, 16mm film size, c1935, 1in (25mm) wide.
£70–140 each APC
Made from Bakelite, this camera was available in five different colours.

A Junior Sanderson large format plate camera, mahogany and brass with red bellows, c1880, 6in (15cm) wide.
£150–180 TOM

A No. 1 Autographic Kodak Junior camera, 120 film size, c1920, 7in (18cm) high.
£25–30 BSA

◄ A Gift Kodak No. 1a camera, special edition with brown leather finish and bellows, Art Deco enamelled front with matching cedar wood box, 1930–31, 4¼in (11cm) wide.
£300–360 APC

A Walter Kunik Petie Vanity camera, with red-enamelled and polished chrome finish, German, c1956, 4¾in (12cm) wide, with original box and instructions.
£700–800 APC
The Petie Vanity is a 16mm camera housed in a make-up compact. The front door opens to reveal a mirror with two cylinders in the top to hold lipstick and rolls of film. The camera was made in a variety of colours and finishes.

▶ An MPP Mk VIII large-format field camera, with f5.6 150mm lens, c1965, 10in (25.5cm) wide.
£350–400 VCL

A chrome Leica M4 35mm camera, with Summicron f2 5cm lens, in original box with lens shade, plastic cap, instructions and service card, c1967, 5¾in (14.5cm) wide.
£850–1,000 Bon

A Linhof monorail camera, with f5.6 105mm lens, c1960, 14in (35.5cm) wide.
£700–800 VCL

A Superfex camera, 127 film size, French, 1945–55, 4in (10cm) wide.
£25–30 BSA

A David White Stereo Realist Model 1041 35mm camera, with f3.5 lenses and original case, American, 1950s, 6in (15cm) wide.
£150–180 APC

A Zeiss Ikon Contaflex twin-lens reflex camera, No. A 46012, with Sonnar f1.5 5cm and 8cm lenses, early 1950s, 4½in (11.5cm) wide.
£550–650 Bon

A Voigtländer Kolibri camera, with Tessar f3.5 5cm lens, 127 film size, 1936, 4½in (11.5cm) wide.
£250–300 VCL

Cats

Innumerable myths and legends surround the cat. In ancient Egypt the goddess Bast was portrayed with the head of a cat, and the cat was a sacred animal, the punishment for killing it was death. In medieval times, the black cat was believed to be Satan's favourite form, and was the chosen familiar of witches, causing the mass extermination of all black cats. Possibly, for this reason those that survived were considered extremely fortunate, hence the lucky black cat. Famous cats in literature include Lewis Carroll's Cheshire Cat, T. S. Eliot's *Practical Cats*, Beatrix Potter's Tabitha Twitchit and Tom Kitten, and Kathleen Hale's Orlando. Perhaps the ultimate cat painter was Louis Wain (1860–1939). Modelled on his wife's pet kitten Peter, Wain's comic anthropomorphised cats first appeared in newspapers in the 1880s and, by the turn of the century, the artist was a household name and President of the National Cat Club. In spite of his huge success, if anyone needed a lucky black cat it was Wain, whose life was marked by tragedy. His wife died in 1887 after only three years of marriage, twenty years later he was sued for debt and forced to move to the USA. After his return he began to show signs of schizophrenia, a family illness. In 1925 he was found in the pauper's wing of a mental asylum, an appeal was launched to move him, and he spent his remaining years in hospital. This section includes Wain's works from postcards to original illustrations, all of which are now highly collectable.

A Victorian clockwork cat, with wooden body and tin mechanism, 3in (7.5cm) long.
£70–80 HAL

A silver-plated pierced metal button, depicting a cat and a lizard, c1880–90, 1¼in (3cm) diam.
£25–30 TB

A French Decamp clockwork cat, with real fur, cries, walks and the tail wags, c1900, 12in (30.5cm) long.
£600–680 DAn

◀ A Cenedese amber glass cat, signed by Elio Raffaeu, Italian, c1960s, 6in (15cm) wide.
£200–220 FMa

A Merrythought Art Silk cat, 1950s, 8in (20.5cm) high.
£30–35 Ann

▶ A Beanie Baby cat, 'Scat', 1998, 7in (18cm) long.
£4–6 BeG

A set of six moonglow glass buttons, in the shape of cats, c1980s, ½in (12.5mm) high.
£3–4 JBB

CERAMICS

A Brownfield majolica model of a kitten, playing with a ball of wool that forms a box, all raised on a turquoise cushion with tasselled corners, box cover missing, damaged, impressed 'Brownfield 1/78', late 19thC, 11½in (29cm) wide.
£200–220 WW

An Aller Vale hollow slipware model of a winking cat, glazed in yellow and with a green glass eye, marked 'Aller Vale Devon', c1920s, 9½in (24cm) high.
£220–240 L(T)

A Goss model of a cat, with City of Bristol crest, c1920s, 2in (5cm) high.
£38–42 TAC

▶ A Royal Doulton model of a cat, 1930–50s, 5in (12.5cm) long.
£25–28 WAC

A set of three Wood's Pussyfoot series teapots, for two, four and six cups, glazed in black with coloured bowties and yellow eyes, 1930s, largest 8in (20.5cm) high.
£75–95 each BEV

An Arthur Wood black and white cat, with green printed globe mark 'Arthur Wood', 1950s, 8½in (21.5cm) high.
£50–60 ES

A Royal Albert model of Mrs Ribby, by Arthur Gredington, wearing a blue and white dress and a pink and white shawl, 1951–present day, 3¼in 8.5cm) high.
£12–15 BBR

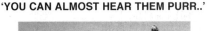

A Beswick model of a ginger kitten, by Colin Melbourne, model No. 1436, 1959–63, 3¼in (8.5cm) high.
£25–30 BBR

A Beswick model of Tabitha Twitchit and Miss Moppet, model No. BP-3b, 1976–93, 3½in (9cm) high.
£50–60 SAS

A Winstanley model of a Siamese blue-point cat, model No. 5, 1998, 12in (30.5cm) high.
£55–65 RIA

A Beswick model of Tabitha Twitchit, by Arthur Gredington, with a blue and white striped dress and a white apron, 1961–74, 3½in (9cm) high.
£35–40 BBR

A Royal Crown Derby model of a seated cat, decorated in Imari colours, base applied with a gilded button, 1980s, 5in (12.5cm) high.
£65–75 GAK

▶ A Wade Collectors Club model of a black and white cat, Burslem, first membership piece, limited edition of 1250, 1994, 3½in (9cm) high.
£85–100 PC
Produced in September 1994 for the Official International Wade Collectors Club, 'The Works Cat 'Burslem'' was given free of charge to fully paid-up members during 1994 and 1995. It was modelled on a stray cat living at the pottery, whose favourite sleeping place was underneath the kilns.

A Worcester model of a ginger cat, by F. G. Doughty, 1962, 4in (10cm) high.
£125–150 WAC

A Royal Worcester model of a white Persian cat, with blue bow and pink pads, 1978, 5in (12.5cm) high.
£85–95 WAC

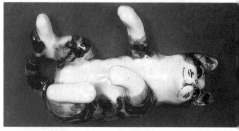

A Winstanley tabby and white cat, marked on base '4 I.Winstanley England', 1990s, 10in (25.5cm) wide.
£40–50 CP

A pair of Winstanley cats, marked on base of feet '3 I.Winstanley England', 1990s, largest 12in (30.5cm) wide.
£30–35 each CP

FELIX

A felt Felix the Cat
fairground prize, c1920s,
12in (30.5cm) high.
£65–80 HAL

A Felix the Cat,
with plush covering,
1920s, 11in (28cm) high.
£180–200 HAL

A pair of Goebel china black and white Felix-style book
ends, the cats seated on orange plinths, with milestone-
shaped backdrop, 1930s, 5¾in (14.5cm) high.
£220–250 CDC

▶ A Felix the Cat
ceramic jug, inscribed
'Please Felix don't shoot',
1920s, 8in (20.5cm) high.
£60–70 MURR

Felix the Cat

The most popular US cartoon character before
Mickey Mouse, Felix the Cat was first introduced
in 1914 by animator Pat Sullivan. He reached the
height of his fame in the 1920s, inspiring a range
of merchandise in both America and Europe.

LOUIS WAIN

Three Louis Wain Christmas series
cat postcards, published by Tuck,
two from series 1735 'The Young
Artists' and 'Paying Visits', the other
from series 8127 'Cinderella',
c1900, 6 x 4in (15 x 10cm).
£90–100 DN

A Louis Wain illustrated saucer,
made by Paragon China,
entitled 'The Clever Tinker',
1920s, 5¼in (13.5cm) diam.
£60–70 HUX

▶ A Louis Wain
(1860–1939) watercolour
and body colour painting,
entitled 'Dinner Please!',
signed and inscribed
with title, 11¾ x 14¾in
(30 x 37.5cm).
£4,000–4,500 C

A Louis Wain (1860–1939)
watercolour painting, entitled
'The One That Got Away', signed,
17¾ x 12¾in (45 x 32.5cm).
£4,250–4,750 C

Ceramics

BESWICK

A Beswick plaque, modelled as a galleon, decorated in blue, yellow and brown, 1930s, 9in (23cm) high.
£175–195 PrB

A Beswick vase, designed by Symcox, decorated in green, blue and brown glaze, 1930-40s, 7¼in (18.5cm) high.
£42–50 OD

◄ A Beswick naturalistic-coloured model of a pigeon, 1955, 5¾in (14.5cm) high.
£100–120 BHA

Eleven Beswick pottery ducks, approved by Peter Scott, 1950s, mallard 4in (10cm) high.
£650–720 SWO
In the 1950s, Beswick modeller Colin Melbourne produced a series of decoy ducks inspired by the birds at Peter Scott's sanctuary at Slimbridge. Scott and art director Jim Hayward selected the various species and today these models are very collectable.

A Beswick Midsummer Night's Dream jug, decorated in colours, 1950s, 9in (23cm) high.
£180–200 BEV

A Beswick Walt Disney model of Goofy, designed by Jan Gramoska, with blue trousers and red sweater, 1953–65, 5in (12.5cm) high.
£250–280 BBR

Two Beswick models of comical pink pigs, 1967–71, 3¾in (9.5cm) high.
£38–45 TAC

► A Beswick Beatrix Potter model of Amiable Guinea Pig, wearing a brown jacket and white hat, backstamp BP–3b, 1967–83, 4in (10cm) high.
£130–160 SAS

▶ A Beswick model of a King Penguin and two chicks, painted in colours, moulded marks 2357, 2398 and 2434, 1970s, tallest 11¾in (30cm) high.
£1,200–1,400 L&T
Designed by Graham Tongue, these penguins were withdrawn in 1976 and are very desirable, either as a group or individually. A single model of the sliding penguin chick, picked up for 20p at a Jersey car boot fair, fetched £390 at a recent BBR auction, making a handsome profit for the eagle-eyed, bird-spotting vendor.

A Beswick Beatrix Potter model of Benjamin Bunny, wearing a dark maroon jacket, c1970–74, 4¼in (11cm) high.
£120–150 SAS

A Beswick model of a Nuthatch, designed by Graham Tongue, No. 2413, decorated in grey, pink and white, 1972–95, 3in (7.5cm) high.
£15–18 BBR

▶ A Beswick Beatrix Potter model of Benjamin Bunny, second version, with brown jacket and green hat, backstamp BP–3b, 1972–80, 4in (10cm) high.
£50–60 SAS

A Beswick Beatrix Potter model of Mrs Tiggy Winkle, designed by Arthur Gredington, wearing a red-brown and white blouse, with green and blue striped skirt and white apron, 1972–present, 5in (12.5cm) high.
£12–14 BBR

A Beswick model of Sir Isaac Newton, with yellow shirt and grey jacket and trousers, backstamp BP–3b, 1973–84, 3¾in (9.5cm) high.
£180–200 SAS

▶ A Beswick model of Mr Jackson, first version, decorated in green with a brown jacket, 1974, 2¾in (7cm)high.
£130–150 SAS

BLUE AND WHITE

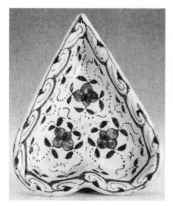

An English delft blue and white heart-shaped pickle dish, painted with flowers within a scrolling border, c1740, 4¼in (11cm) wide.
£700–800 S(S)

A Liverpool blue and white saucer, painted with a bridge connecting two islands, in a Chinese river landscape, slight damage, c1760, 4½in (11.5cm) diam.
£280–320 DN

A Spode blue and white meat dish, Caramanian Series, transfer-printed with The Triumphal Arch at Tripoli, Barbary, impressed 'Spode', early 19thC, 22¾in (58cm) wide.
£1,100–1,300 S(S)

A Liverpool blue and white plate, painted with a seated Chinese figure smoking a pipe and two cockerels, c1760, 9in (23cm) diam.
£300–350 JHo

A Caughley blue and white oval basket, the pierced body decorated with applied rosettes, the base transfer-printed with a pine-cone pattern, c1770, 9¼in (23.5cm) diam.
£675–750 HAM

▶ A Spode blue and white plate, transfer-printed with Castle pattern, 1820, 10in (25.5cm) diam.
£50–55 OD

An Adams blue and white plate, transfer-printed with Blenheim Palace, 1820, 10in (25.5cm) diam.
£200–220 GN

▶ A blue and white Mandarin Opaque plate, marked 'J. Singleton-Dewsbury', 1820–30, 9in (23cm) diam.
£50–55 OD

A Liverpool blue and white flared coffee cup, painted with a fisherman in a boat, a pagoda and trees in a Chinese river landscape, the interior with a trellis band, slight damage, c1758, 2½in (6.5cm) high.
£180–220 DN

A blue and white painted pearlware jug, restored, 1790, 5in (12.5cm) high.
£200–235 IW

A Lockett & Hulme blue and white plate, transfer-printed with Ponte Rotto pattern, marked, 1825, 6¼in (16cm) diam.
£42–50 OD

A Meir blue and white toastwater jug, transfer-printed with Loch Katrine, from the Northern Scenery Series, 1830, 7in (18cm) high.
£220–250 GN

A blue and white transfer-printed lavatory pan, 1850, 8in (20.5cm) high.
£180–220 OD

A blue and white transfer-printed invalid feeder, c1830, 5in (12.5cm) high.
£100–110 OCH

A Staffordshire blue and white tureen, transfer-printed with Grecian Scenery pattern, 19thC, 12in (30.5cm) wide.
£130–160 CoCo

An Elkin & Newton blue and white transfer-printed plate, decorated with Warwick Vase pattern, 1840, 9¾in (25cm) diam.
£25–30 OD

◄ A Thomas Dimmock blue and white chamber pot, decorated with Chintz pattern, 1880s, 5½in (14cm) high.
£60–70 CoCo

A Minton blue and white preserving jar, transfer-printed with Chinese Marine pattern, 1830, 12in (30.5cm) high.
£250–300 GN
The ridge around the neck of this jar is where the paper or muslin lid would have been tied.

A Staffordshire blue and white tankard, transfer-printed with Hunting pattern, 19thC, 6¼in (16cm) high.
£170–200 CoCo

A Copeland Spode blue and white transfer-printed jug and bowl, 1910–20, jug 12in (30.5cm) high.
£450–500 RIA

BRETBY

A Bretby jardinière, decorated in
brown and yellow with floral motif,
1891, 9in (23cm) high.
£400–450 HUN

> **Miller's is a price GUIDE
> not a price LIST**

A Bretby Art Nouveau oval tray, with
interwoven sinuous bands and an iris bloom
in slight relief in bronze colour against a
matt-black ground, impressed 'Bretby
England', numbered '1640', c1900,
13¼in (34cm) wide.
£220–250 DN

◀ A Bretby cloisonné-style vase, decorated
in yellow, pink and white with a bird on a
floral branch, c1910, 12¼in (31cm) high.
£100–120 DSG

BURLEIGH WARE

A Burleigh Ware hors
d'oeuvre dish, decorated
with Dawn pattern, c1930,
8½in (21.5cm) wide.
£55–65 BUR

A Burleigh Ware Parrot
jug, decorated in green
and yellow, 1931,
8in (20.5cm) high.
**£120–150 ERC
This jug was also
produced in a
smaller size.**

A Burleigh Ware coffee pot,
decorated with Sunray pattern,
1930s, 6in (15cm) high.
£85–100 BUR

A Burleigh Ware coffee set,
including six cups, decorated
with Daffodil pattern, No. 4813,
c1935, pot 8in (20.5cm) high.
£420–500 RIA

A Burleigh Ware sauce tureen and stand,
decorated with Tulip Time pattern,
1930s, tray 8½in
(21.5cm) wide.
£70–80 BUR

▶ A Burleigh
Ware Dickens
Series character
jug, Sairey
Gamp, 1940s,
4in (10cm) high.
£55–65 BUR

◀ A Burleigh
Ware Coronation
jug, decorated in
colours with the
coronation of
HRH Princess
Elizabeth, 1953,
8in (20.5cm) high.
£150–180 CoCo

CANDLE EXTINGUISHERS

A Royal Worcester candle extinguisher, in the form of a French cook, painted with coloured enamels, black printed mark, 1820–25, 2½in (6.5cm) high.
£60–70 WW

Two Staffordshire candle extinguishers, in the form of a monk and a nun, c1880, 3¼in (8.5cm) high.
£90–110 each TH

A Royal Worcester candle extinguisher, in the form of a black-faced owl, c1881, 3¼in (8.5cm) high.
£350–400 TH

A Royal Worcester white glazed candle extinguisher, in the form of Swedish opera singer Jenny Lind, c1880, 4½in (11.5cm) high.
£140–160 CAW
This candle extinguisher was also produced as a coloured edition.

A Royal Worcester candle extinguisher, in the form of a monk reading from a bible, painted with coloured enamel, puce factory mark, c1899, 4¾in (12cm) high.
£100–120 WW

A Royal Worcester candle extinguisher, in the form of a nun, 1960s, 3½in (9cm) high.
£100–120 WAC

▶ A Healacraft candle extinguisher, decorated with white glaze with gilded highlights and applied around the base with pink, yellow and blue flowers, marked, 1970s, 3¼in (8.5cm) high.
£65–75 TH

CARLTON WARE

Carlton Ware was the trade name used by the Staffordshire-based firm of Wiltshaw & Robinson (est.1890). The firm specialized in decorative items, toiletware, teaware and crested china. In the 1920s Carlton Ware produced handsome, geometric Art Deco designs along with enamelled and lustre wares, inspired by Oriental ceramics, richly gilded and decorated. Aimed at the top end of the market, today such pieces are highly collectable. Carlton Ware also targeted the middle-market customer with its leaf-moulded tableware, extremely popular in the 1930s. Though some patterns, such as Apple Blossom are comparatively common, others

are rarer and, as such, more expensive to collect. Since these items were designed for everyday use, condition is very important to current value, complete sets will command a premium, and perfect boxed examples are very desirable. In the post World War II years, Carlton Ware created some inventive 1950s designs – such as the organically-inspired Windswept tableware and also produced advertising ceramics for Guinness (*see* page 87). In 1967, the Company was taken over by Arthur Wood & Son, and from the 1970s, became known for a range of novelty designs, including the highly successful Walking Ware designed from 1973 by husband and wife team Roger Mitchell and Danka Napiorkowska.

A Carlton Ware vase, decorated with Chrysanthemum pattern, 1890–94, 12in (30.5cm) high.
£280–350 StC

A Carlton Ware lustre model of a goose, inscribed 'Lucky White Heather from Ryde', 1920s, 2in (5cm) high.
£34–40 MGC

A Carlton Ware match striker, by Fribourg & Treyer, Oxford, 1920, 3in (7.5cm) high.
£42–50 WAC

A Carlton Ware coffee pot, decorated with Eclipse pattern, 1920s, 6½in (16.5cm) high.
£120–140 StC

A Carlton Ware vase, decorated in yellow and black and with gold diamond, 1920s, 5in (12.5cm) high.
£200–220 BEV

A Carlton Ware tobacco jar, decorated with Tree and Swallow pattern, patented by Rumidor Corporation, New York, marked, early 1930s, 4in (10cm) high.
£500–600 StC

A Carlton Ware Art Deco bowl, on three ball feet with separate domed stem holder, decorated with coloured chrysanthemums against deep blue stylized foliage on a powder-blue ground and with part-decorated rim, No. 3413 4/4579, c1930, 10½in (26.5cm) diam.
£350–400 TRL

▶ A Carlton Ware Art Deco Handcraft pattern jug, decorated in deep blue, gold and light blue, c1930, 3¾in (9.5cm) high.
£150–175 StC

A Carlton Ware jug, decorated with Rabbits at Dusk pattern, restored, 1930s, 8in (20.5cm) high.
£550–650 StC

A Carlton Ware Bridge condiment set, decorated in orange, yellow and black, 1930s, 5in (12.5cm) wide.
£180–200 BEV
Introduced to Britain in the late 19thC, Bridge reached the height of its popularity in the 1920s and 1930s. The game was considered a necessary social skill among the upper and middle classes, and a host of related accessories was produced to decorate the Bridge table, from trump markers to ashtrays and score pads. This condiment set reflects the period fashion for card-inspired tableware.

◀ A Carlton Ware candlestick, decorated with Flowering Papyrus pattern, 1930s, 4in (10cm) high.
£155–185 StC

▶ A Carlton Ware Streak Glaze vase, 1930–35, 4¾in (12cm) high.
£80–90 StC

◀ A Carlton Ware bridge ashtray, decorated with playing card patterns, 1930s, 3in (7.5cm) square.
£85–95 BEV

A Carlton Ware three-way tray, decorated with Buttercup pattern, 1936–37, 9½in (24cm) long.
£75–95 StC

A Carlton Ware jug, moulded with Apple Blossom pattern, with yellow glaze, 1930s, 4in (10cm) high.
£50–60 DBo

A Carlton Ware Handcraft inkwell, 1930s, 5in (12.5cm) diam.
£190–220 BEV

A Carlton Ware tennis set, decorated with Anemone pattern in orange, maroon and green on a yellow ground, c1940, cup 3in (7.5cm) high.
£160–180 AOT

A Carlton Ware yellow sugar shaker, decorated with Buttercup pattern, 1937–38, 5½in (14cm) high.
£175–195 StC

A Carlton Ware tea-for-two, decorated with Water Lily pattern in green and yellow, 1939–40, teapot 6in (15cm) high.
£450–500 StC

A Carlton Ware Flowers and Basket sandwich plate, 1940, 11in (28cm) wide.
£45–50 StC

A Carlton Ware Rouge Royale Spider Web jug, c1950, 7in (18cm) high.
£240–270 AnS

A Carlton Ware salad bowl and servers, decorated with Primula pattern, c1945, bowl 8in (20.5cm) wide.
£65–80 StC

◀ A Carlton Ware Rouge Royale Bells dish, decorated with lily of the valley, c1952, 7½in (19cm) diam.
£90–100 StC

▶ Two Carlton Ware flower baskets, one green, one yellow, decorated with pink and yellow flowers and green leaves, 1940s, 5½in (14cm) high.
£80–100 each StC

A Carlton Ware butter knife and dish set, decorated with Buttercup pattern, in original box, c1940, 4in (10cm) wide.
£120–140 AOT

A Carlton Ware ginger jar, decorated with pale orange spiral pattern, with gilt highlights, 1950s, 7in (18cm) high.
£160–180 StC

A Carlton Ware Noir Royale plate, decorated with Wild Duck pattern, in green, pink and orange on a black ground, c1955, 10½in (26.5cm) diam.
£220–250 StC

A pair of Carlton Ware candlesticks, decorated with Rosebud pattern, 1960s, 2¼in (5.5cm) high.
£40–45 StC

► A Carlton Ware butter dish, in the shape of a cat, painted with dark green leaves on a pale green ground, c1960, 7in (18cm) wide.
£85–100 WAC

A Carlton Ware Walking Ware tea cup, with white glaze and green shoes, 1970s, 3½in (9cm) high.
£25–30 BEV

A Carlton Ware mug, depicting Prince Charles, decorated in black on a white ground, 1970s, 4in (10cm) high.
£34–40 BEV

► A Carlton Ware Walking Ware milk jug, with white glaze and black shoes 1970s, 4½in (11.5cm) high.
£58–65 BEV

A Carlton Ware Crocodile three-piece teaset and toast rack, with pale green glaze and painted eyes and features, stamped, 1970s, teapot 8in (20.5cm) high.
£160–180 WBH

A Clarice Cliff Appliqué Avignon fruit bowl, in mauve and green on an orange ground, 1930–34, 6½in (16.5cm) wide.
£500–550 RIA

A Clarice Cliff part tea-for-two, decorated with Original Crocus pattern in orange, yellow, blue and brown, comprising Stamford teapot, cream jug, two Conical cups, saucers and a biscuit plate, printed marks, 1930s.
£900–1,100 RTo

A Clarice Cliff Conical trio, decorated with Cabbage Flower pattern in brown, green, red and yellow, 1934, plate 6in (15cm) diam.
£600–650 RIA

▶ A Clarice Cliff Geometric vase, shape No. 342, decorated in blue, red, mauve and green, 1930s, 8in (20.5cm) high.
£700–800 MD

A Clarice Cliff Fantasque Lotus jug, decorated with Melon pattern, in orange, yellow, blue, mauve and green, printed mark to base, slight damage, 1930s, 11½in (29cm) high.
£850–1,000 CAG
The Melon pattern has been generating considerable interest in recent months, but values depend very much on the shape it is applied to. A six piece Melon coffee set, with a Conical coffee pot, similar in design to the Fantasque service illustrated, is an unusual combination, and at a recent auction achieved £8,500, one of the highest prices ever recorded for a Clarice Cliff coffee set.

A Clarice Cliff Newport Pottery plate, decorated with Autumn pattern in puce, green and blue against a honey glaze, printed marks 'Bizarre, Clarice Cliff, Newport Pottery', slight damage, c1930–35, 10in (25.5cm) diam.
£140–160 Hal(C)

A Clarice Cliff bowl, decorated with Blue Firs pattern, c1936, 6in (15cm) diam.
£400–480 RIA

▶ A Clarice Cliff Conical bowl, decorated in turquoise and yellow, 1930s, 5in (12.5cm) high.
£425–475 MD

CROWN DERBY

A Royal Crown Derby plate, by Ellis Clark, decorated in naturalistic colours with a painting of Chiswick House, Middlesex, with gilt-decorated black rim, c1895, 9in (23cm) diam.
£600–675 GRI

A Crown Derby trio, transfer-printed in Imari colours, with gilt rims, 1903, plate 7in (18cm) diam.
£100–125 RIA

A Royal Crown Derby miniature casserole dish, decorated with Imari pattern, c1912, 2in (5cm) high.
£350–400 GRI

A Royal Crown Derby miniature coal scuttle, decorated with Imari pattern, c1912, 2½in (6.5cm) high.
£325–375 GRI

◄ A Royal Crown Derby miniature casserole dish, decorated with Imari pattern, c1912, 2in (5cm) high.
£350–400 GRI

CROWN DEVON

A Crown Devon Rouge Royal vase, with dark red glaze and gilt rim, decorated in colours with tropical fish, c1930, 11in (28cm) high.
£250–300 TWr

A pair of Crown Devon mirrored cream lustre vases, decorated with fairies in green and lilac, with gilt rims and borders, c1930s, 6in (15cm) high.
£170–200 MD

A Crown Devon Mattajade turquoise vase, enamelled in mauve, green and brown, c1930, 6in (15cm) high.
£360–400 AOT

A Crown Devon Fieldings 15 piece coffee set, decorated with Stockholm pattern in grey and red, printed and impressed marks, incised signature 'Karen', c1930, coffee pot 9in (23cm) high.
£250–300 ES

A Crown Devon vase, decorated with a geometric floral pattern in orange and green, 1930s, 7in (18cm) high.
£265–295 StC

A Crown Devon pale green bowl, in the shape of a tree stump, with a red seated gnome, 1930s, 3in (7.5cm) high.
£42–50 WAC

CROWN DUCAL

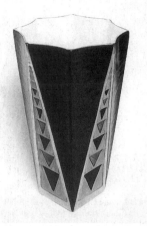

A Crown Ducal teapot, sugar bowl and creamer, decorated with Orange Tree pattern, in orange and grey, c1930, teapot 4in (10cm) high,
£160–185 AOT
The Orange Tree pattern was originally introduced in 1925 as the Red Tree pattern.

A Crown Ducal vase, decorated with Persian Rose pattern in green, yellow blue and pink, 1930s, 5in (12.5cm) high
£150–175 PrB

A Crown Ducal Geometric pattern vase, decorated in black, yellow, orange and blue, 1930s, 9in (23cm) high.
£120–140 CoCo

▶ A Crown Ducal coffee can and saucer, decorated with Lanterns pattern in colours on a black ground, 1930s, 4½in (11.5cm) high.
£42–50 CoCo

CRUET SETS

A Clarice Cliff novelty cruet set, in the shape of fish, with cream glaze and green fins, c1930, 3in (7.5cm) high.
£325–375 MD

A Japanese Maruhon Ware cruet set, modelled as a red bird on a blue basket, the salt and pepper pots in the shape of yellow flowers, 1920s–30s, 3½in (9cm) high.
£22–26 CoCo

Condition

The condition is absolutely vital when assessing the value of a collectable. Damaged items on the whole appreciate much less than perfect examples. However, a rare desirable piece may command a high price even when damaged.

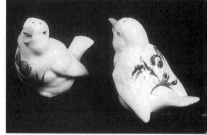

A Mickey Mouse ceramic cruet set, in black, green, brown and gilt, probably German, 1930s, 3in (7.5cm) high.
£85–100 MURR

A Jan Plichta cruet set, in the shape of birds, decorated with green and purple thistles, 1940–50s, 2½in (6.5cm) high.
£75–85 SAA

CUPS & SAUCERS

A Sèvres tea cup, probably Château des Tuileries, decorated with cherubs, with gilt rims and borders, the saucer with a blue ground, c1844, cup 3in (7.5cm) high.
£380–420 GRI

A Copeland Spode coffee cup and saucer, decorated in orange, brown and gold, 1891, 2¼in (5.5cm) high.
£18–22 DBo

A Hammersley coffee can and saucer, decorated with gilded leaf garlands and with blue rims, 1912.
£24–28 DBo

An Irish Carrig Ware Pottery cup and saucer, decorated with clover leaves, c1920s, saucer 5½in (14cm) diam.
£12–15 PC

► A Bavarian porcelain cup and saucer, decorated in shades of brown and yellow, 1910–20, 2½in (6.5cm) high.
£22–25 DBo

◄ A Limoges coffee cup and saucer, decorated with stylized flowers in blue, black and gold, 1928, 2in (5cm) high.
£18–22 DBo

A Royal Staffordshire tea cup and saucer, decorated in underglaze green, c1930, saucer 8in (20.5cm) diam.
£22–25 WAB

◄ A Hammersley cup and saucer, decorated with sweet peas in green, blue, yellow and pink, 1938, 3in (7.5cm) high.
£25–30 DBo

DENBY

A Denby hexagonal brown majolica tobacco jar, c1925, 4in (10cm) high.
£50–60 KES

A Victorian Denby jug, commemorating Queen Victoria's Diamond Jubilee, in the style of a leather blackjack, impressed retailer's mark on base 'Mortlocks, Oxford Street, London', 9½in (24cm) high.
£175–195 KES

A pair of Denby bookends, designed by Donald Gilbert, in the shape of Pastel Blue lovebirds, c1933, 6in (15cm) high.
£100–120 OTT

A Denby tube-lined goblet candlestick, in Electric Blue glaze, c1925, 4¾in (12cm) high.
£125–140 KES

A Denby green stoneware tea urn, with original brass tap, 1920s, 18in (45.5cm) high.
£120–135 KES

◄ A Bourne Denby Kingfisher Pastel Blue bowl, designed by Donald Gilbert, early 1930s, 6½in (16.5cm) high.
£375–395 KES

Cross Reference
See Colour Review

A Denby mug, with Greenwheat design by Glyn Colledge, signed, c1950, 4¼in (11cm) high.
£35–40 ES

A Denby Burlington black jug, shape No. BN833, 1950s, 5¾in (14.5cm) high.
£40–45 PrB

A Denby Burlington yellow jug, shape No. BN839, 1950s, 6¾in (17cm) high.
£40–45 PrB

◄ A Denby Burlington vase, with turquoise glaze, 1950s, 3in (7.5cm) high.
£18–20 PrB

DOULTON

A Doulton saltglaze stoneware jug, by George Tinworth, the baluster body decorated in green and brown enamels with a scrolled seaweed and beaded design with flowerheads, signed with initials, 1874, 9¾in (25cm) high.
£375–425 Bea(E)

A Royal Doulton spill vase, decorated with a polychrome print of sheep in a winter landscape, with gilt rim and handles, printed mark, early 20thC, 8½in (21.5cm) high.
£50–60 Hal

A Royal Doulton oil lamp, decorated in blue and green on a brown ground, with gilt-metal mounts, converted to electricity, impressed mark, 1882, 17in (43cm) high.
£230–260 GAK

▶ A Royal Doulton pear-shaped flask, decorated with portraits and entitled 'Memories', restored to rim, factory lion and crown circle mark, 1906, 8½in (21.5cm) high.
£200–240 BBR

A pair of Doulton Lambeth stoneware vases, the shaft-and-globe bodies decorated with impressed lace and gilt decoration on a yellow-glazed ground, late 19thC, 15½in (39.5cm) high.
£200–240 BR

A Doulton Lambeth silver-mounted salt-glazed stoneware tyg, decorated with blue scrolls and green leaves on a buff ground, impressed 'Doulton Lambeth, 1887' and artist's mark 'HB', 6in (15cm) high.
£260–300 Hal

A Royal Doulton Dickens Series Ware punch bowl, c1915–20, 7in (18cm) high.
£200–250 BRU
All the Series Ware was made in earthenware at Burslem.

▶ A Royal Doulton porcelain vase, with printed and painted decoration depicting a barefooted lady, c1915, 8½in (21.5cm) high.
£250–300 JE

A Doulton hot water jug, decorated with figures on a brown and beige ground, 1895, 8in (20.5cm) high.
£220–250 BRT

A Royal Doulton stoneware jug, commemorating the Diamond Jubilee of Queen Victoria, reserved with green-glazed portraits of the young and old queen on a blue background, impressed marks to base, late 19thC, 7in (18cm) high.
£200–240 TF

A Royal Doulton Bunnykins plate, Issue No. 10, printed mark 'Bunnykins', signed on the front 'Barbara Vernon', c1930-40, 7½in (19cm) diam.
£25–30 ES

A Royal Doulton Touchstone character jug, No. D5613, designed by Charles J. Noke, decorated in maroon, green and light brown, marked, 1936–60, 6in (15cm) high.
£90–100 BBR

A Royal Doulton Treasure Island Collector's jug, No. 41/600, limited edition, designed by Charles J. Noke and Harry Fenton, 1934, 8in (20.5cm) high.
£600–650 TF

A Royal Doulton Parson Brown character jug, designed by Charles Noke, with hallmarked silver rim, marked, c1935, 6½in (16.5cm) high.
£1,500–1,800 BBR

A Royal Doulton Toothless Granny character jug, 1935, 6in (15cm) high.
£250–300 Bea(E)

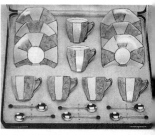

A Royal Doulton porcelain coffee set, comprising six octagonal cups and saucers, decorated with pale green backgrounds and gilded panel with overlapping leaves, in fitted box with spoons, factory marks, 1936.
£180–220 DN

A Royal Doulton group, entitled 'The Perfect Pair', No. HN581, designed by L. Harradine, 1923–1938, 7½in (19cm) high.
£220–250 Bea(E)

A Royal Doulton figure, The Balloon Man, No. HN1954, designed by L. Harradine, marked, damaged, 1940–present, 7¼in (18.5cm) high.
£30–35 BBR

A Royal Doulton Ugly Duchess character jug, No. D6599, designed by Max Henk, decorated in green and purple with a pink flamingo, marked, 1965–73, 7¼in (18.5cm) high.
£300–350 BBR

▶ A Royal Doulton Henry VIII character jug, No. D6642, designed by Eric Griffiths, marked, 1975–present, 6½in (16.5cm) high.
£42–50 BBR

A Royal Doulton Anne Boleyn character jug, No. D6644, designed by Douglas V. Tootle, marked 1975–90, 7in (18cm) high.
£50–60 BBR

LOCATE THE SOURCE
The source of each illustration in Miller's can be found by checking the code letters below each caption with the Key to Illustrations, pages 476–484.

A Royal Doulton model, Mr Bunnykins, No. DB18, designed by Harry Sales, 1982–93, 5in (12.5cm) high.
£60–70 BBR

A Royal Doulton model, The Snowman Tobogganing, 1990–94, 5in (12.5cm) high.
£35–40 WWY

A Royal Doulton model, Aussie Surfer Bunnykins, No. DB133, designed by Graham Tongue, marked, 1994, 4in (10cm) high, with box.
£42–50 BBR

A Royal Doulton George Armstrong Custer/Sitting Bull character jug, No. D6712, designed by Michael Abberly, limited edition of 9,500, marked, 1984, 7in (18cm) high.
£45–55 BBR

A Royal Doulton model, Bunny's Bedtime, LE9500, 1991, 6¾in (17cm) high.
£100–120 WWY

A Royal Doulton model, Magician Bunnykins No. DB126, new colour-way for 1998 in limited edition of 1,500 for Sinclairs, marked, 1984–90, 4¼in (11cm) high, with box.
£120–140 BBR

A Royal Doulton model, Drum Major Bunnykins, No. DB27, designed by Harry Sales, marked, 1984–90, 3½in (9cm) high.
£65–80 BBR

 ▶ A Royal Doulton The Auctioneer character jug, No. D6838, designed by Geoff Blower, limited edition of 5,000, marked, 1988, 6in (15cm) high.
£70–80 BBR

A Royal Doulton The London Bobby character jug, No. D6744, designed by Stanley J. Taylor, marked, 1986–87, 7in (18cm) high.
£85–100 BBR

EARTHENWARE, STONEWARE & COUNTRY POTTERY

A Dutch pottery pot and ladle, 17thC, pot 6in (15cm) high.
£300–350 JHo

A Border Ware green-glazed earthenware chamber pot, late 17thC, 4¼in (11cm) high.
£150–180 IW

A Westerwald salt-glazed tankard, with pewter lid, pre-1840, 8in (20.5cm) high.
£145–165 IW

A Derbyshire salt-glazed stoneware storage jar and lid, 1840, 12½in (32cm) high.
£50–55 OD

A Derbyshire brown saltglaze stoneware grouse mould, 1840, 2¼in 5.5cm) high.
£30–35 OD

A Scottish Seaton pottery bowl, 1886, 17in (43cm) diam.
£400–450 TWr

A West Country glazed earthenware sprigged country jug, handle restored, 1870, 13½in (34.5cm) high.
£300–350 IW

Further reading

Miller's Ceramics Buyer's Guide,
Miller's Publications, 2000

An agateware model of a top hat, inscribed 'Robert Sharp Miles Platting', probably Cliviger, 1889, 4in (10cm) high.
£120–140 IW

A French Donyatt Aldridges Pottery puzzle jug, with English inscription, 1880, 5½in (14cm) high.
£175–200 IW

◀ A Verwood Pottery two-handled earthenware flagon, late 19thC, 7in (18cm) high.
£100–120 IW

A pottery washbowl, possibly from Bridgwater, Somerset, 1900, 5½in (14cm) high.
£100–120 IW

A Donyatt earthenware shaving mug, 1900, 6in (15cm) high.
£100–115 IW

An earthenware bedpan, probably Verwood, early 20thC, 14in (35.5cm) long.
£65–75 IW

A Soil Hill Pottery earthenware cream jug, Halifax, early 20thC, 3¼in (8.5cm) high.
£25–30 OD

A Doulton salt-glazed stoneware jug, c1900, 5¼in (13.5cm) high.
£25–30 IW

A South Wales Pottery earthenware jug, c1900, 11½in (29cm) high.
£42–50 IW

A Weymouth Pottery jug, decorated with incised flowers and a beaded pattern, signed, 1940s, 5in (12.5cm) high.
£18–22 WAC

▶ A slip-decorated earthenware bowl, c1920, 7in (18cm) diam.
£12–15 AL

A pair of Silchester bowls, c1900, 5¼in (13.5cm) diam.
£30–35 IW

A North Devon earthenware pitcher, slight damage, early 20thC, 12¼in (31cm) high.
£65–75 IW

A Dicker Ware slip-decorated pottery jug, inscribed with '1697', c1911, 4¼in (11cm) high.
£40–45 IW

Earthenware, Stoneware & Country Pottery • CERAMICS 119

EGG CUPS

From the 19th century onward, eggs became a standard part of the 'great British breakfast'. Many Victorian potteries made egg cups, but buyer beware! Included below is a salt, which can be confused with an egg cup, as can small spirit glasses and spill vases. If in doubt use a real or dummy egg (the type used to encourage hens to lay) to check the size of the vessel; salts, for example, tend to be larger in size.

For many collectors the golden age of egg cups was the 1920s and 1930s, when innumerable novelty designs were produced for the nursery. Because the surface area of the base is small, egg cups were often unmarked. Many were produced for the British market abroad, in Czechoslovakia, Germany and Japan, but they tend simply to be stamped 'foreign'.

A Spode egg cup, No. 2967, decorated in green, blue and pink, c1820, 1½in (4cm) high.
£45–50 AMH

A hen-shaped ceramic egg cup, mid-19thC, 2½in (6.5cm) high.
£28–35 CoCo

A Staffordshire footed salt, resembling an egg cup, decorated with blue and white Willow pattern, 19thC, 2½in (6.5cm) high.
£38–45 CoCo

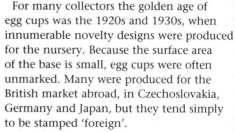

A Continental hand-painted ceramic Toby egg cup, 19thC, 2¾in (7cm) high.
£25–30 CoCo

A pair of Quimper egg cups, decorated in blue, orange and green, with blue rims, marked 'HB', 1904, 2in (5cm) diam.
£25–30 SER

A Quimper egg cup, decorated in blue, green and yellow, marked 'HR', 1904, 2½in (6.5cm) high.
£48–55 SER

A ceramic egg cup, in the shape of a laughing cat, decorated in red, yellow and green, 'foreign', 1920–30, 2½in (6.5cm) high.
£22–28 CoCo

Three egg cups, modelled as two cats and a dog, decorated in colours, marked 'foreign', 1920s, largest 3½in (9cm) high.
£20–30 each CoCo

▶ A Czechoslovakian bird whistling egg cup, decorated in red, yellow, green and blue, 1930s, 2in (5cm) high.
£65–80 BEV

A Czechoslovakian chick and rabbit whistling egg cup, decorated in orange and yellow, 1930s, 3in (7.5cm) wide.
£65–80 BEV

FAIRINGS

A German fairing match holder, late 19thC, 4in (10cm) wide.
£75–85 LeB

A fairing, entitled 'A doubtfull case', c1875, 4in (10cm) high.
£275–325 SAS

A fairing, entitled 'A game of patience', c1890, 4in (10cm) high.
£200–220 SAS

A fairing, entitled 'When mother's at the wash', c1890, 4in (10cm) high.
£190–220 SAS

A pair of German fairing match holders, depicting scenes from the Crimean War, late 19thC, 3in (7.5cm) high.
£200–225 LeB

A fairing, entitled 'Truly every form is not evil', restored, c1875, 3½in (9cm) high.
£330–370 SAS

A fairing, entitled 'A game of patience', c1890, ... of patience.

A fairing, entitled 'Alone at last', c1890, 4in (10cm) wide.
£70–80 SAS

A fairing, entitled 'Waiting for a bus', damaged, c1875, 5in (12.5cm) high.
£180–220 SAS

A Royal Vienna-type fairing, depicting a lady fending off an amorous gentleman, blue spear mark, c1880, 3½in (9cm) high.
£220–260 SAS

A fairing, entitled 'It's a shame to take the Money', c1890, 5in (12.5cm) high.
£150–175 SAS

FIGURES

A Prattware figure of a lyre player, early 19thC, 5¼in (13.5cm) high.
£100–120 SER

A ceramic nodding-head figure of a child holding a puppy, decorated in fawn, cream and brown, marked, 1875, 3in (7.5cm) high.
£65–75 BEV

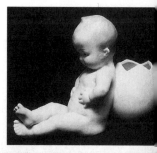

► A Gebrüder Heubach piano baby, leaning against an eggshell, c1900, 6in (15cm) long.
£250–300 DOL

A pair of French pottery Walt Disney dwarfs, Grumpy and Happy, decorated in brown, blue, mauve and white, the backs marked 'Joyeux' and 'Grincheux', inscribed, damaged, 1940–50, 22in (56cm) high.
£300–350 DN

A German bisque group of a boy and girl, decorated in pastel colours, c1925, 6in (15cm) high.
£42–50 YC

A Rosenthal group of two young centaurs, decorated in shades of brown, 1929, 10½in (26.5cm) high.
£650–750 MD

A Bing & Grøndahl group of a boy and girl kissing, decorated in blue, white and gold, 1950, 7½in (19cm) high.
£60–70 FrG

◄ A Runnaford Pottery figure of an old man seated, by Will Young, the back inscribed 'Old Uncle Tom Cobley in his famous chair at Widecombe in the Moor', signed, 1951–70, 3½in (9cm) high.
£100–120 NDCR

A Coalport figure, Melanie, 1988, 8in (20.5cm) high.
£75–85 WAC

A Hummel figure, Chimney Sweep, No. 12/2/0, wearing a black cap and suit, 1970s, 4in (10cm) high.
£60–70 ATH

GOSS & CRESTED CHINA

A Goss Bagware teapot, with Chelmsford and Essex crests, c1880, 4in (10cm) high.
£125–145 JACK

A Goss model of a Guernsey fish basket, with City of Lincoln crest, 1880–1929, 2½in (6.5cm) high.
£30–35 MGC

A Goss crinkle-top ball vase, commemorating the Golden Jubilee of Queen Victoria, 1887, 5in (12.5cm) high.
£50–60 MGC

A Goss model of a Lincoln imp on a pedestal, 1890–1910, 4½in (11.5cm) high.
£90–100 G&CC

A Goss tankard, with John of Gaunt crest, marked, 1900–15, 1¾in (4.5cm) high.
£10–12 ES

The Goss items illustrated on this page are followed by Crested China in alphabetical order.

A Goss model of a Rye cannonball, decorated in grey and yellow, 1910, 3in (7.5cm) diam.
£100–120 CCC

A Goss model of Charles Dickens' house, c1910, 2½in (6.5cm) wide.
£180–200 CCC

A Goss wall posy, in the form of the Brasenose College nose, c1919, 5in (12.5cm) high.
£80–100 HarC
Over the gate of Brasenose College, Oxford, is a brass nose. The word 'brasenose' is a corruption of *brasenhuis*, meaning a brasserie or brewhouse, the College having been built on the site of a brewery.

◄ A Goss nightlight model of Robert Burns' cottage, 1910–20, 6in (15cm) wide.
£100–120 DN

An Alexandra model of a grandfather clock, with Margate crest, 1910–30, 5in (12.5cm) high.
£20–22 G&CC

An Arcadian model statue of Newton, with Grantham crest, 1910–30, 6¼in (16cm) high.
£35–40 G&CC

◄ An Arcadian model of a milking stool, with Herne Bay crest, 1910–25, 1½in (4cm) high.
£10–12 G&CC

► An Arcadian Rock of Ages, with inscribed hymn and Cheddar crest, 1910–30, 3¼in (8.5cm) high.
£15–17 G&CC

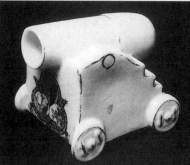

An Arcadian model of a canon, with Dover crest, 1915, 2in (5cm) high.
£24–27 JACK

A Carlton model of a valise, with Portishead crest, 1910, 2in (5cm) wide.
£12–14 JACK

A Carlton model of a pointed-nose British E.9 submarine, with Leeds crest, c1915, 5½in (14cm) long.
£35–40 G&CC

◄ A Czechoslovakian model of a chair, with Clacton-on-Sea crest, 1930s, 4in (10cm) high.
£12–15 CRN

A Carlton model of a spinning wheel, with High Wycombe crest, 1900–20, 3in (7.5cm) high.
£16–20 G&CC

A Carlton model of a treadle sewing machine, 1900–20, 3in (7.5cm) high.
£20–24 G&CC

A Carlton ring tree, with crest, 1902–30, 3½in (9cm) diam.
£8–10 G&CC

A Florentine model of a Jack-in-the-Box, with Herne Bay crest, 1910–30, 4in (10cm) high.
£28–32 G&CC

A Florentine model of a war memorial, with Great Yarmouth crest, 1920, 7in (18cm) high.
£60–70 CCC

▶ A Grafton model of a motor tractor used on the Western Front, No. 456, with Brighton crest, c1915, 3¼in (8.5cm) wide.
£150–170 G&CC

A Longton model of Chesterfield Parish Church, with Chesterfield crest, c1920, 5in (12.5cm) high.
£55–65 JACK

A Rita model of Sir Walter Scott's Chair at Abbotsford, with Briton Ferry crest, 1930s, 4in (10cm) high.
£10–12 CRN

A Foley model of a milk churn, with Sarum crest, 1900–10, 2¾in (7cm) high.
£14–17 G&CC

A Podmore model of a grandfather clock, with Southampton crest, 1910–30, 5¼in (13.5cm) high.
£14–16 G&CC

A Saxony figure of a Gretna Green officiant, with crest, 1900–20, 4¼in (11cm) high.
£25–30 G&CC

A Shamrock pin tray, with Dublin crest, 1940, 3½in (9cm) wide.
£7–9 MLa

◀ A Tuscan model of a drum, with Melton Mowbray crest, c1915, 2½in (6.5cm) diam.
£15–18 JACK

▶ A Willow Art model of 'The Clock Tower, St. Albans', c1910, 5in (12.5cm) high.
£70–80 CCC

A Willow Art 'Model of Burns' Statue', with Leeds crest, 1910–30, 7in (18cm) high.
£28–32 G&CC

A Willow Art model of a monoplane, with rotating propeller, 1914–20, 5¼in (13.5cm) long.
£75–85 G&CC

◀ A Willow Art 'Burns' Chair Dumfries', with Brighton crest, 1930s, 3in (7.5cm) high.
£20–25 CRN

▶ A Willow Art model of a Bull Terrier, with Wolverhampton crest, 1920, 4in (10cm) long.
£28–32 JACK

A model of The Pig That Won't Go, with Inner-leithen crest, 1910–20, 3½in (9cm) long.
£15–20 SQA

Miller's is a price GUIDE not a price LIST

A 'Model of Mary Queen of Scots' Chair at Edinburgh Castle', with South Shields crest, 1910–25, 3in (7.5cm) high.
£15–18 SQA

GOUDA

A Gouda matavaan or grain storage vessel, by Andreas Rijp, decorated with Suled pattern in orange, yellow, blue and green, 1910, 7½in (19cm) high.
£200–225 OO

A Gouda bowl, decorated with Danier pattern, rim restored, c1920s, 6in (15cm) high.
£90–110 BRU

Cross Reference
See Colour Review

A Gouda vase, decorated with Iris pattern in mauve and orange, signed 'Fiona Gouda, Holland', marked 'No. 1042', c1930, 6in (15cm) high.
£100–120 ES

A Gouda miniature vase, decorated with Archipel pattern in green, blue, yellow and orange, c1910, 1¾in (4.5cm) high.
£80–100 OO

A Gouda candlestick, decorated by J. van der Meide, with Bloemen pattern in red, gold and blue, 1926, 11½in (29cm) high.
£225–250 OO

A pair of Gouda clogs, decorated with Rido pattern, c1940, 3½in (9cm) long.
£60–75 OO

A Gouda flat bowl, decorated with Melvin pattern in green, red, blue, yellow and orange, 1921, 10¼in (26cm) diam.
£200–220 OO

A Gouda powder bowl with lid, decorated by J. C. van Leeuwen with Clareta pattern in green and gold, 1926, 5¼in (13.5cm) diam.
£120–150 OO

A Gouda inkwell and tray, decorated with Atrium pattern in green and orange, 1928, 8¼in (21cm) wide.
£100–120 OO

A Gouda ashtray, decorated with Kayanza pattern in yellow, blue and red, 1931, 4¼in (11cm) diam.
£50–60 OO

HANCOCK & SONS

Sampson Hancock & Sons was founded in 1858 and, by the turn of the century, was known for producing tableware and Arts and Crafts-style pottery, particularly Morris Ware. In the 1920s the company introduced a new trade mark, Royal Coronaware. Lustre designs were painted by artists such as Frank X. Abraham and Molly Hancock, while nursery designs were another strong line. Hancock's closed in 1937.

A Hancock & Sons Titian Ware vase, hand-painted in colours by F. X. Abraham, c1920, 14½in (37cm) high.
£250–300 BFR

A Hancock & Sons Royal Coronaware vase, decorated with Autumn pattern in orange, pink, blue and yellow on a brown ground, signed 'Molly Hancock', 1924, 5½in (14cm) high.
£140–160 PIC

A pair of Hancock & Sons Royal Coronaware candlesticks, decorated with Cherry Ripe pattern in red, orange and blue on a green and purple ground, signed 'Molly Hancock', 1924, 2in (5cm) high.
£100–120 PIC

A Hancock & Sons Rubens Ware bud vase, decorated with Pomegranate pattern in red, yellow, green and blue, signed 'F. X. Abraham', 1928, 5½in (14cm) high.
£85–100 PIC

A Hancock & Sons Royal Coronaware vase, decorated with Waterlily pattern in shades of red, yellow, green and pink on a blue ground, 1924, 5½in (14cm) high.
£150–175 PIC

A Hancock & Sons Royal Coronaware jug, decorated with Cremorne pattern in yellow, purple, pink and green on a blue ground, signed 'Molly Hancock', 1924, 4in (10cm) high.
£150–170 PIC

A Hancock & Sons Royal Coronaware vase, decorated with Cherry Ripe pattern in red, orange and blue on a green ground, signed 'Molly Hancock', 1920s, 11½in (29cm) high.
£300–350 BEV

◄ A Hancock & Sons lustre long-neck vase, hand-painted with Storm pattern in shades of blue, green and pink, c1935, 9in (23cm) high.
£140–160 AOT

▶ A Hancock & Sons Royal Coronaware nursery cup and saucer, designed by Edith Gater, decorated with chicks in red, yellow and green, 1930s, saucer 5½in (14cm) diam.
£50–60 BDA

HONEY & JAM POTS

A Wilkinson pottery honey pot, designed by Clarice Cliff, decorated in a honey-glaze pattern in orange, yellow and pink, 1930s, 4in (10cm) high.
£180–200 HUM

A Belleek porcelain honey pot, decorated with bees and shamrocks in yellow and green, c1880, 6in (15cm) high.
£300–350 HUM

Two Japanese pottery jam pots, 1920–30s,
l. Maruhon Ware Fruit Basket, decorated in green and with coloured fruit, 2¾in (7cm) high.
r. Marutomo Ware Orange Branch marmalade jar, decorated in orange and green, 3in (7.5cm) high.
£22–30 each CoCo

▶ A Price Bros honeycomb honey pot, hand-painted with red and blue flowers, c1934, 5in (12.5cm) high.
£45–55 CoCo

◀ Two Japanese jam pots, 1920–30s, 3in (7.5cm) high.
l. Maruhon Ware, inscribed 'Ye Kings Head'.
r. Marutomo Ware cottage.
£30–35 each CoCo

JUGS

A creamware harvest jug, transfer-printed in black with a rural scene, 1790, 9in (23cm) high.
£300–325 OD

Two brown stoneware Drunken Silenus jugs, 1830–40, largest 6in (15cm) high.
l. £100–120
r. £75–90 CoCo

An Elsmore & Forester puzzle jug, decorated with Cockfighting pattern in red, yellow and green, 1858–71, 8½in (21.5cm) high.
£150–175 CoCo

Cross Reference
See Colour Review

A Staffordshire clobbered jug, decorated in orange, green and brown on a blue ground, with copper lustre rim, 1810–40, 5½in (14cm) high.
£120–140 CoCo

A Ridgeway brown milk jug, moulded with figures and animals, 1835, 5in (12.5cm) high.
£100–110 BWA

A T. Dean yellow jug, decorated in green and orange, with dragon handle, 1902, 8½in (21.5cm) high.
£50–60 DBo

A polychrome pearlware jug, with simulated bamboo handle, inscribed 'James Wood 1819.', painted in Pratt enamels with sprays of flowers below a decorative neck and yellow spout, slight damage, 7½in (19cm) high.
£240–280 Bea(E)

A Drabware pottery jug, moulded with Van Ambrugh the lion tamer, c1845, 8in (20.5cm) high.
£75–85 IW

A Myott jug, decorated with red and green leaf pattern on a brown and cream ground, 1930s, 8in (20.5cm) high.
£30–35 DBo

LINTHORPE

A Linthorpe vase, with brown and green flowing glaze, design attributed to Dr Christopher Dresser, 1879–82, 3¾in (9.5cm) high.
£85–100 NCA

A Linthorpe flask vase, designed by Dr Christopher Dresser, decorated with Aztec pattern in brown and green, c1882, 8in (20.5cm) high.
£425–475 HUN

A Linthorpe plate, designed by Dr Christopher Dresser, decorated by Fred Brown with flowers on a yellow and brown ground, marked, 1880s, 11½in (29cm) high.
£220–260 DD

◄ A Linthorpe yellow and brown vase, c1883, 11in (28cm) high.
£325–365 HUN

LUSTRE WARE

A Sunderland lustre plaque, attributed to Moore & Co, Southwick Union Pottery, depicting the *Union*, with pink and gilt surround, 1830, 9in (23cm) wide.
£350–400 IS

A Scottish lustre jug, decorated with pink, blue, red and yellow flowers, c1840, 5in (12.5cm) high.
£180–200 BWA

A Low Lights Pottery lustre scripture plaque, by John Carr, with pink and gilt surround, 1860–65, 9in (23cm) wide.
£150–180 IS

A Pilkington Royal Lancastrian lustre bowl and cover, designed by W. S. Mycock, decorated in red, brown, gilt and yellow, c1915, 7in (18cm) diam.
£400–480 JEZ

A Hollinshead & Kirkham lustre cup and saucer, decorated with fruit in yellow, red and blue on a brown ground, 1930s, saucer 5¼in (13.5cm) diam.
£30–35 CoCo

A Pilkington Royal Lancastrian lustre vase, painted with vertical bands of leaves on a gold-coloured ground, restored, 1903–13, 6¼in (16cm) high.
£240–270 P(Ba)

MAJOLICA

A Minton majolica trefoil-shaped hors d'oeuvre dish, decorated in green with a central water lily and buds, impressed marks for shape No. 1010, 1865, 9¾in (25cm) wide.
£800–900 DN

A Minton majolica leaf-shaped nut dish, the handle in the shape of a squirrel eating a nut, flanked by nuts and leaves, impressed marks for shape No. 1522 and 1869, restored, 9¾in (25cm) wide.
£850–1,000 DN

A majolica dish, decorated in relief with green and blue foliage, with orange and black rim, possibly Minton, c1870, 18in (45.5cm) diam.
£540–600 TWr

► A George Jones majolica garden seat, decorated in relief with leafy foliage, white flowerheads and trailing branches of blueberry blossom in coloured enamels on a green and brown glazed ground, impressed mark 'George Jones & Sons 2', slight damage, 1875–80, 20½in (52cm) high.
£2,200–2,500 Hal

A majolica corn-on-the-cob cream jug, decorated in green and yellow with brown handle and rim, 1880s, 3in (7.5cm) high.
£75–90 CoCo

A majolica corn-on-the-cob jug, with pewter lid, 1880s, 6in (15cm) high.
£90–100 CoCo

MALING

A Maling lustre plate, decorated with Windmill pattern in gilt and colours on a cobalt blue ground, early first period, c1929, 9½in (24cm) diam.
£400–480 AOT

◄ A Maling pin tray, decorated with red, blue, green and yellow flowers, c1935, 4in (10cm) wide.
£24–28 FQA

A Maling rack plate, decorated with Delphinium pattern in pink and pale blue on a cobalt-blue ground, c1930, 11¼in (28.5cm) diam.
£250–280 AOT

A Maling vase, by Norman Carling, decorated with Blossom Time pattern in blues and greens, c1935, 8in (20.5cm) high.
£140–160 AOT

> **Cross Reference**
> See Colour Review

A Maling plate, decorated with Blue Galleon pattern in colours on a blue ground, 1935, 11in (28cm) diam.
£300–350 MD

A Maling rack plate, decorated with Old Mill pattern in colours on a cobalt-blue ground, c1936, 11¼in (28.5cm) diam.
£250–280 AOT

A Maling vase, decorated with a floral pattern in colours on a dark blue ground, c1940, 6in (15cm) high.
£120–150 JEZ

A Maling lustre planter, with green and white floral decoration and pink interior, black transfer mark, c1936, 13in (33cm) wide.
£110–130 FQA

A Maling bowl, decorated in colours with a floral pattern, 1938, 11in (28cm) diam.
£150–180 RIA

A Maling footed dish, decorated with Rosine pattern of yellow roses and pink swirls, c1940, 10¾in (27.5cm) wide.
£90–110 FQA

A Maling teapot, decorated with Anemone pattern on a cobalt-blue ground, c1950, 6½in (16.5cm) high.
£150–180 AOT

A Maling octagonal plate, enamelled with fruit on a matt burnt-orange ground, c1936, 9in (23cm) wide.
£160–180 AOT

A Maling bowl, decorated with pink and green flowers, c1938, 11in (28cm) diam.
£120–150 RIA

A Maling two-handled dish, decorated with flowers in pink, yellow and green on a cobalt-blue ground, c1950, 11in (28cm) wide.
£75–90 AOT

◄ A Maling set of six lustre comports, decorated in green, blue, pink, yellow, light blue and purple with gilt rims, c1950, 3in (7.5cm) high.
£80–90 AOT

MASON'S IRONSTONE

A Mason's Ironstone coffee can, decorated with flowers and leaves in green, brown and pink, 1810, 2½in (6.5cm) high.
£120–140 JP

A Mason's Ironstone miniature coffee pot and cover, with side handle, painted in Imari style in underglaze blue, iron-red and gilt with flowering branches and fences, 1815–20, 2½in (6.5cm) high.
£550–650 DN

A Mason's Ironstone cider mug, with wavy rim, decorated in iron-red and blue, 1820, 5in (12.5cm) high.
£350–400 JP

A Mason's Ironstone drainer, decorated in iron-red and blue, 1830–48, 30in (76cm) wide.
£250–300 JP

A Mason's Ironstone plate, decorated with Chinese Wall pattern in iron-red, brown, black, green and yellow, 1830, 10½in (26.5cm) diam.
£120–140 JP

A Mason's Ironstone soup plate, decorated with yellow, green and pink flowers on a cobalt-blue ground, within a pink band and black and gilt rim, 1830–48, 9in (23cm) diam.
£200–230 JP

Mason's Ironstone

A fine stone china imitating porcelain, Mason's Ironstone was patented in 1813 by Charles James Mason of Lane Delph, Staffordshire.

A Mason's Ironstone jug, decorated in iron-red, blue, black and gilt, 1830–48, 6in (15cm) high.
£250–300 JP

A Mason's Ashworth teapot, decorated with reserves of flowers in colours and gilt on a green ground, 1862–72, 4in (10cm) high.
£350–390 JP
In 1862 Mason's was taken over by G. L. Ashworth & Bros.

A Mason's Ironstone jug, decorated with Bandana pattern in iron-red, black and yellow, 1840–60, 5½in (14cm) high.
£210–240 JP

MOORCROFT

A Moorcroft Florian Ware vase and silver-plated basket stand, decorated with a floral Art Nouveau design in shades of blue, the stand on three bun feet, marked and painted 'WM', c1900, 3¼in (8.5cm) high.
£550–650 Hal

A Moorcroft two-handled vase, decorated with a wisteria pattern in colours on a deep blue ground, 1928, 8in (20.5cm) high.
£1,000–1,200 MD

A Moorcroft MacIntyre Florian Ware two-handled vase, design No. 5, decorated with a butterfly pattern, monogram printed mark, c1900, 11in (28cm) high.
£1,100–1,300 GAK

A Moorcroft vase, decorated with Pansy Nouveau pattern in red and green on a deep blue ground, 1918–26, 11in (28cm) high.
£800–900 TWr

▶ A Moorcroft Flambé vase, decorated with a clematis pattern in reds and browns, c1940, 13in (33cm) high.
£1,700–2,000 TWr

A Moorcroft vase, decorated with a freesia pattern on a deep blue ground, marked, c1935, 5in (12.5cm) high.
£140–160 Hal(C)

A Moorcroft vase, decorated with a pomegranate pattern on a deep blue ground, signed and marked, c1930, 6½in (16.5cm) high.
£400–475 JM

A Moorcroft teapot and cover, decorated with an African lily pattern of pink and ivory flowers on a green-blue ground, marked, c1953, 6in (15cm) high.
£350–400 Hal(C)

A Moorcroft two-handled vase, decorated with a Sally Tuffin carp pattern in colours, marked, signed in green 'J. Moorcroft', c1990, 13½in (34cm) high.
£1,200–1,400 L&T

MUGS

A pearlware porcelain Bacchus mug, decorated in colours on a white ground, slight damage, c1790, 4½in (11.5cm) high.
£100–120 MMa

An Irish spongeware mug, decorated in green and red on a cream ground, slight damage, 19thC, 3¾in (9.5cm) high.
£90–100 Byl

An Edwardian christening mug, with gilt inscription and decoration, 3in (7.5cm) high.
£25–30 WAB

A creamware green and white Bacchus mug, slight damage, c1790, 4½in (11.5cm) high.
£100–120 MMa

A Victorian Mocha ware half-pint mug, decorated with brown, blue and black bands, 4in (10cm) high.
£85–95 WeA

A green glazed mug, modelled as Old Bill, 1918, 4in (10cm) high.
£30–35 HUX

▶ A Dartmouth tankard, 'Widecombe Fair', decorated in relief on a blue ground, 1950s, 5½in (14cm) high.
£25–30 PC

A Derby Neptune mug, decorated with yellow hair and orange and gilt crown, marked, slight damage, c1810, 4in (10cm) high.
£200–240 MMa

A two-handled loving cup, decorated in colours with Ningpo pattern, marked 'Ningpo C.H.', probably by Charles Hobson, 1865–75, 5in (12.5cm) high.
£80–90 IW

A pottery ale mug, decorated with blue bands on a brown and white ground, 1880, 5in (12.5cm) high.
£65–75 WeA

NAUTILUS

The Nautilus Porcelain Company, Possil Pottery, Possil Park, Glasgow, was founded in 1894 by two brothers, John and Daniel MacDougall. The firm produced high-quality porcelain, ranging from elaborate figures and vases to crested pieces, concentrating on Scottish locations.

Nautilus ornamental and table wares were often gilded, decorated with delicately painted flowers and elaborately modelled with frilled rims, raised decoration and curlicue handles. 'The Designs and Decorations being extremely delicate and chaste, and quite a departure from anything else in the market, are well suited for a better class Retail Trade', promised a 1901 advertisement in *The Pottery Gazette*, which also assured potential customers that prices would be found 'extremely moderate'. Despite these attractions, however, the company ceased trading in 1911. Today, with growing interest from collectors, prices for Nautilus porcelain are considerably less moderate.

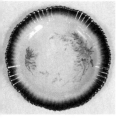

A Nautilus Porcelain plate, decorated with flowers, with a blue and gilt rim, early red mark, 1890s, 6½in (16.5cm) diam.
£120–150 FQA

A Nautilus Porcelain jardinière, with gilt and floral decoration, signed, c1898, 5½in (14cm) high.
£450–500 MMa

◀ A Nautilus Porcelain ewer, with serpent handle, decorated in blue and gilt with red flowers, stamped, c1898, 13in (33cm) high.
£750–900 MMa

◀ A Nautilus Porcelain cup and saucer, 1890s, cup 2½in (6.5cm) high.
£50–60 TWr

◀ A Nautilus Porcelain campana-shaped vase, gilded with blue and floral decoration, 1890s, 7in (18cm) high.
£500–600 MMa

▶ Two Nautilus Porcelain ewers, decorated with flowers and heightened with gilt, c1898, tallest 12in (30.5cm) high.
£350–400 each MMa

Two Nautilus Porcelain plates, with gilt and floral decoration, one signed and one with printed mark, c1898, 8½in (21.5cm) diam.
£100–200 each MMa

▶ A Nautilus Porcelain two-handled vase, the handles modelled as seated putti, decorated with sprays of poppies within gilt borders, printed mark, c1900, 13in (33cm) high.
£600–700 P(Sc)

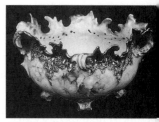

A Nautilus Porcelain jardinière, decorated with sprays of poppies on a cream ground, with blue and gilt border, pierced scroll rim and four scroll feet, printed mark, c1900, 10½in (26.5cm) wide.
£450–550 P(Sc)

A Nautilus Porcelain Gypsy pot, with gilt and floral decoration, transfer mark, c1900, 3in (7.5cm) high.
£120–140 FQA

A Nautilus Porcelain teapot, decorated in flow blue and gilt, stamped, c1900, 5in (12.5cm) high.
£130–150 MMa

A Nautilus Porcelain leaf-shaped tray, with floral decoration, c1900, 11in (28cm) wide.
£250–300 TWr

A Nautilus Porcelain fruit bowl, decorated with pink and purple flowers and gilt rim, c1900, 10in (25.5cm) high.
£450–550 TWr

A Nautilus Porcelain trio, decorated with poppies, with cream and gilt rims, c1900, cup 2½in (6.5cm) high.
£70–80 MMa

A Nautilus Porcelain plate, with Worcester-style floral decoration in yellow and gilt, stamped, c1900, 7in (18cm) diam.
£45–50 MMa

A Nautilus Porcelain teapot, commemorating the Glasgow Exhibition 1901, decorated with poppies and gilt on a white ground, stamped, c1901, 4in (10cm) high.
£85–100 BLA

A Nautilus Porcelain cauldron-shaped fairing, with Larne crest, black transfer mark on base, c1902, 2½in (6.5cm) high.
£25–30 MMa

A Possil Pottery earthenware plate, decorated with a river scene in blue and gilt, stamped, c1905, 10in (25.5cm) diam.
£85–100 MMa

NURSERY WARE

A child's plate, transfer-printed in black, entitled 'April', c1850, 7¼in (18.5cm) diam.
£50–60 IW

A child's plate, with moulded alphabet border surrounding a black and white transfer-print quoting one of Benjamin Franklin's maxims, late 19thC, 6½in (16.5cm) diam.
£50–55 IW

A Maling Cetem ware child's washbowl and jug, decorated with Steiff policemen and Florence Upton gollies, 1920s, bowl 16in (40.5cm) diam.
£600–700 MURR

◄ A baby's plate, entitled 'Teddy caught again', possibly Continental, c1910–18, 7in (18cm) diam.
£50–60 MURR

A doll's house cup and saucer, decorated with a bee and butterfly, 1930s, cup 1½in (4cm) high.
£4–5 SAA

A Royal Doulton Bunnykins jug, 1950s, 5¼in (13.5cm) high.
£120–140 WWY

A Midwinter Stylecraft Classic Shape plate, designed by Peggy Gibbons, 1963, 7in (18cm) diam.
£45–55 BDA

A Coalport Paddington marmalade pot, c1974, 4¼in (11cm) high.
£30–35 WWY

A child's plate, decorated with Sweep, c1980, 6in (15cm) diam.
£6–7 AL

A Pendelfin model, Desmond Duck, wearing a pink cap and mauve boots, 1955–58, 5½in (14cm) high.
£1,000–1,500 AHJ

Miller's is a price GUIDE not a price LIST

A Pendelfin model, Father Kipper Tie, wearing blue trousers and a grey, white and pink tie, 1960–70, 8in (20.5cm) high.
£500–600 AHJ

A Pendelfin model, Rosa, wearing a pink dress, 1982–98, 4in (10cm) high.
£25–30 PSL
Pendelfin also produced a limited edition model of Rosa wearing a blue dress which is worth c£350.

A Pendelfin model, Clanger, wearing a pink jacket and carrying a cream and green bell, 1983–98, 3½in (9cm) high.
£40–50 AHJ

A Pendelfin model, Aunt Ruby, wearing a red, pink and blue dress, from a limited edition of 10,000, 1993–96, 8in (20.5cm) high.
£180–200 AHJ

A Pendelfin model, Herald, wearing a blue bib and carrying a white scroll with a red seal, October 1992–December 1993, 3½in (9cm) high.
£140–170 AHJ
This Pendelfin was a Club Founder-Member gift.

▶ A Pendelfin model, Cookie, wearing blue trousers and a cream chef's hat, 1995–2000, 4½in (11.5cm) high.
£25–30 AHJ

PLATES

A pair of Delft polychrome plates, decorated in manganese, blue and yellow with inscribed entwined hearts within a naively-painted border, 18thC, 8¾in (22cm) diam.
£220–250 HYD

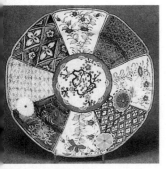

A Spode pearlware octagonal plate, decorated in Kakiemon style with radiating panels of leaves and flowers in underglaze blue, iron-red, green, puce and gilt, impressed mark, c1810–15, 8in (20.5cm) wide.
£140–160 DN

A Hammersley plate, decorated in gilt and with hand-painted exotic birds on a blue ground, c1895, 9½in (24cm) diam.
£135–155 RIA

A creamware plate, transfer-printed in puce with a scene of ancient ruins, late 18thC, 8in (20.5cm) diam.
£160–180 JHo

A Minton plate, with pink and blue lattice rim and hand-painted floral decoration, c1858, 9½in (24cm) diam.
£450–475 GRI

▶ A pair of St Clement fruit plates, decorated in yellow and red, 1920s, 8in (20.5cm) diam.
£85–100 MLL

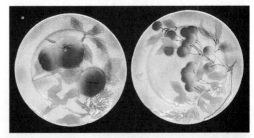

A Grimwades plate, entitled 'The Imp', 1930s, 12½in (32cm) diam.
£85–95 MD

A French faïence pottery plate, decorated with a bird on a branch in blue, yellow and green, 1800, 9in (23cm) diam.
£100–120 OD

A Bo'ness wall plate, decorated with autumn-coloured leaves interspersed with turquoise against a terracotta background, 1880s, 10½in (26.5cm) diam.
£40–45 JEB

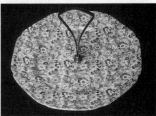

A Parrot & Co pink and blue chintz cake plate, c1935, 9in (23cm) diam.
£35–40 JACK

POOLE POTTERY

A Poole Pottery miniature bowl, decorated in purple, yellow, green and blue, 1920–30, 2in (5cm) high.
£50–60 JEZ

A Poole Pottery bust of a dog's head, 1930s, 6in (15cm) long.
£300–360 HarC
Busts of this type are usually seen as wall hangings.

A Poole Pottery vase, decorated by Mary Brown in shades of brown and blue, 1926–34, 7¼in (18.5cm) high.
£450–500 ADE

◀ A Poole Pottery bust of a dog's head, 1930s, 6in (15cm) long.
£300–360 HarC

▶ A Poole Pottery bowl, decorated by Nellie Bishton, restored, c1944–49, 7in (18cm) diam.
£65–75 UNI

A Carter, Stabler & Adams terracotta ovoid vase, shape No. 973/EB, with stepped handles, decorated by Ruth Pavely with flowers and foliage in purple, yellow, green, blue and pink, impressed and painted marks, 1930s, 7¼in (18.5cm) high.
£350–400 DD

A Poole Pottery plate, decorated with an abstract design in green, mustard and black, 1970s, 6in (15cm) wide.
£50–60 MD

A Poole Pottery vase, by Susan Dipple, the brown body decorated with a carved zigzag pattern, 1972–75, 4in (10cm) high
£100–120 HarC

◀ A Poole Pottery earthenware bottle vase, shape No. A11/1, by Jenny Haigh, the red body decorated with a carved green-glazed spiralling band, impressed factory mark, shape number and artist's monogram to base, 1973–76, 7in (18cm) high.
£120–140 RTo

QUIMPER

◄ A Quimper pot stand, decorated in yellow, blue, red and green with a man and a woman carrying baskets of chickens and turkeys, c1875, 8in (20.5cm) wide.
£110–135 SER

A Quimper jug, 1883–1904, 3½in (9cm) high.
£65–75 SER

A Quimper Soupière bowl with lid, Grand Maison second mark, slight wear, 1883–1904, bowl 9½in (24cm) wide.
£85–100 SER

A Quimper egg stand, decorated in blue, orange and green, marked 'HR Quimper', c1895–1900, 9½in (24cm) wide.
£250–275 VH

A Quimper Malicorne dish, decorated in red, blue and yellow, c1890, 10½in (26.5cm) wide.
£110–125 VH

A pair of Quimper dishes, decorated with a Breton man and woman within a blue and orange patterned border, c1890, 8¾in (22cm) wide.
£200–220 VH

► A Quimper hand bell, decorated with a woman and flowers in blue, yellow, orange and green, signed 'HB', c1900, 4in (10cm) high.
£70–80 CoCo

A Quimper Breton Folk faïence serving dish, c1920, 9¼in (23.5cm) wide.
£75–90 CoCo

A Henriot Quimper cream jug, decorated in orange, blue and green, c1922, 3¼in (8.5cm) high.
£65–75 SER

A Henriot Quimper potager bowl, decorated with a Breton woman in orange, yellow, blue and green, 1922–68, 6½in (16.5cm) wide.
£30–35 SER

A Quimper jug, decorated with a Breton woman in yellow, green, blue and orange, small chip, 1934–60, 6in (15cm) high.
£50–55 SER

A Quimper bowl, with handle, decorated in blue, green and orange, 1943–68, 7½in (19cm) wide.
£17–20 SER

A Henriot Quimper pail, with lid and base plate, decorated in red, blue and yellow, 1922, 4⅛in (11.5cm) high.
£60–70 SER

A Henriot Quimper plate, decorated with musical figures in colours within an orange and black border, 1922–25, 9in (23cm) diam.
£200–220 VH

A Quimper pot stand, decorated with a woman in brown, orange and yellow, 1943–68, 8½in (21.5cm) wide.
£60–70 SER

▶ A Quimper blue and white bowl and plate, 1943–68, plate 6in (15cm) diam.
£30–35 SER

A Henriot Quimper plate, decorated with a Breton figure in blue, orange, yellow and green, 1922–68, 6in (15cm) diam.
£30–35 SER

A Quimper plate, decorated in blue, green and orange, c1930, 6in (15cm) diam.
£40–45 SER

A Quimper two-handled vase, decorated in red, blue, yellow and green, 1943–68, 4½in (11.5cm) high.
£75–85 SER

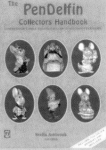

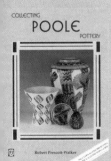

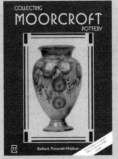

A Baggerley & Ball clobbered jug, 1822–36, 4¼in (11cm) high.
£120–135 CoCo

A Beswick cheese dish, c1930, 7in (18cm) long.
£35–40 FA

A Beswick Beatrix Potter model of Squirrel Nutkin No. BP2, first version, with gilt mark, 1948–80, 3¾in (9.5cm) high.
£25–35 SAS

A Delft blue and white plate, decorated with a Chinese scene, c1740, 10in (25.5cm) diam.
£180–220 JHo

◀ A Beswick Beatrix Potter model of Simpkin No. BP3B, 1975–83, 4in (10cm) high.
£350–400 SAS

A Minton blue and white spitoon, decorated with Florentine pattern, 1825, 4½in (11.5cm) high.
£300–350 GN

◀ An H. Dimmock blue and white lobster dish with strainer, 1828–59, 22in (56cm) long.
£300–360 TWr

A Staffordshire blue and white tankard, decorated with Willow pattern, 19thC, 5½in (14cm) high.
£130–155 CoCo

A pair of Bretby book ends, modelled as polar bears, 1930s, 5in (12.5cm) high.
£250–275 BSA
These book ends were inspired by the two polar bears that were kept in London Zoo during the 1930s.

A pair of Boness parrots, 19thC, 13in (33cm) high.
£150–180 TWr

▶ A Bretby vase, in the shape of an acorn, c1890, 4in (10cm) high.
£165–195 HUN

◄ A double candle extinguisher, c1880, 4in (10cm) high.
£250–300 TH

A Royal Worcester miniature candle extinguisher, Town Girl, c1880, 3¾in (9.5cm) high.
£1,000–1,200 TH

► A candle extinguisher, in the form of a monk, 1910, 5in (12.5cm) high.
£160–190 WAC

A candle extinguisher, in the form of Granny Snow, c1908, 3in (7.5cm) high.
£320–360 TH

◄ A candle extinguisher, in the form of Mr Caudle, 1954, 4in (10cm) high.
£230–260 CAW

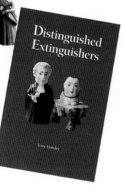

A pair of Carlton Ware vases, decorated with Hydrangea pattern, late 1920s, 12in (30.5cm) high.
£1,000–1,200 MD

A Carlton Ware cruet, in the form of a squirrel and acorns, 1920s, 5in (12.5cm) wide.
£160–180 BEV

A Carlton Ware Waterlily plate, 1930–40, 9in (23cm) diam.
£70–80 MD

A Carlton Ware egg cups and cruet set, 1930s, 5in (12.5cm) wide.
£90–100 BEV

A Carlton Ware Mushroom cruet set, 1930s, 5in (12.5cm) wide.
£140–160 BEV

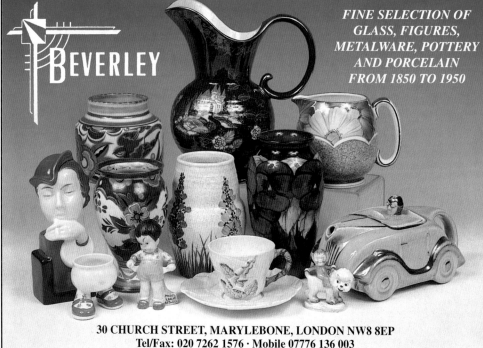

A Clarice Cliff Lynton cup and saucer, 1920s, 3in (7.5cm) high.
£430–480 MD

► A Clarice Cliff Bizarre conical cruet set, decorated with Autumn Crocus pattern, 1928–36, tallest 3in (7.5cm) high.
£500–550 RIA

A Clarice Cliff Bizarre honey pot, decorated with Gayday pattern, 1928–36, 4in (10cm) high.
£400–450 RIA

A Clarice Cliff Original Bizarre jam pot, 1928–30, 3in (7.5cm) high.
£180–220 CoCo

A Clarice Cliff plate, decorated with a geometric pattern, c1930, 10in (25.5cm) diam.
£350–400 MD

A Clarice Cliff plate, decorated with Blue Chintz pattern, 1932–33, 10in (25.5cm) diam.
£450–500 RIA

A Clarice Cliff vase, decorated with a geometric pattern, 1930s, 8in (20.5cm) high.
£875–975 MD

A Clarice Cliff Celtic Harvest sandwich plate, 1930s, 13in (33cm) long.
£245–285 MD

◄ A Clarice Cliff Bizarre coffee set, decorated with Blue Crocus pattern, comprising a coffee pot, sugar bowl, cream jug and six cups and saucers, 1930s.
£2,500–2,800 IM

A Clarice Cliff candle holder, decorated with Forest Glen pattern, 1935–37, 2½in (6.5cm) high.
£450–500 RIA

A Royal Crown Derby miniature saucepan and lid, decorated with Imari pattern, c1912, 2in (5cm) high.
£350–400 GRI

▶ A Crown Devon vase, decorated with trees, 1930s, 15½in (39.5cm) high.
£400–450 MD

A Crown Ducal tankard, 1930s, 7½in (19cm) high.
£155–175 PrB

A Crown Staffordshire model, Melba Finch, by J. T. Jones, 1960–70, 6½in (16.5cm) high.
£80–90 PAC

A Davenport porcelain tray, c1850, 19in (48cm) wide.
£500–600 TWr

A Denby pastel blue vase, by Donald Gilbert, c1933, 7in (18cm) high.
£100–110 OTT

A Doulton Lambeth Art Nouveau jug, by Frank A. Butler, modelled with projecting flower pods growing from a stylized handle, No. 541, marked, 1900s, 8¼in (21cm) high.
£620–700 DD

A Royal Doulton two-handled vase, by J. H. Plant, decorated with a country scene, c1910, 5½in (14cm) high.
£300–350 JE

▶ A pair of Royal Doulton candlesticks, decorated with Gaylee pattern, c1930, 6in (15cm) high.
£145–185 BEV

A Royal Doulton jug, decorated with Gnomes pattern, c1930, 4½in (11.5cm) high.
£300–350 BEV

A Scottish Gallatoun blue and white puzzle jug, inscribed 'Fleming Lillie', damaged, c1830, 7in (18cm) high.
£540–600 BWA

A Gibsons Sheila sugar bowl, cover and stand, 1930s, 4in (10cm) high.
£45–55 CoCo

A Goebbels model of a rabbit and egg, 1930s, 7in (18cm) high.
£85–95 LEGE

A Hancock & Sons Corona ware vase, Cremone, designed by Mollie Hancock, 1920s, 10in (25.5cm) high.
£300–350 BEV

A Sunderland lustre plate, impressed mark Dixon, Phillips & Co', c1840, 8in (20.5cm) wide.
£200–250 IS

A Gouda Gothic-style vase, 1925, 11¾in (30cm) high.
£300–350 OO

▶ A Scottish Alloa majolica jardinière and stand, c1870, 10in (25.5cm) high.
£350–400 TWr

A Maling ware rack plate, decorated with Windmill pattern, c1929, 11¼in (28.5cm) diam.
£280–320 AOT

A Maling ware vase, decorated with multicoloured pansies, 1930s, 7in (18cm) high.
£175–195 BSA

A Maling ware vase, decorated with white flowers and swirls, printed mark, 1930s, 8in (20.5cm) high.
£100–125 SAA

A Marutomo ware honey pot, relief-moulded and hand-painted, with bee finial, Japanese, 1920–30, 3½in (9cm) high.
£40–50 CoCo

A Mason's Ironstone cup and saucer, by Francis Morley, pattern No. 2/101, 1850–60, saucer 6in (15cm) diam.
£60–70 JP

▶ A Midwinter Springtime sugar sifter, with metal lid, 1930s, 6in (15cm) high.
£120–150 BEV
This pattern was later renamed Brama.

A Minton plate, reserved with three rural scenes, c1830, 9in (23cm) diam.
£135–150 GRI

A Minton charger, designed by A. W. N. Pugin, the rim with 'Waste Not Want Not' in Gothic script, base marked '430', c1850, 13in (33cm) diam.
£750–850 DN

◀ A Nautilus basketweave jardinière, c1890, 8in (20.5cm) wide
£350–400 TWr

A Mason's Ironstone coffee pot, decorated with Trophy pattern, 1862–72, 7in (18cm) high.
£240–270 JP

RADFORD

Edward Radford (1882–1969) was born into the ceramics business. His father was a leading potter at Pilkington's Tile Company, where Edward himself trained, before leaving to fight in WWI where his actions gained him the Military Cross.

On his return he worked for Wood & Sons, before setting up The Radford Handcraft Pottery in Burslem, Stoke on Trent. Highly successful during the 1930s, he specialized in hand-thrown, hand-painted wares. One of his selling points was that no two pieces were exactly the same, as everything was done by hand: the potting, the back colourwash, the painting of the flowers and trees, even through to the very end when the pots were hand-dipped in the glaze. The resulting quality is why so many people are interested in Radford ware.

The pottery specialized in ornamental wares using both traditional and modern Art Deco-inspired shapes. Typically pieces were finished with a matt glaze and decorated with floral patterns in delicate pastel colours. Among the most popular designs were Anemone, Clematis, Delphinium and Poppy. Collectors today particularly prize unusual items such as pieces decorated with tree designs, the animal figures produced during the 1930s, and any odd shape or rare pattern. The more Art Deco the design, the more collectable the object.

During WWII production merged with that of Wood & Sons who continued to produce Radford designs until the 1960s. Although 1930s Radford is commanding strong prices today, post-war moulded pieces are more affordable and are likely to be a good investment.

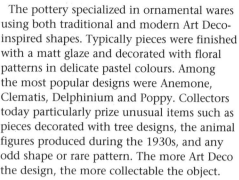

A Radford Art Deco hand-thrown jug, hand-painted with purple flowers on a mottled yellow ground, c1928, 6½in (16.5cm) high.
£150–180 ERCC

A Radford jug, decorated with a landscape in shades of brown, 1930s, 8in (20.5cm) high.
£120–130 BEV

A Radford vase, decorated with a geometric pattern in purple and yellow on a cream ground, 1930s, 5in (12.5cm) high.
£90–100 BEV

A Radford vase, decorated with a geometric pattern in blue on a cream ground, 1930s, 6in (15cm) high.
£120–140 BEV

A Radford hand-thrown vase, decorated with orange flowers on a pale green ground, c1930, 6½in (16.5cm) high.
£90–100 ERCC

A Radford Burslem hand-thrown vase, decorated with purple and orange flowers on a mottled pink ground, c1930, 6in (15cm) high.
£100–120 ERCC

A Radford Burslem hand-thrown vase, hand-painted with Broom design in red and green on a beige ground, c1930, 6½in (16.5cm) high.
£120–150 ERCC

A Radford vase, decorated with orange flowers on a pale green ground, 1930s, 5in (12.5cm) high.
£80–90 BEV

A Radford vase, decorated with Broom pattern in red and yellow on a beige ground, 1930s, 6in (15cm) high.
£80–90 BEV

A Radford jug, decorated with yellow and blue flowers on a pale blue ground, 1930s, 8in (20.5cm) high.
£90–100 BEV

A Radford Burslem hand-thrown vase, decorated with a tree pattern in black, yellow and green on a mottled yellow ground, c1930, 9in (23cm) high.
£200–225 ERCC

A Radford tube-lined vase, decorated with a floral pattern in pink, green and yellow on a mottled pale blue ground, 1930s, 9in (23cm) high.
£90–100 BEV

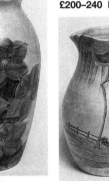

A Radford vase, decorated with pink and purple anemones on a mottled yellow ground, 1930s, 8in (20.5cm) high.
£100–115 BEV

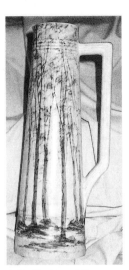

A Radford hand-thrown jug, hand-painted with a tree pattern in browns and green on a yellow ground, c1930, 13in (33cm) high.
£200–240 PC

A Radford jug, decorated with a landscape in colours on a pale green ground, 1930s, 8in (20.5cm) high.
£140–160 BEV

A Radford vase, decorated with a floral pattern in pink and purple on a mottled green and pink ground, 1930s, 5in (12.5cm) high.
£80–90 BEV

A Radford hand-thrown yellow dripware jug, c1930, 7½in (19cm) high.
£110–130 ERCC

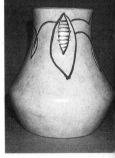

A Radford hand-thrown vase, decorated with sgraffito pattern in blue on a pale green ground, c1930, 6in (15cm) high.
£90–110 ERCC

A Radford hand-thrown jug, decorated with Foxglove pattern in yellow, green and white on a pale green ground, c1930, 6½in (16.5cm) high.
£125–145 ERCC

► A Radford jug, decorated with Zebra Tree pattern in blue, green, black and orange, on a blue ground, 1930s, 5in (12.5cm) high.
£100–115 BEV

A Radford Butterfly Ware jug, decorated with yellow flowers on a dark green ground, c1935, 9½in (24cm) high.
£150–180 ERCC

A Radford vase, decorated with Bamboo pattern in greens on a pale green ground, c1950, 9in (23cm) high.
£55–65 ERCC

A Radford Burslem hand-thrown jug, decorated with orange and purple flowers on a yellow ground, c1930, 5in (12.5cm) high.
£75–85 ERCC

A Radford jug, decorated with yellow, red and blue flowers on a green ground, c1938, 11in (28cm) high.
£145–165 ERCC

A Radford vase, decorated with Strawberry pattern on a pale green ground, c1950, 5in (12.5cm) high.
£35–40 ERCC

► A Radford teapot, decorated with a floral pattern in yellow and blue, 1940s, 6in (15cm) high.
£75–85 BEV

A Radford vase and three trays, decorated with a floral pattern in yellow, red and blue, c1945, largest 13in (33cm) wide.
Vase £42–50
Trays £35–60 each ERCC

CHARLOTTE & FREDERICK RHEAD

A Wood & Sons teapot, designed by Charlotte Rhead, decorated with Seed Poppy pattern in pink and green on a blue ground, c1918, 5¼in (13.5cm) high.
£250–300 ChR

A Bursley Ware tube-lined bowl, designed by Frederick Rhead, decorated with Trellis pattern in brown, orange and white on a blue ground, 1920s, 8½in (21.5cm) high.
£180–220 BDA

A Burgess & Leigh egg set, designed by Charlotte Rhead, decorated in blue, red and yellow, pattern No. 4471, c1930, 7in (18cm) wide.
£150–175 OTT

An Ellgreave pottery cream jug, designed by Charlotte Rhead, decorated in brown and yellow, stamped 'Lottie Rhead Ware', c1924, 2½in (6.5cm) high.
£100–120 BDA

A Wardle & Co Country Life blue and white candlestick, designed by Frederick Rhead, 1920–30s, 7in (18cm) high.
£250–300 BEV

A Crown Ducal jug, designed by Charlotte Rhead, decorated with an orange and brown pattern on a beige ground, c1940, 8in (20.5cm) high.
£120–140 ChR

◄ A Crown Ducal child's plate, designed by Charlotte Rhead, 1930s, 7½in (19cm) diam.
£175–200 LEGE

A Bursley Ware biscuit jar, designed by Charlotte Rhead, decorated with Arras pattern in orange and yellow on a blue ground, 1920s, 5in (12.5cm) high.
£160–180 BDA

A Crown Ducal child's dish, designed by Charlotte Rhead, decorated with 'Polly put the kettle on' pattern, c1934, 6¾in (17cm) diam.
£150–180 BDA

A Wood & Sons jug, designed by Charlotte Rhead, decorated with an orange and brown pattern on a beige ground, 1940s, 8½in (21.5cm) high.
£180–220 ChR

ROYAL WINTON

A Royal Winton cream jug, decorated in blue, black and yellow, 1930s, 5in (12.5cm) wide.
£16–18 DBo

A Royal Winton coffee pot, decorated with Estelle pattern in pink, yellow and green, 1940s, 6in (15cm) high.
£200–250 BEV

A Royal Winton blue lustre grapefruit bowl, with yellow lustre interior, 1930s, 4¾in (12cm) wide.
£35–40 DgC

A Royal Winton chintz compote, decorated in colours with Sunshine pattern, c1937, 7in (18cm) wide.
£85–100 CoCo

A Royal Winton sandwich tray, decorated with pink petunias on a pink ground, c1940, 11in (28cm) wide.
£80–90 AOT

A Royal Winton chintz two-cup teapot, decorated in colours with Sweet Pea pattern, c1940, 4in (10cm) high.
£400–480 AOT
Two-cup teapots in chintz are scarce, hence the price range of this item.

SHORTER & SON

A Shorter & Son hand-painted cake slice, decorated in red, orange and green on a yellow ground, 1930s, 8in (20.5cm) long.
£16–18 WAC

A Shorter & Son dish, decorated with snowdrops in cream and green on a green ground, 1930s, 6in (15cm) wide.
£24–28 WAC

◄ A Shorter & Son Daisy Belle toothbrush holder, designed by Betty Sylvester, c1940, 4in (10cm) high.
£75–90 AOT

► A Shorter & Son tureen, modelled as a red apple, c1940, 5in (12.5cm) high.
£85–100 AOT

A Shorter & Son double-handled dish, modelled as an anemone, decorated in purple and red, c1940, 11in (28cm) wide.
£30–35 AOT

STAFFORDSHIRE

Staffordshire figures were produced in vast numbers during the Victorian era, with animals being one of the favourite subjects. The burgeoning of travelling menageries and fairs stimulated demand for exotic beasts, and as pet ownership flourished, prompted by an expanding middle class and an animal-loving queen, so did the portrayal in pottery of domestic creatures, particularly dogs which are far more easily found than pottery cats.

Staffordshire human figures chronicled the main events and preoccupations of the Victorian age. The Royal Family was, perhaps, the most produced subject. Soldiers and sailors were an important theme, as Staffordshire potters covered contemporary conflicts from the Crimean War (1854–56) to the Boer War (1899–1902) as well as historical battles and heroes. Politicians and religious figures were popular (Nonconformist rather than established Church), as was sport. The Victorian love of melodrama expressed itself not only in theatrical and literary subjects, but even in the portrayal of famous criminals and murderers. Since the turn of the century Staffordshire figures have been widely reproduced, often using the original moulds. Watch out for crude painting, fake crazing and poorly defined modelling. Would-be collectors should familiarize themselves with the subject, see and handle as many pieces as possible, and buy from a reputable source.

A Staffordshire model of a brown foal, c1800, 3¼in (8.5cm) high.
£800–900 JHo

► A pair of Staffordshire pearlware dogs, 'Pointer' and 'Setter', with bocage, c1825, 9in (23cm) high.
£1,600–1,800 JRe

A Staffordshire model of a dog, in brown and white, c1840, 5in (12.5cm) high.
£200–250 JO

► A pair of Staffordshire inkwells, modelled as greyhounds, decorated in brown and black on cobalt blue bases, 1855, 7in (18cm) wide.
£300–350 ACO

A Staffordshire figural group, The British Lion and Napoleon III, c1860, 9in (23cm) high.
£425–475 S(S)

A pair of Staffordshire models of dogs, decorated with black spots and with yellow collars, c1850, 4in (10cm) high.
£300–330 ACO

A pair of Staffordshire models of zebras, c1900, 5in (12.5cm) high.
£450–500 ACO

Staffordshire figure, one of the Four Seasons, possibly by Enoch Wood, 1815, 5in (12.5cm) high.
155–185 SER

A Staffordshire figure, The Showman, with yellow breeches and brown coat, before bocage, 1815–25, 6in (15cm) high.
£200–225 SER

A pair of Staffordshire Obadiah Sherratt-type figures, entitled 'Elijah' and 'Widow', on four-legged bases, early 19thC, 11in (28cm) high.
£380–420 RTo

A Staffordshire pearlware group, entitled 'Songsters', by John Walton, marked, c1820, 8½in (21.5cm) high.
£400–480 G(T)

pair of Staffordshire figures, entitled 'Robt Burns' and 'Highland Mary', decorated in red and shades of green, c1840, 3¼in (33.5cm) high.
400–450 GLO

A Staffordshire figure of Napoleon sitting on a rock, wearing a green and red cloak and blue jacket, 1845, 7½in (19cm) high.
£350–400 ACO

A pair of Staffordshire figures of Queen Victoria and Prince Albert, seated on throne chairs, 19thC, 6in (15cm) high.
£200–220 G(T)

> **Cross Reference**
> See Colour Review

◀ A Staffordshire group of a man and a woman, decorated in dark green, orange and brown, c1855, 12in (30.5cm) high.
£150–175 JO

A Staffordshire group, The Death of Nelson, decorated in red, green and blue, 1845–50, 9in (23cm) high.
£320–380 DAN

A Staffordshire spill vase, modelled as a gentleman wearing a blue coat and purple cloak with a spaniel at his feet, mid-19thC, 13in (33cm) high.
£350–400 S(S)

A Staffordshire figure, entitled 'Will Watch', decorated in pink, blue, orange and cream, 1860, 15in (38cm) high.
£250–300 AnS

A Staffordshire figure of a blacksmith, wearing a fawn apron and red cap, c1860, 17in (43cm) high.
£375–425 AnS

> Miller's is a price GUIDE not a price LIST

A Staffordshire flatback figure of Shakespeare, decorated in red, black and gilt on a white ground, 1870–90, 18½in (47cm) high.
£140–160 Hal(C)

A pair of Staffordshire figures, entitled 'Moody' and 'Sankey', c1880, 14in (35.5cm) high.
£500–600 TWr Dwight Moody and Ira Sankey were American Evangelist preachers who visited England in 1873–75 and 1881–84, preaching the 'old fashioned' Gospel and the Second Coming. The mould for the Moody figure was rediscovered in 1948 and reproductions were cast from it.

A Staffordshire pastille burner model of a house, with an octagonal roof, decorated in blue, red, green and yellow, c1860, 5in (12.5cm) high.
£130–140 ACO

A pair of Staffordshire figures of musicians, decorated in pink, blue, yellow and green, 1860, 9½in (24cm) high.
£450–500 ACO

A pair of Staffordshire groups of boys standing beside girls sitting on horses, decorated in red, green and black, c1880, 13in (33cm) high.
£500–600 ACO

A Staffordshire pastille burner model of a house, decorated in red, green, blue and yellow, 1830, 3¼in (8.5cm) high.
£85–95 OD

Sets/pairs

Unless otherwise stated, any description which refers to 'a set' or 'a pair' includes a guide price for the entire set or the pair, even though the illustration may show only a single item.

A Staffordshire group of a boy and girl with a ram decorated in pink, blue, brown and green, c1860 8in (20.5cm) high.
£200–220 ACO

A Staffordshire figure, entitled 'The Lion Slayer' wearing a cobalt blue jacket, with an orange and red lion, 1855, 17in (43cm) high.
£450–500 ACO

A Staffordshire money box model of a house, with orange walls, red door and green foliage, c1860, 5in (12.5cm) high
£75–90 ACO

A Bernard Leach stoneware flask, with red oriental-style decoration on a grey and cream chequered ground, marked, 1920s, 7¾in (19.5cm) high.
£2,500–2,800 DN
These slab vases were the subject of a forgery scandal in England in 1980–81, when a number of deliberate fakes were produced by inmates in an open prison during their pottery recreational periods. These are often identifiable by their strange glazes and unusual proportions. Most were recovered by investigating police.

A Lucie Rie stoneware cruet set, decorated in chocolate brown with incised linear pattern, 1920s, largest 4¼in (11cm) high.
£600–660 DN

A Winchcombe pottery jug, by Pat Grooms, decorated with a brown and orange pattern, minor chips, 1950s, 6¼in (16cm) high.
£20–25 IW

A pottery slipware jug, decorated by William Fishley Holland, c1950, 6½in (16.5cm) high.
£20–25 IW
Fifty Years a Potter by W. F. Holland, published in 1958, is an account of a country potter's life and work.

Three Seaview Pottery bowls, decorated in orange and dark green, Isle of Wight, 1958–60, largest 3½in (9cm) high.
£9–12 each DSG

A Poterie Arpot dish, by de Crousaz, decorated with a bird in brown and grey on a cream ground, Swiss, c1965, 10¼in (26cm) square.
£250–300 DSG

▶ A David Leach porcelain flared bowl, decorated with a brown and grey tree on a white ground, marked, c1976, 8¼in (21cm) diam.
£340–380 P(B)

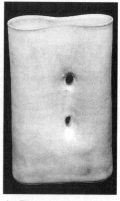

Crowan pottery oil and vinegar bottle, decorated with celadon glaze, 1950s, ¾in (14.5cm) high.
30–35 IW

Miller's is a price GUIDE not a price LIST

◀ A Derek Clarkson pottery vase, decorated with pink and white crystaline effect, 1990s, 6in (15cm) high.
£110–130 PGA

An Eileen Lewenstein porcelain pot, with biomorphic pierced circles, marked, c1978, 7in (18cm) high.
£75–90 P(B)

SYLVAC

A SylvaC green celery jug, No. 5033, 1930s, 7in (18cm) high.
£55–65 TAC

A SylvaC green ribbed jug, No. 1253, 1930–40, 8in (20.5cm) high.
£25–30 AnS

A SylvaC green leaf-moulded jug, No. 1318, with brown rabbit handle, 1936–50, 7in (18cm) high.
£60–70 AnS

A SylvaC brown comical dog, No. 5295, c1950s, 7in (18cm) high.
£42–50 TAC

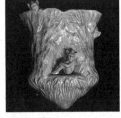

A SylvaC wall pocket, decorated in brown and green with elves, c1950, 8in (20.5cm) high.
£50–60 AnS

A SylvaC green posy vase, applied with a brown pixie, c1950s, 5in (12.5cm) wide.
£25–30 TAC

A SylvaC green dish, No. 1921, decorated in pink and dark green with flowers and foliage, c1960, 8in (20.5cm) wide.
£38–45 AnS

TILES

A set of four Bristol blue and white tiles, c1760, each tile 5in (12.5cm) square, framed.
£400–450 JHo

Ten Dutch Delft tiles, painted in underglaze blue with a swan in the foreground of a twin-turreted building on an island, some damage, 18thC, each tile 5in (12.5cm) square.
£400–450 Hal

◀ A set of 12 Minton tiles depicting scenes from Aesop's Fables, attributed to Thomas Allen, block-printed in brown on a cream ground, c1875, each tile 6in (15cm) square.
£500–550 Bri

A brown and white Dutch Delft tile, 19thC, 5in (12.5cm) square.
£24–28 AOH

A yellow and blue Minton tile, 1900–10, 8in (20.5cm) square.
£60–70 DSG

TEAPOTS & TEA SETS

A Coalport teapot, decorated in Japanese style with terracotta, blue, green and gilt enamels, handle replaced, c1810, 6½in (16.5cm) high.
£50–60 Hal(C)

A Belleek Tridacna teapot, the cream and pink body applied with a pink handle, First Period, c1860, 7in (18cm) high.
£350–400 TWr

A Russian teapot, decorated on each side with a yellow Sirin wearing a gold crown and blue, pink and yellow flowers, heightened with gilt, marked, knop restored, late 19thC, decorated 1921, 6½in (16.5cm) high.
£450–550 WW
A Sirin is a fabled bird-woman from Russian folklore.

A Copeland three piece tea set, decorated in blue with terracotta and gilt, marked, c1880, teapot 6in (15cm) high.
£430–470 GRI

Two Midwinter teapots, c1935,
l. blue and pink, 6in (15cm) high.
r. green and gold, 6½in (16.5cm) high.
£35–40 each AND

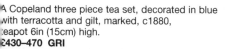

▶ An Old Lady tea set, decorated with brilliant glaze, c1940, 8in (20.5cm) high.
£160–190 AOT

A Thomas Dean & Sons Art Deco teapot, hand-painted with a geometric pattern in orange, yellow, green and black, c1930, 5½in (14cm) high.
£200–240 AOT

A Crown Ducal teapot, decorated in colours and inscribed 'War Against Hitlerism...', 1939, 6in (15cm) high.
£80–100 HUX

◀ A teapot, modelled as a zebra, 1990s, 6in (15cm) high.
£18–20 JBy

A teapot, modelled as 'The Bull' public house in Ambridge from the BBC's The Archers, 1999, 6in (15cm) high.
£16–18 ArA

TORQUAY

Torquay pottery is the generic name given to the wares produced by a group of potteries situated in and around the Torbay area of Devon, including the factories of Aller Vale, Dartmouth, Lemon & Crute, Longpark and Watcombe. Favourite products included motto ware and other items aimed predominantly at tourists visiting the coastal resorts. This year we include a collection of cats belonging to the Torquay Pottery Collector's Society. The lucky cat was a favourite souvenir item, and similar models were produced in crested china.

The Torquay potteries produced a large number of cats in sizes ranging from one and a half to eleven inches and in various colours. Designs were often comical, verging on the grotesque, and favourite poses include the Staring Cat, the Screaming Cat and the Winking Cat with its single glass eye – a same design that appears in crested china where it is known as the Cheshire Cat. These cats were popular in the Edwardian period and remained in production in the 1920s. They are much sought after by Torquay collectors today. (*see* Cats section page 80).

A Torquay plate, decorated with a green glaze and inscribed 'When you finish pouring tea, Place your teapot down on me', c1900, 7¼in (18.5cm) diam.
£34–40 DSG

A Longpark vase, decorated in blue, green, yellow and brown on a cream ground, 1910, 6in (15cm) high.
£55–65 DBo

An Aller Vale Tiny Tim cat, decorated with a yellow eggshell glaze, impressed mark, c1900, 9in (23cm) high.
£250–300 TPCS

An Aller Vale Winking Cat, decorated with a green glaze, with one glass eye, marked, c1910, 6in (15cm) high.
£100–120 TPCS

▶ An Aller Vale Staring Cat, decorated with a green glaze, both glass eyes replaced, marked, c1910, 12in (30.5cm) high.
£225–250 TPCS

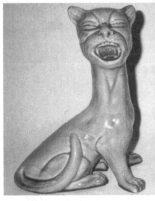

A Watcombe Screaming Cat, decorated with an amber glaze, marked, c1910, 9in (23cm) high.
£150–180 TPCS

A Watcombe motto ware Winking Cat, decorated with coloured circles and inscribed 'Anybody seen our cat', minor chip, c1920, 9in (23cm) high.
£300–350 TPCS

An Aller Vale udder vase, decorated with orange, green and blue pattern on a beige ground, 1920s, 3½in (9cm) high.
£42–50 DBo

A Torquay flowerpot, decorated with blue and green pattern, c1920, 6in (15cm) high.
£90–100 HUN

► A Torquay Pottery jug, decorated with a boat and seascape, in brown, pink, yellow and orange, 1920s, 6in (15cm) high.
£45–55 DBo

► A Longpark jug with cover, decorated with Kingfisher pattern in colours on a bright blue ground, 1920s, 4¾in (12cm) high.
£50–60 DSG

A Torquay vase, decorated with a kingfisher and yellow foliage on a blue ground, c1920, 11¼in (28.5cm) high.
£75–90 DSG

A Lemon vase, with stone-coloured matt glaze, 1930, 6¾in (17cm) high.
£18–20 IW

◄ A Longpark bowl, decorated with Crocus pattern in red, green and yellow on a blue and cream ground, 1930–40, 5¼in (13.5cm) diam.
£15–20 PC

WADE

A Wadeheath jug, decorated with orange flowers on a cream ground, 1930s, 11½in (29cm) high.
£75–85 CoCo

Three Wade animals, Puppy, Calf and Little Laughing Bunny, 1940–50, largest 3in (7.5cm) high.
Puppy £130–150
Calf £100–120
Little Laughing Bunny £50–60 PC

A Wadeheath vase, decorated with mottled beige and green matt glaze, 1930s, 7in (18cm) high.
£30–35 DEC

◄ A Wade Royal Victoria salad plate, decorated with a stylized leaf pattern in red, green, grey and black on a beige ground, 1935–40, 10in (25.5cm) diam.
£20–25 ES

A Wade squirrel, decorated in fawn and holding a brown nut, 1940s–50s, 1¾in (4.5cm) high.
£40–50 PC

A Wade jug, moulded in relief with Art Deco-style pattern, with pale orange matt glaze, 1950s, 5¼in (13.5cm) high.
£18–22 DEC

A Wade model of Bernie & Poo, decorated in brown, white and blue, 1950s, 3in (7.5cm) wide.
£85–100 PC

► A Wade bell-shaped whisky decanter, commemorating the wedding of Prince Andrew and Sarah Ferguson in 1986, with gilt banding, 10in (25.5cm) high.
£85–100 PC

Wedgwood pearlware custard cup, with loop handle, painted in coloured enamels with a couple in a landscape and flowers and insects, beneath a puce scroll band, marked, c1820, 2¼in (6cm) high.
£220–250 DN

A Wedgwood ashtray, designed by Keith Murray, with white matt glaze, 1930s, 4in (10cm) wide.
£70–80 BEV

Wedgwood tankard, designed by Keith Murray, with white matt glaze, 1930s, 4¾in (12cm) high.
£65–70 BEV

Wedgwood vase, designed by Keith Murray, with engine-turned decoration and green matt glaze, 1933–35, 9in (23cm) high.
£420–500 BEV

A Wedgwood blue and white pitcher, late 19thC, 12in (30.5cm) high.
£80–95 MSB

A Wedgwood conical bowl, designed by Keith Murray, decorated with concentric lines and white matt glaze, 1930s, 5½in (14cm) high.
£250–300 BEV

A Wedgwood bowl, designed by Keith Murray, decorated with matt glaze, 1930s, 6½in (16.5cm) diam.
£275–350 BEV

A Wedgwood Ferrara blue and white punch bowl, 1907, 12in (30.5cm) diam.
£300–350 CoCo

A Wedgwood lustre bowl, decorated with blue and gilt fish on a cobalt blue ground, slight damage, 1920s, 11in (28cm) diam.
£225–275 MD

Keith Murray

Keith Murray (1892–1981) was born in New Zealand and moved to the UK in 1906–7. He trained as an architect, but became best known as a designer of glass, silver and ceramics. From 1933 he worked for Wedgwood, where he created a series of designs that reflect both his architectural background and an understanding of Modernism rarely found in British Art Deco ceramics. Though his work included small domestic wares such as ashtrays and mugs, collectors tend to focus on his distinctive bowls and vases, with their clean-lined, ridged geometric forms and monochrome glazes (matt, semi-matt or celadon). Typical colours included white, green and straw. Grey and blue vases are sought after, and black and bronze tend to be the rarest shades. Certain shapes, such as the spherical engine-turned vases (the deep ridges produced by an engine-turned lathe) are also very desirable. The classical purity of form and glaze makes good condition extremely important. Check inside vases for fading, and beware of any restoration which can give a sandpapery feel to the surface.

A Wedgwood vase, designed by Keith Murray, with black matt glaze, c1935, 8in (20.5cm) high.
£1,200–1,500 BEV

A Wedgwood powder bowl and cover, designe[d] by Keith Murray, with white matt glaze, 1930s, 4¾in (12cm) high.
£250–300 BEV

A Wedgwood shoulder vase, designed by Keith Murray, with white matt glaze, 1930s, 7¾in (19.5cm) high.
£350–425 BEV

A Wedgwood vase, designed by Keith Murra[y] with straw-coloured matt glaze, 1933–35, 8¼in (21cm) high.
£200–250 BEV

A Wedgwood vase, designed by Keith Murray, with green glaze, 1933–35, 9in (23cm) high.
£400–500 BEV

A Wedgwood vase, designed by Keith Murray, decorated with concentric lines and green matt glaze, c1935, 6in (15cm) high.
£200–250 SWO

A Wedgwood vase, designed by Keith Murray, with bronze matt glaze, c1935, 8¾in (22cm) high.
£800–900 BEV

A Wedgwood plate, by Eric Ravilious, decorated with Garden pattern, marked, 1950s, 10in (25.5cm) diam.
£42–50 Hal(C)

A Wedgwood jasper ware Portland vase, decorated with applied white low-relief pattern on a light blue ground, marked, 20thC, 8in (20.5cm) high.
£130–150 Hal(C)

A Wedgwood beaker, made for Crabtree & Evelyn, decorated with brown flowers, leaves and foliage on a dotted ground, 1940–45, 4in (10cm) high.
£12–15 ES

WEMYSS

A pair of Wemyss Grosvenor vases, decorated with Purple Iris pattern, c1900, 7in (18cm) high.
£600–700 TWr

A Wemyss match striker, decorated with Sweet Pea pattern in pink, blue and green, c1900, 5in (12.5cm) high.
£250–300 RdeR

A Wemyss plate, decorated with brown Cock pattern and inscribed 'Bon Jour', 1900, 5in (12.5cm) diam.
£150–180 RdeR

A Wemyss tyg, decorated with Roses pattern in red and green, marked, c1925, 9in (23cm) high.
£300–340 Hal

A Wemyss small pig decorated in black and white, late 1930s, 6in (15cm) long.
£200–240 RdeR

A Wemyss Lady Eva vase, decorated with Roses pattern in pink and green, marked, 1920s, 12in (30.5cm) high.
£550–600 AG

WORCESTER

A Worcester bowl, decorated with Queen Charlotte pattern in red, pink, blue, black and gilt, c1765, 6in (15cm) diam.
£300–340 DAN

A Worcester blue and white pickle dish, decorated with flower sprays and birds, slight restoration, mid-18thC, 5¼in (13.5cm) wide.
£200–240 Bea(E)

A Worcester feather-moulded cream jug, decorated in underglaze blue with a floral pattern, the interior with a flowerhead and leaf-scroll band, c1758, 3½in (9cm) high.
£600–700 DN

► A Worcester sparrow-beak jug and cover, decorated with Mansfield pattern in underglaze blue, c1765, 5½in (14cm) high.
£250–300 DN

A Worcester fluted cup and saucer, decorated with flower sprays in pink, mauve, green and yellow, with gilt rims, c1768, cup 2¼in (5.5cm) high.
£600–700 TWr

◄ A Worcester fluted teapot and stand, decorated with flowers on a pale blue ground, with flower finial, c1775, 5in (12.5cm) high.
£300–350 HYD

► A Royal Worcester plate, decorated with sweet peas and daisies in pink, blue, green and yellow, with gilt rim, c1888, 9in (23cm) diam.
£125–135 GRI

A Royal Worcester figure, Down and Out, wearing a brown coat and fawn hat, c1874, 5in (12.5cm) high.
£270–300 GRI

A Royal Worcester trefoil bon-bon dish, with scroll handle, decorated with insects, thistles and flowers in pastel colours on a cream and pink ground, marked, 1895, 12¼in (31cm) long.
£375–425 Bea(E)

A Royal Worcester jug, applied with a green branch-shaped handle, moulded with a green lizard on a cream and green ground, c1900, 6in (15cm) high.
£165–185 WAC

A Royal Worcester flatback jug, decorated with flowers in pink, red, blue, green and cream, with gilt rim and handle, c1901, 5in (12.5cm) high.
£300–330 GRI

A Royal Worcester vase, by J. Stinton, decorated with Highland cattle in a landscape in shades of brown and grey, with gilt feet and rim, c1900, 9in (23cm) high.
£800–900 TF

A Royal Worcester cabinet plate, the centre enamelled in colours with a view of Stratford Church by Harry Davis, the rim with gilt leaf-scroll decoration on a blue ground, marked, 1903, 10¼in (26cm) diam.
£250–300 CAG

A set of Royal Worcester coffee cans and saucers, retailed by Z. Barroclough & Sons, with pierced silver holders and scroll handles, decorated in blue and gilt, in fitted case, 1911.
£350–450 DA

Royal Worcester Crown are vase, decorated th a galleon in blue, llow and red on a rnt-orange ground, 927, 10¼in (26cm) high.
45–385 LEGE

A Royal Worcester model of a Great Tit, decorated in yellow, brown and black, 1930s, 3in (7.5cm) high.
£90–100 WAC

A Royal Worcester bowl, decorated with coloured fruit on a pink and yellow mottled ground, with gilt rim, c1950, 8in (20.5cm) diam.
£700–800 TWr

LOCATE THE SOURCE

The source of each illustration in Miller's can be found by checking the code letters below each caption with the Key to Illustrations, pages 476–484.

◄ A Royal Worcester figure, May, from the Months of the Year Series, by Freda Doughty, with a pale blue dress, c1951, 5in (12.5cm) high.
£240–280 WAC

► A Royal Worcester figure, January, from the Months of the Year Series, by Freda Doughty, with a burgundy coat and beige leggings, 1965, 6in (15cm) high.
£180–200 WAC

Christmas

A Christmas postcard, 'A Christmas Blizzard', decorated in grey, brown, red and black on a white ground, 1905, 5½ x 3½in (14 x 9cm).
£2–3 JMC

A Christmas postcard, 'Hoping You'll Manage to Make a Shift for Yourself and Sew On!', 1912, 5½ x 3½in (14 x 9cm).
40–50p JMC

▶ A Copeland Christmas plate, decorated with green and gilt holly leaves and gilt mistletoe, c1860, 15in (38cm) diam.
£250–300 TWr

A Christmas card, decorated in red, yellow, blue and grey, 1918, 6 x 5in (15 x 12.5cm).
£12–15 COB

Three porcelain Christmas cake decorations, painted in red, brown and green, 1930s, largest 1½in (4cm) high.
£12–14 each AnS

A Bébé du Noel pottery mould, from Alsace, c1930, 14in (35.5cm) lor.
£90–100 B&R

◀ A WWII Christmas card, 'Business as Usual', 5 x 4in (12.5 x 10cm).
£8–10 COB

▶ Two papier mâché Father Christmas tree decorations, decorated in red, green and white, 1950s, 5in (12.5cm) high.
£15–20 each AnS

◀ A Carlton Ware Father Christmas teapot, decorated in red, brown and black, 1970s, 12in (30.5cm) high.
£42–50 UNI

A Royal Doulton Cellist Snowman model, 1988–93, 5½in (14cm) high.
£35–40 WWY

A Royal Doulton Snowman money box, 1990–94, 8¼in (21cm) high.
£50–60 WWY

Comics & Annuals

This section includes comics from auctions in the UK and the USA, where they are highly valued, both artistically and financially. Collectors look out for first issues, special issues (for example holiday and commemorative numbers) and comics containing the first appearance of famous characters.

Condition is crucial to value. Comics are carefully graded; cover, spine, colour of pages etc and, particularly in the USA, provenance can also be a factor. Prices also reflect rarity. Though produced in their thousands, comics were a disposable product and, by their very nature, suffered at the hands of children. Taking the example (illustrated in this section) of Detective Comics No. 27, published in May 1939, and introducing 'The Amazing and Unique adventures of the Batman', only about fifty copies are known to be in existence, making this one of the most desirable American comic books. Britain too has its rarities. Introduced as a cartoon strip by the Daily Express in 1920, Rupert became one of Britain's best loved bears.

Rupert annuals were a favourite children's Christmas present and by the 1970s, print runs were in the region of half a million. Yet it is from this decade that one of the most collectable annuals comes. In 1973, while some 500,000 annuals showed Rupert with a white face, only 12 copies showed him with the brown face traditionally used, until that year, on annual covers. Of the original 12, only a handful are known to exist, one of which, signed by illustrator Alfred Bestall, came up for auction at Hammer 20th Century Books. Purchased for 53p in 1973, less than thirty years later it fetched £18,315.

All Winners Comics,
No. 1, Summer 1941.
£4,000–4,500 S(NY)

The Amazing Spider-Man comic, No. 1, 1963.
£1,700–2,000 CBP

Avengers comic,
No. 2, 1963.
£250–280 CBP

Three *Batman* comics,
Spring, Summer and
Fall 1940, America.
£2,100–2,400 S(NY)

The Beano Comic,
No. 7, 1938.
£700–800 CBP

The Beano Comic,
No. 8, 1938.
£600–660 CBP

The Beano Book,
No. 1, 1940.
£1,600–1,800 CBP

The Beano comic, No. 421,
August 12th 1950.
£8–10 OCB

The Boy's Own Annual, Nos. 1–4, 1879–82, bound in four volumes, 11 x 8in (28 x 20.5cm).
£150–180 CBP

Butterfly comic, 1904–40.
£2–10 each DPO

Conan The Barbarian comic, No. 1, 1970.
£50–60 CBP

◀ Three Daktari Annuals, 1968–70, 11 x 8in (28 x 20.5cm).
£3–5 each YR

The Dandy Monster Comic, 1949.
£400–450 CBP

Prices

The price ranges quoted in this book reflect the average price a purchaser might expect to pay for a similar item. The price will vary according to the condition, rarity, size, popularity, provenance, colour and restoration of the item and this must be taken into account when assessing values.
Don't forget that if you are selling it is quite likely that you will be offered less than the price range.

The Dandy Comic, No. 334, Bumper Xmas Number, 1946.
£3,000–3,500 CBP

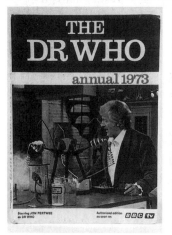

The Dr Who annual, 1973, 11 x 8in (28 x 20.5cm).
£4–5 CMF

Detective Comics, No. 27, May 1939.
£21,000–23,000 S(NY)

The Fantastic Four comic, No. 2, 1963.
£600–660 CBP

Funnies on Parade comic, 1933.
£4,200–4,800 S(NY)

Fireball XL5 Annual, Nos. 1 and 2, 1963–64, 11 x 8in (28 x 20.5cm).
£100–120 CBP

Giles Annual, No. 1, 1946, 6 x 12in (15 x 30.5cm).
£160–180 CBP

Green Lantern comic, No. 1, Fall 1941.
£4,500–5,200 S(NY)

◄ The Hornet comic, No. 1, 1963.
£110–130 CBP

► The Incredible Hulk comic, No. 4, 1962.
£300–350 CBP

Justice League of America comic, No. 1, 1960.
£190–220 CBP

Mickey Mouse Magazine, No. 1, June/August 1935.
£600–660 S(NY)

Miller's is a price GUIDE not a price LIST

► The Magic Comic, No. 2, 1939.
£500–550 CBP

The Rainbow comic, No. 728,
January 28th 1928.
£6–8 OCB

Roxy comic, 13th August 1960.
£4–5 RTT

The New Rupert Book, 1938,
8 x 5in (20.5 x 12.5cm).
£200–240 OCB

Thirty-three Rupert annuals, 1936–69, 4to.
£4,000–5,000 BBA

◄ Superman comic
No. 1, 1939.
£7,500–8,300 S(NY)

The Silver Surfer comic,
No. 1, 1968.
£350–400 CBP

Skippy The Bush
Kangaroo Annual, 1973,
10 x 8in (25.5 x 20.5cm).
£3–5 YR

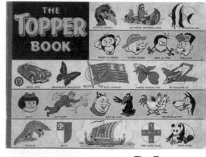

Sparky comics, Nos. 1–5, 1965,
issues 1–3 include free gifts of
Flying Snorter, Big Banger and
Red Rackety.
£240–280 CBP

◄ Finbar Saunders and his Double
Entendres colour sketch, drawn
and signed by Chris Donald and
Simon Thorpe for the first Red
Nose Day charity event by Comic
Relief, 1991, 6 x 8in (15 x 20.5cm),
and The Big Hard One book
featuring VIZ issues, Nos. 1–12.
£65–80 CBP

The Topper
Book, No. 1,
1955.
£70–90 CBP

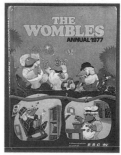

◄ The Wombles
Annual, 1977,
11½ x 8in
(29 x 20.5cm).
£3–4 CMF

Commemorative Ware

A Caledonian Pottery cup plate, commemorating Robert Burns, transfer-printed in blue, c1805, 4in (10cm) diam.
£175–200 SCO

A Staffordshire pearlware pottery mug, commemorating Shakespear's birthplace, transfer-printed in underglaze blue, c1830, 4½in (11.5cm) high.
£450–500 RdV

◀ A Royal Doulton ashtray, commemorating the Wembley Exhibition, decorated with a stylized lion in grey on a blue and grey ground, 1924, 4½in (11.5cm) square.
£50–60 MURR

▶ A Bing & Grøndahl blue ceramic plate, commemorating the Montreal Olympics, 1976, 7in (18cm) diam.
£18–22 MGC

A pottery mug, commemorating the Liverpool and Manchester Railway, transfer-printed in brown, with a view of the locomotive and tunnel, 1840–50, 5in (12.5cm) high.
£580–620 RdV

MILITARY & NAVAL

A Prattware pearlware ceramic jug, commemorating Lord Nelson and Captain Berry, decorated in brown, blue, yellow and red, c1805, 5in (12.5cm) high.
£400–450 RdV

▶ A pottery nursery plate, commemorating Wellington, transfer-printed in black with portrait and inscription 'Wellington as Prime Minister', c1852, 7in (18cm) diam.
£130–150 SAS

◀ A white bisque porcelain bust of the Duke of York, c1820, 8¼in (21cm) high.
£300–330 SAS

▶ A meat-paste jar, commemorating the Dragoon Charge, Balaklava, decorated in red, brown, yellow, green and black, c1855, 3in (7.5cm) high.
£300–350 SAS

An American flag, with 36 stars, stamped 'Annin and Company, NY', inscribed, c1865, 23 x 37in (58.5 x 94cm).
£1,100–1,300 FBG

A Boer War tin, decorated in red, green and black on a yellow ground, 1900, 4in (10cm) wide.
£40–50 WAB
This tin was only issued to Scottish regiments.

A Fieldings miniature chamberpot, inscribed 'Gest-a-po, Flip your ashes on Old Nasty, the Violation of Poland', with caricature of Hitler and a swastika, 1940s, 1¼in (3cm) high.
£30–35 HUX

► A cold-cast bronze resin bust of Field Marshall Montgomery, sculpted by Constance Freedman FRBS, on a wooden plinth with engraved escutcheon, c1960, 12¼in (31cm) high.
£100–120 SAS

A pottery tobacco jar on stand, commemorating the Crimean War, decorated with crossed flags and rustic scenes, enamelled in colours and gilded, damaged, 1855, 10in (25.5cm) high.
£400–450 SAS

A silk bookmarker, depicting Captain HRH Alfred Duke of Edinburgh, in blue, yellow, red and green, c1880, 10in (25.5cm) long.
£70–80 COB

A Staffordshire figure of Lord Kitchener, decorated in brown, red, blue and gilt on a cream ground, c1900, 14½in (37cm) high.
£250–300 BRT

◄ A vase created from a brass field gun shell case, presented to William Leefe Robinson VC, with applied lion's heads and inscription, c1917, 13½in (34.5cm) high.
£630–700 BKS
On 2nd September 1916 thousands of Londoners witnessed dramatic air combat as 21-year-old William Robinson, flying a BE2C, shot down the first Zeppelin SL11. Robinson was awarded the Victoria Cross. He was later transferred to 40 Squadron and subsequently shot down over Germany. He died in December 1918.

A fretwork clock stand, commemorating the centenary of the Battle of Waterloo, the clock compartment surmounted by flags inscribed '1815 Peace 1915', the lower part with two battle scenes, flanked by two lions and the figure of Britannia in the centre, 1915, 36in (91.5cm) long.
£70–85 DN

A porcelain jug, commemorating William Hill's victory at Shrewsbury, transfer-printed in blue with the arms of the city and ribbons, restored, possibly Coalport, 1802, 8¾in (22cm) high.
£2,000–2,400 SAS

A porcelain bust, commemorating George Canning, decorated in dull gilt on a gilded base, c1825, 5¾in (14.5cm) high.
£550–600 SAS

A pink lustre pottery mug, commemorating Earl Grey, transfer-printed in black within an orange and green cartouche 'The Choice of the People & England's Glory, Earl Grey', additionally inscribed 'Ann Addison born Janry 4 18-', c1831, 3¼in (8.5cm) high.
£575–650 SAS

Cross Reference
See Bottles

A Doulton Lambeth salt-glazed stoneware spirit flask, in the form of a man, impressed 'W & G Peters, the late C H Cope of Birmingham' and 'The true spirit of reform', slight damage, c1832, 7in (18cm) high.
£240–280 Hal

A pottery spirit flask, commemorating Lord John Russell, with scroll impressed 'The True Spirit of Reform', decorated in blue, black and gilt, restored, c1832, 6¼in (16cm) high.
£100–120 SAS

A Minton biscuit porcelain figure, Hannah More, seated in a chair, on a scrolling base, c1835, 6¾in (17cm) high.
£330–360 SAS
A strong supporter of emancipation, Hannah More was associated with Wilberforce in his efforts to abolish slavery.

◄ A pair of Victorian Staffordshire figures, Gladstone and Mrs Gladstone, 10in (25.5cm) high.
£160–190 BRT

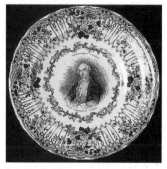

A pottery plate, commemorating Thomas William Coke of Holkham, Earl of Leicester, transfer-printed in black with portrait entitled 'Norfolk's Pride, The Patriot Coke', c1840, 10½in (26.5cm) diam.
£130–150 SAS
Thomas William Coke was born in 1754. He was a pioneer and promoter of improvements associated with the agricultural revolution. He held shows at his estate at Holkham, Norfolk, as early as 1776, which by the end of the century had become major events. He represented Norfolk for the Whigs from 1776–1822 and in the year of Queen Victoria's accession was raised to the peerage.

An oak mace, the head carved with a bust of Benjamin Disraeli, c1870, 21in (53.5cm) long.
£160–180 SAS

A Doulton Lambeth stoneware jug, commemorating William Ewart Gladstone, transfer-printed in brown with a portrait flanked by loyal inscriptions, marked, c1898, 7¼in (18.5cm) high.
£120–140 SAS

A Craven Dunnill portrait tile, depicting Arthur Balfour, glazed in purple, slight damage, c1902, 4½in (11.5cm) high.
£35–40 SAS
A Conservative, Balfour succeeded his uncle, the Marquis of Salisbury, as Prime Minister in 1902, serving until 1905.

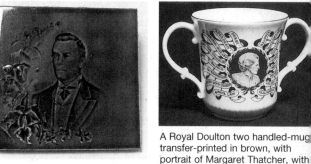

A portrait tile, depicting Joseph Chamberlain, glazed in green, c1900, 6in (15cm) square.
£48–55 SAS

◄ A Luck & Flaw Margaret Thatcher ceramic mug, 1983, 4¼in (11cm) high.
£60–70 SAS

A Royal Doulton two handled-mug transfer-printed in brown, with portrait of Margaret Thatcher, with brown and blue scrolls inscribed with names of previous prime ministers, 1979, 4in (10cm) high.
£34–40 AnS

◄ A Price Kensington pottery gurgling jug, in the form of Harold Wilson smoking a pipe, decorated in black, grey, yellow and gilt, 1980s, 7½in (19cm) high.
£110–130 BRT

► A Luck & Flaw Ronald Reagan teapot, 1981, 10½in (26.5cm) high.
£100–120 GRa

A pair of pottery mugs, transfer-printed in black with named portraits, one inscribed 'Sir Edward Carson MP, We Want No Home Rule', the other with 'Mr John E. Redmond MP, Home Rule For Ireland', c1912, 3¾in (9.5cm) high.
£350–380 SAS

ROYALTY

An enamel patch box, commemorating Princess Charlotte, the Princess Royal, the interior with a mirror, with pale aubergine base, slight damage, c1797, 1¾in (4.5cm) diam.
£850–950 SAS
The eldest daughter of George III was born on the 29th September 1766, christened Charlotte Augusta Matilda and styled Princess Royal. She married Frederick I, King of Württemberg on 18th May 1797, and died without issue on 6th October 1828.

A copper lustre pottery jug, commemorating Queen Caroline, transfer-printed in brown with a half-length portrait, the reverse with a rhyme 'As for the Green-Bag Crew...' and inscribed with the names of her supporters, 1821, 6in (15cm) high.
£450–500 SAS

A Copeland parian bust of Prince Albert, by Theed, c1864, 14in (35.5cm) high.
£400–450 JAK

A stoneware vase, by George Tinworth, commemorating Queen Victoria's Jubilee, moulded with a young head and shoulders and the reverse with an old head, the handles with putti playing musical instruments, restored, signed, 1887, 9¼in (23.5cm) high.
£900–1,000 SAS

A Doulton Lambeth stoneware jug, commemorating Queen Victoria's Diamond Jubilee, transfer-printed in brown with a young and old head, 1897, 8in (20.5cm) high.
£180–200 MGC

A Wallis Gimson & Co pottery plate, commemorating Queen Victoria's Golden Jubilee, transfer-printed in black and coloured, depicting Queen Victoria and HRH The Prince of Wales, inscribed 'The Empire On Which The Sun Never Sets', 1887, 10in (25.5cm) square.
£325–375 RdV

▶ A stoneware jar, commemorating Queen Victoria's Diamond Jubilee, transfer-printed in red with a portrait, 1897, 5in (12.5cm) high.
£60–70 BRT

A Maling pottery mug, commemorating Queen Victoria's Diamond Jubilee, transfer-printed in blue with a portrait, 1897, 3¾in (9.5cm) high.
£65–75 GWR

A pottery mug, commemorating the visit of HRH the Prince and Princess of Wales to St Colomb Minor, June 8th 1909, transfer-printed in red with portraits and flags, 3in (7.5cm) high.
£250–300 BRT

A ceramic nursery plate, commemorating the birth of Princess Elizabeth, transfer-printed in brown with portrait, inscribed 'Our Empire's Little Princess, born April 21st 1926', with gilt rim, 5½in (14cm) wide.
£175–195 BRT

A plaster matt-gold bust of Edward VIII, 1936, 6in (15cm) high.
£34–40 AnS

A tin, commemorating the marriage of the Duke of York and Lady Elizabeth Bowes-Lyon, with scenes of York Minster and Glamis Castle, 1923, 4¼in (11cm) high.
£145–165 BRT

A Paragon porcelain nursery plate, transfer-printed in sepia with a named military portrait of Edward, Prince of Wales, c1927, 8¾in (22cm) wide.
£130–150 SAS

A Paragon porcelain plate, decorated with a heraldic shield in blue, yellow and red, supported by the lion and unicorn, the border inscribed 'Edward VIII King and Emperor, crowned May 12th 1937', 10½in (26.5cm) diam.
£100–120 SAS

▶ A Paragon porcelain mug, transfer-printed in brown with a portrait of Prince Charles, 1953, 3in (7.5cm) high.
£50–60 MGC

A ceramic mug, commemorating the Silver Jubilee of King George V and Queen Mary, May 6th 1935, transfer-printed in black with portraits and coloured in yellow, blue, green and rose, 3½in (9cm) high.
£25–30 AnS

A ceramic mug, inscribed 'HM King Edward VIII crowned May 12th 1937', transfer-printed and coloured with a portrait in red, yellow, blue and grey, 4in (10cm) high.
£30–35 AnS
The Duke of Windsor abdicated in 1936 and was never crowned.

A set of four Coalport boxes and covers, commemorating the 1937 coronation, modelled in the shape of crowns, in crimson, silver and gilt, from a limited edition of 500, largest 3¾in (9.5cm) high.
£400–450 SAS

A Britains coronation coach, in matt-gold and blue, missing eight horses, c1953, 3in (7.5cm) high.
£38–45 UNI

A Lady Grace Limited Edition porcelain mug, commemorating Prince William, inscribed 'Wills goes to Eton, Wednesday 6th September 1995', decorated in brown, green, blue and red, 4¾in (12cm) high.
£25–30 BRT

► A coronation light bulb, with ER-shaped filament, 1953.
£25–30 RTT

A Mamod live steam locomotive, 'Prince of Wales', commemorating the marriage of the Prince of Wales and Lady Diana Spencer, decorated in black, blue and gold, 1981, 8½in (21.5cm) long, with original red and white box.
£220–260 RAR

◄ A Paragon porcelain loving cup, commemorating the 1977 Silver Jubilee, with two lion-shaped gilt handles, decorated in colours, silver and gilt, No. 436 of a limited edition of 750, 5¼in (13.5cm) high, with certificate.
£120–140 SAS

SPACE

◄ A set of badges, commemorating the Apollo Space Project, c1970, in a wooden frame 7 x 9in (18 x 23cm).
£30–35 COB

A porcelain plate, inscribed '1st Moon Landing July 1969 A.D.', transfer-printed in black with a space ship, coloured in green, yellow and blue, 10in (25.5cm) diam.
£25–30 COB

A porcelain mug, commemorating the first moon landing, transfer-printed in black, coloured in green, yellow and blue, inscribed 'July 1969 A.D.', 4in (10cm) high.
£20–22 AnS

Corkscrews

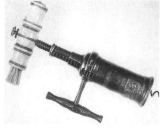

A 'King's Screw' corkscrew, the brass barrel with royal coat-of-arms badge, with turned bone handle and steel side raising handle, maker's name 'R. Jones', c1820, 7¼in (18.5cm) high.
£150–180 CS

A compound folding pocket corkscrew, the faceted bow with eight tools, c1820, 2¾in (7cm) wide.
£80–90 CS

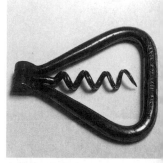

A Farrow & Jackson folding pocket corkscrew, 19thC, 3in (7.5cm) wide.
£35–40 JOL

A Robert Jones First Patent corkscrew, the brass barrel marked '1', with turned bone handle lacking brush, 1840, 7in (18cm) high.
£600–650 P(B)

A peg and worm pocket corkscrew, 19thC, 3in (7.5cm) high.
£90–100 JOL

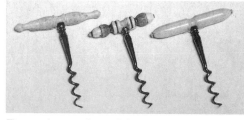

Three corkscrews for medicine, perfume and liqueur, with turned bone handles, 19thC, 2½in (6.5cm) wide.
£90–100 each JOL

A steel pocket corkscrew, with wooden cover, 3½in (9cm) high.
£80–90 JOL

A brass corkscrew, with bone handle, 19thC, 5in (12.5cm) high.
£100–120 JOL

A Lund steel lever-type corkscrew, with detachable worm, the hinge of the handles cast with maker's name 'LUND PATENTEE LONDON' and royal coat-of-arms, 1880, handles 8in (20.5cm) high.
£45–50 CS

► A Rotary Eclipse bar corkscrew, the brass side-winder arm with walnut wood handle, c1890, 16in (40.5cm) high.
£250–275 CS

A folding nickel-plated medicine spoon and corkscrew, the bowl embossed with an advertisement for 'Hazeline Cream', c1900, 4in (10cm) wide.
£18–20 CS

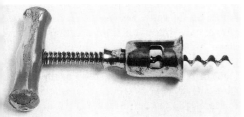

A German chromium-plated spring bell corkscrew, with painted wooden handle, paint worn, 1930s, 7in (18cm) high.
£20–25 BSA

A brass corkscrew, modelled as a pony, 1930s, 2½in (6.5cm) high.
£35–40 BEV

A corkscrew, the red resin handle modelled as a pig, 1940–50s, 4in (10cm) high.
£48–55 JOL

An Art Deco silver-coloured corkscrew, modelled as a cat, with diamanté flower decoration, 4in (10cm) wide.
£50–60 BSA

▶ A brass bar corkscrew, named 'The Don', patented by Chambers in 1903, 13in (33cm) high.
£90–100 CS

An Armstrong concertina corkscrew, Scotland, 1905, 7in (18cm) high.
£100–120 JOL

▶ A brass table set, with lucky leprechaun charm handles, comprising a corkscrew, bottle opener and bottle stopper, 1930s–40s, 7in (18cm) high.
£35–40 JOL

Dogs

This year's section on dogs includes a special feature on Bonzo, created by George Ernest Studdy (1878–1948). The British illustrator was already known for his cartoon canines when, in 1918, *The Sketch* asked him to produce a weekly illustration entitled The Studdy Dog. The dog went through several permutations gradually evolving into a stylized boxer/bull terrier-influenced puppy. Readers complained that it had no name and, on 8 November 1922, The Studdy Dog was relaunched as Bonzo (a name chosen by *The Sketch* editor Bruce Ingram) and a legend was born. Bonzo was a huge success, appearing in newspapers, books and advertisements – one of the first neon hoardings in Piccadilly Circus showed a giant Bonzo dog puffing on a Pinnace cigarette. In 1923 Bonzo made his stage debut in Jack Buchanan's *Battling Butler,* and 1924 saw the premiere of the first Bonzo animated film, attended by King George V and Queen Mary, in what was said to be the first visit by a reigning sovereign to a public cinema. Twenty-six Bonzoland cartoons were made, and their hero was translated into almost every medium. Studdy provided over a hundred different postcard designs for his principle publisher Valentines of Dundee; there were Bonzo games and puzzles, and cuddly velveteen Bonzos were produced by Dean's Rag Book Co and Chad Valley. Bonzo inspired a huge range of ceramics, from ashtrays to water jugs, and from cheap Japanese china to high-quality porcelain models by Royal Doulton and Royal Worcester. For the gentlemen there were Bonzo car mascots, for the ladies Bonzo perfume bottles, and the whole family could enjoy Bonzo biscuits. Bonzo reached the height of his fame in the 1920s and remained popular until Studdy's death from lung cancer in 1948. Bonzo still inspires an avid band of enthusiasts today. Studdy's biography has been published, original watercolours can fetch four-figure sums and period memorabilia is hotly collected.

A Viennese cold-painted bronze model of a puppy, c1872, 2in (5cm) high.
£560–620 ChA

A plaster group of a German Shepherd dog and child, c1925, 15in (38cm) high.
£50–55 JACK

A silver-plated corkscrew, modelled as a dachshund, 1930, 3in (7.5cm) high.
£35–40 BEV

A cast metal advertising model of two scottie dogs on a plinth, inscribed 'Buchanan's Black & White Whisky', 1940s, 10in (25.5cm) high.
£130–150 BBR

◄ A papier-mâché Nipper display figure, with black details and name on his collar, damaged, late 1940s, 36in (91.5cm) high.
£250–280 SK(B)
Nipper was the dog portrayed on HMV record labels.

► A carved wood corkscrew, modelled as a dog, with glass eyes, 1930s–40s, 4in (10cm) high.
£35–40 JOL

CERAMICS

A pair of Boness pottery dogs, Scottish, c1910, 13in (33cm) high, **£350–400 TWr**

A Staffordshire dog, printed in flow-blue on an off-white ground, late 19thC, 12½in (32cm) high. **£90–100 GAK**

A pair of Boness pottery terriers, Scottish, c1890, 7½in (19cm) high. **£150–180 BWA**

A Carlton Ware crested china model of Nipper, His Master's Voice dog, c1920s, 2½in (6.5cm) high. **£100–120 MURR**

A Carlton Ware model of a black bulldog in a kennel, entitled 'The Black Watch', with Cheddar crest, c1915–20, 3½in (9cm) high. **£50–60 ES**

A Crown Devon Perky Pup door stop, 1930s, 7in (18cm) high. **£85–95 CoCo**

TOYS

A black and white mohair pyjama case dog, 1930s, 15in (38cm) wide. **£25–30 HCJ**

A light brown mohair straw-filled dog, 1930, 4in (10cm) high. **£30–35 A&J**

▶ A light brown mohair pyjama case dog, with black ears, 1950s, 16in (40.5cm) high. **£45–55 Ann**

A brown mohair straw-filled toy dog, c1920, 8in (20.5cm) high. **£20–25 AnS**

A Steiff blonde mohair Pekinese dog, c1950s, 4in (10cm) long.
£30–35 A&J

▶ A black and brown Doby Beanie Baby, with original tag, October 1996, 8in (20.5cm) long.
£4–5 BeG

◀ A nodding dachshund, with brushed nylon fur, c1950s, 11in (28cm) long.
£30–35 PPH

A Chad Valley Sweep glove puppet, 1960, 9in (23cm) high.
£10–12 CMF

BONZO

An Arcadian crested china model of Bonzo, 1920s, 3½in (9cm) high.
£90–110 MURR

A German ceramic Bonzo water jug, 1920s, 9in (23cm) high.
£180–200 MURR

A Continental bisque Bonzo string holder, 1930s, 9in (23cm) high.
£110–130 MURR

A Royal Worcester Bonzo model, 1930, 2¾in (7cm) high.
£800–900 BZ

A Japanese ceramic Bonzo ashtray, 1930s, 3in (7.5cm) high.
£45–55 MURR

Bonzo The Life and Work of George Studdy, by Paul Babb and Gay Owen, published by Richard Dennis, 1988, 9 x 12in (23 x 30.5cm).
£18–20 BZ

A Bonzo postcard, entitled 'Fred the Ball Boy', c1923.
£8–10 BZ

A Bonzo postcard, entitled 'Lost Ball', 1925.
£8–10 PC

A collection of 112 Bonzo postcards, including titles 'Havoc', 'The Art School' and 'The Beggars Opera', 1920s.
£1,200–1,400 Bon(W)

▶ A Bonzo postcard, entitled 'Nice Little Bit of Fluff!', 1925.
£8–10 BZ

A Bonzo postcard, entitled 'Still Buzzing Around!', 1925.
£8–10 PC

▶ A Bonzo postcard, entitled 'Say It With Music!', 1926.
£8–10 BZ

A Bonzo postcard, entitled 'Wish You Could Join Me', No. 2282, c1934.
£5–6 JMC

A Bonzo postcard, entitled 'I've Lost My Heart Properly This Time!', c1930s.
£8–10 BZ

A Bonzo postcard, entitled 'Watching And Waiting For Someone!', No. 1906, c1934.
£5–6 JMC

▶ A Bonzo postcard, entitled 'What's This I'm Hearing About You?', 1930s.
£8–10 PC

Dolls

A German shoulder-headed china doll, with original dress, 1850–60, 12in (30.5cm) high.
£260–300 BaN

A poured wax shoulder-headed doll, with blue glass eyes, painted lips and real hair, on a cloth body with wax lower limbs, dressed, with original satin shoes, mid-19thC, 20in (51cm) high.
£220–250 P(Wm)

Three china dolls' heads, recovered from a shipwreck, 1880s, 2in (5cm) high.
£15–20 each SER

Six German miniature china dolls, on a card, early 20thC, 2in (5cm) high.
£110–120 HAL

A German parian shoulder-headed doll, dressed as a seamstress, with moulded hair, wearing original red skirt, with needles, thimble and thread, 1880s, 8in (20.5cm) high.
£425–465 DAn

A Goss sailor doll, with china hands and feet, moveable glass eyes and real hair wig, 1916–18, 15¾in (40cm) high.
£500–600 G&CC

A clay baby doll, dressed in yellow knitted suit and beige scarf, 1930s, 16in (40.5cm) high.
£85–95 Ann

A Diana The Royal Bride cardboard cut-out dressing doll, 1994, 19 x 12in (48.5 x 30.5cm).
£12–15 PC

A Jean-Paul Gaultier porcelain doll, limited edition of 500, La Poupée Gaultier, 2000, 38in (96.5cm) high.
£1,000–1,200 Ann
Created by the self-styled *enfant terrible* of Paris fashion, this doll is wearing a corset dress from Jean-Paul Gaultier's Spring/Summer 1999 collection, using the same materials as the full size original – satin, silk chiffon and girdle fabric. The skirt is hand-sewn with ostrich feathers.

► A pair of wooden dolls, with blonde hair and red shoes, 1950s, 7½in (19cm) high.
£12–15 GRa

BISQUE

A French bisque swivel-headed fashion doll, with fixed blue glass eyes, pierced ears and blonde ringlette wig, kid leather body with bisque lower arms, wearing a green skirt and jacket and a straw hat, c1860, 14in (35cm) high.
£1,100–1,400 Bon(C)

A Kestner bisque-headed doll, with blue sleep eyes and original wig and clothes, German, 19thC, 14in (35.5cm) high.
£450–500 BaN

Cross Reference
See Colour Review

A Simon & Halbig bisque-headed doll, with jointed composition body and original clothing, German, c1900, 18in (45.5cm) high.
£350–400 BaN

A bisque character squeeze toy, with fixed glass eyes and moulded black curly hair, on a wooden body with squeeze box, wearing pink and purple clown suit and painted yellow shoes, probably German, c1900, 11in (28cm) high.
£700–800 Bon(C)
The tambourines bang together when this doll is squeezed.

A bisque Kewpie doll, wearing red, green and black striped dress, 1920s, 6in (15cm) high.
£120–140 AnS

A Kestner bisque Bye-lo *bébé*, with original wig and label, 1910–18, 5in (12.5cm) high.
£400–500 DAn

◀ A Unis bisque-headed doll, with composition body, wearing a cream dress and jacket and yellow hair ribbons, 1920s, 27in (68.5cm) high.
£240–280 RAR

A Heubach bisque doll, wearing original cream dress with lace trim, 1910, 16in (40.5cm) high.
£175–200 Ann

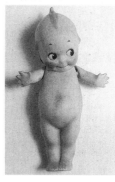

An S.F.B.J. bisque-headed doll, with wood and composition body, wearing a cream dress and blue shoes, marked, c1910, 19in (48.5cm) high.
£400–450 RAR

◀ A Rose O'Neill bisque Kewpie doll, signed, 1920s, 5½in (14cm) high.
£250–300 Ann

CELLULOID

A French celluloid character baby doll, c1920, 8in (20.5cm) high.
£40–50 A&J

A German celluloid doll, wearing a pink and white knitted costume, c1920, 10in (25.5cm) high.
£145–160 AnS

Further reading

Miller's Collecting Dolls & Teddy Bears: Facts At Your Fingertips,
Miller's Publications, 1996

COMPOSITION

A Schoenau & Hoffmeister bisque-headed doll, with wood and composition body and original wig, mould No. 5800, German, c1900, 22in (56cm) high.
£350–400 BaN

Five American composition baby dolls, The Dionne Quintuplets by Madame Alexander, with painted features, jointed five-piece baby bodies, wearing original nappies, vests and bibs with embroidered names, 1930s, 6in (15cm) high, in a painted wooden bed with pillows and linen, original booklet and various newpaper cuttings.
£700–800 Bon(C)

A composition doll, wearing a blue, pink and white floral dress, 1940s, 26in (66cm) high.
£120–150 Ann

A Heubach Kopplesdorf doll, with composition head and fabric body, 1930s, 18in (45.5cm) high.
£90–110 Ann

FELT

A Chad Valley felt doll, 1930s, 12in (30.5cm) high.
£85–95 Ann

A Harwin felt WWI US Officer doll, in the style of Steiff, 14in (35.5cm) high.
£600–700 DAn

▶ Two Norah Wellings WWI felt character dolls, c1930, 11in (28cm) high.
£350–375 DAn

PLASTIC

A Roddy hard plastic doll, with sleep eyes, 1950s, 12in (30.5cm) high.
£25–30 GRa

A Roddy hard plastic doll, c1950, 9in (23cm) high.
£30–40 A&J

A Roddy hard plastic fairy doll, with original dress and box, 1950s, 7in (18cm) high.
£10–12 A&J

A Pedigree hard plastic walkie talkie doll, with original red and white dress, 1950s, 20in (51cm) high.
£100–120 A&J

A Pedigree hard plastic walkie talkie doll, with mohair wig and original clothes, 1950, 23in (58.5cm) high.
£75–100 A&J

◀ An Old Cottage Toys hard plastic headed doll, with felt jointed body, wearing tartan kilt, bonnet and socks, 1960s, 10in (25.5cm) high.
£30–35 A&J

▶ A Twist and Turn Francie doll, wearing First Formal outfit, with gown, pink cape, gloves and blue shoes, 1966–67, 11¼in (28.5cm) high.
Francie £100–120
Outfit £40–50 PC

A Roddy hard plastic teenage walking doll, with pink and white dress, 1950s, 10in (25.5cm) high.
£30–35 GRa

A Pedigree hard plastic doll, with star burst hands, wearing yellow and white dress and brown bonnet, 1950s, 7in (18cm) high.
£20–25 A&J

A Pedigree Sindy doll, with original turquoise and black dress, 1968, 12in (30.5cm) high.
£45–50 CMF

◄ An Action Man Indian Brave doll, with complete medicine man set, 1979–80, 12in (30.5cm) high.
£35–40 CY

A Palitoy Action Man Action Soldier doll, c1966, 12in (30.5cm) high, with original box.
£130–160 HAL

A Trendon Sasha boy doll, Gregor, with brown hair and original green corduroy suit, 1970s, 17in (43cm) high.
£100–110 BGC

◄ A Palitoy Action Man doll, wearing a lancer uniform, incomplete, 1960s, 12in (30.5cm) high.
£50–60 HAL

A Trendon vinyl Sasha baby doll, with original blue corduroy dungarees and white top with red cuffs, 1960–70, 13in (33cm) high.
£60–75 A&J

◄ A Mattel Wayne Gretzky ice hockey doll, c1981, 12in (30.5cm) high, in original box.
£85–95 HALL

DOLLS' CLOTHES

A French 19thC-style doll's outfit, hand-stitched using antique textiles, trimming and beadwork in shades of pink and cream, 1990s, 18in (45.5cm) high.
£200–220 JPr

A lace-trimmed doll's dress, 1890–1910, 24in (61cm) long.
£20–23 Ann

► Three sets of 'Beautiful Clothes for the Happy House Fashion doll', 1960s.
£3–4 each HUX

DOLLS' HOUSES & FURNITURE

A dolls' house glass tea set, comprising two milk jugs, two mugs and a plate, 19thC, largest 5in (12.5cm) high.
£40–45 A&J

A dolls' house wash set, decorated with pink and blue flowers, 1890, 2½in (6.5cm) high.
£35–45 Ann

A German dolls' house cast-metal folding push chair, 1900–20, 3in (7.5cm) high.
£20–25 A&J

A German dolls' house lead tea set, c1900, tray 3in (7.5cm) wide.
£30–36 A&J

◄ A German dolls' house metal telephone, c1920, 2in (5cm) high.
£20–25 A&J

A dolls' house Art Deco-style simulated-wood table and sideboard, 1930, 3in (7.5cm) high.
£30–35 A&J

A dolls' house handmade green-patterned three piece suite, 1930s, 2in (5cm) high.
£20–25 A&J

A dolls' house metal fireplace, 1930, 3in (7.5cm) high.
£15–20 A&J

◄ A dolls' house wooden bedroom suite, decorated with blue, red and white flowers, 1950s, bed 4in (10cm) long.
£20–25 A&J

A Tudor-style four-storey dolls' house, Henley Court, by Robert Stubbs, with stained and painted wood, thatched-effect roof, gable window and skylight, fully timbered front and sides, leaded light windows, opening front sections, electric lighting, 1985–90, 46in (117cm) high, with authentication certificate.
£750–850 AH

► A dolls' house metal vacuum cleaner, 1950, 4in (10cm) high.
£15–20 A&J

Ephemera

A collection of driving licences, 1910–30s.
£5–10 each COB

Four French menus, each hand-painted with a 17thC soldier, late 19thC, 7 x 5in (18 x 13cm).
£350–400 MSB

John Menzies & Co's Ltd Diary 1914, 13 x 9in (33 x 23cm).
£30–35 COB

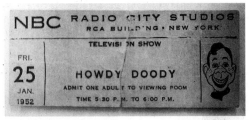

An American Howdy Doody TV show admission ticket, 1952.
£100–120 HALL

Hobdays Cycle Catalogue, 1936, 11 x 9in (28 x 23cm).
£30–35 COB

A New York Blue Line Bus Co sightseeing guide, c1950, 10 x 7in (25.5 x 18cm).
£5–6 RTT

◀ A Waldorf-Astoria menu, 16th December 1951, 11 x 9in (28 x 23cm).
£25–30 MRW

▶ Two Nürburgring race programmes, 1955, 8 x 6in (20.5 x 15cm).
£25–30 DT

AUTOGRAPHS

As our culture grows ever more fascinated by celebrities, so demand for autographs is booming. 'At auction, dealers are paying twice what they paid five years ago and the market is very strong', says dealer Paul Mulvey, from Ink Quest. His own best sellers include what he describes as 'classic boy's heroes': Lord Nelson, Scott of the Antarctic, military leaders, major sportsmen and astronauts. 'Putting a man on the moon was one of the greatest achievements of all time', he enthuses. 'The crew of Apollo XI are now all in their seventies and their autographs are very popular, but watch out for auto-pens – a machine that reproduced their signatures on photographs. Auto-pen signatures are always in the same size and exactly the same place on the photo'. According to Mulvey, Mohammed Ali's is perhaps the most sought-after living autograph, and Nelson Mandela is another figure whose signature appeals across the world. Rock and Pop is a desirable subject and, while The Beatles tend to top the charts, Elvis is also performing well. 'Here again, Presley's prices have doubled in the past few years', claims Mulvey. His tip for investment is artists' signatures – particularly Picasso and Dali, although purchasers should beware of fakes. Increasing prices in the autograph market, can only encourage the activities of fakers, and signatures are not a hard thing to reproduce. Collectors should buy from a reputable source. Don't be afraid to ask dealers about their items, or to ask for a certificate of authenticity.

Buzz Aldrin, a signed colour postcard, full-length, walking on the lunar surface, c1969.
£80–90 VS

Muhammad Ali, a poster of the re-match against Sonny Liston, signed as Cassius Clay, c1964, 20 x 16in (51 x 40.5cm).
£475–575 FRa

Fred Astaire, a signed photograph, three-quarter length standing, in later years, 4½ x 3½in (11.5 x 9cm).
£50–60 VS

Victoria and David Beckham photograph with signature, 1999, 6 x 8in (15 x 20.5cm), framed.
£200–240 SMW

Prince Charles, a signed sepia-toned photograph of Princes William and Harry, inscribed 'To you both from Charles', 1992, 8 x 6in (20.5 x 15cm).
£180–220 Bon(C)

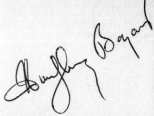

Humphrey Bogart, an album page signed in blue ink, 1940s, 3¾ x 4½in (9.5 x 11.5cm).
£450–500 Bon(C)

◄ Charlie Chaplin, a signed colour postcard, depicted as the tramp, with rolling eyes, 1920s.
£230–260 VS

Prince Charles and Princess Diana, a signed colour photograph of the Prince and Princess and the two Princes on a pony, inscribed in black ink 'To you both from Charles and Diana', 1985, 7¼ x 5in (18.5 x 13cm).
£800–900 Bon(C)

Winston Churchill, a signed letter, congratulating a Mrs Hall on her 100th birthday, on Chartwell writing paper, 1957, 8 x 5in (20.5 x 12.5cm), with original envelope.
£900–1,000 IQ

John Cleese, a signed sepia photograph, as Basil Fawlty, 1980s, 9 x 7in (23 x 18cm).
£120–140 SMW

▶ Diana Princess of Wales, a signed copy of the catalogue for the auction of her dresses, June 1997, No. 74 of a limited edition of 250, signed 'Diana' in blue ink, 17 x 12in (43 x 30.5cm), with invitation and posting box.
£2,300–2,600 Bon(C)

Charles Dickens, a signed one and a half page letter to Miss Barry, 3½ x 4in (9 x 10cm).
£400–480 VS

Salvador Dali, a letter from the Dali Museum with full signature, 1976, 10 x 8in (25.5 x 20.5cm).
£250–275 IQ

Marlene Dietrich, a signed photograph, with first name only, 1949, 11½ x 10½in (29 x 26.5cm).
£200–220 VS

◀ Walt Disney, a signed page from the book *Fantasia*, 1958, 13 x 9½in (33 x 24cm).
£1,000–1,200 IQ

Diana Dors, a signed
postcard, three-quarter
length lying on a tiger
skin, 1950s.
£90–110 VS

Edward, Prince of Wales,
a signed postcard, 1930s.
£220–250 VS

Sir Edward Elgar, a signed
one page letter to his
publishers Novellos,
25 February 1930, 4to.
£350–400 DW

Queen Elizabeth the
Queen Mother, and
Princess Margaret, two
portrait photographs
respectively signed in the
border 'Elizabeth R 1963'
and 'Margaret 1959',
in blue leather-bound
frames bearing the
respective Royal crests,
each 8 x 6in (20.5 x 15cm).
£1,300–1,500 DW

HM Queen Elizabeth and Prince Philip,
a signed colour photograph, wearing Robes
of the Thistle, 1975, 8½ x 6in (21.5 x 15cm).
£90–110 Bon(C)

King George VI, a signed
monochrome photograph of the
King wearing RAF uniform, 1942,
11¾ x 9½in (30 x 24cm).
£320–350 SAS

◄ Mikhail Gorbachev,
a signed colour photograph,
wearing a suit with red
CCCP pin in lapel, 1990s,
4¾ x 3¾in (12 x 9.5cm).
£140–160 VS

Yuri Gagarin, a signed
monochrome postcard,
c1966, glazed and framed.
£1,100–1,300 BKS

Reichsmarshall Herman
Goering, a signed
document, appointing Dr
Fritz Hirsch to the position
of State Veterinary
Surgeon in Silesia,
7th March 1937, folio.
£300–330 DW

► James Hunt, a signed
press photograph, 1977,
8 x 6in (20.5 x 15cm).
£40–50 IQ

Bob Hope, a signed and
inscribed publicity
photograph, 1940s,
10 x 8in (25.5 x 20.5cm).
£40–50 IQ

Jennifer Lopez, a signed
colour photograph, 2000,
7 x 5in (18 x 12.5cm).
£45–50 VS

Nelson Mandela and
F. W. de Klerk, a signed
photograph, with Office of
the President seal, 1999,
7 x 5in (18 x 12.5cm).
180–200 IQ

Edgar Mitchell, a signed colour photograph,
on the lunar surface with the American flag and
shadow of the lunar module and photographer
on 5 February 1971, 1990s,
10 x 8in (25.5 x 20.5cm).
£50–60 VS

Marilyn Monroe, a piece of paper,
signed in blue ink, 1950s,
2½ x 2¼in (6.5 x 5 5cm).
£1,600–1,800 Bon(C)

Iain Prost, a signed
press photograph, 1986,
8 x 6in (20.5 x 15cm).
35–40 IQ

Eva Peron, a signed menu
card from the wedding of
General Franco's daughter,
15th June 1947.
£1,000–1,200 VS

Monty Python, a publicity postcard signed by all six
characters, 1973, 5 x 7in (12.5 x 18cm).
£320–350 IQ

◄ Basil Rathbone, a
signed postcard, three-
quarter length standing,
holding two terrier dogs,
1930s, 7 x 5in (18 x 12.5cm).
£100–120 VS

**LOCATE THE
SOURCE**
The source of each
illustration in Miller's
can be found by
checking the code
letters below each
caption with the
Key to Illustrations,
pages 476–484.

Edward G. Robinson, a
signed and inscribed photograph, three-quarter length
wearing a suit, 1950s,
10 x 8in (25.5 x 20.5cm).
£70–80 VS

Margaret Rutherford,
a signed postcard, three-
quarter length standing,
waving a handbag, 1950s.
£100–120 VS

Peter Sellers, a signed
postcard, head and
shoulders, 1970s.
£60–70 VS

George Bernard Shaw, a signed letter on personal
stationery, mentioning *Man and Superman*, 1947,
with photograph.
£300–330 IQ

▶ The Spice
Girls, signed by
all four, each
with first names
only, full-length
seated together,
c1999, 10 x 8in
(25.5 x 20.5cm).
£70–80 VS

SPICE GIRLS

Phil Silvers, a signed
photograph, in costume
as Sergeant Bilko,
a modern reproduction
signed in later years,
7 x 5in (18 x 12.5cm).
£110–130 VS

Frank Sinatra, a signed
publicity photograph, 1975,
10 x 8in (25.5 x 20.5cm).
£270–300 IQ

Bram Stoker, two original
typescripts, a signed
article 'The Question
of a National Theatre'
and a corrected copy of
'The Russian Professor',
c1913, 4to.
£2,200–2,500 DW

J. R. R. Tolkien,
a signed letter concernir
The Hobbit, 1968,
9 x 7in (23 x 18cm).
£1,500–1,700 IQ

◀ Mae West, a signed
publicity photograph, 1940s,
7 x 5in (18 x 12.5cm).
£130–150 IQ

Mark Twain and Johann
Strauss II, a 16-flight
wooden fan, with 15
other signatures, mainly
musicians, and with
musical quotations,
c1900, 9in (23cm) high.
£500–550 DW

▶ John Wayne,
a signed album
page, 4 x 6in
(10 x 15cm).
£175–200 VS

Kenneth Williams, a
signed photograph, 1970
10 x 8in (25.5 x 20.5cm
£140–160 VS

∖len & Ginter's, Great
ⁿooters Series,
ⁱⁿerican, 1888.
₁00–120 HALL

Duke's Cameo Cigarettes, Rulers, Flags and
Coats of Arms, Prince Bismark, tri-fold card,
from a set of 50, 1888.
£20–25 HALL

Allen & Ginter's, Celebrated
American Indian Chiefs, six from
a set of 50, American, 1888.
£200–250 HALL

Baines & Son,
ⁱanchester City football
∖rd, slight damage, 1897,
x 3in (12.5 x 7.5cm).
ⁱ0–55 KNI

Kinney Bros, Uniform
Soldiers of the World,
from a set of 622, 1889.
£5–8 each HALL

Cohen, Weenen & Co, Cricketers, Footballers and
Jockeys, set of 20, 1900.
£150–180 Bon(W)

⊃hn Player & Sons, Badges & Flags of British
∶egiments, set of 50, 1903.
₃5–95 MAr

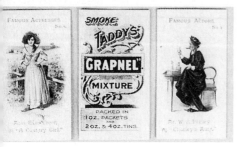

∖ddy & Co, Famous Actors/Famous Actresses,
∶t of 15, 1903.
₂30–260 Bon(W)

Liebig, Astronomers, set of 6, 1906.
£25–30 MAr

W. D. & H. O. Wills, Time & Money in Different
Countries, set of 50, 1907.
£60–70 MAr

Liebig, Aerial Navigation,
set of 6, 1911.
£30–35 MAr

F. & J. Smith, Famous Explorers,
set of 50, 1911.
£300–340 Bon(W)

John Player & Sons, Egyptian
Kings & Queens and Classical
Deities, set of 25, 1912.
£35–40 MAr

W. D. & H. O. Wills, Musical Celebrities, set of 50, 1912.
£95–115 MAr

Cope Bros & Co, Boats of the World, set of 50, 1912.
£400–450 JACK

John Player & Sons, British
Livestock, set of 25, 1915.
£40–50 MAr

W. D. & H. O. Wills, British Birds,
set of 50, 1915.
£40–50 MAr

Ogden's, Boxers, set of 50, 1915.
£150–180 Bon(W)

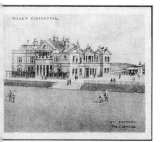

W. D. & H. O. Wills, Golfing,
et of 25, 1924.
130–150 P

W. & F. Faulkner, Prominent
Racehorses of the Present Day,
set of 25, 1924.
£70–85 MAr

Gallaher, Famous Cricketers,
set of 100, 1926.
£200–230 MAr

odfrey Phillips, Famous Cricketers,
et of 32, 1926.
110–130 DA

John Player & Sons,
Football Caricatures by
'MAC', set of 50, 1927.
£50–60 MUR

W. D. & H. O. Wills, Old
Sundials, set of 25, 1928.
£55–65 MAr

John Player & Sons,
Curious Beaks,
set of 50, 1929.
£35–40 MAr

◀ J. Millhoff & Co, Famous
Golfers, set of 27, 1928.
£320–350 P

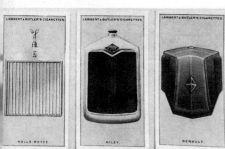

ambert & Butler, Motor Car Radiators,
et of 25, 1928.
0–100 JACK

W. D. & H. O. Wills, Famous Golfers, set of 25, 1930.
£270–300 P

W. A. & A. C. Churchman, Sporting Celebrities, set of 50, 1931.
£80–100 JACK

John Player & Sons, Poultry, set of 50, 1931.
£70–80 MAr

John Player & Sons, Dogs, by Wardle, set of 50, 1931.
£35–40 JMC

John Player & Sons, Butterflies, set of 50, 1932.
£35–40 JACK

John Player & Sons, Aviary and Cage Birds, set of 50, 1933.
£45–50 JMC

W. D. & H. O. Wills, Safety First, set of 50, 1934.
£40–45 MAr

John Player & Sons, Cricketers 1934, set of 50, 1934.
£45–50 MAr

John Player & Sons, Kings & Queens of England, set of 50, 1935.
£55–65 MAr

Carreras, Famous Airmen and Airwomen, set of 50, 1936.
£60–70 MAr

John Player & Sons, Motor Cars, 1st Series,
set of 50, 1936.
£65–70 JMC

John Player & Sons, Wildfowl, set of 25, 1937.
£60–70 MAr

John Player & Sons, Aircraft of the Royal Air Force,
set of 50, 1938.
£40–45 MAr

Lambert & Butler, Dance Band Leaders, set of 25, 1936
£80–90 JACK

John Player & Sons, RAF Badges, set of 50, 1937.
£20–25 JACK

Facchino's chocolate cards, How or Why?,
set of 50, 1937.
£20–25 JACK

John Player & Sons, Cycling,
set of 50, 1939.
£35–40 MAr

John Player & Sons, Animals of the
Countryside, set of 50, 1939.
£10–12 MAr

Gallaher, Army Badges,
set of 48, 1939.
£20–25 JACK

Erotica

Roman phallic badge, 2ndC, 2in (5cm) long.
75–90 GRa

◄ A novelty pottery drink flask, depicting a nude female surrounded by grinning male faces, inscribed 'September Morn', 1920s, 8in (20.5cm) high.
£70–85 MURR

A Murray, Sons & Co set of 25 cigarette cards, Dancing Girls, 1929.
£35–40 VS

A pin-up print, 1920s, 8 x 5in (20.5 x 12.5cm).
£12–15 RTT

A set of five Earl MacPherson sketchbook samples, for Brown & Bigelow pin-up advertising calendars, America, 1940s, 7in (18cm) high, with stand.
£20–25 SpM

An Ernst Bohne porcelain bottle, modelled as mating chickens, decorated in orange, green and gilt on a white ground, 1930s, 3in (7.5cm) high.
£60–70 HT

Foto An International Magazine of Photographic Art pin-up book, with a colour photograph of Marilyn Monroe and monochrome photographs of Betty Page, 1950s.
24–28 SpM

A pack of pin-up playing cards, 1950, 4 x 3in (10 x 7.5cm).
£20–25 RTT

◄ A *Riviera* mail order catalogue, advertising swimwear, nightwear and underwear, Winter 1958/59, 5 x 3in (12.5 x 7.5cm).
£8–12 RTT

A calendar, with a colour photograph of Marilyn Monroe entitled 'Golden Dreams', American, 1955, 14 x 11in (35.5 x 28cm).
£50–60 DW

A *Playboy* magazine, November 1968, 11 x 8in (28 x 20.5cm).
£8–10 RTT

▶ A Playboy money clip, 1970s, 2¾in (7cm) long.
£35–40 PLB

A Playboy medallion, America, 1970s, 1in (2.5cm) diam.
£20–25 PLB

Little Birds, Erotica by Anaïs Nin, published by Book Club Associates, 1979, 9½ x 6¼in (24 x 16cm).
£12–15 PLB

Two erotic books, *The Vice and Spice of the Americas After Dark* edited by Eugene Crammond published by Tallis Press, and *The Kinky Crowd Volume I* by Clavel Brand, published by Riverhaven, 1968–70, 7 x 4½in (18 x 11.5cm).
£8–12 PLB

A Playboy glass mug, America, 1970s, 6½in (16.5cm) high.
£25–30 PLB

A Pirelli calendar, photographed by Terence Donovan, 1987, 23½ x 16½in (59.5 x 42cm).
£40–50 PLB

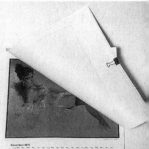

A Fritz Willis pin-up calendar, 1970, 12 x 13in (30.5 x 33cm).
£20–25 RTT

◀ A Playboy glass mug, America, 1970s, 6½in (16.5cm) high.
£25–30 PLB

▶ *Masterpieces of Erotic Photography*, published by Talisman Books, 1977, 12 x 9in (30.5 x 23cm).
£25–30 PLB

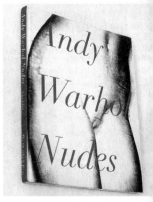

Andy Warhol Nudes, published by The Overlook Press, New York, 1995, 12 x 9½in (30.5 x 24cm).
£35–40 PLB

Eyebaths

Silver and ceramic eyebaths were produced in the early 17th century, and by the late 1670s they were being manufactured in glass, predominantly in the pedestal shape that was to remain standard into the 20th century. Eyebaths were made from clear glass and, from the late 18th century, in coloured glass. Blue and dark green tend to be the most common colours, and the palette expanded in the 19th century to include amber, brown and yellow, as well as more unusual colours such as turquoise and purple. Large numbers of eyebaths were produced in the Victorian and Edwardian period and, while the more common examples can be purchased at very little cost, unusual designs, rare colours, patented models or individual free-blown shapes can command very high prices. Shown here is a selection of rarities.

A ceramic eyebath, transfer-printed in blue, repaired, 1860–70, 2¼in (5.5cm) high.
£800–900 BBR

A clear glass eyebath, 1900–20, 2¾in (7cm) high.
£18–20 DHo

An emerald green freeblown glass eyebath with reservoir, on a chunky circular foot with a pontil base, 1900–10, 2¼in (5.5cm) high.
£290–320 BBR

A green glass eyebath, 1900–20, 2¾in (7cm) high.
£20–22 DHo

◀ A moulded amber glass eyebath, the bowl embossed with a cross, with short stem and kick-up circular foot, 1920–30, 2¼in (5.5cm) high.
£490–540 BBR

A freeblown clear glass eyebath, with a tulip-shaped bowl and thin stem with hook end, 1890–1900, 3¼in (8.5cm) high.
£320–350 BBR

A French cobalt blue glass eyebath, the bowl with vertical ribs, with a faceted stem on a circular foot, 1920–30, 2½in (6.5cm) high.
£550–625 BBR

A cobalt blue freeblown glass eyebath, the tulip-shaped bowl with outwardly turned rim, on a thin stem with a kick-up circular foot, probably French, 1900–10, 3in (7.5cm) high.
£280–320 BBR

A moulded black glass eyebath, with a faceted bowl and stem on a circular foot, 1920–30, 3in (7.5cm) high.
£400–460 BBR

Fifties

Four Ernest Race steel
and plywood Antelope
chairs, 1950s.
£120–140 L
These chairs were
originally designed
for the Festival of
Britain 1951.

A pair of beech armchairs,
with cream vinyl upholstery,
the shaped solid seats
and back rests on swept
back legs and short
splayed tapering front
legs, 1950s.
£1,200–1,400 P(B)

A chrome and vinyl
diner bar stool, 1950s,
21in (53.5cm) high,
on later iron base.
£40–45 TRA

A Charles and Ray
Eames Aluminium
group armchair,
produced by Herman
Miller, 1958.
£200–240 MARK

A Herman Miller brown fibreglass
rocking chair, designed by
Charles Eames, with wooden
rocker and Eiffel Tower metal
base, late 1950s.
£350–425 PLB

An Erance & Sons
two-tier teak
and cane table,
designed by Peter
Hündt and Olga
Molgarrd, Denmark,
late 1950s,
29in (73.5cm) high.
£330–360 GOH

A maple veneer circular
two-tier occasional
table, supported on
three square tapering
splayed legs, 1950s,
31½in (80cm) diam.
£175–200 P(B)

An F. Robert tapestry, Californie, woven in colours
with stylized exotic birds and foliage, on a yellow
ground, signed, 1950s, 45¼ x 117¼in (115 x 298cm).
£500–550 DN

A French tapestry,
Le Chandelier, designed
by Jean Picart le Doux,
depicting a golden
chandelier flanking a
balalaika with moths in
flight and stars and yellow
dots on a red ground,
signed, 1950s, 56¾ x 41in
(144 x 104cm).
£400–460 DN

A mottled grey plastic
lavatory seat, 1950,
21in (53.5cm) long.
£35–45 CRN

A Beswick pottery toast rack, with Circus pattern in blue, red, black and yellow, 1950, 6in (15cm) long.
£12–15 P(B)

An Edelkeramix pottery plate, decorated with dancers in green, brown, yellow and black on a white ground, 1950s, 14in (35.5cm) wide.
£40–50 PrB

A British Flask Co green pottery flask, c1950, 10in (25.5cm) high.
£15–18 FA

A Homemaker pottery tureen, decorated with black household items on a white ground, c1957, 9in (23cm) diam.
£90–100 HarC

A West German black pottery vase, hand-decorated with white stripes, 1950, 7in (18cm) high.
£40–45 V&S

A German green and yellow pottery vase, 1950, 17in (43cm) high.
£50–55 V&S

A Hornsea pottery vase, decorated in black and white on a grey ground, 1950s, 6½in (16.5cm) high.
£30–35 PrB

Auction or dealer?

All the pictures in our price guides originate from auction houses and dealers. When buying at auction, prices can be lower than those of a dealer, but a buyer's premium and VAT will be added to the hammer price. Equally, when selling at auction, commission, tax and photography charges must be taken into account. Dealers will often restore pieces before putting them back on the market. Both dealers and auctioneers will provide professional advice, so it is worth researching both sources before buying or selling your collectables.

A Hornsea pottery blue and white tube-lined flower vase, 1950s, 5¼in (13.5cm) high.
£35–40 PrB

An Italian striated and hand-carved pottery vase, decorated in red and turquoise on a black and grey ground, 1950s, 10in (25.5cm) high.
£45–55 V&S

An Italian textured pottery vase, hand-painted with a glazed portrait in blue, green, white and brown on a red ground, c1950, 8in (20.5cm) high.
£45–55 V&S

An Italian sgraffito-effect pottery vase, decorated in blue and red on a black ground, c1950, 6in (15cm) high.
£45–55 V&S

► A Midwinter tube-lined vase, by Jessie Tait, decorated with Bands and Dots pattern, c1956, 6¾in (17cm) high.
£200–240 BDA

► A Midwinter cup and saucer, designed by Hugh Casson, decorated with a village scene in red, blue, yellow and black, 1950s, cup 3in (7.5cm) high.
£16–20 DBo

A Midwinter dinner set, designed by Terence Conran, decorated with Nature Study pattern, comprising two covered vegetable dishes, six soup bowls and stands, a sauce boat, meat plate, and six dinner, pudding and side plates, 1950s, vegetable dish 10in (25.5cm) wide.
£550–650 DN

A Midwinter Stylecraft plate and cup, decorated with Wild Geese series controlled design by Peter Scott, signed, c1950, plate 9in (23cm) wide.
£16–20 ES

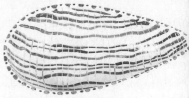

◄ A Rosenthal triangular dish, designed by Raymond Peynet, decorated with a boy and girl in a boat, in blue, pink, green and brown on a white ground, 1950s, 7¾in (19.5cm) wide.
£85–100 RDG

A Rye Pottery avocado dish, decorated with blue and grey stripes on a white ground, 1950s, 5½in (14cm) wide.
£25–30 NCA

1951 FESTIVAL OF BRITAIN

While the Millennium Dome was judged by many to be a forgettable experience, exactly 50 years on people still remember the Festival of Britain as a huge success and a remarkable, joyous event. The Festival was organized to mark the centenary of the Great Exhibition of 1851 and to boost the nation's morale after the austerity of WWII. It celebrated British achievement in every sphere, providing a symbol of optimism and hope for what was to become the New Elizabethan Age.

Though events took place across the country, the centre of the Festival was the Exhibition on London's South Bank, masterminded by Director-General Gerald Barry. A team of architects, led by Hugh Casson and Misha Black, transformed the desolate, urban bombsite into a modern-day pleasure dome with pavilions, piazzas, sculptures and a giant funfair in the Festival Gardens, Battersea Park. Principal structures included the Royal Festival Hall (the one building designed to be permanent) and Powel and Moya's Skylon, an aluminium vertical feature that looked like a giant space-age question mark and reached up into the air without any visible means of support, 'just like Britain', claimed the more cynical visitors. The Festival generated innumerable souvenirs and memorabilia, that are still collectable today. Typically, objects are decorated with the highly distinctive Festival of Britain logo, featuring the head of Britannia in red, white and blue, and designed by graphic artist Abram Games.

A Guinness Festival of Britain red and white wax-paper cup, 1951, 6in (15cm) high.
£10–12 RTT

◄ A Shorter & Son Festival of Britain character jug, in the form of a man with his bulldog, decorated in red, blue, white, yellow and black, 1951, 6in (15cm) high.
£60–70 FBS

Two Paragon Festival of Britain bone china mugs, decorated in white and gilt on turquoise or green ground, 1951, 5in (12.5cm) high.
£70–80 each FBS

A Brentleigh ware Festival of Britain stoneware mug, transfer-printed in brown and green with St. Paul's Cathedral, 1951, 4in (10cm) high.
£40–50 FBS

A Poole Pottery Festival of Britain plate, decorated with flowers in red, yellow, 1951, 10in (25.5cm) diam.
£90–100 FBS

A Gilbey's Festival of Britain metal drinks tray, 1951, 12in (30.5cm) diam.
£30–40 MURR

A Paragon Festival of Britain bone china mug, decorated in white and gilt on a red ground, 1951, 5in (12.5cm) high.
£80–90 FBS

A Swan Brand Festival of Britain aluminium teapot, 1951, 4in (10cm) high.
£15–20 HUX

A Festival of Britain brass jug, 1951, 4½in (11.5cm) high.
£12–15 HUX

A Festival of Britain Singapore United Engineers Closing Ceremony card, 1951, 10 x 6in (25.5 x 15cm).
£20–25 FBS

A Festival of Britain metal tea caddy, 1951, 5in (12.5cm) high.
£15–20 HUX

A Festival of Britain Singapore United Engineers commemorative album, 1951, 11 x 7in (28 x 18cm).
£35–40 FBS

▶ A Festival of Britain brass door knocker, 1951, 5in (12.5cm) high.
£15–20 HUX

◀ A Bryant & May Festival of Britain book of matches, printed in black and white on a red and yellow ground, 1951, 2 x 1½in (5 x 4cm).
£3–4 HUX

A Festival of Britain Skylon biro pen and stand, 1951, 9in (23cm) high.
£50–60 FBS

A Festival of Britain chromium-plated tea caddy spoon, 1951, 3½in (9cm) long.
£6–7 HUX

◀ A Festival of Britain glass paperweight, 1951, 5 x 3in (12.5 x 7.5cm).
£35–45 MURR

A Festival of Britain gold-coloured metal powder compact, 1951, 3½in (9cm) diam.
£25–30 HUX

Pilkington's Lancastrian water jug, in the shape of a grasshopper, 1904, 14in (35.5cm) high.
£1,000–1,200 JEZ

A Poole Pottery Art Deco vase, designed by Truda Carter, decorated by Eileen Prangnell, impressed mark 'Poole England', incised '966', 'GEP' pattern code and painter's mark, c1930, 9½in (24cm) high.
£1,800–2,000 DN

► A Poole Pottery charger, by Angela Wyburgh, with textured surface, 1969–73, 16in (40.5cm) diam.
£540–600 HarC

A Possil Pottery Glasgow flow blue cheese dish, 1890s, 9in (23cm) wide.
£170–200 PC

Henriot Quimper umbrella spill vase, 1895, 16in (40.5cm) high.
£300–330 VH

A Henriot Quimper two-handled vase, 1922–68, 5½in (14cm) high.
£50–60 SER

A Radford hand-thrown hand-painted vase, decorated with Daffodil pattern, shape No. 473, c1928, 6in (15cm) high.
£145–165 ERCC

A Radford hand-thrown two-handled vase, shape No. P23, c1930, 11in (28cm) high.
£220–250 ERCC

Radford vase, 1930s, 8in (20.5cm) high.
£75–90 BEV

A Radford vase, decorated with Hollyhock pattern, 1930s, 7in (18cm) high.
£100–120 BEV

A Radford model of a frog, c1937, 5in (12.5cm) long.
£125–145 ERCC

A Crown Ducal wall plaque, Persian Rose, designed by Charlotte Rhead, pattern No. 4040, c1935, 17½in (44.5cm) diam.
£540–600 **BDA**

A Bursley Ware charger, designed by Charlotte Rhead, pattern No. TL2, 1940s, 14½in (37cm) diam.
£340–380 **BDA**

A Rosenthal group of birds, Chicks, German, 1930s, 4in (10cm) wide.
£150–170 **MD**

A Royal Winton cake plate, decorated with Hazel pattern, on a pedestal foot, 1930s, 6½in (16.5cm) wide.
£75–85 **DBo**

A Royal Winton cheese dish, modelled as a cottage, 1930s, 8in (20.5cm) wide.
£75–90 **JEZ**

A Shelley vase, decorated with Maytime pattern, 1930s, 4½in (11.5cm) high.
£50–60 **DBo**

A Shelley coffee pot, decorated with Maytime pattern, 1930s, 7in (18cm) high.
£165–185 **DBo**

A Shorter & Son character jug, Father Neptune, 1930s, 3½in (9cm) high.
£60–70 **BEV**

A SylvaC model of a dog, 'Joey', 1930s, 8in (20.5cm) high.
£250–300 **JEZ**

A Copeland Spode meat platter, c1924, 10in (25.5cm) wide.
£45–55 **CoCo**

◀ A Shorter & Son butter dish, modelled as a stylized pagoda, c1935, 6in (15cm) wide.
£40–45 **PrB**

A Staffordshire figure of Joshua, c1800, 9in (23cm) high.
£250–300 JHo

A Staffordshire model of a castle, 1810–20, 6in (15cm) high.
£250–300 DAN

A Staffordshire cow creamer, c1840, 7in (18cm) wide.
£290–325 SER

A Walton, Staffordshire group of a shepherd and his dog, before a bocage, 1815–25, 6in (15cm) high.
£200–240 SER

A Sherratt, Staffordshire pearlware model of a cow, before a bocage, c1825, 8in (20.5cm) high.
£1,300–1,500 JRe

A Staffordshire cow creamer, c1840, 10in (25.5cm) wide.
£325–375 SER

A Staffordshire group of two drummer boys from the Crimean War, c1854, 7in (18cm) high.
£250–300 ACO

A Staffordshire model of Sir Robert Peel on horseback, c1850, 12in (30.5cm) high.
£1,500–1,750 ACO

A Staffordshire equestrian figure, c1860, 7in (18cm) high.
£145–165 JO

A Staffordshire figure of a girl with a harp, c1860, 8in (20.5cm) high.
£140–170 DAN

A Staffordshire spill vase, in the form of Red Riding Hood and the wolf, before a tree-trunk, 1880, 10in (25.5cm) high.
£100–120 OD

A Jet Ware teapot, commemorating the Glasgow Exhibition, 1888, 5½in (14cm) high.
£160–180 SQA

A Foley Pottery teapot, modelled as President Kruger, c1900, 5in (12.5cm) high.
£520–580 BRT

An agate-bodied twin-spouted tea pot, commemorating the coronation of King George V, inscribed and dated 1911, 9in (23cm) wide.
£125–145 IW

A Sadler teapot, modelled as a charabanc, with silver-coloured chrome, 1930s, 8in (2.5cm) wide.
£450–500 BEV

◄ A child's 15 piece tea set, commemorating King George V and Queen Mary, in original box, 1911, 12in (30.5cm) wide.
£160–180 HUX

A Staffordshire teapot, modelled as Humpty Dumpty, 1930, 8in (20.5cm) wide.
£60–70 AnS

A Sadler teapot, modelled as a racing car, decorated with children and animals, 1930s, 9in (23cm) wide.
£425–475 DRJ

A Cottage Ware teapot, milk jug and sugar basin, the teapot inscribed 'Festival of Britain 1951', teapot 8in (20.5cm) wide.
£75–85 HUX

A Carlton Ware teapot, modelled as a Hovis loaf, 1970s, 6in (15cm) high.
£25–30 BTB

A Swineside teapot, in the form of a hotel porter carrying cases, 1980–90, 11in (28cm) high.
£35–45 JBy

A teapot modelled as a boiled egg in a cup, impressed mark 'Andy', 1980–90, 9¾in (25cm) high.
£30–35 JBy

A Wadeheath jug, decorated with a galleon, 1930s, 8in (20.5cm) high.
£80–90 PrB

A Wadeheath jam pot, painted with iris, 1930s, 4in (10cm) high.
£35–45 CoCo

A pair of Wedgwood Fairyland Lustre trumpet vases, decorated with Butterfly Women design, marked and numbered 'Z4968', 1920–30, 8in (20.5cm) high.
£2,200–2,500 RTo

A Wedgwood ribbed vase, designed by Keith Murray, c1935, marked, 9in (23cm) high.
£450–500 RUSK

A Wemyss Stuart pot, painted with Roses pattern, c1900, 8in (20.5cm) high.
£300–350 RdeR

A Wemyss lidded bowl, painted with Wild Rose pattern, late 1920s–30s, 3½in (9cm) diam.
£310–350 SAAC

A Chamberlain's Worcester trio, c1821, saucer 6in (15cm) diam.
£380–420 GRI

A Royal Worcester Persian ewer, hand-painted by Harry Martin, 1906, 12in (30.5cm) high.
£800–900 TWr

An Upchurch baluster vase, c1925, 9in (23cm) high.
£450–500 HUN

A Royal Worcester model, Robin, 1930s, 2½in (6.5cm) high.
£60–70 WAC

◄ A Royal Worcester bird group, Yellowhammers, 1950s, 5in (12.5cm) high.
£175–195 WAC

Action Comics, No. 1, June
1938, National Periodical
Publications, restored, America.
£25,000–26,000 S(NY)

The Beano Comic, No. 6, 1938.
£750–850 CBP

The Magic Beano Book, 1948,
11 x 8in (27 x 20.3cm) high.
£180–200 OCB

Eagle comic, 26th December 1959,
13 x 11in (33 x 28cm).
£3–5 OCB

Lucie Attwell's Annual, c1950,
10 x 8in (25.5 x 20.5cm).
£40–45 OCB

The Broons, 1960, 8 x 5in
(20.5 x 12.5cm).
£50–60 OCB

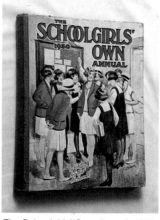

Romeo, teenage romance comic,
21st November 1959.
£4–6 RTT

The Schoolgirls' Own Annual, 1930,
10 x 8in (25.5 x 20.5cm).
£12–15 OCB

Worzel Gummidge Annual, 1980s,
11½ x 8in (29 x 20.5cm).
£2–3 CMF

commemorative tin, decorated
ith portraits of Queen Victoria,
ladstone, Chamberlain and
thers, scratched, c1900,
¼in (17cm) high.
80–100 SAS

A Royal Doulton silver-mounted
stoneware commemorative tyg,
inscribed 'Lord Nelson, Born 1758
Died 1805', 1905, 7in (18cm) high.
£400–480 SAS

An Empire Porcelain Co shaving mug,
commemorating the Coronation of
King George V and Queen Mary,
1911, 3in (7.5cm) high.
£40–45 GWR

knife and spoon, commemorating
e British Empire Exhibition, in
riginal case, 1924, 7in (18cm) wide.
55–65 HUX

A Shelley mug, commemorating the
Coronation of King George VI and
Queen Elizabeth, the reverse with the
Princesses, 1937, 3in (7.5cm) high.
£70–80 MGC

A pottery beehive honey pot,
commemorating the Coronation of
George VI and Queen Elizabeth,
1937, 5in (12.5cm) high.
£80–100 HUM

n American badge, commemorating
e Apollo 11 mission to the moon
1969, 6in (15cm) diam.
12–15 COB

The Sunday Times Magazine,
featuring the Royal Wedding of
Prince Charles and Lady Diana
Spencer, 1981, 11in (28cm) high.
£3–5 RTT

◄ A commemorative mug,
'The Pre-Nuptial Rehearsal Cup',
1990s, 4in (10cm) high.
£20–25 BRT

A Kevin Francis character jug,
depicting Sir Winston Churchill,
1980–90, 9¼in (24cm) high.
£180–200 BRT

A Staffordshire pottery dog, c1800, 4in (10cm) high.
£350–400 JHo

A pottery dog bowl, with flow blue decoration, 1840, 3in (7.5cm) high.
£450–500 GN

A pair of Staffordshire pottery spaniels, 1850, 11in (28cm) high.
£320–340 ACO

A Dean's velour Pluto, with moving tail, marked, 1928–30, 5in (12.5cm) high.
£400–450 DAn

A Poole Pottery free-standing bust of a dog, 1930, 6in (15cm) high.
£300–360 HarC
This model is usually designed as a wall-hanging.

A SylvaC puppy on a slipper, No. 31, c1947, 6in (15cm) long.
£40–50 AnS

A Czechoslovakian whistling egg cup, modelled as a dog, 1930s, 3in (7.5cm) long.
£60–80 BEV

A bisque tobacco jar, modelled as Bonzo, 1920s, 6in (15cm) high.
£200–240 BAO

◄ A Merrythought wind-up musical dog, 1964, 11in (28cm) high.
£55–65 Ann

A Bonzo postcard, 'I'm Struck On This Place', 1930s, 5½in (14cm) high.
£6–10 PC

A brushed nylon nodding Spaniel dog, c1950, 9in (23cm) high.
£25–35 PPH

A wax pedlar doll, with tray containing wares including a small doll, 1850, 14in (35.5cm) high.
£1,200–1,400 DAn

An Oriental jointed doll, with cloth body and composition hands and feet, in original outfit, Japanese, 1890, 11in (28cm) high.
£125–145 Ann

A Oriental souvenir composition boy doll, 1912, 7in (18cm) high.
£55–65 Ann

A German celluloid bent limb doll, 1930s, 16in (40.5cm) high.
£40–50 A&J

A Pedigree baby doll, c1950, 10in (25.5cm) high.
£40–50 A&J

An Old Cottage Toys tartan doll, with hard plastic head and felt jointed body, c1960, 9in (23cm) high.
£35–40 A&J

A Barbie No. 5 doll, dressed in Outdoor Life outfit, 1961, 11½in (29cm) high.
£150–170 PC

An Action Man Lifeguard doll, in original uniform with reproduction sword and spurs, 1978, 12in (30.5cm) high.
£75–85 CY
This Lifeguard's uniform is displayed on an Action Man figure that was first issued in 1978 with realistic hair, moving eagle eyes and gripping hands. The uniform first appeared in the early 1970s and remained unchanged until the line was discontinued in 1984. The reproduction sword and spurs reduce the value of this doll, had these items been original the value would be approximately £125.

A Sigikid artists' doll, Michelle, limited edition, German, 2000, 30in (76cm) high.
£375–395 Ann

A Lines Brothers dolls' house, 1923, 27in (68.5cm) high.
£500–600 HOB

A Brimtoy dolls' house tinplate dresser, 1950s, 4in (10cm) wide.
£12–15 A&J

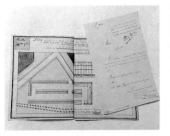

A plan of barracks and document, signed by Napoleon, 1809, 11½ x 8in (29 x 20.5cm).
£2,800–3,000 IQ

The Cliff Richard Show, a signed souvenir programme, 1960s, 11½ x 8in (29 x 20.5cm).
£25–30 BTC

Jim Henson surrounded by television puppets, a signed publicity photograph, 1987, 10 x 8in (25.5 x 20.5cm).
£120–150 IQ

▶ Lennox Lewis, a signed publicity photograph, 1990s, 10 x 8in (25.5 x 20.5cm).
£25–30 IQ

A scrap album, with large number of mounted chromolithographic scraps, including flowers, animals and Prince and Princess of Wales, plus an envelope of unmounted scraps, faded original cloth pages, 1890s, 12in (30.5cm) high.
£180–200 HAM

Elvis Presley, a signed photograph, c1968, 10 x 8in (25.5 x 20.5cm).
£450–500 IQ

A scrap book, 1940s, 16 x 10in (40.5 x 25.5cm).
£8–10 RTT

Buzz Aldrin, a signed monochrome photograph of Buzz walking on the moon, glazed and framed, with certificate of authenticity, c1970, 11in (28cm) high.
£950–1100 BKS

A framed Christmas card, signed by Princess Diana, 1981, 7 x 10in (18 x 25.5cm).
£1,200–1,500 HUX

Two Bergman bronze erotic figures, signed backwards, Vienna, 19thC, 3½in (9cm) high.
£500–600 TWr
Bergman always signed backwards on his erotic pieces, so that his name was not immediately recognized.

▶ A tie, hand-painted with a girl with 3D foam breasts, 1940–50s.
£110–135 SpM

Razzle pin-up magazine, 1949, 8 x 5in (20.5 x 12.5cm).
£3–5 RTT

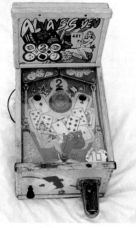

A bar-top pinball machine, decorated with pin-up figures, 1950s, 17in (43cm) high.
£200–240 EDO

Spick glamour magazine, Winter 1958, 7 x 5in (18 x 12.5cm).
£5–6 RTT

A pin-up lighter, in original box, 1950s.
£20–25 SpM

A pack of 'Naked Truth' king size playing cards, 1960s, 7in (18cm) high.
£35–45 PLB

Playboy magazine, October 1966, 11 x 8in (28 x 20.5cm).
£8–10 RTT

A pair of 3D Winky Vari-Vue eyeglasses, American, 1950s.
£38–42 SpM

▶ A Playboy Club glass ash tray, 1970s, 3¾in (9.5cm) square.
£12–15 PLB

A set of four American diner leather and chrome chairs, 1950s, damaged.
£120–140 TRA
In good condition, these items would have been valued at £280–320.

Two rocket lamps, with wooden frames and fibreglass shades, 1950s, tallest 44in (112cm) high.
£40–60 each RAT

◀ A Vallauris jug and set of eight cups, decorated with Le Vaucour pattern, made by Picasso's factory, 1950s, jug 9½in (24cm) high.
£250–300 PLB

An Italian glass vase, 1950s, 11in (28cm) high.
£65–75 PLB

A pair of Italian hand-painted vases, c1950, 9in (23cm) high.
£50–60 V&S

A pair of wall plaques, in the form of ballet dancers, 1950, 11in (28cm) high.
£100–120 pair JEZ

A leather Festival of Britain bag, 1951, 11in (28cm) high.
£50–60 PC

An ivory Barleycorn pattern chess set, c1860, largest 3½in (9cm) high.
£340–400 TMi

A set of Scottish ceramic spongeware carpet balls, c1880, 3in (7.5cm) diam.
£50–60 TWr

A Chad Valley ball game, Cocoa-nut Pitch, c1910, box 13in (33cm) wide.
£60–70 J&J

A Burnett Lucky Race tin board game, c1910, 12in (30.5cm) high.
£50–60 J&J

A Spilli-Wobble game, c1910, box 12in (30.5cm) wide.
£30–35 J&J

A Bystander jigsaw, by Capt Bruce Bairnsfather, entitled 'Now where does this blinkin' bit go?', 1918, 8½in (21.5cm) high.
£85–95 HUX

A Chad Valley Mickey Mouse Ring Quoits game, 1930s, 13½in (34.5cm) square.
£65–80 ARo

A Chad Valley Mickey Mouse Scatter Ball game, 1930s, 11½in (29cm) wide.
£65–80 ARo

A Glevum Games Bounce Ball game, by Roberts & Co, c1930, 8in (20.5cm) wide.
£12–15 J&J

A Waddington's Buccaneer game, 1950s, box 24in (61cm) wide.
£18–20 ARo

A French Tour du Monde en Vespa game, 1950s, box 18½in (47cm) wide.
£34–40 ARo

▶ A Dr Who jigsaw, 1979, box 8¼in (21cm) wide.
£10–12 UNI

A Regency drawn
stem wine glass,
5in (12.5cm) high.
£55–65 HEB

A pair of wine glasses,
on slender stems, 1830–40,
5in (12.5cm) high.
£90–110 HEB

A Bristol glass finger
bowl, c1840,
4¾in (12cm) diam.
£45–55 CB

A Victorian cranberry
glass dimple jug,
8in (20.5cm) high.
£200–225 BSA

A Victorian glass dump,
7in (18cm) high.
£110–130 OCAC

A French double-overlay
glass scent bottle,
c1880, 4in (10cm) high.
£700–800 BHa

A Richardson's hyacinth-
shaped glass vase,
c1885, 6in (15cm) high.
£170–190 GRI

A overlay glass scent
bottle, with silver top,
Birmingham 1890,
5in (12.5cm) high.
£250–300 BAO

A Clutha glass vase,
made for Liberty,
possibly designed by
Dr Christopher Dresser,
c1890, 6in (15cm) high.
£350–400 NCA

► A shaded crystal
glass scent bottle,
c1900, 5in (12.5cm) high.
£50–60 PIL

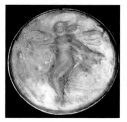

A Lalique glass and
metal button, decorated
with a fairy, c1920,
2in (5cm) diam.
£250–300 JBB

A Liberty Tudric pewter
and glass claret jug,
No. 0238, c1900,
10¾in (27.5cm) high.
£1,200–1,500 PVD

► A Jobling
glass bowl,
decorated with
Jazz pattern,
1930s, 8in
(20.5cm) diam.
£90–110 PIL

A Monart glass vase, 1930,
8in (20.5cm) high.
£100–120 TCG

A Vasart glass basket, signed,
c1950, 5in (12.5cm) high.
£35–40 BSA

A Whitefriars glass vase, 1960s,
6in (15cm) high.
£40–45 PrB

A hand-blown flared cylindrical
vase, 1950s, 12in (30.5cm) high.
£25–30 V&S

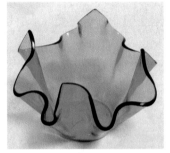

A glass handkerchief vase, 1950s,
4in (10cm) high.
£15–18 CSAC

A Whitefriars glass vase, 1960s,
7in (18cm) high.
£85–100 PrB

◄ An American hand-made cased
and etched glass bowl, Maiori
by Bebe Facente, c1986,
11in (28cm) high.
£500–550 FMa

A Vasart glass posy dish,
c1930, 5in (12.5cm) wide.
£45–55 BLA

An Italian crystal glass ashtray,
1950s, 7in (18cm) wide.
£45–55 V&S

A glass handkerchief vase, 1950s,
4in (10cm) high.
£18–22 CSAC

A Murano glass vase, by Nichetto
c1970, 9in (23cm) high.
£500–580 FMa

Games

Five multicoloured glass marbles, with transparent swirls, 1850s, ½in (18mm) diam.
£30–40 each MRW

A Jamaican palm wood and ebony chess board, 19thC, 19in (48.5cm) square.
£120–140 TMi

A Jacques & Son Staunton ebony and boxwood chess set, 1900, king 4in (10cm) high, with original box.
£500–600 TMi

An M.I.P. Co Home Sweet Home board game, c1910, 16in (40.5cm) square.
£12–15 J&J

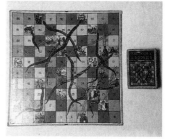

An M.I.P. Co Snakes and Ladders board game, c1920, 14in (35.5cm) square, with original box.
£12–15 J&J

► A Railway Brand Dominoes, in original red box, c1930, box 9in (23cm) long.
£10–12 RTT

A green-painted wooden pinball game, 1940s, 30in (76cm) long.
£40–45 TRA

A Bell Wagon Train game, 1950s, 14in (35.5cm) square.
£10–12 ARo

Cross Reference
See Colour Review

► A TV Sports Football computer game, for an IBM PC, 1988, 9 x 7in (23 x 18cm).
£3–5 MEx

► A brown Bakelite solitaire set, 1940s, 7in (18cm) diam.
£30–35 DHAR

An Atari Lynx Tournament Cyberball game, c1991, 5½ x 4½in (14 x 11.5cm).
£8–10 CGX

CARD GAMES

A Hovis advertising pack of playing cards, 1920–30, 4 x 3in (10 x 7.5cm).
£12–15 RTT

A Worshipful Company of Makers of Playing Cards pack of cards, decorated with soldiers of the Boer War, 1901, 4 x 3½in (10 x 9cm).
£50–60 MURR

A Worshipful Company of Makers of Playing Cards pack of cards, decorated with a classical female figure, 1902, 4 x 3½in (10 x 9cm).
£40–50 MURR

◀ A Ben Truman advertising pack of playing cards, c1960, 4 x 3in (10 x 7.5cm).
£8–10 RTT

▶ A Will's Happy Families card game, decorated in colours, 1920s, 4 x 3½in (10 x 9cm).
£60–75 MURR

JIGSAWS

A Chad Valley Great Western Railway wooden jig saw puzzle, The Cornish Riviera Express, 1920, 6 x 10in (15 x 25.5cm).
£30–35 COB

A Chad Valley official Great Western Railway wooden jigsaw puzzle, Oxford, by Fred Taylor, c1930, 12 x 15½in (30.5 x 39.5cm).
£125–145 DN

A Rowntrees Toffee four-piece paper puzzle, decorated in red, yellow and green, 1920s, 6 x 4in (15 x 10cm).
£40–50 MURR

A Chad Valley Great Western Railway wooden jigsaw puzzle, Henley, 1930s, 11 x 17in (28 x 43cm).
£45–50 COB

A Chad Valley official Cunard wooden jigsaw puzzle, RMS Queen Mary, by William McDowell, 10 x 19in (25.5 x 48.5cm).
£60–70 DN

Garden & Farm Collectables

A Georgian drenching horn, 18in (45.5cm) long.
£24–28 BSA
Drenching horns were used for giving medicine to cattle.

An Irish wooden peat barrow, 19thC, 36in (91.5cm) long.
£125–145 HCJ

A wrought-iron goose crook, with original ash handle, 19thC, 58in (147.5cm) long.
£200–240 MFB

A bone-handled pruning knife, c1860, 9in (23cm) long.
£40–48 Cot

An iron and wood rope-winder or hay-twister, mid-19thC, 17in (43cm) long.
£40–45 NEW

A clay spade, c1880, 57in (145cm) high.
£20–25 HCJ

A Devon pine sack carrier, with traces of original paint, 19thC, 41in (104cm) long.
£70–85 ESA

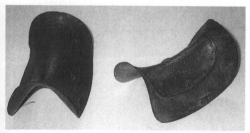

A pair of tin scythe shields, late 19thC, 4in (10cm) wide.
£75–85 AAN

▶ A brass garden syringe, late 19thC, 27in (68.5cm) long.
£25–30 GaB

A miniature straw skep, c1880, 9in (23cm) high.
£35–40 HUM

A stone garden roller, late 19thC, 35in (89cm) high.
£300–350 RECL

A cast-iron lawn roller, with oak leaf decoration, late 19thC, 18in (45.5cm) wide.
£220–250 DOR

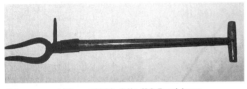

A heavy root lifter, c1900, 34in (86.5cm) long.
£65–75 Cot

A daisy grubber, stamped 'A. & F. Parkes', c1910, 13in (33cm) long.
£30–35 Cot

A French tin apple picker, c1920, 9in (23cm) long.
£30–35 Cot

A Barr's bulb planter, c1920, 38in (96.5cm) long.
£65–75 Cot

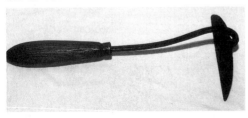

◄ A wooden-handled onion hoe, c1920, 14in (35.5cm) long.
£18–22 Cot

A bine cutter, late 19thC, 81in (205.5cm) long.
£45–55 HCJ

► Three Victorian plant cloches, without glass, damaged, 19thC, largest 19in (48.5cm) square.
£85–100 each HOP

A malt shovel, early 20thC, 43in (109cm) long.
£20–25 HCJ

A hop scuppit, early 20thC, 43in (109cm) high.
£40–45 HCJ

An earthenware flower pot, with glazed bark-moulded surface, c1900, 7in (18cm) high.
£30–35 IW

A hop scuppit, early 20thC, 35in (89cm) high.
£30–35 HCJ

A Carters seed display box, c1920, 22 x 16½in (56 x 42cm).
£85–95 HOP

A French green-painted tin herb collecting box, with three compartments, c1930, 16in (40.5cm) wide.
£35–40 Cot

A youth's or lady's fork, c1930, 37in (94cm) long.
£20–25 GaB

A metal hose winder, c1930, 18in (45.5cm) high.
£20–24 GaB

A Webb miniature lawn mower, 1950, 20in (51cm) high.
£120–150 JUN

◄ A pair of Astor garden shears, c1935, 16in (40.5cm) long.
£20–25 GaB

▶ A Hartley's English Garden Peas cardboard box, c1950, 10 x 12in (25.5 x 30.5cm).
£15–20 HOP

◄ A Rubber Bulb Bowl showcard, c1950, 6 x 9½in (15 x 24cm).
£12–15 HOP

A Covent Garden painted pine sign, c1945, 72in (183cm) long.
£400–450 HOP

SCULPTURE & STONEWARE

A stone trough, late 19thC,
27in (68.5cm) long.
£60–70 BYG

◀ A sandstone trough, 19thC,
36in (91.5cm) long.
£400–450 HOP

A limestone D-shaped
trough, 18thC,
23in (58.5cm) long.
£220–250 DOR

A cast lead and bronze
stand, in the form of
an archangel holding a
bowl-shaped platform,
19thC, 11in (28cm) high.
£275–300 TMA

A Portland stone
finial, surmounted by
a bud finial, 19thC,
56in (142cm) high.
£1,400–1,500 S(S)

A Forest of Dean stone drinking trough, 19thC,
46in (117cm) long.
£450–500 RECL

A pair of cast-iron garden
urns, late 19thC,
24in (61cm) high.
£350–420 CF

A pair of Victorian cast-
iron campana-shaped
urns, on square bases,
19thC, 30in (76cm) high.
£575–650 HOP

A mushroom staddle
stone, 19thC,
28in (71cm) high.
£150–175 HOP

A concrete bird bath,
20thC, 30in (76cm) high.
£200–220 NET

A mushroom staddle
stone, mid-19thC,
40in (101.5cm) high.
£300–350 RECL

▶ A pair of composition
planters, with plinths,
c1950, 36in (91.5cm) high.
£300–350 RECL

A pair of stone millstones, 19thC, 24in (61cm) diam.
£65–75 each HOP

◄ A pair of serpentine coloured marble urns, late 20thC, 19½in (49.5cm) diam.
£450–500 L

An iron garden stork, painted in naturalistic colours, 1920s, 20in (51cm) high.
£170–200 SWO

◄ A reconstituted stone gnome, c1900, 11in (28cm) high.
£40–45 HOP

SEATING

A Victorian wrought-iron garden bench, 73in (185.5cm) wide.
£450–500 DOR

A cast-iron Fern and Blackberry pattern garden bench, probably Coalbrookdale, c1850, 58in (147.5cm) wide.
£850–950 HOP

◄ A white-painted wrought-iron garden bench, with scrolled back and arms and slatted seat, on cabriole legs, 19thC, 50in (127cm) wide.
£475–525 L

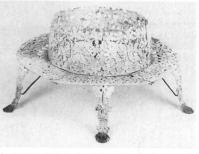

A Staffordshire pottery garden seat, decorated with foliage and flowers in pink, blue, yellow and green on a brown ground, c1840, 18in (45.5cm) high.
£1,000–1,100 JP

A folding mahogany conservatory bench, c1920, 43in (109cm) wide.
£250–300 WRe

A white-painted aluminium circular tree seat, the back cast with fruiting vines, 19thC, 55in (139.5cm) wide.
£230–260 L

Glass

A glass finger bowl, c1810,
5in (12.5cm) diam.
£20–25 PIL

A Yacht-pattern cut-glass cream
jug, with panels of diamonds,
c1815, 3in (7.5cm) high.
£350–400 Del
**Yacht-pattern is a term used for
jugs with a turned-in rim.**

A pair of hand-blown glass knops,
1820–30, 12in (30.5cm) long.
£75–90 WAB

An amethyst glass finger bowl,
1840, 4¾in (12cm) diam.
£60–70 CB

A matching pair of Victorian green
glass dumps, 7in (18cm) high.
£200–230 OCAC
Matching pairs are very rare.

A pair of Victorian green-
painted clear glass obelisks,
4in (10cm) high.
£120–140 HUM

A hand-blown glass
smoke bell, 1850,
5in (12.5cm) high.
£30–35 WAB
**Smoke bells were used
to collect the fumes
from oil lamps.**

A ewer-shaped opal
glass jug, with gilt rim,
1850, 13in (33cm) high.
£100–120 PIL

A Bohemian amber-flashed
glass vase and cover,
etched with a stag
hunting scene, 19thC,
14½in (37cm) high.
£300–360 AH

A pair of cut-glass
decanters, 1850,
11in (28cm) high.
£120–140 PIL

◀ A set of three
Victorian cranberry-
tinted glass light
shades, with
frilled rims and
engraved floral
decoration, largest
9in (23cm) diam.
£200–220 FHF

▶ A French glass lemonade
jug, with silver-coloured
metal mounts and handle,
with parcel-gilt interior,
19thC, 12in (30.5cm) high.
£700–770 HYD

A Victorian white satin glass jug, 6½in (16.5cm) high.
£14–16 TAC

A glass claret jug, with silver-mounted neck and cover with heraldic lion finial, by George Angell, 1850, 11in (28cm) high.
£725–800 L

A Continental green glass wine jug, with loop handle and silver mounts, painted with a coat of arms, reputedly that of Admiral Beatty, with floral spray and scroll work, 19thC, 15in (12.5cm) high.
£220–260 AH

A cranberry glass bell, with clear glass handle, c1875, 11in (28cm) high.
£130–150 GRI

A green glass dump, with internal floral decoration, c1875, 5in (12.5cm) high.
£160–180 GRI

A cut-glass tea caddy, c1880, 4in (10cm) high.
£35–45 WAB

A Clutha bulbous olive green glass vase, by Dr Christopher Dresser, with internal bubbles and gilt and opaque inclusions, 1880s, 8in (20.5cm) high.
£400–450 P(B)

A pressed-glass honey pot, with silver-plated knop in the shape of a bee, 1880, 4in (10cm) high.
£100–120 HUM

◄ A Burtles, Tate & Co press-moulded opalescent pink glass swan, c1885, 4in (10cm) high.
£125–150 CB

A cranberry glass preserve dish, the silver top applied with a leaf, and a silver spoon, c1895, 5in (12.5cm) high.
£100–120 GRI

A cranberry glass preserve dish, with silver-plated holder, probably by Thomas Webb & Sons, c1895, 6in (15cm) wide.
£120–150 GRI

An easel-back mirror, with repoussé pierced rococo silver mounts, Birmingham 1898, 14in (35.5cm) high.
£330–360 WW

A ruby glass scent bottle, encased in silver foliate holder, with a chain for a chatelaine, with a silver top, 1890, 1¾in (4.5cm) high.
£250–300 GRI

Items in the Glass section have been arranged in date order within each sub-section.

A Bohemian jug and two glasses, with white overlay, late 19thC, jug 11in (28cm) high.
£300–360 TWr

◀ A cranberry glass lamp, with white overlay, on a cast gilt-metal base, fitted for electricity, late 19thC, 19¾in (50cm) high.
£475–525 CGC

A glass bell, filled with coloured sands from Alum Bay, Isle of Wight, c1900, 3½in (9cm) high.
£35–40 HUM

A covered glass display jar, c1900, 12in (30.5cm) high.
£165–195 RUL

A Wright & Sons covered glass biscuit jar, c1900, 8in (20.5cm) high.
£50–60 SMI

A cameo glass vase, with ruby ground and white cyclamen pattern, probably by Thomas Webb & Sons, 1900, 6in (15cm) high.
£1,000–1,200 GRI

A cranberry glass ewer, with applied clear glass leaves and handle, probably Bohemian, 1900, 7in (18cm) high.
£150–170 GRI

A Bohemian cranberry glass vase, with Mary Gregory-style enamelled decoration, 1900, 12in (30.5cm) high.
£400–450 GRI

A cranberry glass jug, etched with ferns and vines, with clear glass handle, c1900, 7½in (19cm) high.
£200–220 Oli

A cranberry glass basket, with Art Nouveau-style decoration, c1900, 11in (28cm) high.
£385–450 GRI

▶ A Val St Lambert and Braga cameo glass vase, decorated with green poppies on a frosted ground, on gilt-bronze mount, marked, 1900, 9¼in (23.5cm) high.
£180–220 P(B)

◀ A pair of gourd-shaped cranberry glass vases, overlaid with trailing decoration, with silver rims, Birmingham 1903, 5¼in (13.5cm) high.
£220–260 CGC

An Art Nouveau iridescent glass vase, with pewter mount, 1900s, 10in (25.5cm) high.
£330–380 SWO

A Loetz glass vase, attributed to Michael Powolny, decorated with black vertical bands and neck rim, 1900s, 5½in (14cm) high.
£300–350 DN

▶ An Etling opalescent glass dish, moulded on the underside with frosted bands, moulded mark, 1920s, 13¾in (35cm) diam.
£80–100 DN

A Loetz-type iridescent green glass vase, mounted on an Elkington & Co silver-plated and pierced stand, early 20thC, 8in (20.5cm) high.
£60–70 Hal

A cranberry and clear glass hobnail-cut scent bottle, possibly Baccarat, 1910, 6in (15cm) high.
£180–200 GRI

An amethyst glass finger bowl, 1920, 4in (10cm) diam.
£75–85 HEB

A Carnival glass Vintage bowl, with blue base glass, 1920, 7in (18cm) diam.
£60–70 DBo

▶ A Thomas Webb & Sons Sunshine amber glass bowl, moulded with Old English Bull's Eye pattern, marked, late 1930s, 7¼in (18.4cm) diam.
£25–30 DEC

A wrythen-moulded pedestal bowl, 1920s, 8in (20.5cm) diam.
£190–220 RUSK

A Carnival glass vase, 1920s, 12in (30.5cm) high.
£25–30 TAC

A Daum pink glass bowl, etched mark, 1930s, 9in (23cm) diam.
£85–95 PIL

A Royal Brierley cut-glass flared bowl, designed by Keith Murray, on a faceted pedestal foot, signed, 1930s, 14in (35.5cm) diam.
£500–550 RUSK

A Stevens & Williams
green glass vase,
designed by Keith
Murray, c1930,
13in (33cm) high.
£180–220 PIL

▶ An Orrefors wavy-
edged clear glass bowl,
by Simon Gate, with
black foot, marked,
1930s, 5in (12.5cm) diam.
£45–55 RUSK

A Jobling pink frosted glass bowl,
decorated with Bird pattern,
1930s, 8½in (21.5cm) diam.
£85–95 PIL

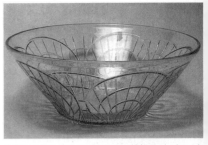

A Royal Brierley conical glass bowl, designed
by Keith Murray, with fan-cut decoration,
signed, 1930s, 12in (30.5cm) diam.
£680–720 RUSK

A Harbridge Crystal Co cut-glass dressing
table tray and matching candlesticks, 1930s,
5in (12.5cm) high.
£75–85 PIL

An Orrefors Graal-decorated
shallow bowl, by Edward Hald,
internally-decorated with
fish among reeds, marked,
1940s, 8¾in (22cm) diam.
£200–230 P(B)

A Murano set of glass sculptures, Fish Tank,
by Alfredo Barbini, depicting coloured fish
among green and brown seaweed, 1950,
largest 10 x 11in (25.5 x 28cm).
Small   £130–150
Medium   £200–220
Large   £2,200–2,500 FMa

A Continental red
and white glass vase,
probably Italian, 1950,
20in (51cm) high.
£50–60 V&S

A Mdina Glass blue
glass vase, 1970s,
10½in (26.5cm) high.
£120–150 MARK

An electroplated tantalus,
with three square cut-
crystal decanters with
silver Brandy, Whisky
and Sherry labels,
Birmingham 1965,
15½in (39.5cm) wide.
£275–300 CGC

A yellow and white
glass handkerchief vase,
1950–60, 5½in (14cm) high.
£12–15 CSAC

▶ An orange, yellow
and brown art glass
vase, by Anthony Stern,
c1994, 8in (20.5cm) high.
£110–130 AND

DRINKING GLASSES

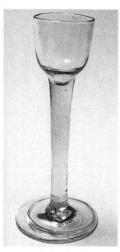

A cordial glass, with an ogee bowl on a plain stem and folded foot, c1730, 6in (15cm) high.
£300–350 JHa

▶ A wine glass, with waisted bucket bowl set on a mercury-gilded single series air-twist stem with a conical foot, c1745, 6in (15cm) high.
£300–360 JHa

A wine glass, with rib-moulded ovoid bowl on a plain stem and folded foot, c1740, 5¼in (13.5cm) high.
£210–240 BrW

A wine glass, on a plain stem with a folded foot, 1740–60, 7in (18cm) high.
£150–175 HEB

A wine glass, with ogee bowl on a plain stem and finely folded foot, c1740, 6¼in (16cm) high.
£150–180 BrW

A wine glass, with round funnel bowl set on a shoulder knopped multi-spiral air-twist stem and conical foot, c1745, 7in (18cm) high.
£300–360 JHa

A pair of wrythen dwarf ale glasses, mid-18thC, 6in (15cm) high.
£135–155 HEB

A wine glass, the round funnel bowl engraved with fruiting vine and a bird, on a plain stem, c1750, 6in (15cm) high.
£210–240 BrW

◀ A John Wilkes firing glass, etched around the bowl with the inscription 'Wilkes and Liberty No. 45', above a slight wrythen pattern, on a thick stem and foot, c1768, 4in (10cm) high.
£430–480 SAS
The drinking of loyal toasts by guests after dinner, followed by the bringing down of the drained glass upon the table with some force, earned these toasting glasses the name of firing glasses because the sound was not unlike that of a volley of muskets.

A wine glass, with faceted stem and foot, c1770, 5½in (14cm) high.
£180–200 HEB

A dram glass, with drawn trumpet bowl and firing foot, c1770, 4in (10cm) high.
£100–120 JHa

A George III wine glass, with double air-twist stem on a semi-domed foot, 5½in (14cm) high.
£130–150 AG

A George III wine glass, with white and plain air-twist stem on a domed foot, 7in (18cm) high.
£120–140 AG

A drinking goblet, c1830, 6in (15cm) high.
£50–60 PIL

A George III wine glass, with double air-twist stem on a semi-conical foot, 6in (15cm) high.
£140–160 AG

A George III green wine glass, with a drawn stem on a folded foot, 5in (12.5cm) high.
£90–110 HEB

◀ A pair of Georgian glass goblets, with thistle-shaped bowls, on baluster stems and square star-cut bases, damaged, engraved and dated 1829, 5in (12.5cm) high.
£220–250 Bea(E)

▶ A rummer, with bucket bowl and bladed knop stem, diamond-point engraved 'W and M Thomas 1838', 5in (12.5cm) high.
£100–120 BrW

A George III ale glass, engraved with wheat ears and vine leaves, with a tapered stem on a semi-domed foot, 5½in (14cm) high.
£200–220 AG

A wrythen-moulded ale glass, c1800, 5in (12.5cm) high.
£50–60 JHa

A drinking goblet, c1860, 6in (15cm) high.
£24–28 PIL

A set of six Continental engraved wine glasses, c1880, 5in (12.5cm) high.
£75–85 PIL

◀ A cranberry glass wine glass, on a clear stem and foot, late 19thC, 5in (12.5cm) high.
£25–30 HEB

A Bohemian flashed cut and engraved glass goblet, 19thC, 5½in (14cm) high.
£120–140 SWO

A green wine glass, 19thC, 5in (12.5cm) high.
£60–70 HEB

A wine glass, with panel-cut bowl, on a hollow-cut stem, probably Bohemian, c1890, 5½in (14cm) high.
£90–110 GRI

◀ A set of eight liqueur glasses, possibly Stuart or Walsh, 1910, 3½in (9cm) high.
£65–75 PIL

▶ An amethyst wine glass, c1930, 5in (12.5cm) high.
£90–110 HEB

A cranberry glass champagne tumbler, with enamelled decoration commemorating Queen Victoria's Diamond Jubilee, 1897, 3½in (9cm) high.
£120–150 GRI

A gilded goblet, possibly French, c1900, 6in (15cm) high.
£100–120 PIL

A Stuart Crystal Prince of Wales Caernarfon Castle goblet, No. 94 from a limited edition of 100, 1969, 9in (23cm) high, with original box.
£140–160 SWO

MONART/VASART

In 1921 Spanish glass maker Salvador Ysart (1887–1955) was employed by John Moncrieff Ltd, Perth, Scotland, to create a new range of art glass. Monart glass (a composite name derived from the factory and the designer) was launched in 1924. Simple, free-blown shapes set off richly-mottled cased glassware, inspired by textile patterns, and flecked with glowing coloured enamels and metallic particles. Monart sold at Liberty's in London and Tiffany's in New York.

In 1947 Ysart and his family set up their own glassworks in Perth called Ysart Brothers. The company made Vasart glass similar in style to Monart, though more standardized and less opulent. In 1956 the factory changed its name to Vasart, and in 1980 it was taken over and renamed Stuart Strathearn Ltd.

A Monart pink glass vase, c1930, 8in (20.5cm) high.
£300–350 TWr

A Monart Glass label.

A Monart glass vase, 1930s, 10in (25.5cm) high.
£145–165 BSA

A Monart yellow, brown and aventurine vase, 1930s, 5in (12.5cm) high.
£165–185 SAN

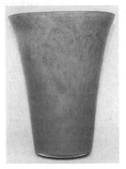

A Scottish green-tinted bubbly art glass vase, ground pontil mark, probably Monart, 20thC, 9¾in (25cm) high.
£90–100 Hal(C)

A Monart orange glass vase, decorated with white swirls, 1930s, 7½in (19cm) high.
£240–280 SAN

A Monart blue and aventurine glass vase, 1948, 8in (20.5cm) high.
£180–220 TCG

A Vasart pale blue lamp base, decorated with red, orange, brown and blue splatter pattern, 1950s, 12in (30.5cm) high.
£100–120 SAN

► A Monart lilac, brown and aventurine glass fruit bowl, 1930s, 7½in (19cm) diam.
£145–165 SAN

◄ A Monart multi-coloured glass vase, mid-20thC, 5½in (14cm) high.
£380–450 TCG

WHITEFRIARS

In 1834, wine merchant James Powell (1744–1840) purchased a glassworks in Whitefriars, London. James Powell & Sons manufactured architectural, industrial and domestic products and specialized in coloured glass. The company developed a yellow uranium glass known as Topaz, and produced stained-glass windows for leading artists of the Pre-Raphaelite Movement, as well as tableware for William Morris. From the 1870s Harry James Powell (1853–1922), a trained chemist, devised more new colours, including straw opal and blue opal, used to make Venetian-inspired flute vases and wavy rim goblets. He created glasses inspired by Roman, Egyptian and other ancient prototypes, as well as Art Nouveau pieces. After his death the factory moved to Wealdstone in Middlesex.

The 1920s and 30s saw the development of ribbed and ribbon-trailed vases in cool clear colours, and simple modernist shapes, as well as brilliantly coloured Cloudy and Streaky glass. In the post-war period, Whitefriars produced Scandinavian-inspired thick-walled glass.

Geoffrey Baxter (1922–95) was recruited as a designer in 1954 and in the 1960s launched his Textured range made from glass blown into textured moulds. Colours varied from cinnamon and pewter, to psychedelic tones such as tangerine and kingfisher blue. Shapes ranged from the cylindrical Bark vases, whose moulded surface resembled tree bark, to abstract designs such as the Banjo and the Drunken Bricklayer vase. In the 1970s Whitefriars focused on studio-inspired glass, and in 1980 the factory closed down.

◄ A James Powell & Sons, Whitefriars, ribbed emerald glass vase, designed by Harry Powell, c1919, 12in (30.5cm) high.
£300–350 RUSK

A pair of James Powell & Sons, Whitefriars, wavy rim glass bonbon dishes, 1910, 4in (10cm) high.
£35–45 PIL

A James Powell & Sons, Whitefriars, ribbon-trailed sapphire blue glass vase, 1930s, 7in (18cm) high.
£60–70 TCG

A James Powell & Sons, Whitefriars, ogee-shaped green glass rummer, on a knopped stem, 1930s, 6in (15cm) high.
£70–80 RUSK

A James Powell & Sons, Whitefriars, blue glass bowl, moulded with a wavy pattern, 1930s, 9in (23cm)
£55–65 BSA

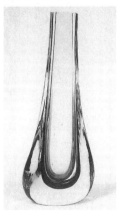

A James Powell & Sons, Whitefriars, amber glass lamp base, moulded with a wavy pattern, 1930, 11in (28cm) high.
£110–125 TCG

▶ A James Powell & Sons, Whitefriars, lobed sapphire blue glass bowl, designed by James Hogan, c1940, 8in (20.5cm) wide, with Manchester Exhibition label, 1996.
£55–65 RUSK

A James Powell & Sons, Whitefriars, amber glass sherry set, designed by Barnaby Powell, marked, 1935, decanter 8in (20.5cm) high.
£175–225 RUSK

A James Powell & Sons, Whitefriars, golden amber glass vase, designed by Frank Hill, with horizontal optical ribbing, 1931, 8in (20.5cm) high.
£100–125 RUSK

◀ A James Powell & Sons, Whitefriars, sea-green-on-blue flared glass bowl, with rigaree foot, 1930s, 13in (33cm) diam
£180–210 RUSK

A James Powell & Sons, Whitefriars, green glass vase moulded with a wavy pattern, 1930, 6in (15cm) high.
£35–45 TCG

A James Powell & Sons, Whitefriars, clear-cased blue glass vase, with blue stars, 1960, 7¾in (19.5cm) high.
£10–15 Law

A James Powell & Sons, Whitefriars, clear-cased brown and green streaked glass vase, 1966, 7¼in (18cm) high.
£15–20 Law

A James Powell & Sons, Whitefriars, blue-tinted Drunken Bricklayer vase, designed by Geoffrey Baxter, 1966, 13½in (34.5cm) high.
£400–450 RUSK

A James Powell & Sons, Whitefriars, clear-cased brown glass vase, designed by Geoffrey Baxter, 1967–73, 6¼in (16cm) high.
£60–75 MARK

Hairdressing & Cosmetics

Whitaker & Co Genuine Bear's Grease pot lid, decorated with a bear in ravine, with gilt-lined rim, slight damage, 1845, 4in (10cm) diam.
£550–600 SAS

A Ross & Sons Genuine Bear's Grease pot lid, decorated with a bear hunting scene, with gilt-lined rim, c1850, 3in (7.5cm) diam.
£250–275 SAS

A Halstaff & Hannaford calamander wood dressing box, with brass borders and initials, the interior with cut-glass and silver-mounted fittings with engraved decoration, including a beaker, canisters, bottles, jars and boxes, 1850–51, 14¼in (36cm) wide.
£1,400–1,600 L

An American multi-coloured ceramic pot lid, probably by Bates, Walker & Co, 'The Buffalo Hunt', slight damage, 1857–78, 5in (12.5cm) diam.
£1,200–1,400 BBR

In the 19th century cold cream, toothpaste and bear's grease (used by gentlemen to oil the hair) were supplied in ceramic pots with transfer-decorated lids. Rare pot lids such as the examples shown here can fetch high sums.

Rimmels Coral Tooth Paste pot lid, decorated in colours with shells within a yellow border, slight damage, 1860–90, 3in (7.5cm) diam.
£550–650 BBR

A Blondeau & Cie Vinolia Shaving Soap pot lid, 1900–10, 3in (7.5cm) diam.
£24–28 BBR

A Portuguese cold cream pot and lid, depicting an Edwardian lady, inscribed in Portuguese, 1900–10, 3½in (9cm) diam.
£375–400 BBR

A seven day cut-throat razor set, in an oak box, c1900, 7in (18cm) long.
£120–135 MB

French hair washing stand, early 20thC, 40in (101.5cm) high.
£350–400 POSH

A bone-handled badger hair travelling shaving brush, 1910, 5½in (14cm) long.
£30–35 DHo

A vanity set, including cut-glass and pink enamel scent bottle and powder jar, brushes, comb and mirror, c1925, 12 x 16in (30.5 x 40.5cm), in original case.
£150–175 JACK

Two face cream tins, Amoline Skin Food and Rose's Cold Cream, 1930s, 2in (5cm) diam.
£5–7 each YR

A plastic comb, with sliding metal cover, 1940s, 4in (10cm) long.
£25–30 CHU

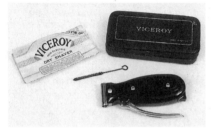

A Viceroy burgundy plastic and chrome clockwork razor, 1940s, 5in (12.5cm) long, with original box.
£35–40 PC

▶ A clockwork razor, with see-through plastic case, made in Monaco, c1950, 4½in (11.5cm) long.
£50–60 PC
This is a demonstration model.

◀ A pair of chrome and purple vinyl-covered hairdresser's chairs, c1960, 38in (96.5cm) high.
£200–240 NET

A Pears' Spraygloss hairspray, 1930s, 3in (7.5cm) high, with original box.
£15–20 YR

A pair of ladies' hair clippers, 1930–40s, 5in (12.5cm) long, with original box.
£15–20 RTT

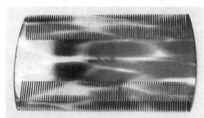

A Fair Maid plastic tortoiseshell dust comb, 1960s, 3½in (9cm) long.
£6–8 CHU

A Rowntrees lady's handbag advertising mirror, 1920s–30s, 3in (7.5cm) high.
£25–30 MURR

A Keika London Whirlwind hair dryer chair, 1950s, 61in (155cm) high.
£350–420 ZOOM

A Stratton plastic comb, in lacquered brass cover, c1950, 4in (10cm) long.
£25–30 CHU

Handbags & Luggage

HANDBAGS

steel-beaded and rochet bag, c1800, n (10cm) long.
80–100 JPr

A crocheted purse, with ormolu baubles and closure, c1820, 5in (12.5cm) long.
£65–80 JPr

A metal-framed beaded handbag, with red, yellow, green and blue pattern, 1820–30, 8in (20.5cm) long.
£220–240 JPr

A steel-framed beaded purse, with mauve, purple, orange and green houses pattern, 1820–40, 4in (10cm) long.
£60–70 JPr

petit point canvas bag, ecorated with pink, ellow and blue floral attern on a beige ground, vith ormolu mount, 1840, 7in (18cm) long.
160–180 JPr

A woolwork silk-lined bag, with red, yellow, black and brown pattern, slight damage, c1870, 8in (20.5cm) long.
£35–40 DE

A beaded sovereign purse, with blue, yellow, red and white pattern, c1840, 10in (25.5cm) long.
£65–80 JPr

► A metal-beaded bag, with gold-plated mount, 1920–30, 9in (23cm) long.
£70–80 JPr

◄ A metal-beaded Art Deco bag, 1930s, 7in (18cm) long.
£85–100 DE

A black velvet handbag, with ornate silver-plated clasp, c1860, 7in (18cm) long.
£55–65 JPr

A petit point bag, embroidered in colours on a black ground, with a metal clasp, c1920, 6in (15cm) high.
£50–60 BAO

A black grosgrain silk bag, with Bakelite frame, 1930s, 8in (20.5cm) long.
£40–45 JPr

A silver-plated chain mail purse, c1930, 4in (10cm) long.
£40–50 JPr

A black suede leather handbag, 1940s, 8in (20.5cm) long.
£35–40 JPr

A black needlepoint bag, with multicoloured pattern, c1950, 6in (15cm) long.
£25–30 DE

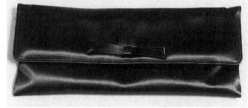

A Jane Shilton brown satin evening bag, 1950s, 12in (30.5cm) wide, with box.
£15–20 DE

A clear lucite handbag, with carved metal top, containing chiffon scarf, 1950s, 10in (25.5cm) wide.
£185–200 ArD

▶ An American straw beach bag, hand-embroidered with coloured yarn 'El Alamo, San Antonio, Texas', 1950s, 18in (45.5cm) high.
£55–65 SpM

LOCATE THE SOURCE
The source of each illustration in Miller's can be found by checking the code letters below each caption with the Key to Illustrations, pages 476–484.

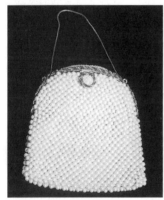

A faux pearl satin-lined evening bag, late 1950s, 8in (20.5cm) long.
£55–65 DE

▶ An American ivory-coloured leather handbag, with working watch and studs, marked 'Mitch' inside, 1950s, 11in (28cm) high.
£200–240 SpM

An American Lite Brite glow-in-the-dark handbag, decorated with a sleeping Mexican pattern in fluorescent beads on fabric, 1950s, 13in (33cm) long.
£70–80 SpM

LUGGAGE & TRAVEL GOODS

leather bucket hat box, 1860,
4in (35.5cm) high.
165–185 SPT

A Wells & Son leather hat box,
1870, 12in (30.5cm) high.
£90–110 SPT

A Coracle wicker railway picnic
hamper, with enamel fittings, 1880,
14in (35.5cm) wide.
£120–150 STS

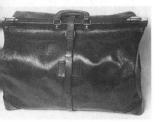

leather bag, with brass fittings,
880, 27in (68.5cm) wide.
250–280 SPT

A metal deed box, inscribed
'J. R. Allsopp', with key, 1890,
16in (40.5cm) wide.
£15–20 AL

A Goyard wooden hat box, 1890,
11in (28cm) high.
£35–45 SPT

brown leather case, containing three glass spirit
ottles with silver tops, London 1906, 6in (15cm) high.
170–200 STS

A French brown leather case
trunk, with brass fittings,
1890, 25in (63.5cm) wide.
£150–180 SPT

hree brown leather collar boxes, 1900s,
argest 8in (20.5cm) diam.
30–35 SPT

A canvas-covered automobile
trunk, 1910, 33in (84cm) wide.
£100–120 CYA

A Drew & Sons tea-for-
two Enroute wicker
travelling hamper, with
ceramic fittings, c1910,
13in (33cm) high.
£340–400 STS

A cream leather suitcase, with fitted toiletries, 1920s, 18in (45.5cm) wide.
£80–100 CYA

A leather luggage container lid, 1920s, 15in (38cm) diam.
£15–20 COB

An A to Z travelling picnic set for two, 1920s, 12in (30.5cm) wide.
£450–500 SPT

A brass soup thermos, with leather travelling case, 1920s, 12in (30.5cm) high.
£160–180 SPT

A Leuchars blue leather vanity case, with brass fittings and cover, 1920s, 11¾in (30cm) wide.
£110–130 SPT

A wooden hat box, 1930s, 11in (28cm) high.
£55–65 SPT

A cream vellum hat box, 1930s, 9in (23cm) high.
£50–60 SPT

▶ A brown leather suitcase, c1930, 27in (68.5cm) wide, with reproduction stickers.
£80–95 BYG

A Barrat & Sons leather glove box and gloves, 1940s, 11in (28cm) wide.
£50–60 SPT

A Brexton picnic set, commemorating the 1953 Coronation, with blue fittings, 19½in (49.5cm) wide.
£100–125 PPH

A Sirram picnic set, in green fitted case, 1960s, 19½in (49.5cm) wide.
£45–55 PC

Heating

Until supplanted by the introduction of television and central heating, the fireplace was the traditional entrepiece of the home. Most of the objects shown here date from the 18th and 19th centuries. Under the influence of Robert Adam, the large stone hearths of the early 18th century were replaced by smaller fireplaces, arched openings and raised metal grates. Cast-iron was a favourite Victorian material because it was durable, could be shaped into innumerable designs and retained the heat. Grates led to the development of free-standing fenders that surrounded the fireplace and prevented hot ash and cinders from spilling over into the room. Made from brass as well as cast-iron, fenders could be extremely elaborate, their pierced borders (some over twelve inches high) were both decorative and practical, protecting long flowing skirts from sweeping into the flames.

A host of furnishings were created for the fireplace. Fire dogs or andirons were used to support logs in the hearth, though as coal began to supersede wood they became increasingly ornamental. The popularity of coal led to the development of coal boxes and scuttles, shown in this section in copper, brass and wood. At the Great Exhibition of 1851, a Mr Purdon showed a portable coal box with a detachable liner and sloping lid that concealed the coal from view and prevented dust escaping. Often produced in wood, with brass fittings, the 'purdonium' became a favourite scuttle in Victorian and Edwardian homes. Fire irons included poker, shovel, tongs and sometimes a brush. When not in use, these were supported on fire-iron rests (developed from andirons). Purpose-built stands, supplied with the sets, did not become commonplace until the 1920s. Pot hangers and chimney cranes were used to suspend pots over the fire, and portable trivets (metal stands) were designed to support anything from kettles to flat irons. Fire screens, often containing fine needlework produced by the ladies of the house, provided a shield from the heat of the flames and concealed the empty fireplace during the summer months. With growing interest in interior decoration, vintage fireplace furniture is very collectable. As with all functional items, purchases should be carefully checked for signs of damage that would render them unusable, and beware of modern reproductions.

COAL BOXES & SCUTTLES

A copper coal scuttle, with swing handle, repaired, 1860, 14in (35.5cm) high.
£140–160 ASH

An early Georgian copper coal scuttle, with swing handle and compartment for shovel, on four brass feet, 14in (35.5cm) high.
£100–120 HCJ

A brass coal bin, c1810, 24in (61cm) high.
£200–230 ASH

▶ A brass coal scuttle, with turned wood handle and coal scoop, 1860, 18in (45.5cm) high.
£300–350 ASH

Cross Reference
See Colour Review

◄ A Benham & Froud brass coal hod, shaped as a seed pod, with a frilled rim and circular hinged lid, with scrolling wrought-iron mounts and supports, c1880, 22¾in (58cm) high.
£330–360 L&T

A copper coal scuttle, c1900, 19in (48.5cm) high.
£200–230 WAC

A mahogany purdonium with brass handle and tin liner, c1900, 16in (40.5cm) high.
£120–140 ASH

FENDERS & GRATES

A cast-iron fire grate, with pot rest, c1750, 23in (58.5cm) high.
£365–395 SEA

A cast-iron fire grate, c1820, 29in (73.5cm) high.
£500–600 WRe

A Victorian cast-iron arched fireplace, 38in (96.5cm) high.
£600–650 WEL

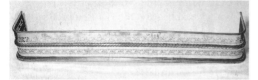

► A cut and pierced brass fender, c1870, 50in (127cm) wide.
£340–380 ASH

A William IV cut brass fender, with ropetwist decoration, 1835, 58in (147.5cm) wide.
£350–380 ASH

A cast-iron fender, with trellis pattern, 1870, 52in (132cm) wide.
£200–230 ASH

An Empire-style cast-iron fender, c1870, 30in (76cm) wide
£230–260 ASH

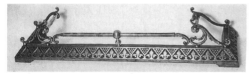

Miller's is a price GUIDE not a price LIST

A cast-iron fender with brass ball and rail supports, 1880, 56in (142cm) wide.
£350–380 ASH

► An Arts and Crafts fire grate with copper detail, 1900, 30in (76cm) high.
£400–450 ASH

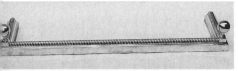

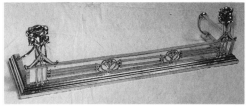

cast brass fender, with ball end stops and gadrooned
etail to the kerb, 1900, 54in (137cm) wide.
20–360 ASH

An Art Nouveau brass fender, c1900,
52in (132cm) wide.
£450–550 NOST

◀ An Art Nouveau cast-iron and copper fender,
c1900, 54in (137cm) wide.
£345–385 ASH

IRE DOGS & FIRE IRON RESTS

pair of cast-iron fire dogs,
3thC, 15½in (39.5cm) high.
350–400 SEA

A pair of Georgian cast-iron fire dogs,
10in (25.5cm) high.
£45–55 HCJ

A pair of wrought-
iron fire dogs, 1780,
12in (30.5cm) high.
£140–160 ASH

pair of brown glazed earthen-
are fire dogs, with mask and
nthemion decoration, mid-19thC,
in (15cm) high.
100–125 MTa

A pair of cast brass fire dogs, with
cabriole legs, log rests replaced,
1860, 24in (61cm) high.
£300–340 ASH

A pair of Victorian cast-iron fire
dogs, 16in (40.5cm) high.
£45–55 HCJ

◀ A pair of Adam-style
brass fire iron rests, c1870,
16in (40.5cm) high.
£190–210 ASH

▶ A pair of late Victorian brass fire
iron rests, 14in (35.5cm) high.
£160–180 ASH

FIRE IRONS

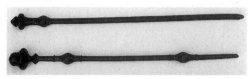

Two Victorian cast-iron pokers, 18in (45.5cm) long.
£12–15 each HCJ

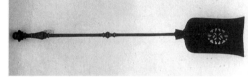

A Victorian fireplace shovel, 31in (78.5cm) long.
£18–22 HCJ

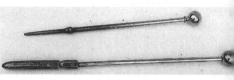

Two brass pokers, 19thC, largest 19in (48.5cm) long
£20–22 each HCJ

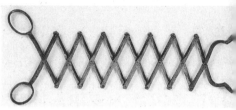

A pair of extendable fireplace tongs, 18thC,
12in (30.5cm) extended.
£250–275 SEA

FIRE SCREENS

An Arts and Crafts copper fire
screen, depicting a sailing ship,
c1910, 35in (89cm) high.
£200–230 WAC

A cast brass and steel fire screen
1920, 30in (76cm) high.
£250–280 ASH

◀ A needlework firescreen, worked
in coloured wools with silk highlights
depicting a bouquet of roses and
other flowers, the Arts and Crafts-
style mahogany frame with narrow
shelf top and splay feet, late
19thC, 34in (86.5cm) high.
£160–180 WW

POT HANGERS

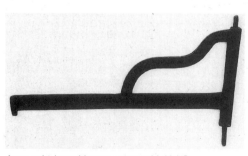

A wrought-iron chimney crane, mid-19thC,
27in (68.5cm) long.
£125–150 SEA

A cast-iron ratchet pot hook, c1710, 45in (114.5cm) long
£365–395 SEA

A cast-iron pot hanger, c1860, 43in (109cm) long.
£40–50 HCJ

STANDS & TRIVETS

An iron trivet, 18thC, 6in (15cm) high.
£30–35 HCJ

An iron pot-warming stand,
18thC, 8in (20.5cm) high.
£40–45 HCJ

◄ A cast brass and wrought-iron
trivet, 1760–80, 8in (20.5cm) high.
£90–110 AnSh

► A Georgian cast brass and
wrought-iron trivet, c1820,
5in (12.5cm) high.
£200–225 SEA

A wrought-iron long-handled pan
trivet, c1750, 18in (45.5cm) high.
£200–230 SEA

STOVES & HEATERS

A French cast-iron
tove, late 19thC,
8in (45.5cm) high.
200–250 B&R
his stove was
robably from a large
ouse where it would
ave been used to
eat flat irons.

A yacht-shaped
hrome-plated electric fire,
950s, 30in (76cm) high.
400–450 ZOOM

A French cast-iron
stove, 19thC,
25in (63.5cm) high.
£150–175 DOR

► A cast-iron
conservatory paraffin
heater, c1870,
21in (53.5cm) high.
£300–375 TWr

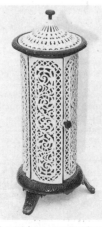

A cast-iron conservatory
heater, c1900,
36in (91.5cm) high.
£120–150 JUN

► A ceramic wood-
burning stove, 1970s,
127in (322.5cm) high.
£300–350 BYG

Horse Brasses

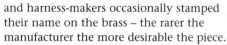

Horse brasses became popular in the 19th century, when it became customary to decorate the harnesses of cart horses with a range of shining plaques, including pendent brasses, studs, nose pieces and swingers or flyers that were attached to the top of the bridle or placed on the saddle. Before 1850 brasses were made of solid metal and pierced by hand. In the second half of the 19th century they were cast in wooden moulds. Innumerable designs were produced. Sun, moon and stars were favourite images, as were playing card motifs (clubs, diamonds, hearts, spades), and appropriate lucky symbols such as the horseshoe. Brewery dray horses might be decorated with barrel-shaped studs,

and harness-makers occasionally stamped their name on the brass – the rarer the manufacturer the more desirable the piece.

Commemorative horse brasses, celebrating royal and military events, can also be very collectable. When the use of working horses declined after WWI horse brasses were increasingly made as tourist souvenirs and decorative pieces, destined to be hung not on horses, but on the walls of houses, hotels and, most typically, pubs.

Modern reproductions tend to be stamped from thin sheets of brass and machine made design details are less sharp; they are lighter in weight and the backs tend to be hollowed out and pitted.

A Victorian brass swinger, with shield design, 3in (7.5cm) high.
£25–30 PJo

A Victorian brass swinger, with wheel design, 3in (7.5cm) high.
£25–30 PJo
Swingers were only made until around 1900. The Scottish swingers were made of nickel and stuck into the straw collars. English swingers were screwed into the leather.

A Victorian brass swinger, with three sun discs, 3in (7.5cm) high.
£25–30 HBr

A set of brewery horse brasses, on original leather martingale, 19thC, 35in (89cm) long.
£120–135 MFB

A cast heart horse brass, c1877, 3½in (9cm) high.
£65–75 HBr

▶ A horse brass, with red and white painted centre, c1880, 3in (7.5cm) diam.
£28–33 MFB

Harness decoration

Swingers or fly-terrets usually fix to the top of the heavy horse bridle. Larger ones, such as multiple bells, were often placed on the saddle. Usually a matching pendent brass was produced, so even horses had matching accessories!

Harness makers advertised their business by placing their names on the newly-completed sets of harness – either on noseband brasses, studs, pendent brasses (or face pieces), rosettes or on the hames.

A swinger, with flowers
of unity design, late
19thC, 4in (10cm) high.
£24–28 HBr

A horse brass, on original
leather strap, 19thC,
11in (28cm) high.
£40–50 MFB

A horse brass, depicting
Lord Baden Powell,
commemorating the
siege of Mafeking,
c1900, 4in (10cm) high.
£40–45 PJo

► A swinger, with
shield design, c1900,
4in (10cm) high.
£18–20 HBr

Two horse brasses, with
crescent and star design,
on original leather strap,
19thC, 10in (25.5cm) long.
£55–65 MFB

A Victorian Scottish
nickel terret, with
geometric design,
5in (12.5cm) high.
£15–20 PJo

Three brewery barrel
studs, late 19thC,
largest 3in (7.5cm) high.
£7–20 each HBr

A horse brass, with
Prince of Wales' feathers
design, late 19thC,
3½in (9cm) high.
£30–35 HBr

A Victorian Scottish
nickel sun disc terret,
5in (12.5cm) high.
£15–20 PJo

A swinger, with two crowns, commemorating the coronation of Edward VII in 1902, 4in (10cm) high.
£55–65 HBr

A commemorative horse brass, painted in red, white and blue, c1910, 3½in (9cm) high.
£30–35 HBr

A donkey brass, with a horse head design, 1930, 3in (7.5cm) high.
£5–8 PJo

▶ A horse brass, depicting Sir Winston Churchill within victory 'V', 1936, 5in (12.5cm) high.
£45–50 PJo

A horse brass, with a central photograph, commemorating the coronation of Edward VII in 1902, 3½in (9cm) high.
£130–150 HBr

A cast hide-shaped horse brass, with maker's name, c1910, 3½in (9cm) high.
£75–85 HBr

A horse brass, with a portrait of Tom Pinch, commemorating Dickens centenary, c1920, 4in (10cm) high.
£5–8 PJo

A pair of heavy horse rosettes, with central photographs, commemorating the coronation of Edward VII in 1902, 3½in (9cm) diam.
£130–150 HBr

A nose-piece horse brass, with harness maker's name, c1914, 3in (7.5cm) high.
£60–75 HBr
The price depends on the scarcity of the maker.

An Isle of Man horse brass, 1920s, 3½in (9cm) high.
£5–8 PJo

A pony brass, with squirrel design within a stirrup, c1930, 2in (5cm) high.
£5–8 PJo

A horse brass, depicting Field Marshall Montgomery, commemorating El Alamein, c1945, 4in (10cm) high.
£25–30 PJo

A horse brass, commemorating the Festival of Britain 1951, 4in (10cm) high.
£20–25 PJo

A beaded evening bag,
with embossed silver
frame, worked with a
village scene, 1820–40,
6in (15cm) wide.
£180–200 JPr

A beaded evening bag, with jewelled
clasp, c1880, 7in (18cm) wide.
£250–280 BAO

A lady's crocodile
Gladstone bag, by Davis,
Piccadilly, with silk
lining and brass fittings,
c1900, 15in (38cm) wide.
£220–250 STS

◄ A beaded evening
bag, early 19thC,
6in (15cm) wide.
£160–180 JPr

A carpet bag, with leather fittings, 1890,
16in (40.5cm) wide.
£40–45 SPT

An Art Deco python-skin clutch bag, c1930,
with original box, 13in (33cm) wide.
£60–70 DE

A German beaded dolly
bag, with drawstring
crocheted top, dated
'1913', 7in (18cm) wide.
£180–200 JPr

A hand-painted silk bag,
by Waldy, London, 1930,
9in (23cm) wide.
£30–35 DE

An Austrian needlepoint
evening bag, 1950s,
7in (18cm) wide.
£75–90 JPr

An American pink fabric
and wooden umbrella-
shaped handbag, with
mirror on inside flap,
1950s, 21in (53.5cm) high.
£250–300 SpM

An American fabric bucket
bag, lined with Pony
Express fabric, 1950s,
11in (28cm) wide.
£75–85 SpM

An American straw
fish-shaped bag, with
blue patent leather
handles, 1950s,
12in (30.5cm) wide.
£85–100 SpM

An iron and copper trivet,
early 19thC, 11in (28cm) high.
£170–190 NEW

An embossed brass double-
hinged coal box, c1870,
19in (48.5cm) high.
£450–550 TWr

A Victorian cast-iron fireplace,
c1880, 38in (96.5cm) wide.
£500–600 WEL

◀ An embossed brass coal bin, with
tin liner, 1880, 18in (45.5cm) high.
£230–260 ASH

A sarcophagus-shaped copper coal
bin, with cast brass feet and acorn
finial, c1880, 26in (66cm) wide.
£280–320 ASH

An Arts and Crafts oak and copper
fire screen, decorated with a
stylized peacock, late 19thC,
18½in (47cm) wide.
£350–400 P(B)

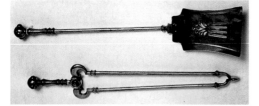

◀ A pair
of copper
fire irons,
c1880, 27in
(68.5cm) long.
£100–120 WAC

A pine, copper and leather pair of
bellows, c1910, 17in (43cm) long.
£45–55 HCJ

An Edwardian copper coal scuttle,
c1910, 19in (48.5cm) wide.
£220–250 WAC

A Sofano electric fire, 1950s,
27in (68.5cm) high.
£200–250 ZOOM

A Calor Gas heater, 1950–60,
14in (35.5cm) high.
£20–25 ZOOM

A Victorian pinchbeck pendant, inset with a cameo, 2in (5cm) wide.
£40–50 AnS

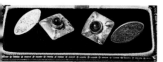

A pair of Arts and Crafts silver and amethyst cufflinks, 1906, ½in (1.5cm) wide.
£70–80 JBB

A silver and enamel buckle and button set, Birmingham 1910, buckle 3in (7.5cm) diam, in original case.
£200–230 JBB

A Christian Dior emerald green crystal necklace, signed and dated 1958, 11in (28cm) long.
£500–550 FMa

A Scottish silver and agate anchor brooch, c1870, 3in (7.5cm) high.
£200–220 BWA

Five silver Scottish kilt pins, 1930s, 3in (7.5cm) long.
£30–40 each BWA

A Miriam Haskell bracelet, in clear and rose pink crystal, signed, 1940s, 8in (20.5cm) long.
£300–350 FMa

A Turku, Finland Sterling silver and chrysophase ring, marked 'M.J.H.', c1960.
£175–200 DID

A Scottish silver and agate brooch, c1880, 2in (5cm) wide.
£140–160 BWA

A silvered-brass tiara, set with paste gems and *faux* pearls, 1924, 6in (15cm) high.
£425–475 JBB
This tiara sold by Christies in 1924, and was part of a collection replicating the Russian Crown Jewels.

A Bakelite cherry necklace, by Anka, with green lucite leaves, 1950s, 22in (56cm) long.
£145–165 FMa

◀ A Georg Jensen enamel and Sterling silver pendant, designed by Henry Heerup, depicting a mother and child, 1974, 2in (5cm) wide.
£350–400 DID

▶ An enamel, paste and gilt-metal brooch, in the form of a tiger, 1980s, 2in (5cm) long.
£20–25 FMa

A Buchan Portobello Pottery butter pot and cover, restored, c1867, 6in (15cm) high.
£220–245 MFB

A copper jelly mould, 1880, 8in (20.5cm) high.
£250–300 WeA

A Walt Disney Dopey ceramic egg timer, 1930s, 4in (10cm) high.
£120–140 JEZ

A copper raised pie mould, 1880, 6in (15cm) wide.
£220–250 WeA

A carved wooden bread board, dated '1897', 12in (30.5cm) diam.
£50–55 SMI

A Carlton Ware lemon squeezer, moulded as a fruit basket, 1930s, 5½in (14cm) diam.
£75–85 StC

A Goebels lemon squeezer, modelled as a chick, 1930s, 3in (7.5cm) high.
£50–60 BEV

▶ An American Juice-O-Mat juice press, 1950s, 7in (18cm) high.
£30–35 TRA

A copper and tin jelly mould, with wheatsheaf design, 1880, 6in (15cm) long.
£90–100 WeA

A De Ve wooden coffee grinder, c1920, 8in (20.5cm) high.
£20–25 TO

A Shelley Harmony Ware hand-painted lemon squeezer, 1930s, 8in (20.5cm) wide.
£60–70 BEV

A brass swan-neck wall gas lamp, with original cranberry glass shade, 1890–1900, 12in (30.5cm) high.
100–120 JW

A Benson brass tripod adjustable lamp, for wall, bed or table mounting, c1900, 13in (33cm) high.
750–850 HUN

Three Edwardian glass hanging lampshades, tallest 6in (15cm) high.
40–60 each JW

An Art Deco chrome table lamp, modelled as an aeroplane, 1930s, 12in (30.5cm) long.
140–160 JBB

A cranberry glass lampshade, c1890, 4½in (11.5cm) high.
£50–60 AL

A Victorian cranberry glass lamp shade, 10in (25.5cm) high.
£250–275 BSA

A Danish Perspex ceiling light, late 1960s, 18in (45.5cm) diam.
£150–175 PAB

A Victorian cameo shell lamp, with silver-plated base, 9in (23cm) high.
£120–140 BSA

A brass two-arm wall sconce, with tinted glass shades, c1900, 15in (38cm) high.
£160–200 JW

A Cenedese glass lamp base, decorated with stylized fish, 1950s, 9in (23cm) high.
£285–325 FMa

◀ A plastic poodle-shaped lamp, 1980s, Dutch, 14½in (37cm) high.
£65–80 PLB

A brass smoothing iron, with wooden handle, mid-19thC, 7in (18cm) high.
£325–375 SEA

A Stevenson's & Co cast-iron mechanically-operated money box, American, late 19thC, 6in (15cm) high.
£200–220 HAL

A Victorian copper pub jug, c1880, 8¾in (22cm) high.
£120–140 AL

◄ A brass hot water can, c1890, 9½in (24cm) high.
£65–75 AL

A Mawson Arts and Crafts copper bowl, late 19thC, 8½in (21.5cm) high.
£475–525 WAC

A Benson scroll-ended elliptical copper tray, with teapot, cream jug and covered bowl, 1896, tray 21in (53.5cm) long.
£500–550 HUN

A brass and horn ear trumpet, c1900, 6in (15cm) long.
£100–120 WAB

A brass kettle on stand, with cane handle and spirit burner, 1900, 13in (33cm) high.
£90–110 P(B)

An Old Hall stainless steel tankard, by Robert Welch, c1958, 3in (7.5cm) high, in original box.
£20–25 GRo

A Harrison Bros boxed carving set, 1930s, box 16in (40.5cm) long.
£25–28 TO

A Lee & Wilkes copper watering can, dated 1918, repaired, 13in (33cm) high.
£90–110 GaB

steel cuirass comprising breast and back plate, 820, 16in (40.5cm) high.
500–600 CYA

Victorian Royal Horse Guards officer's silver-lated helmet, with scarlet yak hair plume, with tin case bearing nameplate.
2,000–2,200 WAL

A David Grieves hand-painted white metal model soldier, depicting a sergeant of the 79th Regiment Cameron Highlanders, Waterloo 1815, 1995, in (10cm) high.
140–165 BONA

▶ A police truncheon, with the Royal Coat of Arms, 19thC, 13½in (34.5cm) long.
£240–280 CCB

A Crimean War medal, unnamed, dated '1854'.
£120–140 Q&C

◀ A Lothian Regiment officer's helmet plate, with gilt, silver and green enamel overlays, 1881–83.
£375–425 DNW

An Imperial Service Medal, 1908–20, in original case, 6in (15cm) high.
£45–55 AOH

A Merryweather fireman's brass helmet, 1880, 13in (33cm) high.
£400–480 CYA

A French fireman's brass helmet, chin-strap missing, 1880–90, 11in (28cm) high.
£300–350 CYA

Ten medals awarded to Major R. N. Rashleigh, Royal Artillery, 1914–37.
£750–850 WAL

A Black Watch busby, with original tin box, 1916, 19in (48.5cm) high, .
£300–350 CYA

A 14th/20th King's Hussars bass drum, post-1952, 30in (76cm) diam.
£400–480 Q&C

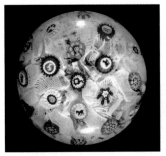

A Baccarat glass paperweight, initial 'B', dated 1847, 3in (7.5cm) diam.
£1,400–1,600 EH

A Whitefriars glass paperweight, 1953, 4in (10cm) diam.
£65–75 PIL

A Paul Ysart glass paperweight, No. 24698, 1970, 1¾in (4.5cm) diam.
£110–130 SWB

A Paul Ysart glass paperweight, No. 24699, 1970, 2¾in (7cm) diam.
£130–150 SWB

A Paul Ysart glass paperweight, No. 24697, 1970, 2¾in (7cm) diam.
£235–265 SWB

A Whitefriars glass paperweight, 1970s, 2½in (6.5cm) diam.
£170–190 PIL

A Victorian fan-shaped wooden photograph frame, with brass stand, hand-painted with forget-me-nots and violets, 6in (15cm) high.
£100–120 AMR

A photograph of the Cosmonauts Preparation Centre, depicting Gagarin, Leonov, Beliaev, Komarov and others, 1960s, 8 x 12in (20.5 x 30.5cm).
£480–530 BKS

An Edwardian mahogany photograph frame, hand-painted with flowers and foliage, 11in (28cm) high.
£60–70 AMR

A French chromolithograph postcard, 'Pavilion des Beaux Arts, Exposition Universelle 1889'.
£18–20 JMC

◄ A dance invitation postcard, 'Casino Maskenball', dated 15th February 1896.
£8–10 JMC

► A French postcard, 'Folies-Bergère', by Walter Hampel, c1900.
£16–20 SpP

An embroidered silk postcard, 'Malines 1914'.
£25–30 JMC

A postcard, 'Shipyards on the Clyde', by H. Cassiers, produced for the Glasgow International Exhibition 1901, one of a series.
£12–15 JMC

► An embroidered regimental postcard, 'Northamptonshire', c1916.
£25–30 SpP

An Imperial Theatre postcard, 'Mr Lewis Waller as Henry V', c1910.
£10–12 JMC

A silk on silk embroidered postcard, 'R.E.', 1916.
£12–15 JMC

A New York World's Fair postcard, '107, Federal Area, Lagoon of the Nations and Surrounding Area', 1939.
£10–12 RTT

A theatrical poster, 'Cruikshank The Fool of the Family', c1920, 31 x 20in (78.5 x 51cm).
£85–100 RTT

An American Warner Bros title lobby card, 'The Oklahoma Kid', 1939, 11 x 14in (28 x 35.5cm).
£350–400 S

An American 20th Century-Fox linen-backed lithographic film poster, 'The Hound of the Baskervilles', 1939, 41 x 27in (104 x 68.5cm).
£5,000–5,500 S

A poster, advertising Mansion Polish, by Harry Rowntree, c1930, 40 x 30in (101.5 x 72cm).
£250–300 RTT

An American Astor Pictures linen-backed lithographic film poster, 'Hell's House', c1938, 41 x 27in (104 x 68.5cm).
£250–300 S

A Belgian Paramount Pictures film poster, 'Le Hold-up du Siècle', 1950s, 12 x 20in (30.5 x 51cm).
£45–55 RTT

▶ An Italian Romulus productions linen-backed film poster, 'Pandora', 1951, 78 x 55in (198 x 139.5cm).
£475–525 S

A Belgian 20th Century-Fox film poster, 'Capitaine Janvier', 1936, 33 x 24in (84 x 61cm).
£500–600 S

An American Universal linen-backed film poster, 'Destry Rides Again', 1939, 41 x 27in (104 x 68.5cm).
£1,000–1,200 S

A National Savings linen-backed poster, by J. H. Dowd, 'For the Future of Our Nation Save Now', 1940s, 30 x 20in (76 x 51cm).
£220–245 Do

An American 20th Century-Fox linen-backed film poster, 'Gentlemen Prefer Blondes', 1953, 41 x 27in (104 x 68.5cm).
£1,000–1,200 S

Two American Universal lobby cards, 'Son of Frankenstein' and 'The Bride of Frankenstein', 1953, 11 x 14in (28 x 35.5cm).
£450–500 S

An American Allied Artists linen-backed film poster, 'Invasion of the Body Snatchers', 1956, 41 x 27in (104 x 68.5cm).
£1,900–2,100 S

An American Universal film poster, 'Touch of Evil', 1958, 22 x 28in (56 x 71cm).
£375–425 S

An American film poster, 'The Checkered Flag', late 1950s, 30 x 16in (76 x 40.5cm).
£40–45 VEY

An American Allied Artists Picture Corporation film poster, 'Tickle Me', 1965, 30 x 40in (76 x 101.5cm).
£100–125 SEY

An Arts Council Exhibition poster, 'Jean du Buffet paintings', 1966, 30 x 20in (76 x 51cm).
£200–240 CJP

A poster, 'Love', by Robert Indiana, 1967, 29in (73.5cm) square.
£100–120 CJP

A Beatles poster, designed by The Fool, published by Apple, to promote The Beatles's shop in Baker Street, 1967, 29 x 21¾in (73.5 x 55.5cm).
£150–180 Bon(C)

A Bob Dylan poster, by Milton Glaser, 1967, 36 x 26in (91.5 x 66cm).
£250–300 CJP

A silkscreen poster, John Lennon, 1967, 29 x 19in (73.5 x 48cm).
£250–300 CJP

A silkscreen poster, Jimi Hendrix, for the Riki-Tik Club, c1967, 29 x 19in (73.5 x 48cm).
£200–220 CJP

A Saville Theatre poster, 'The Jimi Hendrix Experience', by Hapshash and the Coloured Coat, 1967, 29 x 19in (73.5 x 48cm).
£450–550 CJP

A rock concert poster, 'Trips Festival featuring Jefferson Airplane', signed in silver by Bob Masse, 1969, signed, 20½ x 14in (52 x 35.5cm).
£60–70 Bon(C)

A United Artists film poster, 'The Spy Who Loved Me', 1977, 30 x 40in (76 x 101.5cm).
£65–75 SEY

◀ A poster, 'Summer is a Tape Thing', by Peter Max 1971, 36 x 24in (91.5 x 61cm).
£125–150 CJP

A Rank Organisation film poster, 'Silver Dream Racer', 1980, 30 x 40in (76 x 101.5cm).
£20–25 CTO

A Wurlitzer jukebox, 1948, 58in (147.5cm) high.
£6,000–6,600 TRA

A Watkins Rapier 33 guitar, refurbished, 1960s.
£120–150 MG
In original condition, this guitar would be worth £200–240.

Two Melody cards 78rpm discs, 'Birthday Wishes', Nos. M.C. 101 and MC 110, 1960s 7in (18cm) square.
£4–6 each WAB

An Ulster Irish linen Beatles tablecloth, 1964 34in (86.5cm) square.
£65–75 CTO

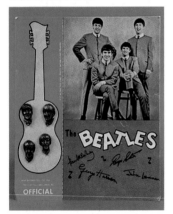

A set of four Beatles tie tacks, on original card, 1964, card 4 x 3in (10 x 7.5cm).
£25–30 BTC

An American dayglow linen-backed film poster, 'The Beatles Come to Town', 1964, 42 x 28in (106.5 x 71cm).
£850–950 S

A Belgian Beatles tapestry rug, maker's label to underside, 1964, 21 x 33in (53.5 x 84cm).
£50–60 BTC

A Beatles campaign book, 'A Hard Day's Night', 1964, 17 x 11in (43 x 28cm).
£50–60 BTC

A PYX 45rpm record carrier, with 16 leaves, depicting the Beatles, 1964, 7in (18cm) square.
£65–75 CTO

◀ A pair of Lybro SlimJeans, complete with flyer, 1960s, size 28
£70–80 BTC

A bamboo plate, depicting The Beatles, 1964–65, 12in (30.5cm) diam.
£42–50 BTC

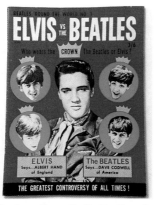

An Acme News Co *Beatles Round the World* magazine, issue No. 3, 'Elvis vs The Beatles', 1965, 11 x 9in (28 x 23cm).
£18–20 CTO

A Cliff Richard souvenir brochure, '*Aladdin and his Wonderful Lamp*', c1964, 11 x 9in (28 x 23cm).
£12–15 CTO

◀ A French Polydor International EP of The Who, '*I'm a Boy*', 1966.
£35–40 CTO

▶ An Anglo Confectionary collection of bubble-gum cards, depicting scenes from The Beatles' film '*Yellow Submarine*', c1967, 3½ x 2½in (9cm x 6.5cm).
£3–4 each CTO

The Monkees jigsaw puzzle, 1967, box 8 x 11in (20.5 x 28cm).
£42–50 CTO

A United Artists stereo LP of themes from '*Thunderbirds*', 1967.
£50–60 CTO

The Verve Massive Attack concert silkscreen advertising poster, designed by Emek, signed, 1998, 30¼ x 22in (77 x 56cm).
£120–150 Bon(C)

A Gibson prototype guitar, signed 'Alex Gregory', 1997.
£650–800 MG

◀ An American Gartlan figural group of The Beatles and the Yellow Submarine, No. 44 of limited edition of 1,968, 1999, 8in (20.5cm) high.
£120–140 BTC

A brass and boxwood drawing set, in a sharkskin etui, c1800, 6½in (16.5cm) high.
£300–330 DHo

A Baker brass compound monocular microscope, c1860, 18in (45.5cm) high, in original box.
£450–500 JeF

► A Mauchline ware sycamore collector's cabinet, with two drawers, c1870, 5in (12.5cm) high.
£350–400 TWr

► A Tartan ware box containing a compass, c1880, 2in (5cm) diam.
£180–200 TWr

A Sikes hydrometer, made by Farrow & Jackson, London, with two boxwood slide rules and a steel thermometer, c1880, 10in (25.5cm) long, in original case.
£140–160 ETO

A Wright & Co lacquered brass stomach pump and enema, with ivory fittings, c1890, 12in (30.5cm) long, in mahogany case.
£375–425 WAC

A compound reversing condensing marine engine, with brass and steel fittings, early 20thC, 18in (45.5cm) long.
£350–400 BKS

A set of six mineral samples under glass domes, by Harrington Brothers, London, c1900, 5in (12.5cm) high.
£100–120 FA

◄ An East German meteorological office brass barograph, with Perspex hinged lid, on a cast aluminium base, c1960, 12in (30.5cm) wide.
£350–400 RTw

A Geographia table-top terrestrial globe, c1900, 15in (38cm) high.
£400–450 CRU

A T. Gerrard & Co anatomy model, c1930, 16in (40.5cm) high.
£95–110 CRN

Jewellery

A Scottish silver and agate bracelet, with blue, brown and black stones and central citrine, c1870, 7in (18cm) long.
£700–800 BWA

A Victorian 9ct gold watch chain, 16in (40.5cm) long.
£250–275 AnS

A Victorian Baltic amber bracelet, 1½in (4cm) wide.
£120–150 Ma

A Victorian gilt-metal sovereign case, c1880, 1¼in (3cm) diam.
£80–90 BHA

A pair of Miriam Haskell crystal drop earrings, with gold filigree mounts, 1960s, 2¼in (5.5cm) long.
£145–165 MAU

◄ An American pearl and glass bracelet, 1950s, 7in (18cm) long.
£7–8 STP

► A Tiffany sterling silver frog earring and bracelet set, c1965, earring 1in (2.5cm) square.
£600–680 FMa

A pair of Tiffany 18ct gold and amethyst earrings, by Paloma Picasso, 1980s, 1½in (4cm) long.
£750–850 DID

A Vivienne Westwood silver articulated armour ring, 1990s, 2in (5cm) long.
£55–65 ID

BROOCHES

A Victorian paste and gilt-metal swallow brooch, c1830, 2in (5cm) long.
£60–75 Ma

An early Victorian tortoiseshell *piqué* brooch, the bi-coloured metal inlay depicting floral and architectural designs, 1½in (4cm) diam.
£100–120 Bon

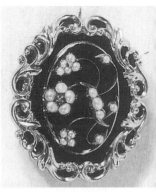

A mid-Victorian half-pearl and rose-cut diamond mourning brooch, decorated with a scroll design on a blue enamel ground, the reverse with glazed compartment and engraved 'Hester Cordy died 22nd March 1849 aged 80'.
£140–160 Hal

A silver plaid brooch, with centre cairngorm stone, c1850, 5in (12.5cm) diam.
£900–1,000 BWA
Cairngorm is a variety of yellow-brown quartz originally found in the Cairngorm Mountains in Scotland. Queen Victoria's passion for all things Scottish helped stimulate the fashion for Highland-style jewellery. In the 1860s, production of silver and Scottish pebble (agate) jewellery developed into a major industry in Edinburgh, demand exceeded production, and Birmingham became another main centre of manufacture.

A Victorian diamond, pearl and enamel mourning brooch, 1in (2.5cm) diam.
£650–700 AnS
Pearls were often used in mourning jewellery, symbolizing tears.

A Scottish silver and agate brooch, with red, brown and black stones, c1860, 2in (5cm) diam.
£350–400 BWA

A Victorian silver and rose-cut diamond brooch, with swallows, set on a gold pin, 2in (5cm) long.
£1,100–1,200 AnS

A late Victorian diamond spiral cluster brooch, set in silver and gold, 1in (2.5cm) diam.
£500–600 Bon

A Scottish silver and agate brooch, with grey and black stones, c1860, 2in (5cm) diam.
£550–600 BWA

▶ A Victorian 18ct gold, ruby and seed pearl stick pin, 2in (5cm) long.
£70–80 AnS

Four Scottish silver clan badges, c1900, 2in (5cm) diam.
£60–70 each BWA

Three silver name brooches, Lillian, Rose and Mona, 1880–90, 1¼in (3cm) diam.
£40–45 each EXC

An 18ct gold stick pin, in the shape of a spaniel, c1900, 3in (7.5cm) long.
£550–750 ANTH

◀ A Murrle Bennett & Co enamelled brooch, with two teardrop-shaped panels of blue and green enamel, marked, damaged, c1900, 1½in (4cm) wide.
£450–500 DN

Four silver name brooches, Miriam, Ethel, Minnie and Dolly, 1900–20, 1½in (4cm) long.
£40–45 each EXC

A silver-gilt brooch, in the shape of a lizard, with green and red paste jewels, c1920, 4in (10cm) long.
£120–140 Ma

◀ A silver paste-set plaque brooch, 1930, 3in (7.5cm) wide.
£120–140 Ma

▶ An eastern European metal and simulated turquoise filigree brooch, 1930s, 2in (5cm) wide.
£8–10 STP

A silver and rhinestone brooch, in the shape of a snail, 1930s, 2in (5cm) long.
£55–65 LBe

A metal and marcasite brooch, in the shape of a flower, 1950, 2½in (6.5cm) long.
£7–8 STP

A Lea Stein laminated plastic brooch, in the shape of a cat with a ball, in brown, grey and black, 1930–40, 3in (7.5cm) high.
£35–40 HT

▶ A Trifari silvered-metal and black enamel brooch, in the shape of a tiger, with faux ruby eyes, 1950s, 2in (5cm) high.
£75–85 FMa

An Eisenberg white-metal paste-set brooch, c1940, 2in (5cm) long.
£60–75 JBB

BUCKLES

A mother-of-pearl belt buckle, c1850, 3in (7.5cm) wide.
£80–90 JBB

◀ A silver belt buckle, the centres depicting putti, Birmingham 1906, 6in (15cm) wide.
£110–130 JBB

A black enamel and metal garment clasp, 1930s, 3in (7.5cm) wide.
£8–10 CHU

A German *Jugendstil* square buckle, the centre with green glass cabochon, probably made in Pforzheim, marked, c1900, 2½in (6.5cm) square.
£150–160 DN

An American Art Nouveau sterling silver two-piece buckle, embossed with the head and shoulders of a maiden emerging from waves, marked, c1900, 3¾in (9.5cm) wide.
£275–300 DN

An Austro-Hungarian Art Nouveau-style enamel clasp, decorated with stylized flower and foliage in red, green, blue and yellow, 1910–20, 4in (10cm) wide.
£70–80 JBB

▶ An enamel and brass clasp, in the shape of two leaves, 1940s, 3in (7.5cm) wide.
£8–10 CHU

CUFFLINKS

A pair of gold cufflinks, set with square 17thC Spanish coins, ½in (1.5cm) square.
£150–170 JBB

A pair of brass, enamel and mother-of-pearl cufflinks, with turquoise centres, 1900–10, ½in (1.5cm) diam.
£35–45 JBB

A pair of French garnet cufflinks, marked, late 19thC.
£250–300 Bon

A pair of Edwardian gold, ruby and mother-of-pearl cufflinks and collar stud set, the rubies set in a button design, with a fitted case.
£625–700 Bon

A pair of French silver cufflinks, depicting a man receiving an enema, late 19thC, 1in (2.5cm) wide.
£140–160 JBB
This is surely one of the most unusual subjects ever to be portrayed on a pair of cufflinks.

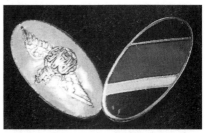

A pair of RAF enamel and metal cufflinks, in red, white, blue and light blue, 1940–50, ½in (1.5cm) wide.
£20–25 JBB

NECKLACES & PENDANTS

A silver and crystal cross pendant on a chain-link necklace, early 18thC, 4in (10cm) high, in original case.
£550–600 JSM

A Victorian 9ct gold, citrine and seed pearl pendant, 1in (2.5cm) wide.
£250–270 AnS

A 15ct gold and turquoise muff chain, 1880, 58in (147.5cm) long.
£300–350 JSM

► A carved ivory cross, with wheatsheaf design, 1870, 5in (12.5cm) high.
£55–65 JSM

A Victorian silver locket engraved with a posy, with chain-link necklace, locket 2in (5cm) high.
£80–90 AnS

► An Arts and Crafts silver necklace, by Arthur and Georgina Gaskin, set with turquoise cabochons, marked, c1900, pendant 2in (5cm) long.
£1,800–2,000 DN

An Edwardian peridot and pearl open-work pendant, 2½in (6.5cm) long.
£700–800 Bon

A Baltic faceted amber bead necklace, c1920, 32in (81.5cm) long.
£150–180 Ma

A Miriam Haskell crystal and copper-gilt necklace and bracelet, 1930, necklace 22in (56cm) long.
Necklace £200–220
Bracelet £160–180 FMa

A faceted cornelian necklace, 1930s, 26in (66cm) long.
£45–50 DEC

A Miriam Haskell green bead and baroque-pearl necklace, with bead flower clasp and gilt chain, early 1960s, 23in (58.5cm) long.
£350–375 MAU

◄ A Vendome crystal and gilt-metal necklace, signed, c1960, 16½in (42cm) long.
£100–120 FMa

► A pale blue and green crystal and silver-gilt necklace and earrings set, by Kenneth Jay Lane, 1960s, necklace 9in (23cm) long.
£420–480 FMa
This design was created for the Duchess of Windsor.

TIARAS

A white metal and paste tiara, c1900, 3in (7.5cm) high.
£250–300 JBB

A white metal and paste tiara, 1920s, 2in (5cm) high.
£75–90 JBB

A wax flower headdress, set with cream flowers and green leaves, 1920s, 6½in (16.5cm) wide.
£25–30 TT

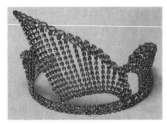

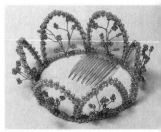

A white metal and paste tiara, 1930s, 4in (10cm) high.
£80–90 JBB

A Perspex and diamanté Alice-band-style tiara, c1935, 6in (15cm) wide.
£65–80 JBB

A pearl-beaded wedding crown, 1940s, 2in (5cm) high.
£75–100 JBB

Kitchenware

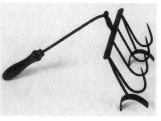

A cast-iron toaster, with wooden
handle, 1870, 18in (45.5cm) long.
£125–150 WeA

A Georgian copper boiler,
20in (51cm) wide.
£100–120 HCJ

A cast-iron toaster, 1830,
16in (40.5cm) long.
£175–200 WeA

▶ A brass ladle, with
steel handle, mid-19thC,
24in (61cm) long.
£160–180 NEW

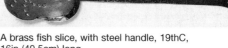

A flour tin, with original
brown and black
paint, mid-19thC,
12in (30.5cm) high.
£125–150 NEW

A brass fish slice, with steel handle, 19thC,
16in (40.5cm) long.
£85–100 NEW

A Scottish cast-iron
bannock turner, 1870,
20in (51cm) long.
£120–140 WeA

◀ A cast-iron
Dutch oven, 1870,
54in (137cm) high.
£800–900 WeA

A tin kitchen slice, with wooden handle, 1880,
15in (38cm) long.
£80–90 WeA

A copper brandy warmer, 19thC, 8in (20.5cm) long.
£90–110 MFB

A Staines Kitchen Equipment pottery Oven Cookery & Household Thermometer, 1900, 6in (15cm) long.
£80–90 WeA

A cast-iron saucepan, early 20thC, 16in (40.5cm) long.
£10–12 HCJ

A Marshall's Patent Ice Cave, c1900, 16in (40.5cm) wide.
£80–90 WeA
From the 1880s until her death in 1905, Mrs Marshall ran a famous cookery school and kitchen equipment shop in London. Her great speciality was ice cream. Among her best selling cookery books were the *Book of Ices* (1885) and *Fancy Ices* (1894), and her shop supplied moulds, freezers and all forms of ice cream making equipment. Mrs Marshall's material is highly sought-after by collectors today.

A metal and brass pastry cutter, c1910, 4in (10cm) diam.
£9–11 AL

A Parisian set of enamel jars and a cafetière, decorated with hand-painted pansies on a pale blue and white ground, c1920, jars 6in (15cm) high.
£150–175 B&R

A French enamel cafetière, hand-painted with flowers in pink, white and green on a blue ground, c1920, 10in (25.5cm) high.
£70–80 B&R

A Lipton's Souvenir brass tea caddy, c1925, 4¾in (12cm) high.
£22–26 AL

A Continental solid fuel cast-iron and enamel Ciney cooking range, 1950s, 42in (106.5cm) high.
£650–750 A&H

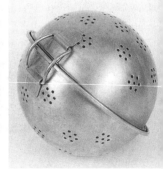

An aluminium rice bowl, c1950, 5¼in (13.5cm) diam.
£10–12 AL

CERAMICS

A Scottish ceramic bread crock, with stylized foliage design, c1870, 17in (43cm) high.
£450–500 TWr

A ceramic cream crock, early 20thC, 10in (25.5cm) high.
£450–500 B&R

► A Maling porcelain lard dish, with brown Cobblestone pattern, c1920, 8in (20.5cm) wide.
£120–140 SMI

A porcelain pie funnel, in the form of a chef, c1920, 4in (10cm) high.
£35–40 SMI

A Royal Worcester pie funnel, in the shape of a bird, decorated in blue on a cream ground, c1950, 5in (12.5cm) high
£30–35 SMI

A spongeware pottery bowl, decorated in green and brown on a beige ground, c1900, 9½in (24cm) diam.
£80–90 MSB

A ceramic milk pail, c1900, 16in (40cm) diam.
£450–500 SMI

A Yorkshire earthenware larding pot, 1900, 5in (12.5cm) high.
£15–18 IW

A Gourmet Pie Cup ceramic pie funnel, c1910, 3¼in (8.5cm) high.
£35–40 WeA

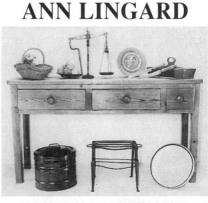

A Cornish Ware blue and white ceramic Barley Sugar storage jar, with original seal and black shield, 1920–60s, 5½in (14cm) high.
£300–350 GeN

A Cornish Ware blue and white ceramic Soap Flakes storage jar, with black shield, 1920–60s, 5½in (14cm) high.
£350–400 GeN

A Cornish Ware blue and white ceramic Cherries storage jar, with black shield, 1920–60s, 3½in (9cm) high.
£100–120 GeN

A Cornish Ware blue and white ceramic rolling pin, with green shield, 1920–60s.
£100–120 GeN

A Cornish Ware blue and white ceramic Bread Crumbs storage jar, with black shield, 1920–60s, 5½in (14cm) high.
£160–175 GeN

◀ A Cornish Ware blue and white ceramic Ginger spice jar, early 20thC, 3½in (9cm) high.
£80–90 TAC

A Cornish Ware blue and white ceramic Vinegar jar with stopper, with green shield, 1920–60s, 7½in (19cm) high.
£90–110 GeN

A Cornish Ware blue and white ceramic coffee pot, marked, 1920–60s, 7in (18cm) high.
£80–90 TAC

◀ A Cornish Ware yellow and white ceramic salt sifter, 1920–60s, 5in (12.5cm) high.
£60–70 TAC

A Cornish Ware yellow and white ceramic storage jar, 1930s, 6in (15cm) high.
£50–60 TAC

◀ A booklet, *Cornish Recipes Old and New*, post-WWII, 9 x 5in (23 x 12.5cm).
£30–40 TAC

CHOPPERS

A herb chopper, with wooden handle, branded with owner's initials, mid-19thC, 8in (20.5cm) wide.
£140–160 NEW

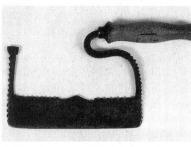

A food chopper, with wooden handle, 1870, 9in (23cm) long.
£80–90 WeA

A food chopper, with wooden handle, 1870, 7in (18cm) high.
£80–90 WeA

A Victorian herb chopper, mounted on a wooden board, 21in (53.5cm) long.
£65–75 HCJ

Further reading

Miller's Collecting Kitchenware, Miller's Publications, 1995

LOCATE THE SOURCE

The source of each illustration in Miller's can be found by checking the code letters below each caption with the Key to Illustrations, pages 476–484.

DAIRYING

A Welsh wooden butter spoon, the handle carved with a marker, 1870, 11in (28cm) long.
130–150 SMI

A brass and tin gill milk ladle, 1880, 5in (12.5cm) high.
60–70 WeA

A pair of wooden butter pat moulders, 19thC, 9in (23cm) long.
£7–8 HCJ

A brass and steel conical milk churn, the side engraved 'Ranelagh Dairy', c1880, 39in (99cm) high.
£700–800 SMI

A sycamore butter skimmer, 19thC, 9in (23cm) diam.
£40–45 MFB

A wooden butter marker, with wheatsheaf design, 1880, 2in (5cm) diam.
£60–70 WeA

A sycamore butter roller, 19thC, 7in (18cm) long.
£80–90 MFB

A wooden butter mould, with wheatsheaf design, 1890, 4in (10cm) high.
£90–110 WeA

A tin and brass cream can, inscribed 'F. Hanson, Thames Ditton', 1890, 2in (5cm) high.
£90–100 WeA

A French enamel milk can, hand-painted with girls playing, in blue and brown on a cream ground, late 19thC, 9in (23cm) high.
£100–120 B&R

A tin milk can, with brass fittings, inscribed 'B. Davies & Son', 1890, 6in (15cm) high.
£80–100 WeA

A sycamore butter marker, carved with 'Maes y Prior Dairy', 19thC, 3in (7.5cm) diam.
£90–100 MFB

A sand-blasted and lacquered metal milk churn, 1920–30, 21in (53.5cm) high.
£40–45 BYG

A Stroud & Son table-top wooden butter churn, c1930, 17in (43cm) high.
£130–150 SMI

A milk can, with brass fittings, inscribed 'D. Wheatley', early 20thC, 9in (23cm) high.
£250–300 B&R

A glass and metal Household Butter Machine, with original blue and white label, c1920, 15in (38cm) high.
£130–150 SMI

KETTLES

In the 17th and 18th centuries tea was an expensive product reserved for the upper classes, and kettles tended to be made from silver. As tea became cheaper and more generally available the kettle, made from copper, brass, cast-iron or enamel became a feature of every kitchen. The traditional stove kettle was gradually supplanted by the electric kettle (introduced in 1921) but today, with the growing popularity of Aga cookers, stove kettles are once again reappearing in kitchens.

A miniature copper kettle, early 19thC, 4in (10cm) high.
£65–75 ALA

A Falkirk No. 1 cast-iron kettle, Scotland, 1880, 8in (20.5cm) high.
£160–190 WeA

A Victorian cast-iron kettle, 16in (40.5cm) high.
£75–85 HCJ

◄ A copper kettle, c1820, 9½in (24cm) high.
£100–120 AL

A Benson copper kettle, on a brass stand with paw feet, and a Mark III burner, c1900, 11in (28cm) high.
£325–375 HUN

A cast-iron grey and white enamelled kettle, c1880, 10in (25.5cm) high.
£50–55 SMI

A Benson copper kettle, with a brass handle, on a brass and cast-iron quadruped stand, with a Mark VI burner, c1900, 32in (81.5cm) high.
£800–880 HUN

LAUNDRY & HOUSEWORK

A steel and brass goffer iron stand, early 19thC, 9in (23cm) high.
£170–190 NEW
Goffer irons were used for crimping ruffles and frills.

A cast-iron lace crimper, with brass rollers, late 19thC, 15in (38cm) wide.
£220–240 SMI
On this crimping machine the rollers are hollow and were heated by having a red hot poker thrust inside them. As with a mangle, the material was wound through and came out corrugated.

▶ A wood, leather and rope carpet flail, c1890, 58in (147.5cm) long.
£50–60 WAB

A French cast-iron iron stand, with eight egg, ball and mushroom finial goffing irons, late 19thC, 15½in (39.5cm) high.
£250–300 B&R

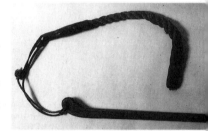

A wooden washboard, late 19thC, 26in (66cm) long.
£25–30 HCJ

A Victorian wooden washing dolly, 36in (91.5cm) high.
£45–55 HCJ

The Northern Queen salesman's sample wooden washboard, with advertising on reverse, Canada, 1886, 9½ x 4½in (24 x 11.5cm).
£65–75 B&R

A wood and cast-iron washing machine, painted red and green, incorporating a mangle, c1900, 52in (132cm) high.
£550–600 BYG

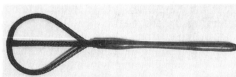

A wirework carpet beater, with a wooden handle, c1920, 24in (61cm) long.
£24–28 B&R

◀ A painted tin hot water jug, inscribed 'Yellow Dressing Room', late 19thC, 15in (38cm) high.
£100–120 B&R

An American Gas Machine Co petrol iron, with attached brass fuel tank, 1910, 9 x 6in (23 x 15cm).
£80–90 FA

MOULDS

With the rise of the middle classes in the 19th century, eating habits became increasingly elaborate. Dinners had more courses and tables were laden with ever-expanding settings of cutlery, crockery and glassware. Food was required to be decorative as well as filling, and an ornamental jelly was a favourite table centrepiece. Moulds were an essential part of the *batterie de cuisine*; there were 500 at Apsley House, the Duke of Wellington's residence, and even the most ordinary middle-class kitchen would have a selection of different designs that were used for both savoury and sweet dishes. Moulds were produced in many different materials, including ceramics, metalware and, from the 1880s, pressed glass. They came in a huge variety of shapes, from castellated forms to rings, fruit, vegetables and animals. The *Book of Moulds*, published in 1886 by cookery writer Mrs Marshall, included over 1,000 designs and sizes.

Copper moulds, produced from c1830 are among the most collectable today. Initially the copper was hand-beaten, then from c1860 machine -pressed. Ice cream moulds were often made from pewter, and can be distinguished from jelly or blancmange moulds by the fact that they close completely, so that the mould could be thrown into the ice box. They should not be used today, since the lead-based metal is toxic. Tin moulds provided a cheap substitute for copper and were popular for chocolate.

Moulds should be checked for condition (beware of rust on tin moulds) and for a registration or retailer's mark that can enhance their value. Whatever the material, the more elaborate the design the higher the price.

Pewter ice-cream mould, in the shape of fruit and a leaf, 1868, 6in (15cm) diam.
£80–200 WeA

A copper ring mould, c1880, 8¼in (21cm) diam.
£260–280 MSB

A copper aspic mould, in the shape of a horseshoe, 1890, 1½in (4cm) wide.
£20–25 WeA

Copper aspic mould, in the shape of a rabbit, 1890, 3in (7.5cm) high.
£0–50 WeA

A tin-plate circular chocolate mould, c1890, 6in (15cm) diam.
£55–65 WAB

▶ A tin chocolate mould, in the shape of a duck, early 20thC, 6in (15cm) high.
£35–40 DHA

A tin chocolate mould, in the shape of a fish, 1900, 8in (20cm) wide.
£40–50 WeA

A ceramic jelly mould, in the shape of a lion, c1900, 8in (20.5cm) wide.
£30–35 AL

A tin chocolate mould, in the shape of a hen, early 20thC, 7in (18cm) wide.
£80–90 MFB

A tin chocolate mould, in the shape of an ocean liner, c1930, 8in (20.5cm) long.
£35–40 AL

A tin chocolate mould, in the shape of a train, c1930, 6¼in (16cm) long.
£35–40 AL

Four Continental tin double-sided chocolate moulds, early 20thC, largest 10in (25.5cm) high.
£70–80 B&R

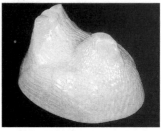

A Greens Newstyle Jellies ceramic mould, in the shape of a chicken, c1910, 6¼in (16cm) long.
£40–50 AL

An Elsheimer & Co tin chocolate mould, in the shape of 18 Emerick's Taxis, New York, c1930s, 11½ x 13½in (29 x 34.5cm).
£110–120 MSB

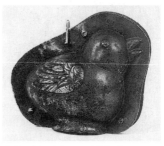

A tin chocolate mould, in the shape of a chick, c1930, 4½in (11.5cm) high.
£35–40 AL

A tin chocolate mould, in the form of John Bull, early 20thC, 5½in (14cm) high.
£80–90 B&R

A Van Emden tin candy mould, in the shape of a rabbit with a basket, marked 'NY', Germany c1920, 20½in (52cm) hig
£450–500 MSB

A tin chocolate mould, in the form of a girl, c1930s, 8in (20.5cm) hig
£50–55 B&R

SCALES

A pair of sycamore butter scales, 19thC, 21in (53.5cm) wide.
£340–380 MFB

A pair of polished steel kitchen or shop scales, with copper pans, early 19thC, 19in (48.5cm) wide.
£130–150 NEW

A pair of iron kitchen or shop scales, with complete set of weights, late 19thC, 18in (45.5cm) wide.
£130–150 NEW

► A pair of brass and iron bread scales, 1870, 13in (33cm) high.
£110–130 WeA

◄ A Salter's cast-iron Butter Balance, with brass face and tin tray, c1920, 10in (25.5cm) high.
£90–100 SMI

A Salter's brass and iron quadrant scale, c1870, 14in (35.5cm) high.
£100–120 SMI

A Salter's spring balance egg scale, c1920, 8in (20.5cm) high.
£50–60 SMI

SPICE CONTAINERS

A wooden spice tower, with compartments for ginger, nutmegs and cinnamon, 1860, 5in (12.5cm) high.
£160–190 WeA

A tin spice container, c1820, 4½in (11.5cm) high.
£55–60 AL

A tin double spice container, c1870, 8in (20.5cm) high.
£140–160 WeA

SQUEEZERS & JUICERS

A cast-iron lemon press, late 19thC, 8¼in (21cm) long.
£45–50 B&R

A green enamel lemon press, early 20thC, 8½in (21.5cm) long.
£35–40 B&R

A Crown Devon lemon squeezer, decorated in yellow and green, 1930s, 4in (10cm) high.
£60–70 BEV

A Crown Devon lemon squeezer, decorated in orange and green, 1930s, 4in (10cm) high.
£45–50 CoCo

A cast-iron fruit juicer, with blue and white ceramic funnel, c1880, 12in (30.5cm) high.
£70–80 FA

▶ A Westbourne treen citrus press, early 20thC, 7in (18cm) long.
£55–60 MFB

A Japanese hand-painted ceramic lemon squeezer, in the shape of a duck, decorated in blue, green, yellow and brown, 1930s, 5in (12.5cm) long.
£55–60 BEV

A Carlton Ware lemon squeezer, decorated with Pink Buttercup pattern, in pink and green, 1930s, 6in (15cm) wide.
£225–250 BEV

A Juice King, chrome and painted metal juice press, America, 1950s, 7in (18cm) high.
£30–35 TRA

A Royal Winton lemon squeezer, decorated with Gera pattern, in pink, blue, green and yellow, 1930s, 5in (12.5cm) wide.
£50–60 BEV

A Carlton Ware lemon squeezer, decorated with Fruit Basket pattern, 1930s, 5in (12.5cm) high.
£90–100 BEV

▶ A Juice King chrome and painted metal juice press, America, 1950s, 7in (18cm) high.
£25–30 TRA

UTENSILS

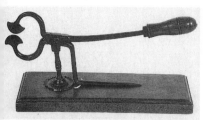

A pair of iron table sugar snips, with wooden handle, on treen base, c1800, 11in (28cm) long.
£245–265 SEA

A pair of W. Bullock & Co cast-iron sugar snips, 1843, 14in (35.5cm) long.
£200–220 WeA

An iron apple parer, 1856, 8in (20.5cm) high.
£70–80 FA

A wood and ivory cucumber slicer, 1860, 9in (23cm) long.
£130–150 WeA

A brass and wood pastry marker, inscribed 'JG 1858', 11in (28cm) long.
£180–200 WeA

A Kite cast-iron tin opener, modelled as a bull, c1880, 5½in (14cm) long.
£15–18 JOL

A cast-iron tin opener, modelled as a fish, c1880, 6in (15cm) long.
£35–40 SMI

A tin-plate tongue press, c1880, 10in (25.5cm) high.
£18–20 FA

An iron knife sharpener, c1880, 10 x 12in (25.5 x 30.5cm).
£55–65 WAB

A metal vegetable cutter and grater, c1910, 4¾in (12cm) long.
£4–5 AL

► A wall-mounted iron and brass coffee grinder, with wooden handle, c1900, 11in (28cm) wide.
£90–100 B&R

A Silent Machine Co, Sheffield, steel sausage-making machine, 1940s, 46in (117cm) long.
£35–40 A&H

WHISKS

A Dover steel egg whisk, c1890, 10in (25.5cm) long.
£30–35 WeA

A Bournville Cocoa wire whisk, with a wooden handle, 1910, 9in (23cm) long.
£20–25 WeA
The wire band around the beaters could be moved to adjust the width of the whisk to fit the size of the cup or bowl being used.

A Bunny aluminium whisk, with a green handle, c1930, 10in (25.5cm) high.
£25–30 SMI

A Ladd steel whisk, with a wooden handle, c1940, 11in (28cm) high.
£15–18 SMI

WOOD

A sycamore grain scoop, late 19thC, 13in (33cm) long.
£30–35 ChA

A pastry pricker, with steel spikes and a sycamore handle, late 19thC, 5in (12.5cm) high.
£18–20 NEW

An oak ewer, with iron bindings, late 17thC, 17in (43cm) high.
£300–350 OCH

▶ A steel bread knife, with a wooden coin-decorated handle, 1880, 12in (30.5cm) long.
£24–28 WeA

A sycamore dairy bowl, late 19thC, 14in (35.5cm) diam.
£350–400 NEW

A wooden chopping block, with attached knife holder, c1900, 17in (43cm) wide.
£400–450 SMI

A wooden bread board, carved 'Give Us This Day Our Daily Bread', early 20thC, 14½in (37cm) wide.
£70–80 B&R

Lighting

CANDLESTICKS

The cheapest form of candle lighting was the rush light, formed by soaking a rush in kitchen fat. Rush lights also had the advantage of being exempted from the candle tax that was imposed in 1709 and not repealed until 1831, which prohibited the manufacture of candles without a licence. Candles were made from tallow, beeswax (more expensive and less smelly than animal fat) and spermaceti (whale oil), which burned with a bright, white flame. The 19th century saw the invention of composite candles, made from coconut oil and stearine (animal fat), which were also known as 'snuffless' candles, because their plaited wicks burnt away without having to

be trimmed. In 1857 the first paraffin wax candles appeared on the market. Bright as beeswax and spermaceti but more affordable, paraffin wax gradually became the most commonly used material. Candlesticks were produced in a large variety of styles, ranging from large table candlesticks to portable or chamber candlesticks, with a handle and a large pan for catching the grease. Sconces and hanging candelabra were generally confined to wealthier homes. Metal was a favourite material and the following selection ranges from humble cast-iron rush lights made by the local village blacksmith for cottage use, to smart silver candlesticks, designed for the gentry.

A brass Heemskirk candlestick, with a domed base and central drip tray, Holland, late 17thC, 8in (20.5cm) high.
£375–425 S(S)

An iron rush light holder, c1759, 9in (23cm) high.
£400–450 SEA

An iron rush light holder, late 18thC, 11in (28cm) high.
£275–300 WeA

A pair of silver fluted square column Adam-style candlesticks, c1770, 11in (28cm) high.
£350–375 SEA

A pair of brass seamed candlesticks, c1740, 7½in (19cm) high.
£450–500 SEA

◄ A pair of brass Heemskirk candlesticks, with knopped stems and central drip trays above domed circular bases, Holland, late 18thC, 10in (25.5cm) high.
£350–400 S(S)

A George III silver circular chamber candlestick, with an aperture for snuffers and detachable nozzle, and a similar conical extinguisher, marked 'I.M.', London, 1793, 5½in (14cm) diam, 9oz.
£400–450 Bea(E)

A French wood, bone and steel spiral candlestick, c1800, 7½in (19cm) high.
£120–150 AnSh
The lever at the side was used to push the candle up as the wax burnt down.

A pair of George III silver table candlesticks, by T. & J. Settle, Sheffield, with cylindrical stems, the circular bases with gadroon borders, 1814.
£750–850 L

A pair of gun-metal candlesticks, 19thC, 13in (33cm) high.
£100–120 WAC

A tin candle mould for eight candles, 1860, 11in (28cm) high.
£100–120 WeA

A pair of metal taper tongs, c1860, 14in (35.5cm) long.
£12–15 AL

▶ A black-painted candle tin, c1870, 11in (28cm) long.
£130–150 WeA
Tallow candles rotted if exposed to the air for too long and so were stored in tin candle boxes.

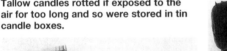

A pair of cut-steel Gothic Revival candelabra, c1870, 17in (43cm) high.
£165–185 RUSK

A pair of Brighton Buns brass candlesticks, c1880, 3¼in (8.5cm) diam.
£150–175 SEA

A silver-plated chamber candlestick, by William Hutton & Sons, c1895, 6in (15cm) wide.
£115–130 ASAA

A Liberty Tudric pewter candlestick, c1900, 7in (18cm) high.
£375–425 ANO

A John Pearson copper candlestick, the circular sconce centred in a square base, with angled flap-like sides, embossed with fleur-de-lys, signed 'JP 1901', 6¾in (17cm) wide.
£250–275 DN

▶ A pair of silver candlesticks, by Fordham & Faulkner, with fluted tapering columns on oval stepped bases, Sheffield 1904, 8in (20.5cm) high.
£600–660 FHF

CEILING LIGHTS

A gilded and patinated ceiling lamp, designed for gas and candles, with original white glass shades, 1850–70, 47in (119.5cm) high.
£600–700 JW

A Dutch brass chandelier, the ball and vase stem supporting two tiers of six dolphin-scrolled arms, 19thC, 25in (63.5cm) high.
£1,200–1,400 S(S)

An opaque glass hanging light shade, with floral decoration, complete with brass chain and ceiling rose, early 20thC, 9in (23cm) wide.
£125–145 LIB

▶ An orange, blue and green marbled glass ceiling bowl, 1930s, 12in (30.5cm) diam.
£35–40 TWa

An Edwardian cast-brass three-branch hanging lamp, 22in (56cm) high.
£300–350 JW

An Edwardian brass three-arm central hanging lamp, with original glass shades, 13in (33cm) high.
£300–350 JW

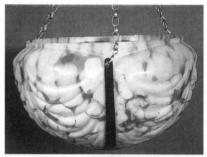

An Edwardian pendant lamp with wrought iron acanthus leaf fitting, with plain white glass bell-shaped shade, 10in (25.5cm) high.
£60–70 JW

A Holophane hanging light shade, with original brass fittings, c1910–30, 8in (20.5cm) high.
£25–30 JW

◀ A spelter ceiling lamp, in the form of a fairy, with Vaseline glass tear-drop shades, c1920, 28in (71cm) high.
£900–1,000 JW

Items in the Lighting section have been arranged in date order within each sub-section.

▶ A Murano glass hanging light, the hand-made shades formed from flowers, early 1970s, 23in (58.5cm) high.
£440–480 PAB

LANTERNS

A Georgian sheet-metal street lantern, converted to a hanging light, 25in (63.5cm) high.
£280–320 AnSh

A tin lantern, with horn panes, 1830, 17in (43cm) high.
£170–200 WeA

◄ An Art Nouveau hammer-beaten copper hall lantern, with vaseline glass shade, 17¾in (45cm) high.
£90–120 P(B)

▶ An oxidized copper hall lantern, with original glass, 1920–30, 9in (23cm) high.
£45–50 JW

A tin lantern, with protective metal grille, 1870, 11in (28cm) high.
£80–100 WeA
The candle was protected by a metal grille to prevent fire risk.

A Masthead brass fishing boat lamp, c1880, 8in (20.5cm) high.
£270–300 TWr

A Christopher Collins iron candle lamp, 1915, 12in (30.5cm) high.
£80–100 SMI

OIL LAMPS

A Crusie cast-iron hanging oil burner, Scotland, 1830, 27in (68.5cm) high.
£180–200 WeA

A WMF silver-plated oil light, c1900, 9½in (24cm) high.
£165–185 WAC

▶ An Edwardian brass oil lamp, with acid-etched glass shade, 23½in (59.5cm) high.
£350–400 CHA

An Edwardian brass columnar oil lamp, with cut glass font and etched shade, 28in (71cm) high.
£350–400 CHA

TABLE & DESK LAMPS

▶ A Royal Doulton Polly Peachum table lamp, No. HN549, the figure wearing a red dress, with cream shade, on a mahogany base, marked, c1930, 21in (53.5cm) high.
£100–120 SAS

An American Arts and Crafts table lamp, the globular base patinated in green with silvered linear design of vine leaves and tendrils, the conical shade green-patinated and pierced with vines in silhouette and having a fabric inner-lining, early 20thC, 9¾in (25cm) high.
£240–280 DN

▶ A pair of adjustable Reflectorlite table lights, 1950s.
£300–350 ZOOM

An Edwardian brass banker's lamp, with a green glass shade, 15in (38cm) high.
£140–160 JW

Cross Reference
See Colour Review

◀ An Art Deco patinated metal lamp, modelled as a young girl rolling a frosted glass snowball shade, inscribed 'A. J. Scottie', c1930, 9in (23cm) high.
£150–175 DN

WALL LIGHTS

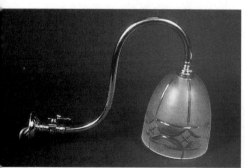

A pair of brass swan-necked wall lights, with etched glass shades, originally for gas lighting, early 1900s, 12½in (32cm) high.
£240–270 LIB

▶ Three Farraday & Son silver-plated double-arm wall lights, c1910, 12in (30.5cm) long.
£240–260 JW

A pair of French gilded-brass wall sconces, c1900, 13in (33cm) high.
£90–120 JW

An Arts and Crafts lacquered copper wall light, c1900, 17in (43cm) high.
£280–320 WAC

◀ A pair of brass wall sconces, with frosted glass shades, c1920, 12in (30.5cm) long.
£120–150 JW

Lithophanes

A lithophane is a translucent porcelain plaque, presenting an indistinct and opaque moulded surface until held up to the light, when a three-dimensional grisaille picture appears. The word comes from the Greek *litho* (stone) and *phanes* (appearance). The complex process which involved making a wax model of the image, encasing it in plaster of Paris and then producing a metal mould used for the slip or liquid porcelain, was invented by Baron Paul de Bourgoing in France in 1827. The Baron granted licences to various factories throughout Europe and the Royal Berlin Factory became one of the major manufacturers.

Lithophane plaques, which were made until c1900, were popular as decorative items. They were hung on windows, incorporated into lights and occasionally on the underside of cups, so that when the tea cup was drained a magical image would be revealed.

A Victorian lithophane plaque, depicting a cherub, 5¾in (14.5cm) diam.
£55–60 JMC

A lithophane plaque, depicting an angel flying in clouds above a landscape, 5 x 4in (12.5 x 10cm).
£60–70 JMC

A lithophane plaque, depicting St Elizabeth, Queen of Hungary, c1880–90, 5¾ x 4¾in (14.5 x 12cm).
£250–300 PC
While she was distributing bread to the poor, St Elizabeth was challenged by her husband, who opposed her charitable work. Miraculously, the loaves had been turned into roses.

A late Victorian lithophane plaque, depicting Mount Vesuvius, Naples, c1880, 6½ x 5in (16.5 x 12.5cm).
£250–275 PC

A Victorian lithophane plaque, depicting an Austrian boy bearing a posy of flowers and dancing in a pastoral landscape, 2½ x 3in (6.5 x 7.5cm).
£45–50 JMC

A lithophane plaque, depicting angels, 1880–90, 5¼ x 4½in (13.5 x 11.5cm).
£225–250 PC

LOCATE THE SOURCE
The source of each illustration in Miller's can be found by checking the code letters below each caption with the Key to Illustrations, pages 476–484.

▶ A German nickel-plated table stove, with four lithophane panels, each depicting country buildings, c1900, 5in (12.5cm) wide.
£80–90 SK(B)

A cup with lithophane base, depicting an angel, the cup decorated in gilt and white and inscribed 'A Present from Hastings', 1910, 3in (7.5cm) high.
£50–55 TAC

Medals

COMMEMORATIVE

A silver medal, commemorating the death of Princess Louisa, by N. Roettier, with a bust of James III with long hair, the reverse with a bust of Princess Louisa, 1712, 52mm diam.
£220–250 BAL

A white metal medal, commemorating the death of Matthew Boulton FRS, in the style of P. Rouw, with a draped bust of Boulton and two cherubs holding a model of the Soho Mint building, the reverse with inscription, 1809, 46mm diam.
£110–130 BAL

A silver prize medal, inscribed 'The General Agricultural Society Assembling at Doncaster Instituted 1813', by W. Turnpenny, with a large bull standing next to a tree surrounded by three sheep, inscribed 'Prize Medal, Guineas', the reverse with farming implements and a sheaf of corn, 73mm diam.
£650–750 BAL

◄ A white metal medal, commemorating the completion of Birmingham Town Hall, by E. Thomason, with a view of the Town Hall, the reverse with inscription, 1834, 73mm diam.
£50–60 BAL

A bronze gilt medal, commemorating Bebington Horticultural Society, by J. Isaac, with a bowl of flowers with a legend around, the reverse inscribed 'Prize Medal' within a wreath, 1843, 45mm diam, in original case.
£40–50 BAL

A silver medal, commemorating the Prince of Wales' visit to India 1875–76, with a bust of Prince Albert, the reverse with Prince of Wales feathers, surrounded by the Royal Garter and inscription, damaged, 61mm high.
£150–175 DNW

An American silver bar medal, insribed Boston Bicycle Club Wheel About The Hub, above a monogrammed pendant star, suspending the medal by chains, with pendant No. 22 attached, 1879, 32mm diam.
£1,500–1,700 S
The Boston Bicycle Club sponsored the first official bicycle ride in the United States in September 1879. This medal was for rider number 22.

A bronze medal commemorating, Augustus Pitt-Rivers, by Pinches, with a theodolite, pick-axe, skull and shield, the reverse inscribed 'Opened by A. Pitt-Rivers FRS', 1880, 38mm diam.
£125–150 BAL
Augustus Pitt-Rivers (1827–1900) changed his surname from Lane Fox after inheriting his great-uncle's estates. After a career in the army, he devoted his life to archaeology. Several of these medals were dated and then buried in barrows that had been excavated by Pitt-Rivers.

A French cast-bronze medal, commemorating the Siege of the Bastille, by P. F. Palloy, with a view of the siege, with integral loop for suspension, 1789, 78mm diam.
£35–45 DNW

A gold prize medal, commemorating the English Jersey Cattle Society, with the head of a Jersey cow, the reverse with wreath border, 1883, 44mm diam.
£260–300 BAL

Prices

The price ranges quoted in this book reflect the average price a purchaser might expect to pay for a similar item. The price will vary according to the condition, rarity, size, popularity, provenance, colour and restoration of the item and this must be taken into account when assessing values. Don't forget that if you are selling it is quite likely that you will be offered less than the price range.

A plated-bronze medal, commemorating the Association Française Pour l'Avancement Des Sciences, by L. O. Roty, with a female seated under a tree reading a book, the reverse with figures of France and Science in greeting, 1890, 68mm diam.
£110–130 DNW

A bronze medal, commemorating William Gladstone, The Member of Parliament for 1894, by L. C. Lauer, with a bust of Gladstone, the reverse with an inscription listing the members of the House for the year, 95mm diam.
£130–150 BAL

A uniface cast bronze medal, commemorating Rene Pallix, by L. Desvignes for Canale, with Pan playing pipes, the reverse inscribed, 1907, 100mm diam, mounted on a plinth.
£170–200 DNW

A gilt prize medal, commemorating Crufts Dog Show, with a bust of a dog, the reverse inscribed 'Won by G. E. Pridmores, Bashfuldi', fine ring mounted with a crown above and held within a glass lunette on the reverse, 1910, 41mm diam.
£65–75 BAL

► A bronze medal, commemorating the 75th Anniversary of the Société Générale, by P. Turin, with female bust, the reverse with two cornucopiae and inscription, 1939, 31mm diam.
£90–110 DNW

A cast-bronze trial for a medal, commemorating the 700th Anniversary of the Death of Saint Francis of Assisi, by P. Turin, with a bust of St Francis and artist's signature on the right, the reverse with St Francis ministering to a flock of birds, 1926, 87mm diam.
£90–110 DNW

A silver-gilt award medal, commemorating the 25th Anniversary of the Chambre Syndicale des Industries Aeronautiques, by C. Mascaux, the reverse with inscription, 1933, 68mm diam.
£160–180 DNW

A German cast-bronze medallic jeton or members' pass, for Bodo Goeke, Dortmund, with a female baring her behind, marked, 1950s, 38mm diam.
£100–120 DNW
Bodo Goeke was a men's club.

MILITARY & CIVILIAN

A Baltic war medal, awarded to members of the Royal Navy, 1854–55.
£130–150 Q&C

► Two medals, awarded to Thomas William Wisdom, George V Imperial Service Medal, and George VI Imperial Service Medal.
£25–30 RMC

A pair of WWI medals, awarded to Private J. W. Poole, Royal Warwickshire Regiment, complete with box and slip of issue.
£40–50 RMC

Three Canadian medals, awarded
to Sergeant R. Thompson,
Canadian General Service Medal
with Fenian Raid bar 1886,
Afghanistan 1878–80, Army Long
Service and Good Conduct Medal
with scroll suspender.
£420–460 WAL

Four medals, awarded to Capt.
D. Hardy, Royal Field Artillery,
Military Cross 1917, 1914–15
Star, British War Medal and
Victory Medal.
£525–575 RMC

Three medals, awarded to Sergeant
S. F. Tandy, Royal Field Artillery,
Military Medal 1919, British War
Medal and Victory Medal.
£180–220 RMC

Six WWI medals, awarded to Sergeant F. W. Francis,
Essex Regiment, Military Medal George V first type,
1914–15 Star, BWM, Victory, IGS 1908, North West
Frontier with bar, 1930–31, Army Long Service and
Good Conduct Medal.
£275–300 WAL

Five WWI medals, awarded to Sergeant P. E. Todd of
the Royal Garrison Artillery, 1914–15 Star, 1914–15
War Medal, Victory Medal, Defence Medal, Army Long
Service and Good Conduct Medal.
£60–70 RMC

Two medals, Hartlepool Special Constabulary Medal
inscribed 'Borough of Hartlepool Special Constable,
Bombardment 1914, Air Raids 1915–18, Zeppelin
Destroyed 1916', with original claw and straight bar
suspension, and a Special Constabulary Long Service
Medal, GVR with bar, The Great War 1914–18,
possibly awarded to Anthony D. Short.
£270–300 DNW

Six WWII medals, awarded to Marine R. A. Jessop,
Royal Marines, 1939–45 Star, Atlantic Star,
Africa Star, Italy Star, War Medal, Naval General
Service Medal.
£200–220 RMC

▶ A Mine Rescue Bronze Medal, awarded
to William Jenkinson, with a bust of King
George V in naval uniform, the reverse
inscribed 'South Kirby, Featherstone &
Hemsworth Collieries Ltd, Awarded for Bravery
in the South Kirby Mine, February 1922', with
original Fattorini & Sons presentation case.
£375–425 DNW

◀ A George VI Coronation Medal,
lady's issue, 1937, in original box.
£15–20 AOH

Metalware

A leaded bronze steelyard weight, or weight of Auncel, the body cast with three armorial shields, the English Three Lions, the Poitou Lion Rampant, and the Hansa double-headed Eagle, 13thC, 3in (7.5cm) high.
£550–650 S(S)

A Hand in Hand Fire Office lead firemark, with clasped hands surmounted by a crown and with policy No. 84687 below, early 19thC, 7in (18cm) wide.
£375–400 DN
Firemarks were nailed on buildings as proof that they had insurance.

An iron coaching jack, early 19thC, 28in (71cm) high.
£180–200 SEA

A steel tobacco cutter, mid-19thC, 4in (10cm) long.
£60–70 ALA

A toleware tea tray, with painted and gilt chinoiserie decoration depicting three figures surrounded by flowers, mid-19thC, 33in (84cm) wide.
£300–350 TMA
The term toleware derives from the USA and was used to describe objects made from tinplate and then covered with black alsphatum varnish and painted with decorations, in imitation of oriental lacquer.

A cast-bronze armorial bearings of the City of Chester, 19thC, 20in (51cm) wide.
£300–350 Hal(C)

An Old Hall stainless steel coffee pot, Campden Range, designed by Robert Welch, c1956, 7in (18cm) high.
£30–35 GRo
Robert Welch was one of Britain's leading craftsmen in silver and metalware. In 1955 he was appointed consultant designer to Old Hall. Inspired by Scandinavian design, he produced a range of contemporary tableware in stainless steel, previously considered an industrial material. Both the Campden Range of the 1950s and the Alveston tableware of the 1960s, are becoming increasingly collectable.

A pair of metal knife rests, 1885, 3in (7.5cm) long.
£15–18 WAC

◀ A metal and brass bird cage, c1920, 19in (48.5cm) high.
£80–90 FA

A pair of brass nutcrackers, 18thC, 4in (10cm) long.
30–35 WAC

A Dutch brass and copper tobacco box, the top and sides engraved with figures and inscriptions, c1780, 6in (15cm) wide.
£200–220 OCH

A brass skimmer, with an iron handle, 1780, 28in (71cm) long.
200–250 SEA

An Islamic embossed brass scroll case, 19thC, 4¼in (11cm) long.
£35–40 WAC

A brass four-letter combination lock, with the combination letters ATE, mid-19thC, 1½in (4cm) wide.
75–85 WAC

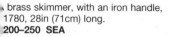

A brass postal scale, c1920, 5in (12.5cm) high.
35–45 WAB

A brass hot water can, c1890, 9½in (24cm) high.
£65–75 AL

Victorian brass knife sharpener, with cast decoration, maker's crest to the base, 5in (12.5cm) wide.
150–170 NEW

A brass fire engine bell, 1954, 11in (28cm) high.
110–130 CRN

Four Friendly Society brass pole heads, the largest engraved with a two-masted sailing ship, 1880–1910, largest 13in (33cm) high.
£130–150 DN
Friendly Societies – voluntary groups formed to protect members against debts incurred through accident, illness, old age and death – sprang up in the 17th and 18th centuries and flourished during the Victorian period. From their influence developed trade unions and life insurance companies. These brass pole heads were fixed to ceremonial staves carried during Friendly Society processions and are sometimes decorated with the symbol of the public house or tavern where the society held its meetings.

COPPER

An L. Lumley & Co copper quart haystack measure, 19thC, 6in (15cm) high.
£200–220 MFB

A copper hot water boiler, with lid and brass tap, mid-19thC, 12in (30.5cm) high.
£220–240 NEW

A copper charcoal burner, c1880, 16in (40.5cm) high.
£235–265 WAC

A Benson copper three-pint conical thermos, with horn knop, copper handle and tin base, c1900, 11in (28cm) high.
£165–185 HUN

◄ A copper ale muller, with an iron handle, 19thC, 11in (28cm) high.
£80–90 SEA

► A copper nameplate, 1950s, 9 x 14in (23 x 35.5cm).
£12–15 FA

PEWTER

Pewter, an alloy of tin, often with traces of lead, antimony and copper, was used for tableware and ornamental objects from Roman times until the end of the 18th century, when ceramics, glass and other forms of metalware provided increasingly popular and affordable alternatives. In the Victorian period, pewter remained popular in pubs, where drinkers required unbreakable tankards, and in the kitchen to produce objects such as ice cream and confectionery moulds. At the turn of the 19th century there was a revival in decorative pewter, particularly among Arts and Crafts and Art Nouveau designers. As the following selection shows, 18th century pewter sadware (the term used for plates, dishes and bowls) and hollow ware (tankards, pots etc) can still be collected at comparatively reasonable prices for simpler items. By law, manufacturers had to apply a mark, known as a 'touch', to their products, which was registered at the pewterer's local guild. Thanks to these touches, makers and dates can often be identified.

A Queen Anne pewter dish, by Leonard Terry of York, c1710, 9¼in (23.5cm) diam.
£240–260 AnSh

An Irish pewter plate, c1760, 9½in (24cm) diam.
£70–80 AnSh

► A Scottish pewter tappit hen, c1760, 12in (30.5cm) high.
£500–600 TWr
A tappit hen was the name given to a Scottish measure (a vessel designed to fill drinking cups in taverns), that held one Scottish pint, the equivalent of three English pints.

A Continental pewter bowl, with L. B. Finck touch mark, 18thC, 11in (28cm) diam.
£220–240 AnSh

▶ A pewter spice or pepper pot, c1800, 4½in (11.5cm) high.
£35–40 AnSh

A late Georgian pewter tobacco or 'tae' box, c1790, 5in (12.5cm) high.
£35–40 HEB
Tae meaning tea.

A George IV pewter pint measure, 4¼in (11cm) high.
£85–95 AnSh

A Samuel Locks pewter bowl, 1799–1820, 9½in (24cm) high.
£30–35 AnSh

A pewter quart tankard, late 18thC, 6in (15cm) high.
£120–140 AnSh

◀ A pewter spoon, by Thomas Yates, mid-19thC, 9in (23cm) long.
£30–35 AnSh

A pewter and brass gunpowder flask, c1840, 4in (10cm) high.
£75–90 WAB

A Victorian pewter half-pint mug, by James Yates, 5½in (14cm) high.
£50–55 AnS

A pewter hot water jug and cover, with leather-bound loop handle and hinged domed cover with thumb rest, owned and used by Charles Dickens, 1870, 8in (20.5cm) high.
£1,800–2,000 Hal
The cover of this jug is inscribed 'Purchased at the Sale at Gadshill August 11th 1870, Number 325 in Catalogue. This was constantly used by Charles Dickens in the preparation of his celebrated gin punch, brewed by the great author himself'.

A pewter confectionary mould, in the shape of a crown, 19thC, 3in (7.5cm) high.
£35–40 NEW

▶ An Art Nouveau WMF circular wall plaque, the shaped edge decorated with florets, the dished centre with the profile of a maiden within a band of vine leaves and grapes, marked, c1900, 12¼in (31cm) diam.
£450–500 DN

◀ An Art Nouveau WMF pewter vase, decorated with a child resting on a tree branch and a merman resting against the neck rim, c1900, 11½in (29cm) high.
£250–300 DN

An Art Nouveau WMF pewter centrepiece, in the form of a maiden wearing diaphanous robes that extend to form four linked dishes, marked, c1900, 10in (25.5cm) high.
£650–750 DN

STATUETTES & MODELS

A Tula cast-iron stag group, after P. J. Mene, Russia, c1865, 5½in (14cm) high.
£500–550 ChA

A Coalbrookdale cast-iron group of a mare and stallion, in the style of P. J. Mene, damaged, late 19thC, 14in (35.5cm) high.
£400–450 Hal(C)

A Viennese cold-painted bronze figure of an African boy, c1880, 4in (10cm) high.
£400–480 TWr

A French bronze model of St Joan of Arc, in the style of Chapu, with mid-brown patination, stamped 'F. Barbedienne Fondeur', 19thC, 21in (53.5cm) high.
£1,100–1,300 Hal(C)

◀ A Lorenzl painted bronze figure of a dancing girl, wearing a silver skirt and jacket with three red buttons, on a green columnar marble base, 1925, 11in (28cm) high.
£800–900 P(B)

▶ A Benin bronze bust of a queen of the Ifa period, wearing a tall headdress and with a coiled necklace, early 20thC, 18in (45.5cm) high.
£400–450 HYD

Militaria

horn gunpowder flask,
arly 18thC, 7in (18cm) long.
80–90 BSA

King's Dragoon Guards
opper miniature kettledrum,
ith embossed crest, c1900,
n (20.5cm) diam.
600–750 Q&C

A pair of Machine Gun
orps engraved silver
nd niello napkin rings,
914–18, 2in (5cm) wide.
28–32 each AOH

A Continental brass side drum,
c1800, 15in (38cm) high.
£120–140 CYA

A chrome clockwork flash gun,
c1910, 7in (18cm) high.
£35–40 WAB

◄ An Odiham RAF
Gunnery School
Sergeants' Farewell
Dinner menu, decorated
in colours with a WWI-
era fighter plane and a
dove, with signatures,
dated 20th February
1920, folio.
£55–60 DW

◄ A Trench
Art bi-plane,
made from
ammunition,
1914–18,
9in (23cm) long.
£75–100 COB

A major part of the silk Regimental
Colour of the 2nd North British
Militia, Ross-shire, the centre
embroidered in colours on both
sides with the Regimental title
on a crimson escutcheon,
within a circular wreath of
thistles and roses and with a
shamrock spray below, together
with fragments of the King's
Colour, c1805, 66 x 56in
(167.5 x 142cm).
£400–480 WAL

A German NGDAP enamel war sign, from Bergen, Norway, 1944, 20in (51cm) square.
£375–450 COB

Field Marshal Montgomery, a signed photograph, half-length in a tank watching the progress of the Battl of El Alamein, signed 22 May 1972, 8 x 10in (20.5 x 25.5cm).
£170–200 VS

A Dutch East Indies WWII gift of tea to occupied Holland, the cotton bag containing tea, with label in Dutch 'Holland will rise again. Greetings from the Free Netherlands Indies. Keep in good heart', c1941, bag 2in (5cm) wide.
£150–170 DNW
During March and April 1941, about 4,000 pounds of tea, a gift from the Dutch of Batavia, were dropped by British bombers over Holland in small cotton bags. The reaction of the Dutch people to the gift, as reported by their Naval Attaché in London, was 'why not bombs?'. The Free French, however, were more impressed, and asked for coffee to be dropped over France! Ten crates, suitably sub-divided, were accordingly distributed by various Operational Training Unit crews.

A military flag kit, containing red, orange and green flags, c1950, 33in (84cm) long.
£35–40 WAB

▶ A white metal figure, Coldstream Guard Drummer, by D. Grieves, 1990s, 4in (10cm) high.
£40–45 BONA

ARMOUR & UNIFORMS

▶ A Dutch lobster-tail helmet, with four-piece articulated neck guard and adjustable nasal bar, ear flaps missing, mid-17thC.
£900–1,000 WAL

A Spanish morion helmet, with brass rosettes round the base, late 16thC, 11½in (29cm) high.
£1,400–1,600 WAL
Morion was the name given to helmets worn in the 16th and 17th centuries without a visor or face guard, known as a beaver.

A Scottish breastplate, with articulated shoulders, 16thC, 15in (38cm) high.
£550–650 CYA

▶ A Victorian 25th Lanarkshire Rifle Volunteers officer's blue cloth helmet, with gilt fittings, in original japanned tin, 16in (40.5cm) high.
£275–325 P(Sc)

319

A pair of junior battalion company officer's full dress box epaulettes, 28th Regiment, North Gloucestershire, retailed by W. & T. Buckmaster, 1840–55, 3in (7.5cm) long, with original chamois-lined carrying tin.
£350–400 DNW

A Scottish cross sword belt, with silver-plated buckle, c1880, 4in (10cm) wide.
£70–80 BWA

▶ A French cuirassier's brass helmet, with red plume and black horsehair tail, c1920, tail 32in (81.5cm) long.
£650–750 CYA

A German double-decal M40 Organization Todt combat helmet, with leather lining and chinstrap, dated 1941.
£250–280 WAL

◀ A WWII German full-length leather coat, by Leder Mollath, Nürnberg, 1930s.
£250–350 CYA

▶ An RAF bandsman's moleskin busby, with blue horsehair plume, post-1952.
£110–125 Q&C

BADGES, BUCKLES & PLATES

A Royal Glamorgan Light Infantry Militia officer's shoulder-belt plate, with gilt back-plate, 1812–30.
£550–600 Gle

A King's Own Light Infantry Militia, Tower Hamlets, officer's gilt shako plate, 1844–55.
£475–525 Gle

◀ A Long Range Desert Group bronzed cap badge, with scorpion design, c1943.
£150–170 WAL

▶ A 2nd/21st Aboyne Highland Rifle Volunteers OR's glengarry badge, c1865.
£450–500 WAL

A Royal Scots 5th Volunteer Battalion officer's silver-plated helmet plate, with gilt and green enamel overlays, 1890–1901.
£450–500 DNW

A 9th Lanarkshire Rifle Volunteers silvered white metal helmet plate, 1880–90.
£180–200 DNW

EDGED WEAPONS

A Continental trooper's sword, with double-edge blade with maker's incised device, the iron hilt with twin pierced guards with raised borders and woven copper wire-bound grip, 17thC, blade 31¾in (78.5cm) long.
£600–660 **WAL**

A Highland dirk, with silver-mounted foil-backed citrine stones, c1780, 19in (48.5cm) long.
£2,000–2,300 **BWA**

A French cuirassier's sword, with brass hilt and steel scabbard, c1813, 40in (101.5cm) long.
£630–700 **CYA**

An Indian axe, from Chota Nagpur, on a steel-mounted wooden haft, 19thC, blade 8in (20.5cm) long.
£150–170 **WAL**

An Indian copper-gilt *jambiya*, from the Hindu Kush, with copper hilt chiselled with flowers and foliage, 19thC, blade 5½in (14cm) long.
£120–140 **WAL**

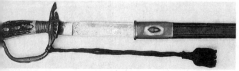

A Nazi Forestry Service cutlass, by WKC, the blade etched with deer and a dog stalking a fox, in a brass-mounted black leather scabbard, 1935, blade 13in (33cm) long.
£350–400 **WAL**

FIREARMS

A percussion pistol, with Tower of London markings, 1850, 16in (40.5cm) long.
£250–350 CYA

A brass-barrelled flintlock blunderbuss, with brass mounts and foliate engraved, pineapple-finialled trigger guard, c1815, 29½in (75cm) long.
£600–650 WAL

▶ A .577 Enfield P56 rifled second model percussion holster pistol, with later detachable shoulder stock, lock dated 1859, barrel 10in (25.5cm) long.
£500–550 WAL

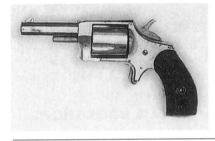

◀ An American five shot .32 RF Defender SA pocket revolver, the barrel, frame and cylinder nickel-plated overall, the black ebonite grips embossed with American eagles, c1880, 6½in (16.5cm) long.
£200–220 WAL

An STR model anti-aircraft gun, c1915, 11in (28cm) long.
£120–150 BKS

POLICE & FIRE BRIGADE

▶ A collection of Fire Brigade memorabilia, relating to fireman H. Hughes of Westcliffe on Sea, Essex, comprising a brass helmet, medals, and a framed and glazed photograph, early 20thC.
£550–600 TMA

A St Pancras police officer's truncheon, decorated with a crown and inscription in red, gold and yellow on a black ground, 19thC, 17½in (44.5cm) long.
£200–230 CCB

A fireman's axe, with painted wooden haft, red ribbed grip and copper plate stamped 'Fire 1807 Exon 3', 25in (63.5cm) long.
£110–130 WAL

An Indian Police sword, with leather case and belt, 1920s, 40in (101.5cm) long.
£270–300 BWA

A pair of California Highway Patrol Police Motorcycle Unit boots, America, 1965, 18in (45.5cm) high
£110–130 COB

Money Boxes

An American Creedmore Bank cast-iron mechanical money box, by James Bowen, with a man in a blue jacket and red trousers, 19thC, 10in (25.5cm) long.
£300–350 HAL

A cast-iron money box, modelled as a County Bank, 1891, 5in (12.5cm) high.
£200–220 MFB

A Continental pottery money box, modelled as a pig lying on a couch, in brown and cream, restored, c1900, 4in (10cm) long.
£40–45 HAL

A Victorian cast-iron novelty money box, in the form of a bust with an open mouth, 7in (18cm) high.
£60–70 HAL
This style was made by various manufacturers.

◄ A brown and cream stoneware money box, made for J. S. Carpenter, born 1889, 7in (18cm) high.
£200–230 MFB

A Lloyds Bank red leather book-shaped money box, c1955, 5in (12.5cm) long.
£12–15 HUX

A cast-iron money box, modelled as Blackpool Tower, c1907, 7in (18cm) high.
£200–220 MFB

A Mickey Mouse tin mechanical money box, decorated in red, yellow, orange and black on a yellow and green ground, 1930s, 7in (18cm) high.
£9,000–10,000 HAL

Newspapers & Magazines

The Daily Gazetteer, Tuesday,
21 October 1746, reporting
the war in Sardinia, 16 x 10in
(40.5 x 25.5cm).
£40–50 HaR

The Illustrated London News,
Saturday, 19 November 1859,
reporting the war in Morocco,
16 x 11in (40.5 x 28cm).
£5–6 HaR

Six copies of *Le Petit Parisien,*
containing six coloured illustrations
of early aviation interest on the
front or rear covers, 1910–11, folio
£150–170 DW

An American pamphlet,
*The National League for
the Civic Education of
Women,* giving details of
lectures, literature and
meetings, with a list of
Board members on the
back cover, 1911–12,
5¼ x 3¼in (13.5 x 8.5cm).
£150–170 VS

The Sphere, 20 April
1912, the front cover
with a photographic
impression of the *Titanic*
near icebergs.
£55–65 ONS

A *Weekly Illustrated*
magazine, Saturday,
18 January 1936,
the front cover depicting
Gertrude Lawrence
and Noel Coward,
16 x 11in (40.5 x 28cm).
£8–10 RTT

A *Melody Maker* magazine
16 October 1948,
17 x 11in (43 x 28cm).
£4–5 RTT

**LOCATE THE
SOURCE**

The source of each
illustration in Miller's
can be found by
checking the code
letters below each
caption with the
Key to Illustrations,
pages 476–484.

▶ An *In Focus*
magazine, depicting
James Bond 007, brown
and black on a white
ground, 1964, 10 x 8in
(25.5 x 20.5cm).
£6–8 CTO

◀ A *Rave* magazine, No. 2
1964, the cover depicting
Cliff Richard, in naturalistic
colours on a dark ground,
11¾ x 8¼in (29 x 21cm).
£12–15 BTC

Paper Money

A Pennsylvania six shillings note, printed in orange on a cream ground, America, dated 1777.
£85–95 NAR

A Pembrokeshire Bank five pound note, with a vignette of a castle by a river, 1830s.
£85–100 NAR

A Standard Bank, Mafeking Branch two shillings voucher, signed by Captain Greener, February 1900.
£60–70 WP
Mafeking in South Africa was besieged by the Boers from 16 October 1899 to 17 May 1900. When the bank ran short of coins, Garrison Commander Robert Baden-Powell, later founder of the Boy Scout movement, issued money vouchers. Vouchers were also produced in the town of Kimberley during the Boer war, but for food rather than money.

South Africa Kimberley Siege soup voucher, 1900, 2¼in (5.5cm) wide.
£100–120 NAR

A National Bank of Scotland one pound note, printed in yellow, orange and blue on a white ground, 1917.
£130–150 WP

An Iceland Bank five kronur note, printed in red and black on a white ground, 1920.
£100–120 NAR

A Bank of England five pound note, signed by B. S. Catterns, Chief Cashier, Leeds, 1929, ¼in (21cm) wide.
£180–200 WP

A States of Jersey WWII occupation one shilling note, printed in brown on a cream ground, 4½in (11.5cm) wide.
£60–70 WP

A Clydesdale & North of Scotland Bank one pound note, printed in orange and black, with a shipyard and rural vignettes, 1955, 6in (15cm) wide.
£25–30 WP

Lucky find!

The habit of hiding money under the bed, or in other secret places, can mean that people forget where they put it. Still, one man's loss is another man's gain. After buying an antique desk for £500, one lucky purchaser found a secret compartment containing a hand-written £100 Bank of England note, dated 12 October 1790, that had lain there undisturbed for more than two centuries. The note was sold at a recent Spinks auction, where it fetched £40,250.

◀ A German WWII Buchenwald canteen voucher, 4in (10cm) wide.
£40–50 NAR

A Seychelles five rupees note, printed in pink and green on a white ground, 1942.
£145–165 NAR

A New Zealand Postal Note, two shillings, printed in orange and black on a white ground, 1963, 6¾in (17cm) wide.
£12–15 WP

A Central Bank of Ireland £100 note, printed in orange and black on a white ground, 1973, 8in (20.5cm) wide.
£150–170 WP

A Central African Republic 500 franc note, printed in orange, yellow and brown on a white ground, 1974, 6in (15cm) wide.
£85–95 NAR

Paperweights

green glass dump,
60, 3½in (9cm) high.
5–90 JBL

Wedgwood glass
per-weight, modelled
a pink elephant,
o. 28368, 1969–84,
in (11.5cm) high.
0–55 SWB

Correia glass paper-
ight, with a black cat
one side of a gold fish
wl, in pink, green and
aque glass, America,
99, 2½in (6.5cm) high.
80–200 SWB

A Ferro & Lazzarini,
rano, glass paperweight,
mmemorating the first
drogen sealed-balloon
ht on 19th September
84, in pink, green,
uve and white, Italy,
00, 3¾in (9.5cm) diam.
0–35 SWB

A green glass dump, with
flower-shaped inclusions,
1860, 5½in (14cm) high.
£230–250 JBL

▶ A Caithness Glass Planet Set
No. 1, depicting Mars, Mercury,
Saturn and Venus, from a limited
edition of 500, 1969.
£1,400–1,500 Cai
**When they were first issued
in 1969, the price for the set
of four was £45.**

A Baccarat glass paper-
weight, with sweet peas
and a ladybird in pink
and green on a green
speckled ground, from
a limited edition of 200,
1985, 3in (7.5cm) diam.
£250–275 SWB

Cross Reference
See Colour Review

A green glass dump,
with a rooster inclusion,
1860, 3in (7.5cm) high.
£100–120 JBL

A North Queensland
Insurance Co advertising
glass paperweight,
inscribed in red and black,
c1900, 3in (7.5cm) diam
£20–25 SWB

Photography

The photography market is currently extremely buoyant. Recently a number of record auction prices have been achieved including £343,750 for a photograph of the Ford Detroit car works, by 20th century American photographer Charles Sheeler, and an astonishing £460,000 for a Mediterranean landscape by 19th century French photographer Gustave Le Gray. As these results show, demand is strong for both early academic works by the pioneers of photography, as well as for later, avant garde and artistic compositions. The small selection shown here includes a couple of the greatest and most collectable names in photography.

While the photographer is one major issue, another is the subject, and prices are also strong for albums of topographic views, interesting historical themes, and portraits of notable personalities. Though some of the prices include four-, five- and even six-figure sums, equally we show Victorian and Edwardian photographs for under £100, and much can still be found at affordable price levels.

An American 1/6th plate daguerreotype, in a leather-covered velvet-lined case, c1850, 3½ x 2in (9 x 5cm).
£50–60 APC

Three papier mâché and mother-of-pearl daguerreotype cases, 1850s, 4 x 3in (10 x 7.5cm).
£150–180 APC

A photogenic drawing, Plant Impression, by William Henry Fox Talbot, c1839, 9 x 7in (23 x 18cm).
£130,000–150,000 S
William Henry Fox Talbot is known as the father of photography. He produced and developed the idea of the negative/positive system, allowing unlimited amounts of positive images to be reproduced from a master negative.

A set of 12 shikar photographs, by Lt Col Willoughby Wallace Hooper, mounted on old album leaves, numbered and captioned in ink, c1870, 7 x 9in (18 x 23cm).
£1,500–1,700 DW
Lt Col Hooper (1837–1912), 7th Madras Light Cavalry, concentrated on photographing life in India from c1860 and often collaborated with veterinary surgeon George Watson.

A photograph album, containing 3 views of Devon, Dorset, Kent and Ireland, 19thC, 6 x 8in (15 x 20.5cm).
£150–170 SWO

A group portrait of Sir William Mansfield and his staff, taken at Simla, 1867, attributed to Bourne & Shepherd Studios, the albumen print mounted on card, 7 x 11½in (18 x 29cm).
£400–450 DW

◀ A Lauer's Patent Revolving Photo-graph Cabinet, by Taft & Schwane, Chicago, the incised wood case with curved glass top and maker's label on base, 1860–70, 10in (25.5cm) high.
£800–900 SK(B)

A collection of 65 photographs of York, including the railway station and street scenes, some on album leaves, 1870–90, largest 7 x 13in (18 x 33cm).
£450–500 BBA

A photograph of the South Notts Hounds Crossing the Trent, c1890, 14 x 9in (35.5 x 23cm).
£55–65 WAB

A photograph of King Edward VII, in a wooden frame, 1908, 6 x 8in (15 x 20.5cm).
£45–50 COB

A walnut Megalethoscope, by Charles Ponti, complete with viewing and field lenses, mirror, photo racks, adjuster and instruction label, on cradle stand, with 26 albumen print views, c1875, 36in (91.5cm) long.
£2,800–3,300 SK(B)

A photograph of the St Ives Fire Brigade, 1893, 11 x 9in (28 x 23cm).
£75–85 WAB

A photograph of Prince George, Prince of Wales, signed 'George P', 1908, 7 x 11in (18 x 28cm).
£550–600 AEL

◄ A school football team photograph, inscribed 'J. E. Moss Esq, House Eleven, 1911', 18 x 15in (45.5 x 38cm)
£35–45 WAB

Two albumen print studies of Oscar Wilde, by Napoleon Sarony, mounted on card, one with photographer's facsimile signature, 1882, largest 6 x 4in (15 x 10cm).
£4,000–4,500 S

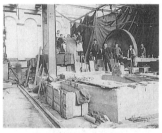

A blue calf album containing platinum and gelatin silver prints, depicting the building and construction trade, c1898–1908, with family photographs, compiled by J. R. Swales, largest 7½ x 9½in (19 x 24cm).
£120–150 Bon

A photograph of a group of Edwardian nurses, 21 x 14in (53.5 x 35.5cm).
£40–50 WAB

A collection of 47 black and white photographs, relating to aircraft, loosely mounted in a contemporary cloth album, 1922–23, each photograph 8 x 6½in (20.5 x16.5cm).
£280–320 DW

A silver print, by Man Ray, Noire et Blanche, mounted on card and signed and dated in the negative, and on the mount, 1926, 8 x 11in (20.5 x 28cm).
£150,000–180,000 S
Few of Man Ray's vintage prints have survived, and this, showing his muse, model and mistress Kiki de Montparnasse, is one of the artist's most famous images.

A signed presentation photograph of Prince Philip, in a black leather frame, 1973, 7 x 10in (18 x 25.5cm).
£450–500 AEL

PHOTOGRAPH FRAMES

A silver photograph frame, 1896, 3½in (9cm) high.
£170–190 SWO

A Victorian carved oak photograph frame, 44 x 27in (112 x 68.5cm).
£250–275 AMR

An Art Nouveau wooden free-standing photograph frame, embellished with metal flowers, 7 x 8in (18 x 20.5cm).
£60–70 AMR

◄ A bronze picture frame, decorated with a rural landscape scene, waterfall and flowers, 1910, 8¼ x 6½in (21 x 16.5cm).
£125–145 CHAP

A Victorian mahogany photograph frame, 4 x 3in (10 x 7.5cm).
£35–40 AMR

A wooden propeller blade photograph frame, containing a portrait of a soldier, 1940s, 12in (30.5cm) high.
£65–75 SPT

Postcards

A French postcard, 'Souvenir de Paris', depicting Notre Dame in muted colours, c1900.
£6–8 JMC

A 'Girls Own Picture' postcard, with coloured vignette of a young woman, c1900.
£10–12 JMC

A base relief postcard of HM Queen Alexandra, from Photo Alliance Series No. 21422-95, 1900–10.
£12–15 ES

A photographic postcard, 'Boer War, The 10th Hussars', published by Picture Postcard Co, London, c1899.
£12–15 JMC

A photographic postcard, 'Boer War, Rhodesian Horse', published by Picture Postcard Co, London, c1900.
£12–15 JMC

◀ A postcard, 'A Champion Skuller', from the George Cruikshank Series, published by Raphael Tuck & Sons, 1901.
£8–10 JMC

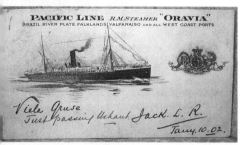

A Pacific Line postcard, depicting RM Steamer *Oravia*, in blue, yellow, red and black on a white ground, 1902.
£15–20 JMC

◀ A photographic postcard, depicting two Oxfordshire Steam Ploughing Company steam-rollers with a group of workmen, c1910–20.
£65–75 DN

Two photographic postcards of delivery carts, one cart belonging to G. Briggs, Baker and Confectioner, postmarked Gainsborough 1907, the other cart to Jarvis & Sons Model Bakery of Tickhill, postmarked 1909.
£55–65 DN

A photographic postcard of a horse bus at the Coach Office at Ilfracombe, 1910.
£20–25 JMC

A WWI coloured silk embroidered greetings card, 'Yours Always', with a front pocket for a message, 1916–20
£7–8 GAA

Two Pit Disaster photographic postcards, the Universal Pit at Senghenydd in 1913, and a scene of the Wattstown Disaster, National Colliery, c1910–15.
£30–35 DN

◀ A real photo postcard of SS *Titanic* in dock at Southampton, photographed by H. Symes, 1912.
£160–180 DN

A WWI coloured silk embroidered postcard, The Queens Own Cameron Highlanders, unused.
£45–50 SpP

A WW1 coloured silk embroidered postcard, 'A Kiss from Belgium'.
£10–15 GAA

▶ A Mabel Lucy Attwell postcard, 'I'se Making a Bit of a Splash Here', in brown, yellow and red on a white ground, 1920.
£8–10 MEM

Posters

A GPO poster, an Imperial Airways Flying Boat at Croydon, by H. S. Williamson, printed in fawn, white, blue and green, 1934, 25 x 20in (63.5 x 51cm).
£180–200 DAL

An American MGM lobby card, '*The Wizard of Oz*', printed in red, yellow, blue, green and black on a cream ground, 1939, 11 x 14in (28 x 35.5cm).
£1,300–1,500 S

A coloured poster, 'Richmond on the London & North Eastern Railway', by Fred Taylor, printed by Adams Bros, c1930, 40 x 25in (101.5 x 63cm).
£380–420 ONS

An American MGM film poster, '*The Pirate*', printed in blue, red, yellow, black and green, 1948, 41 x 27in (104 x 68.5cm).
£500–550 S

A British Railways coloured lithographic poster 'Cornwall', by Gyrth Russell, printed by Jordison & Co, c1950, 40 x 50in (101.5 x 127cm).
£650–700 ONS

An American 20th Century Fox linen-backed film poster, '*The Big Noise*', printed in blue, red, yellow, black and green, 1944, 41 x 27in (104 x 68.5cm).
£400–450 S

► A Belgian Universal linen-backed film poster, '*Frankenstein*', printed in red and green, 1950s, 22 x 14in (56 x 35.5cm).
£500–600 S

An American Warner Bros film poster, '*A Star is Born*', printed in red, purple, blue and white, 1954, 41 x 27in (104 x 68.5cm).
£350–400 S

An American 20th Century Fox film poster, '*Love Me Tender*', printed in blue and red on a yellow ground, 1956, 30 x 20in (76 x 51cm).
£200–240 Bon(C)

A German Paramount linen-backed film poster, '*Psycho*', printed in yellow, red and blue on a beige and black ground, 1960, 33 x 23in (84 x 58.5cm).
£500–550 S

An American MGM film poster, '*The Time Machine*', printed in colours on a black and yellow ground, 1960, 41 x 27in (104 x 68.5cm).
£250–300 S

An Art Council Exhibition poster, 'Miro at the Tate', printed in red, black, yellow and green, 1964, 20 x 30 (51 x 76cm).
£330–400 CJP

A Hammer film poster, '*Slave Girls*', printed in pink and black, 1966, 30 x 40in (76 x 101.5cm).
£80–90 Bon(C)

An American concert poster, Arthur Conley, printed in yellow and black, 1968, 22 x14in (56 x 35.5cm).
£85–100 CTO

A film poster, '*One Million Years BC*', printed in pink, brown and grey, 1966, 30 x 40in (76 x 101.5cm).
£130–150 Bon(C)

An American concert poster, Simon & Garfunkel, by Milton Glaser, printed in black, blue and green, 1967, 25 x 38in (63.5 x 96.5cm).
£120–150 CJP

A Tigon Pictures film poster, '*Witchfinder General*', printed in white, orange and black, 1968, 40 x 30in (101.5 x 76cm).
£40–50 SEY

334   **POSTERS**

An Italian First International Pop Festival coloured poster, by Hapshash and the Coloured Coat, 1968, 21 x 31in (53.5 x 79cm).
£1,000–1,200 CJP
Hapshash and the Coloured Coat was the studio name of design team Michael English and Nigel Waymouth, who produced some of the most important psychedelic posters of the 1960s. Waymouth was also the founder of Granny Takes a Trip, in the Kings Road, one of the most fashionable and alternative boutiques of swinging London.

A United Artists film poster, 'Midnight Cowboy', printed in brown, yellow, black and white, 1969, 40 x 30 (101.5 x 76cm).
£100–120 SEY

A 20th Century Fox film poster, 'Return of the Jedi', printed in colours on a black ground, 1983, 40 x 30in (101.5 x 76cm).
£90–100 SEY

An American Paramount Pictures coloured poster, 'Barbarella', 1968, 41 x 27in (104 x 68.5cm).
£250–300 REEL

A 20th Century Fox film poster, 'Le Mans', printed in red, blue, yellow and black on a white ground, 1971, 40 x 30in (101.5 x 76cm).
£400–470 VEY

A United Artists film poster, 'Rocky', printed in brown, cream and white on a black ground, 1977, 40 x 30in (101.5 x 76cm).
£25–30 SEY

A Universal Picture film poster, 'E.T.', printed in brown, blue and white, 1982, 40 x 30in (101.5 x 76cm).
£50–60 SEY

An American poster, '3' by Robert Indiana, printed in red, white and blue, 1968, 19 x 38in (48.5 x 96.5cm).
£170–200 CJP

A film poster, 'The Cars that Ate Paris', printed in pink, black and white, 1974, 40 x 30in (101.5 x 76cm).
£55–65 VEY

An autographed Aerosmith concert poster, Monsters of Rock, signed in gold and silver marker by the band, 1994, 29½in x 20in (75 x 51cm).
£90–100 Bon(C)

Puppets

Two coloured cardboard clown marionettes, 1950s, 13in (33cm) high.
£35–40 AnS

A Chad Valley Noddy glove puppet, red with a blue hat, 1950s, 9in (23cm) high.
£20–25 GAZE

▶ A Pelham Magic Roundabout Mr Rusty glove puppet, with blue coat and green hat, 1966, 6in (15cm) high.
£16–18 TAC

A Pelham string puppet, Lulabelle, with wooden limbs, 1950s, 20in (51cm) high.
£70–80 ARo

A Pelham Magic Roundabout rod puppet, Florence, with large head and shoes, in original yellow box, 1960s, 14in (35.5cm) high.
£40–50 ARo

▶ Two Pelham string puppets, Cat and Mouse, with original yellow boxes, c1960s, 7in (18cm) high.
£40–45 GAZE

A Pelham Junior Range string puppet, Father, with blue trousers and red checked shirt, in original yellow box, 1970s, 10in (25.5cm) high.
£20–25 J&J

Two Pelham string puppets, Hansel and Gretel, with wooden limbs, in original yellow window box, 1970s, 12in (30.5cm) high.
£60–70 ARo

Radios & Sound Equipment

A home-built three valve radio,
in wooden box, 1928,
28in (71cm) high.
£150–170 FA

A Zenith brown Bakelite radio,
1930s, 10in (25.5cm) wide.
£140–160 SWO

A model RR 56 brown and
cream Bakelite radio, 1930s,
11in (28cm) wide.
£60–70 SWO

► An Airline brown Bakelite radio,
1930s, 10½in (26.5cm) wide.
£80–90 SWO

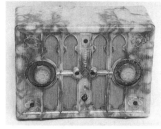

An International Kadette mottled-
cream Bakelite radio, in Gothic-
style cabinet, America, 1932,
7in (18cm) high.
£450–500 GAD
**This was the first American
Bakelite radio to be produced.**

◄ A Philips
model G30A
Bakelite Local
Station Receiver,
Holland, 1931,
18in (45.5cm) high.
£450–500 GAD

An Ekco model R53
Bakelite cabinet radio,
1931, 18in (45.5cm) high.
£550–600 GAD
**This model was the
first to have printed
station names.**

► An Emerson brown
Bakelite radio, 1930s,
10in (25.5cm) wide.
£80–90 SWO

A Philips model G64AS
Butterfly Bakelite radio,
Czechoslovakia, 1933,
10in (25.5cm) high.
£350–400 GAD

An Ekco model AD36 brown 'sad face' Bakelite radio, 1935, 14in (35.5cm) high.
£550–600 GAD

An RCA brown Bakelite book radio, with yellow lettering, Chile, 1938, 4in (10cm) high.
£1,300–1,500 GAD
RCA produced a number of highly inventive novelty radios.

A Fada model 652 Temple radio, in butterscotch Catalin case, America, damaged, 1930s, 11in (28cm) wide.
£225–250 SK(B)
Catalin is cast phenolic resin.

A Bendix model 526C radio, in green Catalin case, America, 1946, 11in (28cm) wide.
£600–700 GAD

A Fada model 200 Streamliner or Bullet radio, in pale green Catalin case, America, 1945, 10in (25.5cm) wide.
£1,000–1,200 GAD

Condition

The condition is absolutely vital when assessing the value of a collectable. Damaged items on the whole appreciate much less than perfect examples. However, a rare desirable piece may command a high price even when damaged.

► A Sonorette brown Bakelite radio, France, 1950, 8in (20.5cm) high.
£450–500 GAD

◄ A Crosley 'Bullseye' orange Bakelite radio, America, 1951, 9in (23cm) wide.
£225–250 GAD

► A Roberts model R300 transistor radio, finished in brown leather, 1960, 9in (23cm) wide.
£70–80 PPH

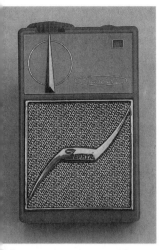

A Zephyr pale grey model AR 600 pocket transistor radio, Japan, 1961, 4½in (11.5cm) high.
£90–100 OVE

A Spica blue model ST 600 pocket transistor radio, Japan, 1965, 5in (13cm) high.
£50–60 OVE

▶ A Realtone Comet black model TR-1088 pocket transistor radio, Japan, 1962, 4½in (11cm) high.
£90–100 OVE

An Imperial black pocket transistor radio, Japan, 1963, 4½in (11.5cm) high.
£20–25 OVE

Cross Reference
See Colour Review

▶ A Precor black pocket transistor radio, Hong Kong, c1970, 5¼in (13.5cm) high.
£12–15 OVE

TELEVISIONS

A Bush brown Bakelite valve television, 1950s, 12in (30.5cm) high.
£200–220 SWO
In the 1950s this television cost £35.10s, equivalent to more than an average month's wage.

A Panasonic TR-005NR television, early 1970s, 12in (30.5cm) diam.
£900–1,000 MARK

A JVC Videosphere white television set, incorporating an alarm clock and radio, 1970, 10in (25.5cm) diam.
£350–400 MARK

GRAMOPHONES

A Columbia Type BG graphophone, with four-spring motor, 6in (15cm) mandrel, nickeled mechanism, in mahogany case, horn and reproducer missing, c1900, 12in (30.5cm) wide.
£450–500 SK(B)

A Columbia Type AK disc graphophone, with wooden case, brass-belled black horn, single-spring motor and 7in (18cm) turntable, c1900, 12in (30.5cm) wide.
£800–900 SK(B)

A Victrola X gramophone, with No. 2 soundbox, in mahogany case, motor defective, early 1900s, 20in (51cm) high.
£325–350 SK(B)

A Victor 6 gramophone, No. 2757, with Hawthorne & Sheble flower horn, gilt fittings, on a mahogany case, restored, 1905–10, 16in (40.5cm) square.
£2,100–2,300 SK(B)

A child's tin-plate gramophone, probably German, 1920s, 9in (23cm) high.
£110–130 GAZE

An HMV chrome used-record-needle holder, c1930, 3in (7.5cm) diam.
£25–30 FA

A Russian portable wind-up gramophone, in a wooden case, 1930s, 11in (28cm) long.
£165–185 JUN

An HMV 102 portable gramophone, in green leatherette case, 1930–50s, 16in (40.5cm) long.
£125–150 HHO

▶ An HMV wooden-handled record cleaner, 1930s, 4in (10cm) long.
£25–30 FA

An Excelda travelling gramophone, in blue leather case, c1950, 11in (28cm) wide.
£150–180 HHO
This gramophone in black leather would be in the range of £100–120.

Railwayana

Sustained by a small but tremendously dedicated band of British private collectors, the railwayana market remains consistently strong. Rarities can command huge prices and, at the time of writing, the auction record for a loco nameplate is £34,600 for the LMS Duchess of Devonshire nameplate, sold by Sheffield Railway Auctions.

Salvaged when a locomotive was sent to the scrap yard, nameplates are certainly the most desirable, and often the most costly, examples of railwayana. Loco numberplates, which were mounted on the cab sides or the smoke box door, are also popular as are works plates bearing the name and address of the manufacturing company and the date of production. In addition to objects that formed part of the loco itself, there is also huge interest in all other forms of railway memorabilia, from posters, to ephemera, to station vending machines and enamel signs.

The expansion of the railways from the 1830s onwards led to the production of a vast and varied amount of material and even for the non-enthusiast, these objects can still conjure up the romance of the age of steam, when Britain's railway system was a source of pride and trains were expected to run on time.

A Birmingham Derby Railway Inspector's gilt-brass tip-staff, with ebony central collar, 1850, 7¼in (18.5cm) long.
£1,450–1,600 CCB

A North Eastern Railway silver-plated presentation teapot, inscribed 'Presented with A Purse of Gold to Mr Wm Rutherford Inspector under the NE Ry Co N & C Section by Workmen under his Charge for a Term of Years, Haltwhistle 20th November 1869', 8in (20.5cm) high.
£100–110 SRA

Four steel railway carriage keys, 1880–1950, largest 4in (10cm) long.
£8–10 each WAB

A metal railway lunch box, with brass fittings, c1920, 12in (30.5cm) wide.
£90–100 SMI

A Miller's Official Tourist Guide, North British Railways West Highland Railways, 1907, 5 x 7in (12.5 x 18cm).
£12–15 RTT

A Canadian Pacific Railway menu card, 1956, 8 x 11in (20.5 x 28cm).
£10–12 COB

NAMEPLATES, NUMBERPLATES & WORKS PLATES

A Great Western Railways Atbara Class brass combined name and numberplate, 'Kekewich 4129' , polished and with original black paint, the rim stamped with the engine and boiler details, the reverse impressed with the original number '3383', 26in (66cm) wide.
£18,500–20,000 SRA
Named after General Robert George Kekewich, officer in charge of the British Forces during the Boer War at the defence of Kimberley.

► An LMS Royal Scott Class cast brass and black nameplate, 'Royal Engineer', 1927, restored, 48½in (123cm) long.
£17,000–18,500 SRA

◄ A Natal Government Railways brass works plate, 'Durban Works 1899', carried by NGR Class H No. 21 built by Robert Stephenson, 1882, 12in (30.5cm) wide.
£2,000–2,200 SRA
This is the only known surviving 19thC works plate from the NGR

A Great Central Railway Class 11F cast brass and black nameplate, 'Prince of Wales', with a black ground, 1920, face restored, 50in (127cm) long.
£16,500–18,000 SRA

A Great Central Railway Class 11F cast brass nameplate, 'Prince Albert', face polished and repainted black, 1920, 53in (134.5cm) long.
£15,000–16,500 SRA

A London & North Eastern Railway Class B17/2 cast brass nameplate, 'Kimbolton Castle', 1931, 59in (150cm) long,
£12,500–13,500 SRA

An LMS Jubilee Class cast brass and red nameplate, 'Prince Edward Island', 1934, 49in (124.5cm) long.
£19,000–21,000 SRA
This is one of only five three-word single-line Jubilee nameplates.

An LMS Patriot Class cast brass and black nameplate, 'Sir Frederick Harrison', named in 1937, face restored, 52in (132cm) long.
£15,500–17,000 SRA
Sir Frederick Harrison entered LNWR employment in 1864, became Assistant Superintendant in 1875 and a Director in 1909.

A London & South Western Class cast brass and red nameplate, 'Newport', built 1891, sent to the Isle of Wight in 1947, face polished, with original bolts, 34in (86.5cm) long.
£7,750–8,250 SRA

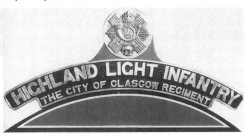

An LMS Royal Scott class cast brass and black nameplate, 'The Highland Light Infantry The City of Glasgow Regiment', with Regimental badge, mounted on a red, black and yellow painted replica wheel splasher, 1949, 48in (122cm) long.
£26,000–28,000 SRA

A Great Western Railway 6959 Modified Hall class brass and green nameplate, 'North Aston Hall', 1950, 78in (198cm) wide.
£11,000–12,000 SRA

A BR Type 4 Class 43 diesel locomotive alloy nameplate, 'Superb Warship Class', in raised letters on a red ground, 1961, 31in (78.5cm) long.
£3,300–3,600 SOL

A BR BoBo diesel elecric HST power car cast aluminium and red nameplate, 'Heaton', 1984, 27in (68.5cm) long.
£1,700–1,900 SRA

A BR Class 59 diesel loco alloy and red nameplate, 'Vale of Evesham', 1996, 36½in (92.5cm) long.
£2,200–2,600 SOL

A smokebox numberplate, as carried by ex-LSWR Class M7 locomotives, c1948, 24in (61cm) long.
£550–600 RAR

A smokebox numberplate, '63838', with a black ground, 1949, 22in (56cm) long.
£350–400 SRA

An East African Railway Governor Class cast brass and red nameplate, 'Sir John Hall', 1954, 54in (137cm) long.
£600–660 SRA
Named after Governors of the East African territories, these lightweight engines worked on the track between Kampala and Kasese to Soroti on the Northern Uganda Line and the Nairobi to Nanyuki Branch line.

POSTERS

A poster, commemorating the 'Opening of the New Southern Railway Graving Dock' by King George V and Queen Mary, 1933, 11 x 9in (28 x 23cm).
£20–25 COB

An LMS linen-backed poster, 'The Irish Mails', by Bryan de Grineau, printed in orange, blue and black on a beige ground, c1930, 40¼in x 50in (102 x 127cm).
£1,800–2,000 ONS

▶ A British Railways poster, 'Progress Every Week, British Railway's Modernisation Plan Goes Further Ahead', by Terence Cuneo, printed in colours by Waterlow, c1960, 40¼in x 50in (102 x 127cm).
£450–500 ONS

An LNER poster, 'The Coronation', by Doris Zinkeisen, printed in green and brown, 1937, 40¼in x 50in (102 x 127cm).
£2,700–3,000 ONS

SIGNS & TOTEMS

A BR(S) totem station sign, 'Cannon Street', white on a green ground, from the SE & CR London terminus opened in 1866, 36in (91.5cm) wide.
£1,500–1,700 SRA

A BR(Sc) totem station sign, 'Gourock', white on a blue ground, 1889, 37in (94cm) wide.
£550–650 SRA
This totem is from an ex-Caledonian terminus station on the Firth of Clyde that opened in 1889, closed in 1973, to be re-opened almost immediately, and finally closed in 1993.

A Great Northern Railway cast-iron plate, 'Public Warning Not to Trespass', white on a red ground, 1896, 28in (71cm) wide.
£75–85 JUN

A Somerset & Dorset Joint Railway cast-iron sign, white lettering 'S. & D. J. R. Beware of Trains', on a red ground, 1903, 16½in x 25¾in (42cm x 65.5cm).
£170–190 DN

◀ A Southern Railway enamel sign, 'Special Train to London (Waterloo)', white on a green ground, from Southampton Docks, 1940s, 60 x 30in (152.5 x 76cm).
£475–525 RAR

A London & South Western Railway cast-iron sign, 'L. & S. W. R. Trespassers Will be Prosecuted', painted white, c1920, 15¾ x 24¾in (40 x 63.5cm).
£90–110 DN

> **Miller's is a price GUIDE not a price LIST**

A Brazil Railway Company 4½ percent First Mortgage 60-year Gold Bond, with vignette of a steam train on an iron bridge, 1909.
£30–35 GKR

A Soldiers Bounty Fund Bond No. 2 6% Bond, issued by the County of New York, with vignette of a General on horseback and soldiers, dated July 1864.
£40–50 GKR
This Bond was issued to raise funds to pay the volunteers for the Union Armies.

An A la Reine d'Angleterre share certificate in Parisian Perfume Company, with vignette of Queen Victoria in the 1840s when she visited France, dated '1924'.
£30–35 GKR

A Cadbury card, Olympic and Titanic, a single card set, 1907, 2¾ x 1½in (7 x 4cm).
£35–40 JACK

► A Chad Valley cardboard 'Take to pieces' model of RMS Queen Mary, c1950, 12in (30.5cm) long, with original box.
£110–130 HUX

A ship in a bottle, 1930s, 12in (30.5cm) long.
£40–45 COB

A tin ship, 'Normandie', c1935, 22in (56cm) long.
£300–350 HUX

A Stratton powder compact, decorated with Cunard's Caronia, 1950–60, 3in (7.5cm) diam, in original box.
£45–50 BAf

A Bensons English Choice Confections sweet tin, decorated with RMS Queen Mary, c1955, 12in (30.5cm) wide.
£30–35 HUX

A Royal Copenhagen porcelain plate, decorated with a freighter, 1960s, 11in (28cm) diam.
£120–140 COB

A Merrythought RMS Titanic bear, from a limited edition of 5,000, 1992, 9in (23cm) high, in original box.
£110–130 COB

A silver snuffbox, with gilt interior, hallmarked, 19thC, 3in (7.5cm) wide.
£100–120 MB

A set of silver-plated fish servers, by William Hutton & Sons, with bone handles, in fitted case, c1885, 14in (35.5cm) long.
£200–225 ASAA

A silver flatwear set, by Hillard & Thomason, Birmingham 1863, 9in (23cm) long.
£250–300 CoHA

A WMF Art Nouveau silver-plated card games note pad holder, c1900, 7in (19cm) long.
£120–150 WAC

A pair of silver sugar nips, by Nathan & Hayes, in the form of a harlequin, Chester 1900, 4in (10cm) high.
£160–190 HEB

An Edwardian silver seal, Birmingham 1906, 3in (7.5cm) long.
£50–60 WAC

An Edwardian silver pin cushion, in the shape of a lion, Birmingham 1907, 2½in (6.5cm) long.
£675–725 FHF

▶ A set of silver and coloured enamel coffee spoons, Birmingham 1930, 4in (10cm) long, in original fitted case.
£100–110 JACK

A Sterling silver trinket box, Birmingham 1916, 5in (12.5cm) wide.
£200–220 BWA

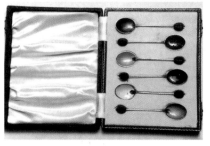

A silver working pepper mill, by Mark Stevens of Warwick, in the shape of a hot air balloon, on a wooden plinth, from a limited edition of seven, Birmingham 1997, 5in (12.5cm) high.
£700–850 MRW
One of these was made in 9ct gold for the birthday of King Hussain of Jordan, another for Richard Branson.

An Artifort Ribbon stool, designed by Pierre Paulin, 1966 onwards.
£800–900 MARK

An Aero miniature transistor radio, model G-607, Hong Kong, 1961, 3in (7.5cm) high, in original box with leather case and earpiece.
£30–35 OVE

A St Michael's floral print cotton mini-dress, 1960.
£12–15 DE

◄ A psychedelic stool, late 1960s, 19in (48.5cm) diam.
£50–60 MARK

► A St Ives Troika pottery vase, c1965, 10in (25.5cm) high.
£250–280 HUN

Four Poole Pottery pin trays, 1960s, 4in (10cm) diam.
£20–25 each HarC

A Murano glass ashtray, 1960s, 6in (15cm) wide.
£80–95 ZOOM

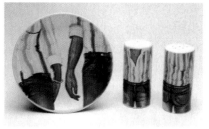

A Carlton Ware pottery plate, decorated with Denim pattern, with matching salt and pepper, 1970s, plate 6¼in (16cm) diam.
Plate   £20–25
Salt and pepper £40–45 StC

An Aladdin Industries Charlie's Angels lunch box, America, 1978, 8in (20.5cm) wide.
£35–40 TBoy

A Snoopy & Woodcock moulded plastic telephone, 1970s, 14in (35.5cm) high.
£220–240 AnSh

A Corgi Magic Roundabout clockwork carousel, c1972, 7in (18cm) high.
£130–150 RAR

A Panasonic plastic Bangle radio, 1970, 6in (15cm) high.
£85–95 PLB

A Toppi bubble gum wrapper, depicting James Bond Moonraker, 1979, 3 x 2⅓in (7.5 x 6.5cm)
£5–7 YR

A Scottish horn snuff mull, the silver top mounted with a cairngorm, c1800, 5in (12.5cm) long.
£450–550 BWA

A Scottish cowrie snuff box, with silver lid, unmarked, c1880, 4in (10cm) wide.
£250–300 BLA

A German plaster tobacco jar, in the form of a Boer War soldier's head, c1900–01, 9in (23cm) high.
£75–90 MURR

A Tyler's Honey Dew tobacco tin, c1890s, 5in (12.5cm) wide.
£240–280 MURR

A Muratti's Bouquet Gold Tipped Cigarettes cardboard show card, c1910, 4in (10cm) wide.
£95–110 MURR

A Linsden Bakelite cigarette box and match tidy, 1925, 6in (15cm) wide.
£50–60 GAD

A Lambert & Butler's Waverley Mixture tobacco tin, c1920, 4in (10cm) wide.
£10–12 WAB

A British Fillalita Shell lighter fuel dispenser, 1920s, 20in (51cm) high.
£450–480 JUN

A Polo Swift Action cigarette lighter, 1930s, 2in (5cm) high, with original box.
£20–25 RTT

An American Art Deco Bakelite cigarette box, Cleopatra, 1935, 6in (15cm) wide.
£220–250 GAD

▶ A Exclusiv Pipe Tobaccos rubberoid figure of a guardsman, 1950s, 22in (56cm) high.
£150–180 DBr

The Grand National at Aintree,
a watercolour painting, unsigned,
late 19thC, 13½ x 21in (34.5 x 53.5cm),
in period gilt frame.
£200–240 DW

A Stevengraph, entitled 'The First
Set', No. 172, 1881, 5 x 8in
(12.5 x 20.5cm), framed.
£700–800 VINE

An Allen & Ginter's The World's
Champions cigarette card,
Hugh McCormack, Skater,
from a set of 50, 1888.
£110–125 HALL

An American baseball cigarette
advertising fabric badge, Walter
Johnson, 1914, 5in (12.5cm) square.
£75–90 HALL

A J. Baines, Bradford shield-
shaped trade card, depicting Bristol
Rovers, 1897, 3in (7.5cm) high.
£50–55 KNI

A Fry's Chocolate Golf Balls
& Footballs box, 1918–25,
10in (25.5cm) wide.
£90–110 MURR

A set of 50 W. A. & A. C. Churchman's cigarette cards, Rugby Internationals, 1935.
£65–75 MAr

A pair of Stanley Matthews' football boots, both signed, 1950s, with various press cuttings.
£900–1,000 LT

A painted wooden football rattle, c1955, 10in (25.5cm) long.
£25–30 WAB

A signed photograph of Pele, 1960s, 10 x 8in (25.5 x 20.5cm).
£175–200 SMW

An American Bowman Gum baseball card, Mickey Mantle, 1952.
£600–660 HALL

A Stanley Matthews Number 7 Shirt, used when playing for the British XI vs European XI, 1955.
£6,000–7,000 LT

A Ridgeway Jolly Jinks child's beaker, decorated with rabbits playing various sports, 1950–60, 3in (7.5cm) high.
£25–30 KNI

▶ A Mastermatic Master Football Game, 1957, 26in (66cm) high.
£100–120 AMc

◀ An American bobbin head doll, Willie May, early 1960s, 7in (18cm) high.
£100–120 HALL

A pottery figure of Lord Harris, the cricketer, inscribed '1851–1932', 1950s, 12in (30.5cm) high.
£80–95 BRT

An illumination presented to Stanley Matthews by the Football Association to commemorate his having played 44 International matches for England, dated April 1946, mounted and framed.
£2,000–2,400 LT

A signed photograph of Muhammad Ali, Joe Frazier and Don King, from a limited edition of 100, 12/13 June 1998, 20 x 16in (51 x 40.5cm), framed.
£550–600 SMW

▶ A signed photograph of Sally Gunnell after winning the Olympic gold medal for the 400m hurdles, 1993, 15 x 11in (38 x 28cm).
£90–110 SMW

A signed photograph of John McEnroe, 1980, 8 x 9in (20.5 x 23cm).
£120–140 SMW

A signed photograph of Anna Kornikova, 1999, 9 x 8in (23 x 20.5cm).
£100–120 SMW

▶ A signed photograph of David Beckham, 1999, 10 x 8in (25.5 x 20.5cm).
£120–140 SMW

A pair of Selby Shoe leather Swaggers golf shoes, 1960s.
£30–35 SPT

A print of Stanley Matthews, by Michael Dudash, limited edition of 650, signed by Matthews and Dudash, 1996, 24 x 16in (61 x 40.5cm).
£250–300 SMW

A Canadian Opee Chee Gum hockey card, Bobby Orr, 1967.
£110–125 HALL

An American HJ College jacket, by Hamilton, 1970s.
£55–65 TRA

An American football Super Bowl sweatshirt, 1997.
£20–25 TRA

An Everlast boxing glove, signed by seven world champions, Hollyfield, Tyson, Norton, Frazier, Ali, Holmes and Foreman, c1999, 14in (35.5cm) long.
£400–480 SMW

Rock & Pop

A concert programme, Count Basie with Joe Williams, printed in red, black and white, 1957, 15 x 10in (38 x 25.5cm).
£12–15 CTO

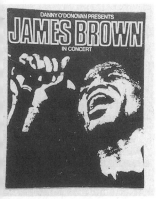

A James Brown in Concert programme, 1973, 10 x 8in (25.5 x 20.5cm).
£8–10 CTO

◀ A Jimi Hendrix oriental-style jacket, decorated with dragons and pagodas in brown, black and yellow on a green ground, c1967.
£35,000–40,000 S
Jimi Hendrix (1942–70) was one of the most influential guitarists of the 20th century. His flamboyant clothes reflected both his personality and performance and are hugely sought-after by collectors today.

A Beach Boys autographed drumskin, 1977–80, 20in (51cm) diam.
£300–350 Bon(C)

A Dire Straits autographed postcard, in black and white on a cream ground, with blue signatures, 1980s, 5¾ x 4in (14.5 x 10cm).
£120–150 Bon(C)

A Marc Bolan and T-Rex signed paper, dated 1976, 7in (18cm) square.
£100–120 BTC

A Doors and Jefferson Airplane double-sided handbill, 1968, 10 x 8in (25.5 x 20.5cm).
£150–175 CTO

A Buddy Holly and the Crickets Coral Recording Artist signed promotional card, 1958, 5¾ x 3¼in (14.5 x 8.5cm).
£700–800 Bon(C)

An adjustable piano stool, used by Elton John on tour, by Paul Jansen & Son, with black leatherette covering, 1992, 20in (51cm) high.
£275–325 Bon(C)

A Chanel brown double-breasted velvet jacket, owned and worn by Lulu, signed, 1990s.
£200–220 Bon(C)

A Bob Marley autographed concert poster, 1980, 31 x 41in (78.5 x 104cm).
£2,000–2,400 S

A Cliff Richard and The Shadows flyer, printed in red, pink and black on a white ground, 1965, 11½ x 5½in (29 x 14cm).
£25–30 BTC

A Las Vegas Hilton menu, autographed by Elvis Presley, with letter of authenticity, 1973, 7in (17.5cm) diam.
£300–350 Bon(C)

A Rolling Stones autographed paper, 1960s, 4 x 6in (10 x 15cm).
£300–350 Bon(C)

A Pink Floyd UFO Club poster, by Hapshash and The Coloured Coat, printed with yellow, orange, blue and silver metallic colours, published by Osiris Visions, 1967, 29¾ x 19¼in (75.5 x 49cm).
£200–240 Bon(C)

A pair of Britney Spear's autographed silver shoes, with letter of authenticity, 1999.
£600–660 Bon(C)

A Sex Pistols concert poster, 1976, 27½ x 29¼in (70 x 74.5cm).
£675–725 S

A Woodstock black and white photographic poster, by Bruce Gowens, 1969, 25 x 23in (63.5 x 58.5cm).
£160–200 CJP

THE BEATLES

A Beatles autographed concert ticket, 1963, 3½ x 4½in (9 x 11.5cm).
£2,000–2,400 S

A Beatle wig, by Lowell Toy Manufacturing Corporation, with original red, white and black packaging, 1963–64.
£40–50 BTC

A Beatles ceramic plaque, by Proudholme Products, Brighton, black on a white ground, 1964, 4in (10cm) square.
£12–15 BTC

A Beatles ticket and folder, for the Kerridge Odeon, New Zealand, 1964, 5½in (14cm) wide.
£125–150 BTC

A Beatles framed black and white photograph, with autographs, 1960s, 19 x 18in (48.5 x 45.5cm).
£800–1,000 BTC

Two Beatles mugs, by Broadhurst Brothers, Burslem, transfer-printed in blue and black, 1960s, 4in (10cm) high.
£35–45 CTO

A Rave magazine, No. 3, with coloured cover depicting Paul McCartney, 1964, 11¾ x 8¼in (29.5 x 21cm).
£12–15 BTC

A Beatles window card, for the Odeon, Southend, 31 May 1963, 10 x 12¾in (25.5 x 32.5cm).
£2,200–2,400 S

A set of four Beatles dishes, by Washington Pottery, transfer-printed in blue and black, with gold fluted edges, early 1960s, 4½in (11.5cm) diam. **£330–400 MTM**

A Cavern Club compliments slip, printed in brown and black on a white ground, 1960s.
£12–15 BTC

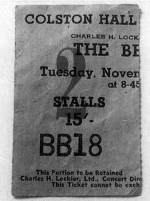

A Beatles concert ticket, for Colston Hall, Bristol, printed in red and black on a pink ground, 1964, 3 x 2in (7.5 x 5cm).
£35–45 CTO

A Beatles *Showtime* magazine centrefold calendar, printed in naturalistic colours on a pink ground, 1965, 12 x 9in (30.5 x 23cm).
£12–15 RTT

◄ A Beatles family tree booklet, by Achievements, printed in blue, green, brown, orange and black on a white ground, 1966, 10 x 7in (25.5 x 18cm).
£12–15 CTO

A Paul McCartney psychedelic silkscreen poster, 1960s, 48 x 36in (122 x 91.5cm).
£120–150 Bon

An album of eight black and white photographs, from the Albert Marrion Photographic Collection of 1961, limited edition of 5,000, 1990s, 16 x 12in (40.5 x 30.5cm).
**£150–175 MTM
Albert Marrion ran a photographic studio in the early 1960s. He was commissioned to photograph the Beatles for their first ever photoshoot on 17 December 1961, featuring their then drummer Pete Best.**

Three Beatles reel-to-reel tapes, 1960s, 5in (12.5cm) square.
£15–20 each BTC

▶ A Beatles green velvet jacket, from Apple Shop, Baker Street, with yellow lining and multicoloured Apple label, 1968.
£80–100 BTC

INSTRUMENTS

A Gibson Custom L-5 CES electric guitar, with maple back and sides, spruce top and mother-of-pearl markers, restored, 1940s.
£5,000–6,000 MG

A Fender Stratocaster electric guitar, with maple fingerboard, ash body, and white plastic scratch plate, restored, 1956.
£4,000–4,800 MG

A Hofner Committee accoustic guitar, with bird's-eye maple back and sides, ebony fingerboard and mother-of-pearl inlays, restored, 1950s.
£1,200–1,500 MG

A Gibson Les Paul Gold Top guitar, with mahogany back and sides, maple top, rosewood fingerboard and mother-of-pearl inlays, restored, 1958.
£13,000–15,000 MG

A Gibson Super 400 CES accoustic guitar, No. A28256, the ebony fretboard with mother-of-pearl and abalone block inlays, marbled scratch plate with original controls, two PAF pickups, in original case, 1958.
£9,000–10,000 Bon(C)
This guitar was formerly the property of Albert Lee, the British Country and Rock guitarist, and is accompanied by a letter of authenticity from Albert Lee.

A Hofner violin bass, with maple back and sides, spruce top, rosewood fingerboard and dot inlay, restored, 1962.
£3,000–3,600 MG

A Vandre electric guitar, painted blue, with rosewood fingerboard, Italy, 1960s.
£1,100–1,300 MG

A Gretsch Chet Atkins Tennessean electric guitar, the top, back and sides of maple, with rosewood fingerboard, restored, 1964.
£1,300–1,500 MG

A Fender Musicmaster electric guitar, painted red and with rosewood fingerboard and ash body, restored, 1965.
£200–300 MG

A Vox Phantom electric guitar, with white-painted ash body, white plastic scratch plate, and rosewood fingerboard, restored, 1966.
£650–800 MG

A Gibson Les Paul six string electric guitar, the simulated-ivory asymmetrical body with four volume/tone controls, mother-of-pearl inlaid fingerboard and brass machine heads, with Fender amplifier and metal travelling case, c1980.
£600–700 DN

A B. C. Rico six string classical guitar, the wooden body with marquetry bands and simulated tortoiseshell scratch plate, with mother-of-pearl inlaid fingerboard and chrome machine heads, marked, c1980, with simulated-leather travelling case.
£150–180 DN

A Yamaha maple custom tom-tom, with six pairs of Yamaha special hickory wood tipped signature sticks, Yamaha stand, and stencilled cardboard travelling case, property of Cozy Powell, 1985–90s, 15in (38cm) high.
£140–160 DN

A tambourine, from a Prince tour, the gold symbol and rim on a black ground, 1990s, 10¼in (26cm) diam.
£220–250 Bon(C)

A Roland Juno-6 polyphonic synthesizer, with five octaves, the instrument panels with red, blue, white and yellow stripes on a black ground, 1970.
£275–325 CGX

► A Korg monophonic synthesizer, Model No. MS10, 1979–80, 20in (51cm) wide.
£300–360 CGX

359

JUKEBOXES

A Wurlitzer 1400 jukebox, with multicoloured panels, 1951–52, 60in (152.5cm) high.
£2,900–3,200 HALB

A Seeberg Selecto-o-Matic jukebox, with 200 selections, with green, red and white front plate, 1957, 62in (157.5cm) high.
£7,500–8,500 JU

A Rock-Ola 1478 Tempo II Stereo jukebox, with blue and white panels and logo, 1960.
£3,000–3,300 HALB

A Chantal Meteor jukebox, with 200 selections, in silver, black and chrome, 1957–59, 60in (152.5cm) high.
£6,000–6,600 MARK
Although it was designed in Switzerland, this is one of the few jukeboxes made in England.

RECORDS

A Chuck Berry 7in EP single record, 'Reelin' and Rockin', by London Records, in yellow, white and black on an orange ground, 1958.
£100–120 TOT

An Art Blakey & the Jazz Messengers LP record, by Blue Note Records, in red, orange, yellow, blue and white on a brown and black ground, America, 1962.
£50–60 TOT

A Blind Faith LP record, by Polydor Records, made for distribution in Eire, in black on a white ground, 1969.
£250–300 MVX

◀ A Curved Air-Airconditioning LP Picture Disc, by Warner Bros Records, in purple, blue, pink, red and white, on a black ground, 1970.
£8–10 MVX

A Dave, Dee, Dozy, Beaky, Mick & Tich 7in single record, 'Loos of England', by Fontana, decorated in yellow, orange and colours on a blue and grey ground, 1967.
£22–25 TOT

A Depeche Mode promotional CD, 'Ultra', by Mute Records, in purple, white and brown on a black ground, unopened, 1997, 11in (28cm) wide.
£80–100 MVX

Cross Reference
See Colour Review

A Jimi Hendrix 12in LP record, 'Jimi plays Berkeley', in orange, red, yellow and green on a black and white ground, French, 1970.
£60–70 TOT

A Blind Lemon Jefferson 10in LP record, 'The Folk Blues of Blind Lemon Jefferson', by Riverside Records, in black and white on a grey ground, America, 1953.
£80–100 TOT

A Derrick Morgan 12in mono LP record, 'Moon Hop', by Pama Records, photographic cover, 1969.
£65–75 TOT

An Elvis Presley 7in EP record, 'A Touch of Gold', by RCA, in yellow, gold and blue on a black ground, 1960.
£90–100 TOT

A Major Lance mono EP record, 'Um Um Um Um Um Um', by Columbia, in red, green and white on a black and white ground, 1963.
£30–35 CTO

◄ A Small Faces EP record, 'Sha-La-La-La-Lee', by Decca, in yellow, red and black on a white ground, French, 1966.
£30–35 CTO

A 'Mr Spock Presents Music from Outer Space' stereo LP, by Rediffusion, in blue, pink, white and orange on a black ground, 1973.
£10–12 CTO

A Paul Weller promotional 12in LP record, 'Live at the Hayward Gallery London 1997', in blue and white on a black ground.
£40–50 TOT

Scandinavian Design

There is currently huge interest in Scandinavian design, and auction houses are even beginning to hold sales dedicated to Scandinavian decorative arts. This section focuses on works produced in Denmark, Sweden, Norway and Finland, ranging from traditional, hand-crafted wooden items made by a 19th century agricultural society, to objects by the pioneers of the 20th century modern movement.

Finnish architect Alvar Aalto (1898–1976) was among the first Scandinavian designers to achieve international fame in the 1930s. His innovative bent wood furniture and glass designs such as the wavy-rimmed Savoy vase, combined a modernist approach, with natural materials and a curving, organic line that paved the way for fifties style. Leading figures after WWII included Danish designers Arne Jacobsen (1902–72) and Verner Panton (b.1926), who experimented with new shapes and man-made materials, and helped promote 'Scandinavian Modern' style across the world.

In every media from furniture to glass to jewellery, Scandinavian design became the height of fashion in the fifties and sixties. Many of the classic designs from this period still remain in production today and thanks to the influence of Ikea (est. 1944), the world's largest furniture chain, Scandinavian design now decorates homes across the globe

FURNITURE

An Artek blond wood and laminate tea/serving trolley, model No. 98, with grey and black shelves, designed by Alvar Aalto, Finland in 1935–36, 1970s edition, 21⅛in (54.5cm) wide.
£550–600 PLB

A wood and black leather webbed armchair, designed by Alvar Aalto, Finland in 1946.
£520–560 PLB

A Kandya Jason plywood chair, by Karl Jacobs, c1950.
£140–160 PLB

A Swan cast-aluminium and turquoise fabric upholstered armchair, designed by Arne Jacobsen for Fritz Hansen, marked, 1960s.
£240–280 DN

► A yellow fabric cone chair, designed by Verner Panton for Plus-Linje, manufactured by Fritz Hansen, 1959.
£650–750 PLB

A black wood and metal Grandprix chair, designed by Arne Jacobsen for Fritz Hansen, 1972.
£75–85 PLB

GLASS

A blue glass Savoy vase, designed by Alvar Aalto, Finland in 1937, produced in 1950s, 4in (10cm) high.
£80–100 MARK

An Orrefors glass vase, designed by Heinrich Wollman, decorated with stylized flowers and foliage in pink and red on a pale pink ground, 1914–16, 9¼in (23.5cm) high.
£550–650 Sck

► An amethyst glass vase, designed by Tapio Wirkkala for Iittala, Finland, signed, 1960s, 11in (28cm) high.
£160–180 PLB

An Orrefors blue and gold glass vase, designed by Sven Palmqvist, 1946–48, 10½in (26.5cm) high.
£220–250 Sck

An Orrefors glass bowl, designed by Ingeborg Lundin, decorated in green on a light green ground, 1967, 6¾in (17cm) diam.
£400–450 Sck

A Swedish hand-blown sea-green glass vase, c1950, 13in (33cm) high.
£40–45 V&S

Two Lassi glass vases, in green and in red, Finland, 1970s, 12in (30.5cm) high.
£40–50 each PLB

◄ An Orrefors lilac glass vase, Sputnik, designed by Lars Hellsten, 2000, 6½in (16.5cm) high.
£225–255 HaG

An Orrefors red glass Tulip vase, designed by Nils Landberg, 1950s, 17¾in (45cm) high.
£250–280 Sck

A Swedish clear glass vase, Skruf, by Bengt Edenfalk, 1974, 9in (23cm) high.
£70–80 MARK

► An Orrefors clear glass triple candle-holder, 1970s, 10in (25.5cm) wide.
£65–75 PIL

JEWELLERY & METALWARE

A Georg Jensen silver pepper pot and salt, numbered, marked, 1928–32, pepper pot 1½in (4cm) diam.
£550–600 DN

A Georg Jensen silver brooch, with eight cut diamonds, marked, 1963.
£175–200 Bea(E)

A pair of Danish lapis lazuli and silver cuff links, designed by Arne Jacobsen, c1960.
£100–120 DID

A sterling silver bangle, designed by Bent Gabrielsen Pedersen for Hans Hansen, Denmark, 1960s, 3in (7.5cm) diam.
£300–350 DID

A stainless steel coffee pot, designed by Arne Jacobsen for Stelton, with wooden handle, mid-1960s, 8in (20.5cm) high.
£100–120 MARK

A Dansk Designs black-painted metal candle-holder, 1970s, 4in (10cm) diam.
£20–25 PLB

POTTERY & PORCELAIN

A Gustavsberg Argenta vase, designed by Wilhelm Käge, with stylized mermaid on a jade green ground, 1930s, 10¼in (26cm) high.
£600–700 MARK
Argenta ceramics were designed by Wilhelm Käge (1889–1950), the artistic director of the Gustavsberg Porcelain Works in Sweden during the 1930s.

A Rorstrand vase, designed by Gunnar Nylund, in brown with a blue-green speckled pattern, 1950s, 6¼in (16cm) high.
£90–100 MARK

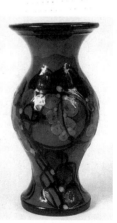

A Danko pottery vase, decorated with flowers and foliage in green, blue, yellow and black on an orange and red ground, 1950s, 7¼in (18.5cm) high.
£65–75 DSG

A Lotte hand-painted pottery plate, decorated with a couple in traditional dress in pink, blue, green and yellow, Norway, 1960s, 9¾in (25cm) high.
£18–20 PrB

> Miller's is a price GUIDE not a price LIST

WOOD

A Swedish birchwood herb grinder, late 18thC, 8in (20.5cm) high.
£180–200 NEW

A Norwegian carved wooden box, decorated with acanthus motifs, the lid with loop handle, 19thC, 5in (12.5cm) wide.
£450–500 AEF

A Scandinavian banded wooden flour tub, with lid, with original green and black paint, mid-19thC, 13in (33cm) high.
£130–150 NEW

A Swedish bentwood box, with snap-on lid, mid-19thC, 11in (28cm) long.
£160–175 NEW

▶ A Scandinavian 'dug out' birchwood dairy funnel, mid-19thC, 18in (45.5cm) long.
£70–90 NEW

Scent Bottles

A Viennese porcelain scent bottle, modelled as a boy and goat holding a fruiting vine stock, in black, blue, green and brown, with gilt-metal screw-on stopper, marked, 1840, 2¾in (7cm) high.
£200–220 RTo

A clear glass scent bottle, with silver-gilt chased mount, c1850, 3½in (9cm) high.
£440–480 SOM

A Stevens & Williams dark red *verre de soie* scent bottle, with silver top, c1889, 5in (12.5cm).
£500–600 ALiN
***Verre de soie* is a type of art glass with a silky iridescent surface made by reheating the glass object and spraying it with stannous chloride.**

A Maderas de Oriente scent bottle, with green and grey tasse, and original wooden box, c1900, 5in (12.5cm) high.
£90–100 BAO

A Lalique clear glass scent bottle, with raised weaved pattern, embossed 'R. Lalique' to base, c1910–20, 1¼in (3.25cm) high.
£100–120 BBR

A German ceramic perfume lamp, in the form of a lady draped in red material, on a green and gold base, 1920, 9in (23cm) high.
£270–300 BAO

A white ceramic scent bottle, modelled as a frog, c1920, 2¼in (5.5cm) high.
£35–40 AL

A pineapple-cut clear-glass scent bottle, with pump action atomizer, star-cut base, silver-plated top, decorated with yellow enamel, c1930, 6in (15cm) high.
£40–45 MED

Two Schuco mohair and felt monkey scent bottles, 1920s, largest 3in (7.5cm) high.
£200–250 each BAO

A Vivienne Westwood scent bottle, Boudoir, with cream felt drawstring bag, from a limited edition of 500, 1998, 4in (10cm) high.
£90–100 ID

A Lalique scent bottle, Klytia, with moulded wavy lines, signed 'R. Lalique France', c1930, 3¾in (9.5cm) high.
£1,000–1,200 DN

Science & Technology

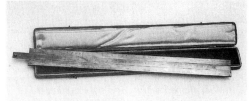

A brass Roget slide rule, by Rooker of London, with original red leather-covered silk-lined case, c1820, 10in (25.5cm) long.
£650–800 TOM

A Berge brass transit theodolite, signed on the horizontal plate 'Berge London Late Ramfden', c1800–10, 11in (28cm) high.
£800–1,000 Bon

A stained-ivory and silver spy glass, with original case, 1840, extended 4in (10cm) long.
£275–325 CHAP

▶ A Dring & Fage brass saccharometer, the thermometer and saccharometer signed and numbered '5340', in mahogany case with inscribed ivorine plaque, c1850, 14 x 4in (35.5 x 10cm).
£145–165 WAC
A saccharometer is an instrument which measures the amount of sugar in a solution.

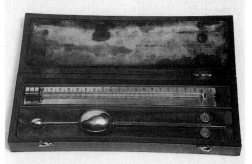

A set of French microscope slides, retailed by Stanley, London, in a pine wood box, 1867, 8in (20.5cm) long.
£200–250 BWA

A Victorian mahogany collectors' cabinet, with a glazed front and enclosing 16 drawers, 12in (30.5cm) high.
£550–600 TWr

An American painted-wood patent model of a washing machine, by H. Grandjean, New Berlin, Illinois, with metal gears and patent tags No. 15256, dated 30 June 1874, 10in (25.5cm) high.
£650–750 SK(B)

A brass stoicheiometric gas mixer, by Abbots, Burks & Co, late 19thC, 11in (28cm) long.
£30–35 WAC
Stoicheiometry is the process of calculating the atomic weight of elements in a chemical experiment.

A Micrograph miniature microscope, with nickeled body, nine microphotograph slides, tweezers and instructions, in original wooden box, late 19thC, box 6in (15cm) wide.
£160–180 SK(B)

A lacquered brass aneroid barometer with thermometer, by M. Pillischer, London, in original weighted wooden case, late 19thC, 7in (18cm) high.
£400–450 WAC

A Bryan Corcoran chondrometer, No. 852, with lacquered brass balance, mahogany case, and trade label giving weights and instructions, early 20thC, case 12¼in (31cm) wide.
£190–210 Bon

A French chrome anemometer, by Jules Richard, in original leather case, c1920, 11in (28cm) long.
£350–400 ETO

Miller's is a price GUIDE not a price LIST

◄ A four-drawer Ministry Issue telescope, with leather case, c1920, 34in (86.5cm) extended.
£190–220 CRN

A Keen & Frodsham lattice frame sextant, with silvered scale and vernier, magnifier, and two sets of mirrors and shades, with accessories in original mahogany case, damaged, early 20thC, radius index arm 7½in (19cm) long.
£275–325 Bon

An American Baroscribe disk barograph, by Bacharach, Pittsburgh, in a brown Bakelite case with hinged and glazed front, 1930, 8in (20.5cm) high.
£350–400 RTW

An Addmaster mechanical adding machine, with black, red and gilt front plate, 1930–40, 7in (18cm) long.
£15–20 TOM

◄ A Zeiss lacquered brass and black enamel microscope, with original case, c1920, 12in (30.5cm) high.
£200–220 WAC

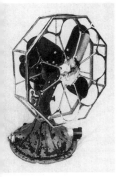

A Crompton chrome and cast-iron electric fan, 1930s, 16in (40.5cm) high.
£50–55 JUN

▶ A liquid-filled wrist compass, as used in WWI and WWII, initialled 'WBT', possibly made by James White, on a leather strap, 3in (7.5cm) wide.
£150–175 WAC

A wooden globe, on a Bakelite base, 1930, 18in (45.5cm) high.
£80–120 CYA

◀ A WWII liquid-filled brass military compass, 2¼in (5.5cm) diam.
£110–130 DHo

An American Tempscribe disc thermograph, by Bacharach, Pittsburgh, in a brown plastic case with hinged and glazed front, the graph in green on a white ground, 8in (20.5cm) high.
£180–200 RTW

A Mattel Electronics Intellivoice Voice Synthesis Module, with original blue and white box, late 1970s, 6in (15cm) wide.
£25–30 CGX
The first synthetic voice synthesizer.

An ENIAC Decade ring counter, the black steel chassis with 27 (of 28) vacuum tubes, various wires, busses and connections, labelled on reverse 'Front Office, J. P. Eckert', 45in (114.5cm) wide, together with a schematic diagraphic from the Moore School of Electrical Engineering, University of Pennsylvania, dated 20 November 1943, for the Accumulator Decade Unit.
£45,000–50,000 SK(B)
This unprepossessing object is a decade ring counter from ENIAC, the world's first digital computer. During WWII, the US army asked the University of Pennsylvania to produce an advanced calculating machine, and J. P. Eckert and John Mauchly designed ENIAC, The Electronic Numerical Integrator and Computer. It weighed 30 tonnes, covered 1800sq ft and cost over $500,000. According to legend, when it was first turned on, lights dimmed across the whole of Philadelphia, but it was 1000 times faster than any other calculator and launched the computer revolution. ENIAC contained 20 of these decade rings, which enabled electronic pulses to be converted into numbers. This example came from the estate of the Eckert family, and when sold at auction in the USA attracted huge interest. Eckert and Mauchly went on to found the world's first computer company and to build the famous UNIVAC computer.

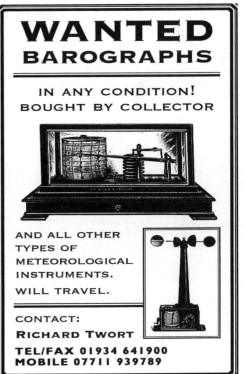

MEDICAL INSTRUMENTS

An ivory probe, 1800, 5in (12.5cm) long.
£55–65 DHo

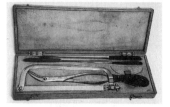

A set of steel amputation tools, by Charrier, in original wooden case, c1830, 16in (40.5cm) long.
£1,300–1,400 BWA

A mahogany and brass pill-making machine, by Maw & Son & Thompson, London, with three boxwood pill rollers and a double-ended powder measure, c1870, 16 x 9in (40.5 x 23cm).
£365–395 WAC

An American domestic homeopathic medicine chest, by Boericke & Tafel, Philadelphia, with a part set of bottles and a portable balance, in fitted mahogany case, with contents list in lid, late 19thC, 9¼in (23.5cm) wide.
£200–220 SK(B)

A French gilt-metal antiseptic disperser, with double burner and pivoting dispenser, on four ball feet, late 19thC, 8¾in (22cm) high.
£140–160 Bon

A child's brown leather and steel orthopaedic foot brace, c1880, 8in (20.5cm) high.
£85–90 BWA

▶ An American plaster phrenology head, by S. R. Wells & Co, American Institute of Phrenology, with divided cranium and paper identification and instruction labels, together with a plaster human skull, with brass label, J. F. Olson & Co, Skarpaline, Cambridge, Massachusetts, the forehead stencilled 'Iota', c1900, head 10in (25.5cm) high.
£170–190 SK(B)

A brass breast pump, in mahogany case, 18thC, 3¼in (8.5cm) high.
£330–370 DHo

A brass and ivory enema set, in original pine wood case, late 19thC, case 10in (25.5cm) wide.
£200–220 BWA

A Down Bros sphygmomanometer to measure blood pressure, lacking armbands and bulb, in original leather case, c1895–1905, 13in (33cm) high.
£100–120 WAC

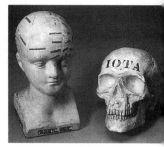

Scripophily

An Elizabeth I manuscript vellum recovery document, dated Michaelmas Term (2–5 November 1596), with small fragment of the Royal Seal attached to the original vellum tag.
£330–400 DW
Recovery documents were issued for the purchase of land. Nominally at least, the reigning monarch owned all English territory necessitating a legal transaction document when land was purchased by a private individual or body. Often highly decorative, these recovery documents are becoming increasingly collectable today.

A £20 share certificate, for Charles Laffitte & Co Ltd, No. 52508, printed in black on a cream ground, 1866, unissued.
£10–12 GKR
Charles Laffitte was an offshoot company of the famous Jacques Laffitte, an influential French banker during Napoleonic times. He became Prime Minister under Louis Phillippe in 1830 but resigned in 1831. This company was involved in much of the financing of French railways and other industries.

A Selma, Marion & Memphis Railroad Co $1000 uncancelled bond, with vignettes of cotton workers and a train, signed by N. B. Forrest, President, dated 1869.
£850–950 P
Nathan Bedford Forrest (1821–77) was a Confederate General, slave trader and plantation owner. He was famous for his raids at Shiloh and Chicakamauga, and became a Klu Klux Klan leader after the war.

> Miller's is a price GUIDE not a price LIST

▶ A James II vellum recovery document, with a portrait of the King contained in an elaborate initial 'J' and extensive scrollwork decoration to top border, with a small portion of the Royal Seal, 1687.
£200–250 DW

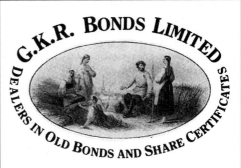
A 500 francs share certificate, for Compagnie Imperiale Chemins de Fer Ethiopiens, with a vignette of the Emperor and his court awaiting the arrival of a steam train, 1889, with two similar certificates.
£180–200 P

A 187.50 roubles bond, 5% loan of the City of Moscow, printed with the city crest, in blue, black and red on a cream ground, 1909.
£14–16 GKR

An Imperial Chinese Government Hukuang Railways Sinking Fund Gold Loan £20 bond, countersigned by J. P. Morgan & Co and three other American banks, slight damage, 1911.
£1,100–1,300 P
Only 150 bonds of this type were ever issued.

A Whitehead Aircraft (1917) £1 Preference share certificate, with vignettes of biplanes, printed in black on a blue ground, restored, 1918.
£170–200 P

A Compagnie des Mines de Bruay 500 francs bearer share certificate, printed in blue and black on a white ground, 1939.
£12–15 GKR

Prices

The price ranges quoted in this book reflect the average price a purchaser might expect to pay for a similar item. The price will vary according to the condition, rarity, size, popularity, provenance, colour and restoration of the item and this must be taken into account when assessing values. Don't forget that if you are selling it is quite likely that you will be offered less than the price range.

◀ A Casino des Fleurs de Beaulieu 500 francs share certificate, with a vignette of a casino overlooking the sea, printed in blue and black on a pink ground, 1929.
£30–35 GKR

▶ A Kato Aromatic 1000 Egyptian pounds unissued certificate, depicting figures and Egyptian script, printed in black and white on a brown ground, c1930.
£16–18 GKR

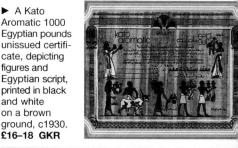

An American Playboy Enterprises Inc red $100 specimen share certificate, with vignette of a reclining nude Playboy Bunny Girl, and facsimile signature of the founder, Hugh Hefner, 1960s–70s.
£150–170 P

Sewing

This year's guide includes a special section on sewing machines. The first experimental sewing machine was designed in 1790 by Thomas Saint of London, launching a host of inventions. In 1830, Barthelemy Thimonnier of Paris produced 80 machines to make army uniforms, which were destroyed by a mob of rioting tailors who feared unemployment. The American Elias Howe improved upon this design, and his lock-stitch sewing machine (patented 1846) was widely copied, but the man most responsible for introducing the sewing machine into the family home was American Isaac Merritt Singer (1811–75). Singer had wanted to be an actor and only turned to invention to fund an unsuccessful theatrical career and ever-expanding family,

which was eventually to include two wives, some 24 children and numerous mistresses. In 1850, he created Singer's Perpendicular Action Sewing Machine, which could sew continously a straight, curved and angled seam. Singer advertised widely, used pretty girls to demonstrate the models, and in 1856 introduced the hire-purchase system. Singer became the best-known name in the field and revolutionized sewing. Prices for vintage sewing machines depend on age, rarity and visual appeal. Competing manufacturers often made machines extremely decorative both to attract purchasers and avoid infringing patents. Serious collectors are more likely to be interested in obscure models that were unsuccessful at the time rather than the most popular, mass-produced machines.

A carved wooden knitting sheath, c1800, 7in (18cm) long.
£175–195 **AEF**

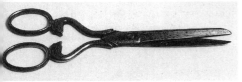

A pair of steel Victorian scissors, with bird neck handles, 7in (18cm) long.
£25–30 **WAC**

Three metal pin-cushion animals, a brown bear, an elephant and a dachshund, 1890–1910, largest 1¾in (4.5cm) high.
£40–50 each **VB**

► A tortoiseshell needle and thimble case, c1880, 2in (5cm) high.
£230–260 **CHAP**

A silver bodkin, c1600, 5in (12.5cm) long.
£50–55 **BSA**

SEWING MACHINES

A Singer cast-iron Perpendicular Action Sewing Machine, with steel parts, 1854, 17in (43cm) high.
£6,000–6,800 WSM

A Clark's Foliage sewing machine, Serial No. 879, 1859.
£3,200–3,500 KOLN

A Grove & Baker cast-iron sewing machine, with steel parts and rosewood base, USA, 1862, 13in (33cm) wide.
£700–800 WSM

A Globe cast-iron sewing machine, with steel parts, gilt-painted scrollwork and coloured floral transfer, 1868, 9in (23cm) high.
£300–350 WSM

A Shaw & Clark sewing machine, with painted flowers and foliage in fawn and pink, with gilt trim, America, 1864.
£4,700–5,000 KOLN

A Royal treadle cast-iron sewing machine, on carved mahogany stand with claw feet and gilt-painted treadle, 1865, 38in (96.5cm) high.
£2,300–2,600 WSM

A Moldacot steel and brass Patent Sewing Machine, No. 8921, in original blue and white tin with instructions under the lid, 1876, 8in (20.5cm) high.
£340–380 WSM

An Elliptic treadle sewing machine, No. 4070, with vertical arm, glass pressure foot and gilt decoration, in a walnut cabinet on a cast-iron stand, with tools and accessories, c1870, 33in (84cm) high.
£300–350 SK(B)

A Brevete & Co La Queen sewing machine, with table brace, Continental, 1868, 8in (20.5cm) high.
£525–565 WSM

▶ A Willcox & Gibbs sewing machine, with rosewood base and original pine carrying box, 1876, box 14in (35.5cm) high.
£200–250 WSM

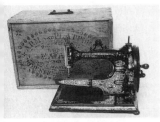

An Arm & Platform cast-iron Domestic Sewing Machine, with steel parts, gilt scrolling, and original pine carrying case, 1878, box 16in (40.5cm) wide.
£600–700 WSM

A cast-iron Hannum Pinking Machine, with steel parts, and a table brace, 1897, 7in (18cm) high.
£90–100 FA

An American Singer Machine Co sewing machine, c1910, 8in (20.5cm) high.
£80–90 BWA

A Foley & Williams Reliable Sewing Machine, with gilt decoration and clamp, in original wooden box, America, c1900, 7in (18cm) high.
£220–250 SK(B)

◄ A British United Shoe Machinery Co 'A1' treadle sewing machine, for leather boots and shoes, with cast-iron frame and mahogany table, 1884, 32in (81.5cm) high.
£500–550 WSM

▶ A Singer hand and treadle cast-iron sewing machine, No. 29K53, Boot Patcher, 1926, 27in (68.5cm) high.
£320–360 WSM

A Singer multipurpose treadle cast-iron sewing machine, No. 31K15, with attached light fitment, plywood table, tool box and Singer work stool, c1937, 42in (106.5cm) high.
£100–120 WSM

◄ A Reece keyhole, eyelet and buttonhole cast-iron treadle sewing machine, with plywood table, c1926, 48in (122cm) high.
£2,250–2,500 WSM

▶ A Singer Featherweight aluminium gear-driven electric sewing machine, No. 221, with a laminated-plywood carrying case, 1962, 13in (33cm) wide.
£300–350 WSM

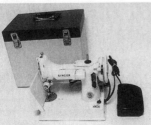

Shipping

A vellum royal warrant, empowering George Whitehead, commander of the cutter *The Eagle*, to take and seize vessels of the French Republic, with a portrait of George III and Royal coat-of-arms, 1803.
£320–360 DW
This document of the Napoleonic Wars was issued just two years before Nelson's decisive defeat of the French navy at Trafalgar.

An enamelled picture brooch, RMS *Celtic*, in blue, white and black, c1910, 1in (2.5cm) wide.
£175–200 DMW

A White Star Line cruise itinerary, printed in black on a white ground, 1934, 13 x 9in (33 x 23cm).
£20–25 COB

A Paget angle sextant, No. 894, by H. Hughes & Son, in a mahogany case, c1890, 7in (18cm) high.
£300–350 WAC

A brass shackle paperweight, c1900, 6in (15cm) wide.
£140–160 REG

A coloured postcard, 'Royal Navy 10 Inch Gun in Action', 1900.
£8–10 JMC

An enamel Cunard Line plaque, decorated in colours on a dark blue ground, c1925, 6½ x 9½in (16.5 x 24cm).
£250–300 HUX

A cast-brass ship's bell, *Orestes*, mounted between two brass fish, on a wooden base, 1894, base 28in (71cm) wide.
£600–700 ONS

A monochrome poster, In Memoriam *Titanic*, printed by Spelman, 1912, 15 x 20in (38 x 51cm).
£190–220 ONS

A White Star Line Third Class ceramic sugar bowl, 1915, 6in (15cm) diam.
£1,300–1,500 BSA
This bowl was recovered from the *Arabic Royal,* a United States mail steamer sunk by the German U-boat U-24 in 1915.

An EPNS souvenir basket dish, RMS *Niagara,* with red and blue enamel name badge, 1930s, 4in (10cm) diam.
£35–40 Baf

A French photographic postcard, SS *Normandie*, c1935, 7 x 10in (18 x 25.5cm).
£18–20 COB

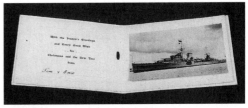

A Christmas card, with a photograph of the cruiser HMS *Leander*, 1930s, 4 x 5in (10 x 12.5cm).
£7–8 Baf

A pair of Frank Art Inc metal book ends, modelled as sailing boats, America, 1940, 6½in (16.5cm) high.
£100–120 REG

A cardboard E.F. Training Sextant, by Einson-Freeman, with a simple telescope, America, 1940s, in original box, box 10½in (26.5cm) square.
£25–30 SK(B)

◀ A Ministry of Defence Hydrographic Department deck watch, in original wooden case, c1940, case 5in (12.5cm) wide.
£400–480 HARP

An American US Navy thermo-hygrograph,
by J. P. Friez & Sons, in a metal case,
dated 1944, 12in (30.5cm) wide.
£250–300 RTW

A *Queen Mary* felt penant, c1950, 12in (30.5cm) long.
£6–8 HUX

An R. J. Series *Queen
Mary* wooden puzzle,
c1955, 5in (12.5cm) high.
£12–15 HUX

▶ A Ronson white-metal
lighter, with red and blue
enamel flag, c1960,
3in (7.5cm) wide.
£35–40 DAC

A brass marine compass, pillar-
mounted on a brass and oak base,
1949, 12in (30.5cm) wide.
£350–400 REG

A Walker's painted-metal Excelsior IV
Patent Log, in original pine box, 1950s,
box 15in (38cm) wide.
£170–200 NC

◀ A Spode
ceramic plate,
HMS *Ark Royal*,
decorated in
colours on a
white ground,
with navy-blue
and gold rim,
from a limited
edition of 1,000,
1978, 11in
(28cm) diam.
£100–120 COB

▶ A ceramic
plate film prop,
from *Titanic*,
decorated in
red, blue and
gilt on a white
ground, 1998,
7in (18cm) diam.
£100–120 COB

Shoe Trees

Every subject, however obscure, has its enthusiasts. Most of the shoe trees shown here come from a private collection. Natalie Giltsoff, an artist, bought her first pair for £2.50 at a football club jumble sale in 1979. 'I thought they were a wonderful sculptural shape,' she explained, 'and I loved the colour of the wood.' Natalie began looking out for shoe trees in antiques markets and junk shops, and as her collection grew, so did her interest in their history. 'There are just so many different materials and mechanisms,' she enthused. 'Once you get into it, it's a fascinating subject. Honestly!' As Natalie explained, 'The last manufacturing process that gives footwear its final shape is called 'treeing' and it is from this that the shoe tree gets its name.' Her earliest examples date from the 19th century, when ladies and gentlemen (or rather their servants) were expected to look after their clothes. 'Everyone who can afford it should have his own boot trees at home to preserve his boots in proper shape,' advised Mr James Dowie in 1861. But apart from the odd reference in household management books, very little has been written about shoe trees, and Natalie has assembled her own research. Today her collection includes over 50 different models and she continues to search for new and unusual designs.

► A boxwood shoe tree, the toepiece for a girl's flat pumps, 1860–1900, 5½in (14cm) long.
£12–15 NG

A pair of wooden straights shoe trees, 1830–80, 10in (25.5cm) long.
£10–12 NG
Straights were shoe trees that would fit either foot.

► A pair of beech four-piece riding boot trees, made for a pair of hand-made boots, 1870–90, 15in (38cm) high.
£30–35 NG

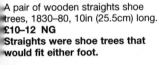

A pair of men's patent leather ankle boots, by C. Moykope, with three-piece wooden shoe tree, stamped 'Size 2', with brass pull ring, c1890, 11¼in (28.5cm) long.
£20–25 NG

A pair of beech four-piece boot trees, with separate heel and central shaft, and articulated toe section, 1870–90, 11in (28cm) long.
£25–30 NG

A pair of wood and iron women's shoe trees, for narrow feet, 1880–1900, toe 6in (15cm) long.
£20–25 NG

A pair of wooden shoemaker's moulds, 19thC, 8in (20.5cm) long.
£80–90 MFB

A pair of combined boot trees and dryers, probably poplar wood, with adjustable foot, 1890–1915, foot 8in (20.5cm) long.
£10–12 NG

A pair of Skyline white-metal adjustable shoe trees, 1900–30, toe 4in (10cm) long.
£6–8 NG

A pair of wooden shoe formers, c1930, 11in (28cm) long.
£20–25 Cot

A pair of lady's shoe stretchers, 1940, 10in (25.5cm) long.
£10–12 Cot

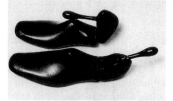

A pair of black-lacquered wooden shoe trees, the undersides cut away, 1890–1920, 10½in (26.5cm) long.
£10–12 NG

A pair of black-lacquered adjustable iron shoe trees, 1900–20, foot 5in (12.5cm) long.
£6–8 NG

A pair of wooden shoe trees, with brass pull ring, 1930s, 11in (28cm) long.
£25–30 WAB

A pair of red Ronning electric footwear dryers, 1930–40, 8½in (21.5cm) long.
£18–20 NG

▶ A pair of Mobbsmiller wooden advertising shoes, 1970s, 5in (12.5cm) long.
£20–25 NG

A pair of beech three-piece boot trees, shaped for left and right feet, 1890–1910, 11in (28cm) long.
£25–30 NG

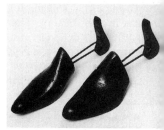

A pair of four-ply wooden shoe trees, with iron foot-adjusting device, 1915–40, 11in (28cm) long.
£8–10 NG

A pair of Lotus brown leather lady's shoes, with gilt-wood and sprung-steel shaft shoe trees, 1920–40, tree 11½in (29cm) long.
Shoes £12–15
Trees £1–1.50 NG
Originally the shoe trees would have been covered with pink satin.

Silver & Silver Plate

A George III silver milk jug, with thread edging and engraved crest, London 1799.
£300–330 Bea(E)

A Victorian silver-gilt chalice and paten, by George Adams, the paten engraved with a sunburst around the letters 'IHS', London 1863, 4in (10cm) high.
£130–150 CGC
A paten is the shallow, circular silver dish on which the bread is laid at the celebration of the Eucharist.

LOCATE THE SOURCE
The source of each illustration in Miller's can be found by checking the code letters below each caption with the Key to Illustrations, pages 476–484.

A Victorian silver-plated coffee pot, c1880, 9in (23cm) high.
£175–195 ASAA

A George III silver wine funnel and strainer, by Peter & William Bateman, with reeded decoration, London 1809, 5in (12.5cm) high.
£350–400 CGC

A William IV four-division silver egg cruet, probably by William Eaton, with gadroon edging, the stand on four winged paw feet, marked, London 1830.
£475–525 Bea(E)

A Victorian silver vine leaf Sherry label, by Joseph Willmore, Birmingham 1885, 3in (7.5cm) wide.
£120–140 CoHA

A Sheffield plate dish and cover, c1830, 14in (35.5cm) wide.
£100–120 ASAA

A pair of Victorian silver sandwich boxes and plates, by Thomas Johnson, inscribed with a monogram enclosed by a garter with the Royal motto and the coronet of an Earl above, 1875.
£1,400–1,600 P(B)

A Victorian silver mustard pot, by Aldwinckle & Slater, with blue glass liner, London 1884, 2¾in (7cm) high, with a fiddle-and-thread pattern mustard spoon by J. & A. Savory, London 1852.
£275–300 CGC

▶ A Victorian silver vesta case, Birmingham 1892, 2in (5cm) long.
£65–75 CoHA

An Edward VII sugar caster, possibly by Henry Stradford, with spiral reeded and fluted decoration, London 1902.
£320–350 Bea(E)

A silver christening tankard, Sheffield 1915, 3in (7.5cm) high.
£200–240 CoHA

An Edward VII silver vesta case, with fox mask pattern, Chester 1907, 2in (5cm) high.
£500–600 Bea(E)

An Edward VII silver tea caddy, by Nathan & Hayes, with wrythen finial and gadroon-edged base, with paw feet, Chester 1907.
£220–260 Bea(E)

A Regency-style three-piece tea service, by The Goldsmiths & Silversmiths Co, with egg-and-dart and shell cast border, London 1914.
£300–350 HYD

A pair of cut-glass and silver knife rests, Chester 1928, 3¼in (8.5cm) long, with fitted case.
£200–240 CoHA

An Art Nouveau-style silver-mounted red glass preserve jar, engraved with flowers and leaves, and a matching three-handled butter dish, Birmingham 1907, jar 4¾in (12cm) high.
£375–425 DN

A sterling silver calling card case, with engraved scrollwork and a monogram, Chester 1908, 3in (7.5cm) wide.
£60–70 BWA

A silver mustard pot, with a blue glass liner, and spoon, Birmingham 1923, 1½in (4cm) high.
£50–60 CoHA

Cross Reference
See Colour Review

A Dunhill silver table cigarette lighter, marked 'W & C', London 1928, 4in (10cm) high.
£440–480 CGC

An Art Deco four-piece silver tea service, with ebonized spur-capped handles, Birmingham 1934–39.
£300–350 HYD

CUTLERY

A George II silver marrow scoop, by Ebenezer Coker, London 1741, 8in (20.5cm) long.
£275–295 BEX

A Regency silver stilton scoop, with ejector, Birmingham 1824, 9in (23cm) long.
£245–265 HEB

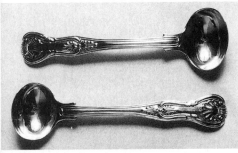

A pair of Victorian silver King's pattern salt spoons, by George Adams, London 1863, 4½in (11.5cm) long.
£85–95 BEX

Condition

The condition is absolutely vital when assessing the value of a collectable. Damaged items on the whole appreciate much less than perfect examples. However, a rare desirable piece may command a high price even when damaged.

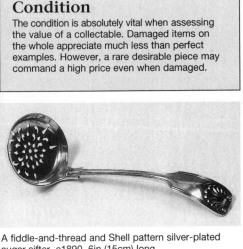

A fiddle-and-thread and Shell pattern silver-plated sugar sifter, c1890, 6in (15cm) long.
£30–35 ASAA

A silver Fiddle pattern gravy spoon, London 1822, 13in (33cm) long.
£165–185 HEB

Fiddle pattern was an English cutlery design, consisting of a shaped stem, broad top and notched shoulders at the base. The pattern could be plain or threaded around the edges (fiddle-and-thread pattern), and a stylized scallop shell was sometimes stamped on the cutlery.

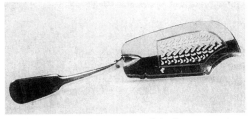

A William IV silver Fiddle pattern fish slice, by Jonathan Hayne, with pierced curved blade, London 1835.
£130–150 GAK

A Victorian silver-plated Queen's pattern stuffing spoon, by James Dixon & Son, c1890, 14in (35.5cm) long.
£60–65 ASAA

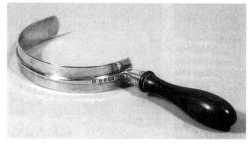

A Scottish silver presentation cream scoop, by Hamilton & Inches, with turned hardwood handle, Edinburgh 1899, 11¼in (28.5cm) long.
£170–200 CGC

A pair of silver-plated pickle forks, by Mappin & Webb, c1900, 7in (18cm) long, with fitted case.
£45–50 ASAA

▶ An Edwardian silver sauce ladle, by Brewis & Co, London 1908.
£110–130 BEX

A Victorian silver-plated Fiddle pattern soup ladle, with engraved crest, c1890, 13in (33cm) long.
£60–70 ASAA

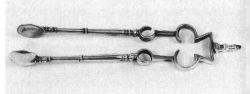

A pair of silver sugar tongs, Birmingham 1899, 5in (12.5cm) long.
£25–30 MRW

A set of six Art Nouveau silver and blue enamel spoons, marked 'JF', Birmingham 1906, 4½in (11.5cm) long, with fitted case.
£270–290 DN

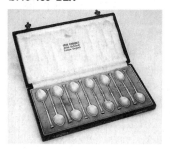

A set of 12 silver spoons, by Omar Ramsden, marked, London 1933, with original wooden retail box.
£750–850 DN

A set of six silver-plated pastry forks with matching server, c1930, with fitted case.
£40–45 ASAA

A silver tea caddy spoon, by T. Bradbury & Son, with shell-fluted bowl, the handle with an oval shield cartouche, Sheffield 1933.
£80–90 WW

Sixties & Seventies

A set of six glasses, Smoke, designed by Joe Colombo, 1964, ½in (14cm) high.
£350–400 **MARK**

An Arkana mushroom stool, with white plastic base and black fabric seat, 1960s.
£60–75 **MARK**

An American poster, 'The MOD Ball' at The Rainbow Room, by Joe Eula, printed in red and black on a white ground, 1965, 25 x 38in (63.5 x 96.5cm).
£170–200 **CJP**

A festival poster, 'UFO Coming', by Hapshash and the Coloured Coat, printed in yellow and purple, 1967, 30 x 19in (76 x 48.5cm).
£300–350 **CJP**

A signed Andy Warhol card, Marilyn, 1967, 6 x 4in (15 x 10cm).
£250–285 **VS**

An Eero Saarinen-style miniature plastic table and four tulip chairs, 1960s, 4in (10cm) high.
£55–65 **PLB**

An ABS Plastic Kartell Stacking Unit, designed by Anna Castelli Ferrieri, 1968, 30in (76cm) high.
£140–160 **PLB**

An Italian chrome and red fabric lounge chair, 1960s, 29in (73.5cm) long.
£225–265 **PAB**

◄ A beige plastic and chrome ashtray, 1970s, 20½in (52cm) high.
£35–40 **ZOOM**

A German poster, 'Look at Vasarely', 1969, 35 x 26in (89 x 66cm).
£120–150 **CJP**

A Tabacoff smoked-Perspex and chrome chair, with cream vinyl padded covers, Belgium, early 1970s.
£200–240 MARK
In clear Perspex the price range would be £300–350.

▶ A Pirelli black plastic breast plate, by Allen Jones, 1972, 13in (33cm) high.
£4,500–5,000 MARK
Allen Jones (b.1937) was one of the best-known British pop artists of the 1960s and 70s. Much of his imagery was sexual and fetishistic in nature, and this breast plate (where the accent is definitely on the breasts!) was designed for a Pirelli calendar in 1972.

▶ Two Nagel Variante sculptures, S70 and S71, with chrome base and adjustable silvered-plastic spheres, West Germany, early 1970s, 33in (84cm) high.
£100–120 PAB

CERAMICS

A Royal Worcester ceramic plate, by Scottie Wilson, decorated with stylized birds in a landscape in black on a white ground, with a grey and white geometric border, signed, c1960, 10in (25.5cm) diam.
£85–95 DAD

A Poole Pottery red earthenware vase, shape No. A20/3, by Carol Cutler, decorated with four carved green-glazed castellated bands, marked, c1975, 5in (12.5cm) high.
£100–120 RTo

A Portmeirion cup and saucer, Jupiter, decorated with blue-black circles, 1960s, 3¼in (8.5cm) high.
£35–40 LEGE

A Troika vase, decorated in orange and cream on a blue-grey speckled ground, c1970, 9in (23cm) high.
£250–280 HUN

A Portmeirion coffee pot, decorated with Phoenix pattern in gold on a dark brown ground, 1960s, 13½in (34.5cm) high.
£25–30 LEGE

A Carlton Ware ashtray, decorated with Denim pattern in blue and brown on a white ground, c1978, 6¼in (16cm) diam.
£25–30 StC

A Carlton Ware biscuit barrel, decorated with Denim pattern in blue and brown on a white ground, with a bamboo handle, 1970s, 12in (30.5cm) high.
£35–40 StC
Reflecting the contemporary fashion for jeans, Carlton Ware launched their Denim Ware range c1978. The couple wear matching unisex jeans and cheesecloth shirts a classic example of seventies style, accurate down to the open shirt buttons. Denim Ware is becoming increasingly collectable today, particularly the more unusual items such as this biscuit barrel.

LIGHTING

A Franco Albini chrome and white glass table lamp, early 1960s, 26in (66cm) high.
£550–600 MARK

A metal multibranch plant lamp, 1960s, 69in (175.5cm) high.
£400–450 ZOOM

An Italian table lamp, with chrome base and black glass mushroom shade, early 1970s, 26in (66cm) high.
£200–240 ZOOM

◄ A Visconti spun-fibre-glass light shade, designed by Achille Castiglioni, produced by Gavina, Italy, 1960, 26in (66cm) diam.
£450–500 MARK

A chrome arc lamp, with gold-coloured shade, c1970, extended 78in (198cm) high.
£350–400 ZOOM
This design was based on the Arco lamp created by the Castiglioni brothers in 1962. The Italian designers were much imitated and copies of the Arco lamp appeared in homes around the world. A Castiglioni original could be worth double this amount.

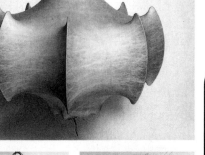

A chrome-on-metal Sputnik hanging light, probably French, 1970s, 32in (81.5cm) high.
£175–200 MARK

An Italian chrome and glass chandelier, 1970s, 40in (101.5cm) high.
£550–650 PLB

Smoking

A German ceramic tobacco jar, in the form of a child in a basket, decorated in brown, pink, yellow and pale green, 19thC, 7in (18cm) wide.
£200–225 LeB

A Meerschaum pipe, carved with two owls on a branch, with inset glass eyes, 19thC, 7in (18cm) long.
£250–300 RTo

▶ A Dean Bros metal cigarette dispensing machine, 1920s, 33in (84cm) high.
£180–200 JUN

A Bigg's Own Cigarettes glass change tray, decorated in brown and black, 1920s, 4in (10cm) wide.
£60–75 MURR

A ceramic match holder, in the form of a wide-mouthed man with smiling feet, decorated in pink, red and black, possibly German, c1930, 3½in (9cm) high.
£50–60 MRW

A chrome combined date and match striker, 1930s, 4⅛in (11.5cm) high.
£30–35 HarC

A Wendell August Forge aluminium ashtray, The Hindenberg, with pivoting glass vial in the form of the Zeppelin, marked, 1936, 6¼in (16cm) diam.
£750–850 SK(B)

A Michelin black and white Bakelite advertising ashtray, 1940s, 5in (12.5cm) high.
£100–120 GAD

A Colibri metal combined lighter and cigarette case, 1950s, 4in (10cm) high, in original box.
£20–25 RTT

Spectacles & Optical Equipment

A pair of silver-framed four lens spectacles, with clear and blue-tinted glass and original red leather case, c1850, 5in (12.5cm) wide.
£200–220 BWA

Four lens spectacles were invented by the British optician J. R. Richardson in 1797. They were produced with clear and tinted lenses, the additional lenses folding back against the sides to form protective goggles.

A Victorian double-folding horn magnifying glass, 6in (15cm) long.
£30–35 WAB

An optician's eye-testing kit, in original box with purple lining, c1870, 5in (12.5cm) wide.
£70–80 BWA

A pair of gold-rimmed spectacles, with original leather case, c1880, 7in (18cm) wide.
£35–40 BWA

A pair of French brass and mother-of-pearl adjustable opera glasses, c1880, 5in (12.5cm) wide.
£100–120 WAB

A tortoiseshell lorgnette, 1900, 12in (30.5cm) long.
£35–40 DHo

A white-gold Art Deco sprung lorgnette, 1935, 3¼in (8.5cm) long.
£550–600 WIM

A pair of glitter-fleck plastic sunglasses, 1940s.
£35–40 SpM

A pair of American pink plastic sunglasses, with original price tag of $3.98, 1940s.
£35–40 SpM

A pair of Polaroid sunglasses, with original black case, 1950, 6in (15cm) wide.
£8–10 RTT

Sport

A Leeds St John's Football Club season's fixture card, with gold embossed decorative boards, 1886–87.
£140–160 MUL

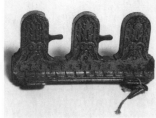

A Victorian cast-iron snooker cue holder, 7in (18cm) wide.
£30–35 WAB

A bamboo shooting stick, with brass fittings, 1890, 29in (73.5cm) long.
£100–120 SPT

An Olympic Games London silver and enamel Steward's badge, by Vaughton, pin missing, 1908.
£725–800 DNW

A wood and metal mountaineer's ice pick, 1920s, 44in (112cm) long.
£75–85 SPT

◄ A pair of metal and leather ski poles, c1920, 48in (122cm) long.
£14–16 AL

A painted-metal bowls scoring board, c1920, 31in (78.5cm) high.
£25–30 AL

A wood and leather lacrosse stick, 1930, 44in (112cm) long.
£40–50 SMW

A pottery hockey mug, decorated in green and black on a brown ground, 1920s, 5½in (14cm) high.
£120–130 BRT

◄ A wooden croquet set, in original box, c1930, box 40in (101.5cm) wide.
£180–200 AL

► A German chrome-steel official torch for the first Olympic torch relay to Berlin from Olympus, by Krupp, lacking funnel, inscribed, 1936, 22in (28cm) high.
£1,800–2,000 MUL

A pair of lady's leather and steel ice skates, 1940s, 12in (30.5cm) long.
£24–28 **SPT**

A pair of Cooper leather ice hockey gloves, Canada, 1960s, 15in (38cm) long.
£30–35 **TRA**

A Bowman Gum football card, The Great Sammy Baugh, printed in brown and orange on a green ground, 1950.
£60–65 **HALL**

A Spalding leather American football, 1970s.
£20–25 **TRA**

A signed black and white photograph of Roger Bannister after breaking the four-minute mile, with Chris Chataway and Chris Brasher, 1954, 8 x 10in (20.5 x 25.5cm).
£180–200 **SMW**
The neurologist Roger Bannister (b.1929) was the first man to run a mile in under four minutes (3 min. 59.4sec) at Oxford University on 6 May 1954.

Further reading

Miller's Antiques & Collectables: The Facts At Your Fingertips,
Miller's Publications, 1996

BASEBALL

A black and white photograph, Lou Gehrig, 1928, 10 x 8in (25.5 x 20.5cm).
£100–110 **HALL**

A National Chiclet Gum coloured baseball card, Diamond Stars Series, Carl Hubbell, 1934.
£55–60 **HALL**

◄ A leather baseball glove, 'Super 5837', 1950s.
£30–35 **TRA**

► A Topps Gum card, Roberto Clemente, printed in red, brown, white and black on a green ground, 1955.
£550–600 **HALL**

An official American League leather baseball, autographed by Babe Ruth, mid-1940s.
£1,200–1,500 **HALL**

◄ A leather and fabric baseball body protector, 1950s, 31in (78.5cm) high.
£25–30 **TRA**

A Topps Gum card, Ted Williams, printed in blue, brown, red and yellow on a brown ground, 1956.
£230–250 HALL

A fibreglass ice-baseball backcatcher's mask, 1960s, 10in (25.5cm) high.
£20–25 TRA

A Rawlings leather baseball glove, 1970s, 11in (28cm) wide.
£25–30 TRA

BOXING

Life of Tom Sayers, published by George Newbold, 1860, 8vo.
£160–200 DW

▶ A collection of about 107 boxing programmes, some damaged, most contests promoted by Jack Solomons, c1931–66, 4to.
£375–425 DW

A collection of about 250 boxing press photographs, c1930–59, approx 8 x 10in (20.5 x 25.5cm).
£375–425 DW

A pair of child's leather boxing training gloves, 1910.
£35–40 DQ

A Mecca Cigarettes card, Jack Johnson, printed in brown, white and red on a green ground, 1910.
£55–60 HALL

Sets/pairs

Unless otherwise stated, any description which refers to 'a set' or 'a pair' includes a guide price for the entire set or the pair, even though the illustration may show only a single item.

A signed colour photograph, Evander Hollyfield after the Tyson fight, showing bitten ear, 1998, 10 x 8in (25.5 x 20.5cm).
£120–150 SMW

CRICKET

A wooden cricket bat, damaged, c1875,
34in (86.5cm) long.
£300–330 **SMW**

A black and white photograph, the Australian
cricketing team, by The London Stereoscopic &
Photographic Co, 1888, 3½ x 5in (9 x 12.5cm).
£180–200 **DW**

A black and white
visiting-card photograph,
George Parr, by McLean
& Haes, 1845–70,
4 x 2½in (10 x 6.5cm).
£150–175 **KNI**

A leather-covered
cricket ball, c1880,
3in (7.5cm) diam.
£160–180 **SMW**

► A solid bronze statue,
William Gilbert Grace,
playing a defensive shot
off the front foot,
12in (30.5cm) high.
£275–300 **KNI**

◄ *Laws of
Cricket*, by
Charles Crombie,
with 12 colour
plates, original
cloth-backed
pictorial
boards, 1907,
oblong folio.
£350–400 **BBA**

► A pair of
white leather
cricket shoes,
size 8, c1960.
£8–10 **AL**

Items in the Sporting
section have been
arranged in date
order within each
sub-section.

◄ A signed black and
white photograph,
Sir Don Bradman, 1950s,
15 x 11in (38 x 28cm).
£200–240 **SMW**

FISHING

The Angler's Vade Mecum, by Chetham James, third edition, bound in 20thC half-leather with marbled boards, 1700, 8 x 5in (20.5 x 12.5cm).
£475–525 MUL

▶ A cut-glass Allcock-style lure, No. 328, with cut glass to both sides held on to fish-shaped nickel-silver body by 14 claws, c1871, 1¾in (4.5cm) long.
£1,000–1,200 MUL

A Flexible Jointed Cleopatra brass lure, by Gregory of Birmingham, 1880, 5in (12.5cm) long.
£700–900 OTB

◀ *The Compleat Angler*, volumes I and II, by Izaak Walton, The Lea & Dove edition, limited to 500 copies signed by Marston, 1800, 11 x 9¼in (28 x 23.5cm).
£850–950 OPB

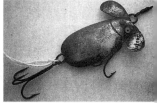

A Gregory glass-eyed Colorado spoon lure, with two treble hooks, c1890, body 2in (5cm) long.
£500–550 MUL

A Ramsbottom of Manchester brass and gunmetal trout fly reel, with bevelled face plate rims, 1895, 2½in (6.5cm) diam.
£50–60 OTB

A brass Malloch's Patent side casting reel, by H. Moore, c1900, 4in (10cm) wide.
£220–250 SMW

A glass-eyed nickel-silver-plated Clipper Bait, possibly by Gregory of Birmingham, c1900, 2½in (6.5cm) long.
£150–175 OTB

The Science of Dry Fly Fishing, by Fred G. Shaw, the Amateur Champion, published by Bradbury, Agnew & Co, 1906.
£25–30 HBo

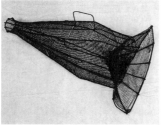

A metal eel trap, c1920, 24in (61cm) long.
£25–30 AL

◀ An Allcock Aerial six-spoke alloy ventilated reel, with brass foot, twin ivorine handles and on/off check, marked, 1920s, 3in (7.5cm) diam.
£550–600 MUL

An Allcock Waterwitch plated-brass pike and salmon lure, 1920, 2in (5cm) long.
£65–80 OTB

Hardy's Angler's Guide, 46th edition, with a green cover showing J. J. Hardy on the Orchy, 1924.
£90–100 MUL

A wooden fishing chair, with a slatted seat, c1920.
£20–25 AL

◀ A metal bait can, c1920, 7in (18cm) wide.
£20–25 AL

A Robert Turnball leather fly wallet, the interior with pouched pages for flies, gilt-embossed, 1905–14, 6in (15cm) wide.
£60–70 P(Sc)

A bottle of Hardy's Anti-Midge oil, with a nickel-silver capped stopper, in original waxed-card box, c1920, 3in (7.5cm) high.
£120–150 OTB

A chrome-steel and Bakelite game reel, c1930, drum 6in (15cm) diam, with wooden carrying case.
£175–225 WAB

A landing net, with wood and brass handle, 1930s, 61in (155cm) long.
£45–55 SPT

A wood and brass reel with star back, c1930, 5in (12.5cm) diam.
£200–225 SMW

A Mercury Trotting Reel, with open-cast caged ball-bearing drum, and black handle, c1938, 4in (10cm) diam.
£80–100 MUL

► A metal line winder, with wooden handle, c1930, 16in (40.5cm) long.
£35–40 AL

◄ A wicker creel, 1940s, 16in (40.5cm) wide.
£160–185 SPT

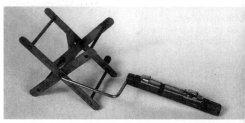

A Hardy brass lipstick-style rod ferrule greaser, c1930, 2¼in (5.5cm) long.
£20–25 OTB

◄ A Brown-Robertson Lock Joint Tool, for undoing Lock Fast rod ferrules, 1940s, 3½in (9cm) long, in original box.
£10–12 OTB

A Hardy Harlaw fountain-pen-style dry fly oiler, in original card box, 1960s, 5½in (14cm) long.
£75–90 OTB

FOOTBALL

A leather football, c1910.
£175–200 SMW

A wooden football rattle, c1890, 10in (25.5cm) wide.
£120–130 SMW

A pair of leather soccer boots, c1920.
£175–200 SMW

A Southampton v. Tottenham Hotspur team card, with black and white and red cover, 26 December 1903.
£1,600–1,800 S

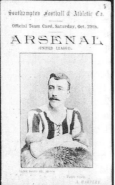

A Southampton v. Woolwich Arsenal team card, 29 October 1900.
£800–1,000 S

▶ A Tottenham Hotspur stadium fibreglass cockerel mascot, decorated with bronze-effect paint, 25in (63.5cm) high.
£2,750–3,000 S
The cockerel and ball first appeared in 1909 when a former player, W. J. Scott, cast a copper centrepiece to perch on the new West Stand at the White Hart Lane ground. The West Stand was redeveloped in 1980.

Cross Reference
See Colour Review

A plaster figure of a footballer, finished in bronze, with folded arms and ball under his left foot, c1910, 21in (53.5cm) high.
£375–425 MUL

A gilt-metal and enamel medal, by Thomas Fattarini, awarded to Stanley Matthews by the English Schools' Football Association for being selected to play for the North v. South, in red, blue, white and gold, 1929, 1½in (4cm) wide.
£1,800–2,000 LT
This was the first medal ever to be awarded to Stanley Matthews. He was then aged 13.

A blue Birmingham City FA Cup Final shirt, worn by Ned Barkas, long-sleeved, with white button-up collar and blue and cream embroidered badge, 1931, with a black and white press photograph of the Duke of Gloucester shaking hands with the Birmingham team.
£2,000–2,200 S

An Arsenal Football Club programme, for Arsenal v. Birmingham matches in 1933–34 and 1934–35, printed in black and red, 9 x 5in (23 x 12.5cm).
£65–75 KNI

An FA Cup Final Tie programme, Arsenal v. Sheffield United, 1936.
£275–300 MUL

◄ A right football boot, belonging to Stanley Matthews, possibly worn in the 1953 Cup Final.
£650–700 LT

A Football League War Cup Final programme, Arsenal v. Charlton Athletic, 1943, 8vo.
£220–250 DW

◄ A white Tottenham Hotspur No. 4 FA Cup Final jersey, worn by Alan Mullery, with embroidered black cockerel club crest and inscription, 1967.
£1,700–1,900 S

A World Cup coloured photograph, signed by all the England team players and Alf Ramsay, 1966, framed and glazed, frame 28 x 26in (71 x 66cm).
£2,800–2,000 SMW

A blue England v. Bulgaria international cap, with a gold tassel, 1968–69.
£1,100–1,300 S

A signed black and white photograph, Tom Finney at Stamford Bridge, 1956, 7 x 9in (18 x 23cm).
£85–100 SMW

A black and white football, signed by Pele, 1990s.
£220–250 SMW

► A signed colour photograph, Alan Shearer, Captain of Newcastle and England, 1999, 10 x 6in (25.5 x 15cm).
£75–100 SMW

GOLF

A gutta-percha golf ball, 1840.
£250–275 SMW

A transitional golf club, by J. Morris, with gutta-percha inset and bone protection, c1895.
£450–500 SMW
When the gutty ball (made from gutta-percha) replaced the softer feather ball in the mid-19th century, a new 'transitional' club was introduced with a thicker neck and a shorter head.

British Golf Links, edited by Horace Hutchinson, first edition, 1897, 4to.
£500–550 DW

A Pope's short-head putter, with hickory shaft, c1905.
£1,000–1,100 S

▶ *Ladies' Golf*, by May Hezlet, first edition, 1907, 8vo.
£450–500 DW

A Bramble golf ball, c1895.
£250–275 SMW

▶ A Rowland Hilder lithograph, 'Come to Britain For Golf', printed in colours by W. S. Cowell, for the Travel Association of Great Britain and Northern Ireland, framed and glazed, c1950, 29½ x 19½in (75 x 49.5cm).
£750–850 S

MISS MAY HEZLET

A wooden golfing figure, in the style of John Hassal, with a red coat and brown cap and plus fours, 1930s, 7in (18cm).
£100–120 BEV

A black and white photograph, Bobby Jones holding a trophy, 1930s.
£100–120 HALL

ROWING

A pair of ornamental blades, blue with red stripe, and black, 1930s, 18in (45.5cm) long.
£40–50 WAB

▶ A Stevengraph, entitled 'The Final Spurt', No. 170, early 1881, 5 x 8in (12.5 x 20.5cm).
£300–330 VINE

◀ Two Selwyn College Cambridge black and white rowing photographs, 3rd May Boat, 1950, framed and glazed, frame 12 x 21in (30.5 x 53.5cm).
£60–75 WAB

A section of a wooden rowing skiff 1970s, 23in (58.5cm) wide.
£80–100 NC

TENNIS

A pine lawn tennis box, with inscribed label, and down poles, net, guy ropes, pegs and mallet, and two later convex wedge rackets, 19thC, 38in (96.5cm) wide.
£900–1,000 MUL

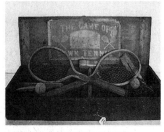

A Spalding Olympic tennis ball box, with used balls, 1950s, 8in (20.5cm) wide.
£18–20 WaR

A pair of Victorian wood and parchment bats, 19in (48.5cm) long.
£40–45 SPT

◀ A Slazenger Special Demon lawn tennis racket, with mahogany convex wedge and scored and grooved fish-tail handle, c1885.
£170–200 DW

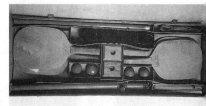

A Parvo tennis set, in original fitted wooden case, c1920, box 35in (89cm) long.
£120–150 TWr

◀ A signed black and white photograph, Billie Jean King, 1960s, 12 x 11in (30.5 x 28cm), framed and glazed.
£80–100 SMW
Billie Jean King was four times Wimbledon Champion.

Swimsuits

While 19th-century ladies would take a sea-cure by immersing themselves in water from a bathing machine, swimming itself did not become acceptable for women until the early 20th century. The first bathing suits followed the fashions of outerwear and were almost as substantial; the knee-length dress, stockings, pumps and a turban, were severely impractical for anything more than a soggy paddle. After WWI came the introduction of the knee-length, jersey one-piece suit, similar to a male costume and daringly clinging. 'Far greater latitude than ever before seems to have been given to the designers of bathing suits,' commented *Vogue*. As beach holidays became increasingly fashionable among the bright young things of the 1920s, so costumes became shorter, revealing the arms, the back and the legs and reflecting the new fashion for sun tanning. In the 1930s new elasticated fabrics made costumes more figure hugging. For the first time bathing suits could be body-shaped, leading to a growing emphasis on fitness.

The post-war period saw the growing popularity of the two-piece bathing suit, and in 1946, French designer Louis Reard launched the bikini, named after Bikini Atoll, where the USA had detonated the atomic bomb, and which created an equally far-reaching fashion explosion.

The introduction of the Miss World contest in 1951 brought bathing beauties into the living room and raised the profile of the swimsuit (bikinis were not permitted). Fifties style veered from girlish frills, skirts and rompers, to boned and padded strapless suits that emphasized womanly curves. With the 1960s came psychedelic fabrics, cutaway bathing suits and daringly sexy swimwear, epitomized by the bikini-clad James Bond girls. In 1964 designer Rudi Gernreich introduced the topless swimsuit, paving the way for topless bathing.

A ceramic Tipperary bathing machine, by Wiltshaw & Robinson, decorated in orange and gilt on a cream ground, c1910, 3in (7.5cm) wide.
£28–32 JACK

A boy's Sensola navy-blue machine-knitted cotton one-piece bathing costume, 1920–30.
£12–14 DE

◄ A multicoloured Crocus Swim Suits stand-up card advertisement, by Patons & Baldwins, 1920s, 14¾ x 9¾in (37.5 x 25cm).
£50–60 BBR

A ceramic bottle, transfer-printed with a beach beauty wearing a bikini, in red, brown, gilt and blue on a cream ground, possibly French, late 1950s, 5in (12.5cm) high.
£18–22 SpM

A Slix black spandex swimsuit, 1950–60.
£10–12 DE

A pair of men's brown and green cotton elasticized swimming trunks, 1950–60.
£8–10 DE

A Debenhams black and white nylon swimsuit, with padded cups, 1960s.
£6–7 DE

A cotton two-piece swimsuit, possibly home-made, in blue, red and white on a green ground, late 1950s.
£12–15 DE

A Bri-nylon swimsuit, with blue and white flowers on a navy ground, early 1960s.
£6–8 DE

A Sinney nylon swimsuit, with orange, yellow and brown flowers on a white ground, 1960s.
£8–10 DE

▶ A Brigitte Bardot pink and white gingham bikini, with a padded top and original label, 1960s.
£150–175 SpM

◀ A *Photoplay* magazine, with full-colour cover featuring Sean Connery and a bikini-clad Bond girl, 1966.
£5–6 CTO

A Slix black and white one-piece nylon swimsuit, 1960.
£6–8 DE

▶ A Denys Fisher Miss World Game, printed in colours on a navy ground, 1972, 13 x 22in (33 x 56cm).
£50–60 TBoy

A Triumph nylon Elastene foto-print bikini, with purple, green and blue flowers on a multicoloured ground, Austria, 1970s.
£20–25 SpM

Tattooing

▶ Five photographic postcards of tattooed Maori chiefs, c1900, 5 x 3in (12.5 x 7.5cm).
£16–20 BTM

Three black and white photographic postcards of tattooed ladies, c1900, 5 x 3in (12.5 x 7.5cm).
£8–10 BTM

Three brass and chrome-over-brass tattoo machines, 1950, 6 x 5in (15 x 12.5cm).
£16–20 each Ram

A Johnny-Two-Thumbs of Singapore twin-coil vibrating tattoo machine, 1940, 6 x 4in (15 x 10cm).
£120–150 Ram

Four black and white photographic postcards of tattooed Maori women, 1910–20, 5 x 3in (12.5 x 7.5cm).
£8–10 Ram

▶ Memoirs of a Tattooist, by George Burchett and Peter Leighton, 1953, 9 x 6in (23 x 15cm).
£16–20 Ram

Two tattoo machines, by Cindy Ray, Australia, 1960s, 6 x 5in (15 x 12.5cm).
£25–30 Ram

Teddy Bears & Soft Toys

A beige fabric straw-filled Humpty Dumpty, with a painted face, early 20thC, 11in (28cm) high.
£55–65 DAn

A Steiff mohair teddy bear, with centre seam, original excelsior filling, wearing a blue and white sailor suit, 1905–8, 19in (48.5cm) high.
£1,800–2,000 Ann

A Steiff mohair teddy bear, wearing a knitted navy and white suit, pads and paws repaired, 1910–12, 13in (33cm) high.
£600–700 Ann

A Steiff blonde plush bear, with a pointed snout, bead eyes, long arms and hump back, with Steiff ear button, c1920, 25in (63.5cm) high.
£1,800–2,000 HYD

A German blonde plush teddy bear, with excelsior filling, button eyes, and re-covered foot pads, early 20thC, 13in (33cm) high.
£800–900 DAn

A yellow plush teddy bear, with button eyes, early 20thC, 3¾in (9.5cm) high.
£60–70 TMA

A Steiff mohair rabbit, with glass eyes, early 20thC, 6in (15cm) high.
£130–150 TMA

> **Cross Reference**
> See Colour Review

A genuine fur tiger cub, copy of a Steiff, 1920–30, 16in (40.5cm) long.
£50–60 Ann

A German mohair teddy bear, with glass eyes, restored, 1920, 21in (53.5cm) high.
£300–350 A&J

A felt hedgehog, in the style of Steiff, with red and white clothes and white knitted jacket, c1930, 8in (20.5cm) high.
£15–20 A&J

A mohair lion, with glass eyes,
1930–50, 16in (40.5cm) long.
£40–50 A&J

A Steiff mohair rabbit, with excelsior filling, c1950s, 5in (12.5cm) long.
£30–35 A&J

A mohair teddy bear, with Rexine pads and glass eyes, 1930s, 21in (58.5cm) high.
£120–150 A&J

▶ A Dean's Mickey and Minnie Mouse soft toys, Mickey with red shorts and green buttons, Minnie wearing a green cotton skirt and yellow and green felt hat, numbered, 1935–40, 6½in (16.5cm) high.
£350–400 DN

A Chiltern Hugmee mohair teddy bear, with painted glass eyes, 1930s, 21in (53.5cm) high.
£230–260 TMA

A Dean's mohair black bear cub, with a red leather collar, 1950s, 14in (35.5cm) high.
£3,000–3,300 Ann

A mohair monkey, with velveteen hands and feet, c1950, 13in (33cm) high.
£20–25 A&J

◀ A Pedigree mohair teddy bear, 1950s, 20in (51cm) high.
£200–220 Ann

A Steiff Jacko mohair monkey, with excelsior filling, c1950, 7in (18cm) high.
£35–40 A&J

A Steiff Rocky mohair goat, with pressed-felt horns and glass eyes, 1950s, 6in (15cm) high.
£30–35 A&J

A Steiff mohair ram, with pressed-felt horns and glass eyes, 1950, 6in (15cm) high.
£30–35 A&J

A mohair panda, dressed in top hat and tails and with a monocle, 1960s, 3½in (9cm) high.
£200–240 TED
This panda was specially dressed for F. A. O. Schwarz in New York and I. Magnin in San Francisco.

A Muppet Bendy Toy, Gonzo, with blue, yellow, white and turquoise face, wearing a beige suit with a red collar, 1970–80, 12in (30.5cm) high.
£18–22 TAC

A Muppet Bendy Toy, Chef, with a cream suit, red bow tie and white cap, 1970–80, 17in (43cm) high.
£24–28 TAC

A fur fabric Orinoco womble, with white body, yellow face and paws, and black hat, 1970s, 18in (45.5cm) high.
£10–12 UNI

A Canterbury Bears mohair teddy bear, wearing a tartan scarf, from a limited edition of 1,000, 1999, 17in (43cm) high.
£90–100 Ann

A fur fabric Madame Cholet womble, with brown face and paws, grey fur, white apron and pink and white satin hat, 1980s, 14in (35.5cm) high.
£16–20 CMF

▶ A nylon-fur and felt emu hand puppet, with orange body, yellow legs and beak, and black face, 1975, 37in (94cm) high.
£16–20 UNI

Prices

The price ranges quoted in this book reflect the average price a purchaser might expect to pay for a similar item. The price will vary according to the condition, rarity, size, popularity, provenance, colour and restoration of the item and this must be taken into account when assessing values. Don't forget that if you are selling it is quite likely that you will be offered less than the price range.

Telephones

A red and white enamel Post Office public telephone sign, c1916, 15 x 20in (38 x 51cm).
£100–120 COB

A black Bakelite candlestick telephone, model No. 150, with wooden bell set No. 1a, in a wooden telephone valet, 1920s, 16in (40.5cm) high.
£400–450 DHAR

A black Bakelite telephone, model No. 232, mounted on Bakelite bell set No. 26, 1920–30s, 9in (23cm) wide.
£160–180 DHAR

◀ An ivory Bakelite telephone, model No. 162, mounted on a Bakelite bell set, 1920–30s, 8in (20.5cm) wide.
£420–475 DHAR

A black Art Deco GECO telephone, 1930s, 8in (20.5cm) wide.
£170–190 DAC

A Belgian cast-iron wall telephone, with Bakelite handset, 1940–50s, 8in (20.5cm) high.
£140–170 DHAR

A red Bakelite telephone, model No. 312, 1930–40s, 9in (23cm) wide.
£375–400 DHAR

A French white Bakelite desk telephone, with mother-in-law piece, 1940s, 9in (23cm) wide.
£120–150 DHAR
A mother-in-law piece is a listening device at the back of the telephone.

◀ A black Bakelite series 200 telephone, with bell set 64d, 1934–50, 9in (23cm) wide.
£350–400 OTC

▶ A cream Bakelite GPO telephone, model No. 232, 1930s, 7in (18cm) wide.
£375–400 GAD

◀ A black Bakelite 300 series telephone with bell, on/off button and cheese drawer, 1940s, 4 x 8in (10 x 20.5cm)
£180–200 DAC
Cheese drawer is the name given to the pull-out section in the base used for telephone numbers.

▶ A Stromberg-Carlson black telephone, America, 1949, 8in (20.5cm) wide.
£55–65 AnSh

An American Western Electric bell system 500 series telephone, 1950s, 9in (23cm) long.
£45–50 DHAR

An Ericsson black Bakelite telephone, 1950s, 9in (23cm) wide.
£70–80 DHAR

A Northern Telecom cream plastic round telephone, 1960s, 9in (23cm) diam.
£80–100 ZOOM

▶ An Ericsson cream Ericofon, Sweden, 1960s, 8½in (21.5cm) high.
£85–95 PLB
Also known as the Cobra Phone, this was the first one-piece telephone, and was designed in 1954 by L. M. Ericsson. The dial and circuitry were lodged in the base and the design came in various colours.

A Carl grey metal Telephone List Finder, in original red, yellow and black cardboard box, c1960, 8in (20.5cm) high.
£12–15 RTT

◀ An Italian BoBo cream plastic telephone, early 1980s, 9in (23cm) wide.
£150–175 PLB

▶ A set of five South African coloured phone cards, The Big Five, water buffalo, cheetah, elephant, rhinoceros and lion, 1993.
£5–10 JCa
If unused, these cards would be in the £25–30 range.

Textiles

A pair of early Georgian needlepoint tapestries, worked in coloured wools and silks, depicting exotic birds and nests of eggs amongst branches and floral sprays, in bowed octagonal mahogany frames, 12 x 11in (30.5 x 28cm).
£380–420 WD

A painted silk picture, 'Lavinia', worked in coloured silks, depicting a young girl with an apron full of corn, in a glazed gilt-gesso oval frame, late 18thC, 9 x 6½in (23 x 16.5cm).
£240–280 WW

A late Georgian silkwork picture, embroidered in coloured silks and wools, depicting a parrot perched in a tree, framed and glazed, 11½ x 8in (29 x 20.5cm).
£640–680 WW

A George III sampler, worked with a verse above Adam and Eve beside the Tree of Life, flanked by birds, fruit and trees, and 'Ann Stimson 1807', in a glazed mahogany frame, 17½ x 12½in (44.5 x 32cm).
£4,000–4,500 S(S)

A William IV sampler, worked with a verse, a house, animals, birds and flowers, and 'Elisa Grylls aged 10 years June 12th 1832', in a rosewood frame, 16½ x 13in (42 x 33cm).
£650–750 AG

A Berlin woolwork tapestry, depicting rustic figures in a wooded landscape, framed, 19thC, 27 x 24in (68.5 x 61cm).
£220–260 Mit

A Victorian patchwork quilt, composed of 2 x 1in diamond patches in printed and plain cottons, the border of large and small diamonds, with lappet-style ends and wavy sides, lined, 101 x 77in (256.5 x 195.5cm).
£300–350 WW

A late Victorian North Country patchwork quilt, the centre design of red, white and green flowers, bordered by blue and cream, with orange zig-zag border, 83 x 74in (211 x 188cm).
£500–600 JJ

Items in the Textiles section have been arranged in date order within each sub-section.

◀ A plushwork and needlework picture of a King Charles spaniel, in raised tan and white woolwork, with textured body, black bead eyes and seated on a red cushion, in a glazed gilt-painted frame, 19thC, 23½in (59.5cm) square.
£730–800 WW
This needlwork was executed in Turkey and was a gift of Their Imperial Highnesses Prince Ali Vassib and Princess Mukbile of Turkey.

A Victorian red velvet table-cloth, with embroidered red and white border, and red wool tassels, 68 x 60in (172.5 x 152.5cm)
£100–120 DE

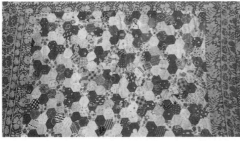

A Victorian patchwork quilt, worked in six-sided red, white and blue patches with hand-stitched buttons, the reverse on a green ground with similar patches, 42in (106.5cm) square.
£100–120 DE

An Indian dhurrie, the ivory field with section of a multiple medallion design with central mid-blue diamond, surrounded by four yellow-green and pink stylized blossoms, wide ivory ground border with long cartouches and rosettes in blue, pink, green-yellow and white, c1950, 127 x 84in (322.5 x 213.5cm).
£1,500–1,700 WW

A Brussels lace appliqué flounce, c1870, 100in (254cm) long.
£180–200 JuC

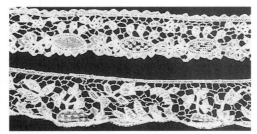

Two Irish needle-lace edgings, c1890, 3in (7.5cm) wide.
£30–35 each JUC

A Honiton bobbin-lace handkerchief, c1880, 15in (38cm) square.
£40–45 JuC

A cotton crewelwork wall hanging, worked in red, orange and cream silks, depicting parrots in a flowering tree, c1880–1900, 92 x 50in (233.5 x 127cm).
£120–150 DE

An American quilt, worked in red and white star pattern, c1890, 82in (208.5cm) long.
£300–350 JJ

A Dutch Arts and Crafts hanging, worked in wool and silk, with stylized Tudor roses in green and blue with yellow centres on an orange-brick ground, the base with a wide frieze of roses and tulips on a cream ground, early 20thC, 95 x 63in (241.5 x 160cm).
£240–260 WW

A pair of Art Deco gold silk machine-lace bedspreads, 88 x 62in (223.5 x 157.5cm).
£60–70 DE

A pink and green needle-work sampler, worked in wool by Jessie Dalxall, c1920s, 12 x 10in (30.5 x 25.5cm).
£90–100 DE

A Ruskin brown and cream pin-cushion, c1900, 5½in (14cm) square.
£65–75 ChA

A cream linen drawn-thread runner, c1910, 79 x 23in (200.5 x 58.5cm).
£40–45 JUC

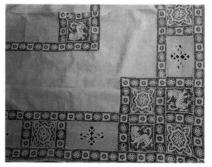

An American log cabin cotton quilt, in bright colours, by Patsy Ferguson, c1920, 73 x 67in (185.5 x 170cm).
£350–400 JJ

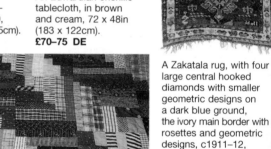

A linen filet and cut-work bedspread, c1920, 102in (259cm) square.
£250–300 JUC

An Irish linen bolster case, with hand-embroidered open-work design and scallop border, c1910, 72in (183cm) long.
£40–45 AIL

An Edwardian chenille tablecloth, in brown and cream, 72 x 48in (183 x 122cm).
£70–75 DE

A Zakatala rug, with four large central hooked diamonds with smaller geometric designs on a dark blue ground, the ivory main border with rosettes and geometric designs, c1911–12, 52 x 33in (132 x 84cm).
£250–300 WW

> **Cross Reference**
> See Colour Review

An Irish linen tablecloth embroidered in blue with a hand-worked peacock, with four napkins, c1920s, 42 x 24in (106.5 x 61cm).
£40–45 DE

A pair of Regency cream kid leather shoes.
100–120 **JUC**

A Swiss or German woollen bonnet, decorated with coloured beads, c1820, 11in (28cm) wide.
£160–180 JUC

A blue velvet and cream lace lady's head decoration, 1860, 48 x 6in (122 x 15cm).
£100–120 JUC

A Victorian black chiffon bonnet, decorated with metal-work and feathers, by D. Merrell, Bristol, in (23cm) diam.
160–180 JUC

A woven wool Paisley shawl, in crimson, black and gold, c1880, 130 x 66in (330 x 167.5cm).
£400–450 DE

◀ A late Victorian printed Paisley shawl, in red, blue and green on a ginger ground, 65 x 58in (165 x 147.5cm).
£65–70 DE

A late Victorian cotton lawn petticoat, with lace detail.
65–75 **DE**

▸ A lady's cotton camisole and petticoat combination, with lace trim, c1890.
35–40 **JUC**

A black wool lady's day wear jacket, c1890.
£180–200 DE

A Chinese mid-blue silk damask robe, embroidered in floss silks with flowers and birds, edged with woven metal-thread braid and black satin ribbon, one toggle to neckline, lined in pale blue silk, late 19thC.
£60–80 WW

A muslin and lace christening robe, c1900, 43in (109cm) long.
£100–120 JUC

A child's lace matinee jacket, c1900.
£30–35 JUC

▶ An Edwardian black straw and ostrich feather hat, with black velvet trim, by Marshall & Snellgrove, Leeds, 19in (48.5cm) diam.
£55–65 DE

An Edwardian girl's woollen three-piece suit, in gold on a turquoise ground.
£100–120 DE

A top hat and a pair of gloves, in original box, c1910, 13 x 7in (33 x 18cm).
£80–90 BWA

Three gentleman's lightweight cotton waistcoats, c1914
£30–40 each DE

A black dévoré coat, with cut sleeves, 1920.
£80–90 DE

A Chinese hand-embroidered piano shawl, decorated with coloured silks, 1920s, 48in (122cm) square.
£140–160 JPr

▶ A straw boater, 1930s, 11in (28cm) wide.
£35–40 SPT

A pair of brown kid leather and snakeskin shoes, 1920s.
£55–65 DE

◄ A pair of peep-toe cream suede shoes, by Lotus, 1930s.
£35–40 DE

A satin wedding dress, with beaded decoration around the neck and waist, late 1930s.
£120–140 TT

Three school caps, brown and blue, black and green, and black with red crest, 1930s.
£25–30 each SPT

A pair of brown and tan snakeskin high-heeled shoes, with utility mark, 1940s.
£25–30 DE
Wartime shortages in Britain led to the Utility Scheme, which included clothing. Designers had to use less material, fewer fastenings and simpler techniques. Regulations stipulated no more than three buttons to a jacket, the heels of shoes could be no more than two inches high and peep-toes were banned. Utility wear was marked with the trademark 'CC41', 'CC' standing for Civilian Clothing, and '41' for the year Utility was introduced.

A gentleman's two-piece fawn woollen suit, 1940.
£60–65 DE

◄ A brown wool crêpe Fitzwear suit, with utility mark on skirt, 1940s.
£45–50 TT

Miller's is a price GUIDE not a price LIST

◄ A lady's black felt and net hat, 1940s.
£35–40 L&L

► A gentleman's brown felt hat, c1940s.
£25–30 DE

A cream and green felt and straw hat, by Mitzi Lorenz of London, 1950.
£25–30 DE

A black and white wool tweed Dolly Rocker dress and skirt, with cotton inserts, designed by Sambo, 1960.
£30–35 DE

A black and white taffeta evening dress, with pink and white butterfly decoration, 1950.
£35–40 DE

A pair of Stilo Venice Girl brown and tan snakeskin shoes, with kitten heel, c1960.
£25–30 DE

A pair of Bluebird stockings, in original coloured box, 1950s, 10 x 7in (25.5 x 18cm).
£12–15 YR

A black and white tie, decorated with a Daliesque mermaid pattern, 1940s.
£65–70 SpM

◄ A blue and white floral cotton mini jacket dress, 1960s.
£15–20 DE

LOCATE THE SOURCE

The source of each illustration in Miller's can be found by checking the code letters below each caption with the Key to Illustrations, pages 476–484.

A Pierre Cardin green-checked woollen two-piece suit, with flared trousers, 1970.
£60–65 DE

A pair of High Brow blue and white sports platform shoes, 1970s.
£25–30 DE

A pair of black leather 'rocking horse' shoes, by Vivienne Westwood, with high wooden platforms and thong ties, 1990s.
£80–100 ID

A 'Bride of Fortune' black felt hat, by Vivienne Westwood, printed with gold foil, c1986.
£100–125 ID

► A Chiltern mohair Hug Me range teddy bear, with replacement eyes, 1920s, 15in (38cm) high.
£200–220 Ann

A mohair teddy bear, possibly Chad Valley or Farnell, 1920s, 17in (43cm) high.
£360–400 BaN

► A Pedigree mohair teddy bear, Bobby Boy, 1937, 18in (45.5cm) high.
£180–200 Ann

A Dean's felt Mickey Mouse, c1928, 18in (45.5cm) high.
£470–520 DAn

► A Steiff mohair lion, well worn, 1950s, 9in (23cm) high.
£25–30 A&J

A Merrythought mohair teddy bear, late 1930s, 21in (53.5cm) high.
£270–300 Ann

A Steiff mohair Bambi, 1950s,
6in (15cm) high.
£35–40 A&J

A Chad Valley Mr Toffy mohair
teddy bear, 1953, 9in (23cm) high.
£250–300 Ann

A Dean's golly, 1950s,
16in (40.5cm) high.
£25–35 A&J

A Modern Toys battery-operated
teddy bear on a rocking chair,
Japan, 1960, 9in (23cm) high.
£120–140 HAL

A Gabrielle Designs Paddington
bear, 1970s, 20in (51cm) high.
£60–70 Ann

A Muppet Bendy Toy, Miss Piggy,
1970–80, 16in (40.5cm) high.
£22–26 TAC

A Street Kids Corporation
'Socks the White House Cat',
1993, 14 x 8in (35.5 x 20.5cm).
£50–60 TBoy

Two Dean's Artist Showcase teddy
bears, limited edition, 2000,
Jim Junior 12in (30.5cm) and
Sam Sock 10in (25.5cm) high.
£180–200 each Ann

◄ A Steiff Walt Disney Fantasia
Mickey Sorcerer's Apprentice,
limited edition, 2000, 14in (35.5cm)
high, in original packing.
£180–200 Ann

A printed cotton mini beach dress, c1960.
£16–20 **DE**

A Dianna Warren gold-sequined and beaded woollen dress, early 1960s.
£60–70 **DE**

A Bernard Frères cotton dress, 1970s.
£30–35 **DE**

A Vivienne Westwood Time Machine Collection tweed armour jacket, with denim gauntlet-style sleeves and orb motif on shoulder, c1988, 27in (68.5cm) long.
£250–300 **ID**

▶ A pair of men's cotton swimming trunks, 1950s.
£8–10 **DE**

A cotton peek-a-boo-midriff swimsuit, 1940s.
£40–45 **SpM**

A pair of Mabel Lucy Atwell patterned child's knickers, c1994.
£12–15 **MEM**

▶ A cotton swimsuit with elasticized back, 1950s.
£10–12 **DE**

A Bernhard Altmann Pucci-style one-piece swimsuit, Austria, 1970s.
£22–27 **SpM**

A Kittiwake polka-dot cotton one-piece swim suit, with boned bodice, c1950.
£18–20 **DE**

An Orchider patterned cotton bikini, with lace-up sides, 1950s.
£30–35 **SpM**

▶ A Mary Quant-style bathing suit, with cutaway sides and daisy motif, 1960s.
£20–25 **HarC**

A carved polychrome carousel horse, attributed to Armitage Herschell Co, with original paint, late 19thC, 41in (104cm) high.
£4,200–5,000 SK(B)

A Schuco clockwork clown drummer boy, dressed in felt, Germany, 1910–20, 4in (10cm) high.
£85–100 A&J

A Lehmann WWI tin plate clockwork van, Germany, c1918, 7in (18cm) long.
£300–350 HAL

A pull-along plush-covered horse, 1920s, 27in (68.5cm) high.
£350–400 BaN

A Lehmann EPL679 'ITO' clockwork sedan car, with tin plate Lehmann flag to bonnet, Germany, 1920s, 7in (18cm) long.
£650–700 Bon(C)

A Britains lead figure, Village Idiot, 1930s, 2¼in (5.5cm) high.
£200–220 RAR

◀ A Dinky Toys Hall's Distemper No. 13 lead advertising figural. 1930s, 5¼in (13.5cm) high, with original box.
£150–175 RAR

A Heyde lead horse and rider, depicted jumping a fence, Germany, c1920, 3in (7.5cm) wide.
£35–40 HAL

A Hornby 0 gauge clockwork No. 2 special LMS locomotive, 1930s, 10in (25.5cm) long.
£100–130 HAL

A Tipp & Co tin plate racing car, with electric light, driver missing, Germany, 1920–30, 12in (30.5cm) long.
£420–500 HAL

A Hornby 0 gauge clockwork No. 2 special 4-4-0 LNER locomotive and tender, hunt class Bramham Moor RN201, mid-1930s, 15in (38cm) long.
£350–400 WAL

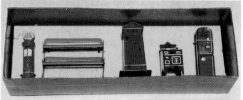

A set of Hornby 0 gauge No. 3 platform machines, in original box, 1938, box 8½in (21.5cm) long.
£130–150 RAR

A Meccano two-seater sports car, 1930s, 8¼in (21cm) long, with original box.
£500–550 RAR

Teddy painted steel pedal car, 1948, 36in (91.5cm) long.
£420–500 JUN

A Hornby No. 1 clockwork LMS tank engine, 1939–40, 7in (18cm) long, complete with keys, lamps and guarantee card, boxed.
£180–220 HOB

A Dinky Toys Jaguar XK120 Coupe, c1950, 4in (10cm) long, with original box.
£75–90 HAL

A Triang painted metal pedal car, restored, 1950s, 42in (106.5cm) long.
£1,200–1,500 JUN

Four Lumar pressed-metal yo-yo's, from poor to mint condition, c1950, 2⅛in (5.5cm) diam.
£4–20 each YO

Four Matchbox Series cars, c1950, 2in (5cm) long, with original boxes.
£15–20 each HAL

A set of Britain's African Zulu Warriors, No. 147, 1950s, box 14¾in (37.5cm) wide.
£110–130 RAR

A Dinky Supertoys Leyland Octopus wagon, No. 934, c1950, 7in (18cm) long, with original box.
£140–180 HAL

A Dinky Toys Nestle's Austin Van, No. 471, 1950s, 3in (7.5cm) long, with original box.
£60–75 HAL

A Dinky Toys Kodak Bedford Van, No. 480, 1950, 3in (7.5cm) long.
£70–85 HAL

A Pyramid Toys 00 gauge Trackmaster clockwork N2 goods train set, 1950s, box 9 x 14in (23 x 35.5cm).
£65–75 RAR

An American plastic and metal pick-up truck, 1950s, 8in (20.5cm) long.
£35–40 RTT

A Roadmaster tin plate battery-powered car, late 1950s, 8in (20.5cm) long, with original box.
£65–75 RTT

A Dinky Toys Opel Kapitan car,
No. 177, late 1950s, 4in (10cm)
long, with original box.
£50–60 HAL

A Denzil Skinner Nuffield tractor,
1950–60, 7in (18cm) long,
with original box.
£360–400 RAR

A Yon Japan battery-powered
Jumbo the Bubble Blowing
Elephant, 1950s–60s,
7in (18cm) high, with original box.
£120–150 HAL

A Corgi Toys Ford 5000 Super
Major Tractor, 1960,
4in (10cm) high, with original box.
£65–80 HAL

A Yon Japan battery-powered tin
plate Moon Explorer, 1960,
11in (28cm) long.
£130–160 HAL

A Dinky Toys Thunderbirds Lady
Penelope's FAB1, pink Rolls
Royce, 1960s, 6in (15cm) long,
with original box.
£225–245 CWO

A Dinky Toys Captain Scarlet Spectrum Pursuit
Vehicle, 1960s, 6in (15cm) long, with original box.
£125–150 HAL

A Modern Toys battery-powered tin plate Planet
Explorer, Japan, 1960s, 9in (23cm) long.
£110–130 HAL

Two tin plate clockwork motorcycles and riders, 1965–75.
l. 7in (18cm) long.
r. Russian, 8in (20.5cm) long, with original box.
£60–70 BLH

A Corgi Toys E-Type Jaguar,
No. 312, 1960s, 4in (10cm) long,
with original box.
£65–80 HAL

A Corgi Toys Volkswagen 1200, in East African Safari Trim, No. 256, c1972, 6in (15cm) long, in original box.
£130–150 RAR

A Hornby Minic Ships diecast 1:1200 scale Naval Harbour Set, 1972, 12 x 11in (30.5 x 28cm).
£50–60 COB

A Marx Toys Danny Reid and Little Bear fully jointed action figures, from the TV Lone Ranger series, 1975, 9in (23cm) high, in original boxes.
£60–75 TOY

▶ A Smurf plastic Emperor model, 1978, 2½in (6.5cm) high.
£6–8 CMF

Three Mattel *Masters of the Universe* figures, Hordak, Tri-Klops and Roboto, on original cards, 1984, card 11 x 6in (28 x 15cm).
£12–15 each PC

A *Star Wars* Hammer-head figure, 1977, 4½in (11.5cm) high.
£6–7 UNI

A *Star Wars* television series Ewok figure, Wicket W. Warwick, 1984, 2in (5cm) high.
£7–8 UNI

A *Star Wars* carbonite chamber Han Solo figure, from *The Empire Strikes Back*, 1980s, 4in (10cm) high.
£50–60 HAL

A Dapol *Dr Who* Mel figure, on original card, 1987, card 7¾ x 5¼in (19.5 x 13.5cm).
£3–4 UNI

A balsa wood model of a 1930s Swordfish plane, 1980s, 45 x 59in (114.5 x 150cm).
£380–450 CYA

A Mondial Injection Came-yo, by Harry Baier, aluminium yoyo with rubber buffers, Germany, c1998, 2½in (5.5cm) diam.
£100–110 YO

going, going, gone-on-line.

A French spelter aviation clock, commemorating the Wright brothers' first flight, engraved 'Le Premier Vol', 1908, 16in (40.5cm) high.
£800–900 PC

A Jaz Bakelite clock, France, 1936, 10in (25.5cm) high.
£450–500 GAD

An International Watch Co 18ct white gold watch, 1930s.
£330–400 JoV

► An Ingersoll Mickey Mouse chromium-plated pocket watch, 1950s, 2½in (6.5cm) diam.
£120–150 BBR

A Roidor 9ct gold cased watch, with automatic movement and two-tone dial, 1950s, in original case.
£150–175 JoV

An 18ct gold watch, with fusee movement, London 1851, 2in (5cm) diam.
£650–800 AOH

A plastic Smiths Sectric electric wall clock, 1950, 8in (20.5cm) high.
£18–20 RTT

A Smiths Timecal Noddy alarm clock, 1960s, 5in (12.5cm) diam.
£30–35 GAZE

A Marcel Boucher base metal and gilt bangle watch, with 17 jewels, Switzerland, 1950s, 1¼in (3cm) wide.
£120–150 LBe

◄ A Vivienne Westwood Pop Swatch plastic watch, from a limited edition of 40,000, in orb-shaped presentation case, 1980s, box 4in (10cm) high.
£265–285 FMa
This watch was sold from very few outlets, one being Harrods.

A Heuer Autavia GMT chronograph, with additional hour hand for reading different time zones, c1973.
£900–1,100 HARP

A Welsh pine spoon rack, with nine sycamore spoons, 19thC, 14in (35.5cm) high.
£400–460 CoA

A Gaudy Welsh cup, saucer and bread plate, decorated with Bethania pattern No. 1155, 1820–90, plate 10¼in (26cm) wide.
Cup and saucer £80–90
Plate £50–60 CoHA

A pair of Carmarthenshire oak farmhouse chairs, c1780.
£600–700 CoA

A Welsh brass footman, 19thC, 18in (45.5cm) wide.
£250–280 CoA
A footman is a trivet designed to hang on the bars of a grate.

A Gaudy Welsh cup and saucer, decorated with Waggon Wheel pattern No. 91, 1820–90, saucer 4½in (11.5cm) diam.
£50–60 CoHA

A Welsh beech wood potato masher, c1820, 12in (30.5cm) high.
£70–75 SEA

A North Wales slip-decorated dish, 19thC, 13in (33cm) long.
£240–265 CoA

A late Victorian Cardiganshire velvet and silk crazy patchwork quilt top, 59in (145cm) square.
£250–300 JJ

◀ A Welsh Thomas & Williams brass miner's lamp, early 20thC, 10in (25.5cm) high.
£90–100 CoA

▶ A Goss cream jug, in the form of a Welsh lady, 1920–30, 3½in (9cm) high.
£65–75 MGC

A Welsh wide loom plaid and fringed wool blanket, c1930, 90 x 78in (228.5 x 198cm).
£60–70 JJ

A Victorian agate seal, carved with a coat-of-arms, 3¼in (8.5cm) high, with sealing wax stick.
£60–70 HBC

An oak inkstand with drawer, with silver-plated mounts and two glass inkwells with glass stoppers, 1890, 12in (30.5cm) wide.
£225–275 MB

A Victorian ormolu ink and pen stand, mounted with Scottish agate, 7in (18cm) wide.
£650–750 TWr

◀ A brass desk seal, the handle in the shape of a serpent, 19thC, 2¾in (7cm) high.
£40–45 WAC

▶ A Williams No. 1 typewriter, with round keyboard, America, 1891.
£4,250–4,500 KOLN

A metal pig inkwell, c1900, 6in (15cm) wide.
£55–65 SER

A Scottish carved wood and staghorn silver-mounted writing stand, Edinburgh 1908, 13in (33cm) wide.
£1,800–2,000 BWA

A white metal owl letter clip, with brass eyes and beak, c1920, 5¼in (13.5cm) high.
£18–20 AL

◀ An H. A. Coombs's Young Artist's Crayons, with original contents, c1905, 3in (7.5cm) long.
£20–25 WAB

An inkwell, moulded with two frogs, the stopper moulded with an insect, 1920s, 6in (15cm) wide.
£280–300 MD

A lead novelty frog pen wipe, 1930, 2in (5cm) high.
£25–30 HAL

An Artemide plastic penholder, designed by Emma Schweinberger, 1970, 3½in (9cm) high.
£25–30 PLB

A Swiss postcard, with vignette of Hotel Generoso-Kulm, 1900.
£4–5 JMC

A Colgate & Co Dactylis perfume, America, 1920–30, 1in (2.5cm) diam.
£4–5 RTT

A painted metal and glass brooch, 1945–55, 1in (5cm) wide.
£4–5 STP

▶ *Practical Gardening and Food Production in Pictures*, by Richard Sudell, published by Odhams, 1945.
£4–5 RTT

A Babycham cardboard mat, 1960s, 3in (7.5cm) square.
£2–3 BSA

A Miller's Baking Powder tin, c1920, 3in (7.5cm) high.
£4–5 YR

Robinson Crusoe, by Daniel Defoe, published by Blackie & Son, c1930.
£4–5 AnS

A selection of toffee bars, 1960s, largest 5in (12.5cm) long.
£1–3 each YR

Four bread tins, for Youma, Procea, Sunray and Cremalt, 1930s, largest 11in (28cm) long.
£4–5 AL

Four J. Wix & Son Kensitas cigarette cards, Silk Flowers, 1933.
£2–2.50 each MAr

A pair of painted metal daisy earrings, 1960, 3in (7.5cm) diam.
£4–5 STP

A selection of airline match books, c1960.
£2–3 each RTT

▶ A packet of Golden Wonder Smokey Bacon Flavour Crisps, 1966, 7 x 5in (18 x 12.5cm).
£4–5 YR

A Caledor Productions 'Who Wants to be a Millionaire?' game, 2000, 10½ x 14in (26.5 x 35.5cm).
£29.99 Woo
'Who Wants to be a Millionaire?' has been the TV success story of the turn of the century, attracting an audience of millions, introducing popular catch phrases: 'But I don't want to give you that.'

A Hasbro UK 'Big Brother' game, 2000, 10 x 12½in (25.5 x 32cm).
£19.99 Woo
Another innovative TV hit, Big Brother, was followed by a sell-out auction of objects from the house and the creation of Big Brother merchandise.

A Millennium Dome ceramic sugar bowl, by James Sadler, 2000, 5in (12.5cm) diam.
£12 MMa
While the Dome was not an unqualified success, some of the merchandise was more appealing. This bowl is part of a set including matching teapot and milk jug.

A Tiger Woods signed colour photograph, framed and glazed, 1999, 17 x 12in (43 x 30.5cm).
£300–360 SMW
The market for contemporary autographs is currently booming and Tiger Woods is one of today's most sought-after sporting figures.

A Micro folding aluminium skate-scooter, Swiss designed, made in China, 1999–2000, 32in (81.5cm) high.
£99 ROU
Micro scooters were the craze of the year and, like Pokemon cards, were banned from many school playgrounds. This is the classic model.

A *Vogue* magazine, 'The Gold Issue', December 2000, 11 x 9in (28 x 23cm).
£3 PC
***Vogue* produced a silver issue for Xmas 1999 and a gold issue for Xmas 2000, both already collectable for devotees of the fashion bible.**

The Amber Spyglass, by Philip Pullman, published by David Fickling Books, imprint of Scholastic Press, 2000.
£14.99 SCP
With Harry Potter books already fetching vast sums (*see* Books section) look out for the first editions of Philip Pullman's hugely popular Dark Materials Trilogy: *Northern Lights* (1995), *The Subtle Knife* (1997) and *The Amber Spyglass*.

◄ A BBC VHS video boxed set, Dr Who, *Attack of the Cybermen, The Tenth Planet*, limited edition, 2000, 8 x 5in (20.5 x 12.cm).
£25 ONY
Dr Who still attracts legions of fans, and this is an attractively packaged set. But will the popularity of DVD eventually transform videos into collectable rather than everyday items? Watch this space...

► A Caithness pink rose glass paperweight, No. 27591, Elizabeth of Glamis, commemorating the 100th birthday of Elizabeth the Queen Mother, 2000, 2in (5cm) diam.
£99 SWB
The Queen Mother's 100th birthday inspired a massive celebration and a host of commemorating items.

Tools

A leaf iron, with wooden handle, c1860, 8in (20.5cm) long.
£135–155 MFB
Leaf irons were used in the fashion industry.

A rosewood and brass bow drill, by Buck, c1880, 12in (30.5cm) long.
£100–120 TOM

A wooden moulding plane, by Sims, 19thC, 9in (23cm) long.
£5–6 WO

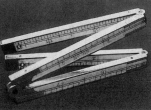

A Stanley ivory four-fold ruler, bound in nickel-silver, No. 88, c1890, 12in (30.5cm) long.
£60–80 TOM

A pair of iron dagging shears, 19thC, 12in (30.5cm) long.
£8–10 HCJ

An iron thatching needle, c1880, 23in (58.5cm) long.
£40–45 HCJ

An iron-pronged bag hook, with a wooden handle, 19thC, 5½in (14cm) long.
£10–12 WO

An iron wheelwright's adze, with a wooden handle, by Gilpin, early 20thC, 25in (63.5cm) long.
£20–25 WO

◄ A Norris A5 dovetail steel smoothing plane, with rosewood infill and patent adjuster, 1920s, 9in (23cm) long.
£250–300 TOM

A brass paper caliper, c1920, 3in (7.5cm) long.
£12–15 WAB

A wire, rope and chain measure, by Smallwood, made from wood and brass, 1964, 7in (18cm) long.
£35–40 WAB

Toys

A German wooden bow-bottomed Noah's Ark, with sliding panel to one side, straw-work windows and border, and a selection of about 200 carved animals, with Noah, his wife and family all with painted faces and carved hats, mid-19thC, 23in (58.5cm) wide.
£2,500–3,000 Bon(C)

An Edwardian Fleischmann battleship, in grey and black, with a brown deck, with gun emplacements, four lifeboats, lacking masts, 20in (51cm) long.
£900–1,100 P(Wm)

A Snow White and the Seven Dwarfs toy theatre set, with lithographed figures and scenes on plywood with wooden stands, late 1930s, backdrop 26in (66cm) wide.
£450–500 Bon(C)

A pair of tin cap guns, c1920, 5in (12.5cm) long.
£20–22 WAB

A Durable Toy & Novelty Corporation Popeye menu bagatelle board, with lithographs of various foods, late 1930s, 23in (58.5cm) high.
£200–220 SK

A Meccano No. 1 Aero constructor set, comprising a full set of silver-finished parts for six models shown on instruction sheets, in original coloured box, 1930s, box 17in (43cm) wide.
£175–200 WAL

An Irish plastic musical Rupert Bear, wearing a red coat and black boots, 1960s, 11in (28cm) high.
£30–35 HUX

A wooden pond yacht, Bowman Racing Yacht, c1930, 18in (45.5cm) high.
£25–30 AL

▶ A Queen Elizabeth II Coronation wooden bus, with hinged top, in green with a yellow stripe, 1953, 25in (63.5cm) long.
£60–80 CYA

A Dam Things rubber giraffe, in brown with dark brown patches, Denmark, 1962, 12in (30.5cm) high.
£90–100 PLB

A Dam Things rubber troll, wearing a green shirt and yellow apron, Denmark, 1960s, 5½in (14cm) high.
£30–35 PLB

Dam trolls

Trolls became a fashion fad in the 1960s. The troll was a figure from Norse mythology, and the most collectable trolls were produced by Dam Things in Denmark. Thomas Dam carved large wooden trolls for funfairs, and these proved so successful that the family began producing troll figures, made from natural rubber, filled with wood shavings, wearing handmade felt clothes and with real sheepskin hair. Dam trolls were marked and often dated on the foot. Trolls were launched in the UK toy market in 1964, promoted by the unlikely figure of Diana Dors, and were produced by a range of different manufacturers.

A Dam Things rubber troll, with pink shirt, the gold label inscribed 'I'm an iggynormous, one of the Thomas Dam Family', Denmark, 1964, 11in (28cm) high.
£80–100 PLB

A Dam Things rubber lion, with dark brown mane, Denmark, 1960s, 8in (20.5cm) long.
£25–30 PLB

A Peyo plastic Smurf, Gardener, with blue body, white hat and boots, green apron and brown wheelbarrow, 1960–70, 2¾in (7cm) high.
£9–10 CMF

A set of Corgi Magic Roundabout figures, decorated in colours on blue and yellow bases, c1972, 3in (7.5cm) high.
£320–350 RAR

A ProYo Ultimate black and white yo-yo, 1995, 2¼in (5.5cm) diam.
£20–25 YO

A McDonalds plastic Witch, wearing a black hat and blue jacket, 1992, 4in (10cm) high.
£1–2 CMF

◀ A Marx Toys plastic clockwork Tom and Jerry, Tom with blue body and pink ears, with yellow and red barrow, in original coloured box, 1977, 3in (7.5cm) wide.
£30–40 HAL

DIECAST VEHICLES

A Dinky Chrysler Airflow saloon, No. 30a, in mid-green with black hubs, 1930s, 4in (10cm) long.
£110–120 WAL

A Dinky Foden 14-ton tanker, No. 504, in pale blue with dark blue cab, late 1940, 7in (18cm) long, with original red, white and green box.
£140–180 HAL
This toy originally cost 8s 6d.

◄ A Matchbox Series metallic-red Aston Martin DB2–4 Mk 1, No. 53, late 1950s, 2½in (6.5cm) long, with original box.
£450–500 WAL

► A Matchbox Series metallic-copper Vauxhall Cresta, No. 22, with silver plastic wheels, late 1950s, 2½in (6.5cm) long, with original box.
£110–130 WAL

A Dinky Supertoys Guy van, with gold inscription 'Slumberland Spring Interior Mattresses', 1950s, 5in (12.5cm) long, with original orange, white and blue box.
£140–180 HAL

◄ A Matchbox Series light green Ford Thames Singer van, No. 59, with silver plastic wheels, late 1950s, 2in (5cm) long, with original box.
£230–260 WAL

A Matchbox Series orange and yellow Coca-Cola lorry, No. 37a, with grey plastic wheels, late 1950s, 2in (5cm) long, with original box.
£150–175 WAL

A Matchbox Series red Maserati 4CLT/1948, No. RN 52, with wire wheels and black plastic tyres, late 1950s, 2½in (6.5cm) long, with original box.
£230–260 WAL

A Dinky USA Ford Fairlane Police car, No. 258, in black with white door panels, inscribed 'Police' to front, white interior and spun wheel hubs, 1960s, 5in (12.5cm) long, with original box.
£110–130 WAL

A Dinky South African issue Jaguar 3.4 saloon, in blue-grey with white interior, 1960s, 4½in (11.5cm) long, with original box.
£450–500 WAL

A Matchbox Models of Yesteryear Horse-Drawn Fire Engine, with black horses, red carriage and gold pumps, early 1960s, 3in (7.5cm) long, with original box.
£90–110 HAL

A Corgi The Man From UNCLE blue Oldsmobile, No. 497, with yellow interior, c1966, 4½in (11.5cm) long, with original box and display insert.
£100–120 WAL
This car also came in white, which was rarer than the blue version.

A Corgi Toys red and black Rambler Sports Fastback, 1960, 4in (10cm) long, with original yellow and blue box.
£20–25 HAL

A Dinky Captain Scarlet's metallic-red Spectrum patrol car, with aerial, 1960s, 5in (12.5cm) long.
£80–90 WAL

A Corgi Toys Simon Snorkel red fire engine, 1960s, 9in (23cm) high, with original coloured box.
£40–50 HAL

A Dinky green Shado 2 Mobile tank, Gerry Anderson's UFO Series, 1970, with original green, orange and brown box.
£60–80 HAL

A Corgi Toys James Bond's silver Aston Martin DB5, with original blue, yellow, black and red box, 1960s, 4in (10cm) long.
£120–150 HAL

LUNCH BOXES

Lunch boxes are a popular American collectable and enjoyed a huge boom in the 1980s. They date back to the 19th century when utilitarian tin food containers were used by farm and factory workers. The decorated children's lunch box first appeared in the 1930s, and Walt Disney issued a Mickey Mouse example in 1935, but the golden age was the 1950s and 60s, when lunch box sales topped an astonishing 120 million. Pioneering manufacturers included Aladdin who, in 1950, introduced their first character box illustrated with Hopalong Cassidy, which sold 600,000 units and introduced TV (still a comparatively new medium) as a favourite decorative theme. Other major producers include Ohio Art and Thermos/King Seeley. Shapes ranged

from rectangular to dome-lidded boxes, popular with collectors today, and designed to hold a thermos. Many lunch boxes came with a matching vacuum flask (invented in 1913), which will enhance the value of a box. Prices are also affected by condition (the lithographed steel surface was prone to scratching) and subject matter. Cult TV shows, pop and space themes can all fetch high prices, and lunch boxes provide a visual catalogue of children's entertainment and interests in the 1950s and 60s.

The vinyl lunch box was introduced in 1959 and, initially ignored by collectors, is now popular if the condition and subject are good enough. Vinyl is a less durable material than metal, so beware of cracks and tears.

A Ham Fisher New York tin Lunch Kit, decorated on five sides with illustrations of Joe Palooka and his pals in colours on a red ground, with blue handles, 1948, 7in (18cm) wide.
£45–55 CBP

▶ A Thermos metal lunch box, decorated in colours with Trigger, 1957, 9in (23cm) wide.
£330–350 SK

A Thermos metal lunch box, decorated with Roy Rogers' Chow Wagon, with domed top, 1958, 10¼in (26cm) wide.
£140–160 SK

An Aladdin tin lunch box, decorated with Tom Corbett Space Cadet, with matching thermos, 1954, 10in (25.cm) wide.
£250–275 SK

An Adco metal lunch box, decorated with Howdy Doody, with detached handle, 1955, 10½in (26.5cm) wide.
£110–130 SK

An Omni Graphics metal lunch box, VW Bus, with domed top, in cream and red with black wheels, with matching thermos, 1960, 10¾in (27.5cm) wide.
£450–525 SK

◀ An Aladdin metal lunch box, decorated with The Flintstones and Dino, with matching thermos, 1962, 10½in (26.5cm) wide.
£190–210 SK

A yellow metal lunch box, decorated with Huckleberry Hound and his friends, c1960, 10in (25.5cm) wide.
£55–65 HALL

An Ohio Art metal lunch box, decorated with Mod Tulip pattern, with a domed top, 1962, 10in (25.5cm) wide.
£50–60 SK

A Thermos vinyl lunch box, decorated with Junior Nurse pattern, with matching thermos, 1963, 11in (28cm) wide.
£60–70 SK

An Aladdin blue metal lunch box, decorated with The Beatles, with instructions and sticker, and matching thermos, 1965, 10in (25.5cm) wide.
£800–900 SK

An Ohio Art metal lunch box, decorated with Bond XX Secret Agent, 1966, 10½in (26.5cm) wide.
£50–55 SK

An Aladdin purple vinyl lunch box, decorated with Twiggy, with matching thermos, 1967, 10¾in (27.5cm) wide.
£100–110 SK

► A Thermos white vinyl lunch box, decorated with The Monkees, with a red handle, with matching thermos, 1967, 11in (28cm) wide.
£120–140 SK

◄ An Ohio Art olive green metal lunch box, decorated with Underdog, 1974, 10in (25.5cm) wide.
£1,700–1,900 SK

► An Aladdin blue vinyl lunch box, decorated with The World of Dr Seuss, with a matching thermos, 1970, 10in (25.5cm) wide.
£190–210 SK

MODEL SOLDIERS, FIGURES & BUILDINGS

A Britains King's 3rd Hussars King's Own Set No. 13, with four troopers carrying carbines and an officer on a rearing horse, damaged, in original box, c1930, 3in (7.5cm) high.
£200–240 P(Wm)

A Britains Officers & Petty Officers of the Royal Navy Set No. 207, in natural colours, in original black, red, cream and blue box, 1930s, box 15in (38cm) long.
£150–170 RAR

A Heyde brown lead polo pony, the rider with red shirt and cream breeches, Germany, c1920, 3in (7.5cm) high.
£40–50 HAL

Five Britains Argentine naval cadets and an officer, from Set No. 1835 of eight figures, 1930s, 3½in (9cm) high.
£200–240 P(Wm)

◄ A Britains composition Farm Cottage Set No. 43F, 1930s, 6in (15cm) high.
£200–240 P(Wm)

A Britains Royal Corps of Signals Motorcycle Despatch Rider Set No. 1791, in olive green with brown boots, wearing blue and white arm bands, 1950s, bikes 2in (5cm) long.
£160–180 WAL

A set of solid-cast copies of Britains Guards, wearing winter greatcoats, 1960s, each 2¾in (7cm) high.
£50–60 UNI

A Women's Royal Army Corp 17-piece band, decorated in natural colours, on green bases, c1990, 2¼in (5.5cm) high.
£90–100 IE

PEDAL & PUSH-ALONG

A Lines Bros WWI aluminium pedal aeroplane, with steel balloon-type tyres that also move the propeller, ailerons, rear wheel and rudder, damaged, 1920s, 53in (134cm) long.
£750–900 CARS

A metal-framed three-wheeled wooden push-cart, with cream-painted box, green frame and red and black wheels, 1920s, 17in (43cm) high.
£50–60 GAZE

◄ A French metal pedal car, with red body and wheels and white tyres, 1930s, 39in (99cm) long.
£250–300 JUN

A Jocker metal pedal car, with red body and wheels, 1930, 53in (134cm) long.
£900–1,000 JUN

A Triang metal pedal car, with red body and white and black wheels, c1960, 36in (91.5cm) long.
£80–100 JUN

► A Triang doll's push-chair, with red handle, blue frame and cream seat, 1950s, 23in (58.5cm) high.
£30–40 GAZE

A Triang Vanwal pedal racing car, with red body, black and silver wheels and white number, 1960, 39in (99cm) long.
£180–200 JUN

ROBOTS

The word robot comes from the Czechoslovakian word *robota*, meaning forced labour, and was first used to describe the mechanical creatures which appeared in the 1921 story *R.U.R. (Rossum's Universal Robots)* by Czechoslovakian author Karel Capec. The development of robot toys coincided with the space race in the 1950s, which took off in earnest in October 1957, when the first Sputnik satellite orbited the earth. While the USA and the USSR battled for galactic supremacy, Japan was the earthly leader in the robot market. The lithographed tinplate toys were produced first with friction or wind-up mechanisms, then later with batteries, and were widely exported to the USA. Style and subject matter were influenced by American science fiction movies and TV shows; famous examples include Robbie the Robot, from the film *The Forbidden Planet* (1956), whilst the TV series *Lost in Space* (1965–68) also inspired robotic toys.

The 1960s saw plastic replacing metal, as even alien robots had to conform to human health and safety regulations. Vintage robots are highly collectable today. Condition is very important to value as is the presence of a box, which was often handsomely decorated, and which, if the robot itself is unmarked, is important for identifying name and maker. Major manufacturers include Masudaya, Nomura and Yonesawa.

A Cragstan Mr Robot, c1959, 10½in (26.5cm) high.
£400–450 AG
Cragstan was an American importer who sold Japanese robots under his own label.

An Asahi wind-up Radar Robot, with blue and yellow body, and red arms and feet, Japan, 1960s, 6in (15cm) high, in original coloured box.
£15–20 PLB

A Yoshiya Space Dog tin robot, in red, with black flapping ears, opening mouth and ball eyes, c1960, 8½in (21.5cm) high, with original box.
£420–460 SK

An Attacking Martian battery-operated tin robot, in black, with red feet and red, silver and blue front panel, 1960s, 11in (28cm) high.
£85–95 PLB

A Nomura X-70 Tulip Head Robot, in lilac and silver, with orange plastic arms, three lowering head panels revealing rotating camera and screen, c1960, 9in (23cm) high.
£1,000–1,200 SK

▶ A Billiken wind-up Mirror Man tin robot, with white suit, red cloak, orange boots and gloves, and gold face, Japan, 1991, 9in (23cm) high, with original coloured box.
£125–150 TOY

A battery-operated tin robot, with silver body, red feet and blue, pink, yellow and green front panel, 1960s, 11in (28cm) high.
£85–95 PLB

ROCKING, HOBBY & CAROUSEL HORSES

◀ A wooden hobby horse, comprising a carved head, the legs and hooves forming forks for the wheels, horsehair tail and padded saddle, 1820s, front wheel 23in (58.5cm) diam.
£5,800–6,300 BKS

◀ A Victorian child's hobby horse tricycle, with dappled grey body, horse-hair mane and tail, iron wheels and steering bars, 18in (45.5cm) high.
£800–1,000 BKS

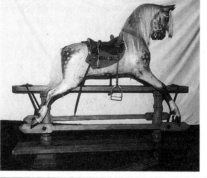

▶ A Victorian carved wood rocking horse, with dappled grey body, horsehair mane and tail, brown leather saddle and bridle, on a pine trestle base with turned supports, dated 'January 29th 1880', 61in (155cm) long.
£1,000–1,200 CYA

A Victorian carved wooden and gesso grey rocking horse, on a wooden trestle base with turned supports, 37in (94cm) high.
£750–850 SWO

A child's pine hobby horse, with a light brown body and darker mane and tail, original paint, 1895, 23in (58.5cm) high.
£100–120 OLM

An American carved and painted carousel-type rocking horse, with dappled grey body, brown and yellow carved saddle, and green blanket, on a decorated red platform, early 20thC, 48in (122cm) long.
£800–1,000 SK(B)

A painted wooden rocking horse, with a dappled grey body, horsehair mane and tail, leather harness and amber glass eyes, with wrought iron suspenders on a painted wood trestle base with turned supports, early 20thC, 57in (145cm) long.
£200–240 AH

A children's carved wooden carousel horse, 'Ringo', with a pale yellow body and red saddle, 1910, 45in (114.5cm) long.
£550–600 JUN

◀ A Lines Bros wooden rocking horse, with a dappled grey body, original paint and horsehair mane, leather saddle and bridle, on a trestle base with turned supports, c1910, 50in (127cm) long.
£2,000–2,400 BaN

A wooden rocking horse, with a dappled grey body, white mane and tail, tan leather saddle and bridle, blue velvet cloth, mounted on green-painted bow rockers, fully restored, 1910, 79in (200.5cm) long.
£900–1,000 DN

A Stevenson Bros first rocking horse, No. 007, with a dappled brown body, leather saddle and bridle, on a wooden trestle base with turned supports, 1982, 60in (152.5cm) long.
£1,800–2,000 STE

◄ A wooden rocking horse, with a dappled grey body, tan leather saddle and bridle, red saddlecloth, supported on a wooden trestle base, 1950–60, 56in (142cm) long.
£450–500 STE

SPACE, SCI-FI & TV

▶ A Marx battery-operated Black Dalek, complete with fittings, c1967, 6in (15cm) high, in original box.
£230–250 GTH

Three *Thunderbird* coloured plastic friction-drive model vehicles, Nos. 1, 2 and 3, by JR 21 Toys, 1960s, largest 10in (25.5cm) long, in original boxes.
£200–220 GAZE

▶ A Lady Penelope's Fab 1 plastic friction-drive car, by JR 21 Toys, c1967, 9in (23cm) long, in original box.
£120–140 GTH

A *Star Wars* Bossk figure, with a brown body and yellow shirt, 1978, 4in (10cm) high.
£8–10 UNI

A *Star Wars* Bespin Guard, figure, from *The Empire Strikes Back*, wearing a black suit, 1980, 3¾in (9.5cm) high.
£8–10 UNI

◄ A *Star Wars* At-At-Commander figure, from *The Return of the Jedi*, on original blue and black card, 1980s, 4in (10cm) high.
£18–20 HAL

A *Clash of the Titans* Perseus action figure, by Mattel, in original brown, black and cream box, 1980s, 9in (23cm) high.
£40–45 OW

A *Star Wars* moulded green rubber Yoda figure, wearing a brown cloak, 1980s, 8½in (21.5cm) high.
£25–30 PLB

▶ A Dapol *Doctor Who* Dalek model, silver and blue, on original coloured card, c1987, 8 x 5¼in (20.5 x 13.5cm).
£4–5 OW
Made in the 1980s, Dapol's *Doctor Who* unsold stock figures are still available from specialist shops today.

A *Star Trek* Mr Spock action figure, by ERTL, with a white and red jacket and black trousers, 1984, 3¾in (9.5cm) high.
£6–8 OW

TINPLATE

A Lehmann tinplate clockwork EPL686 Berolina convertible car, painted in blue and red, with spoked wheels, brown cotton hood and Lehmann flag to bonnet, slight wear, German, c1920, 6¾in (17cm) long.
£700–800 Bon(C)

An automated tinplate toy drunkard, Le Pochard, in working order, c1900, 8in (20.3cm) high, with original box.
£230–260 DA

A Lehmann tinplate clockwork horseless carriage, the figures dressed in green and red, in a brown and cream carriage, German, c1900, 6in (15cm) high.
£1,000–1,200 HAL

◄ A Doll & Cie tinplate clockwork convertible car, hand-painted in maroon with cream lining, tin radiator surround, tan cotton hood, white rubber tyres, driver missing, Germany, 1920s, 20in (51cm) long.
£1,800–2,000 Bon(C)

A tinplate clockwork car, Express Transport, in yellow and red with blue windows, c1930–40, 6in (15cm) long.
£50–60 RTT

WALLIS & WALLIS Est. 1928

WEST STREET AUCTION GALLERIES, LEWES, SUSSEX, ENGLAND BN7 2NJ
TEL: +44 (0)1273 480208 FAX: +44 (0)1273 476562

Britain's Specialist Auctioneers of Diecast Toys, Model Railways, Tin Plate Toys & Models

2001 AUCTION SALES

Sale 89 February 12th	Sale 93 July 22nd
Sale 90 March 19th	Sale 94 August 28th
Sale 91 April 30th	Sale 95 October 8th
Sale 92 June 11th	Sale 96 November 19th

A 4½" gauge 4-2-2 GNR live steam locomotive (RN79) and tender. Realised £1250

Catalogues £6.50 incl. postage. Overseas (Airmail) £7.50 inc. postage

"Get to know the real value of your collection"

Our last 10 sales catalogues are available at £2.00 each, including postage, complete with prices realised.

TO ENTER ITEMS FOR AUCTION PLEASE ASK FOR ENTRY FORM

email: grb@wallisandwallis.co.uk   web site: http://www.wallisandwallis.co.uk

447

A tinplate clockwork auto-giro, in red and yellow, marked 'Germany DRGN', 1930s, 3¼in (8.5cm) long.
£65–85 RAR

A Wells Brimtoy tinplate clockwork police van, in dark green with white tyres, c1940s, 7in (18cm) long.
£70–80 HAL

Two Triang Minic tinplate clockwork double decker buses, one in red as No. 14 Putney, one red and cream as No. 177 Mitcham, 1950s, 8in (20.5cm) long.
£110–130 WAL

▶ A Triang Minic tinplate clockwork Bentley tourer, in dark green with white seats, 1950s, 1½in (4cm) long.
£80–90 WAL

A Mettoy friction-drive tinplate ambulance, in black, white and red, 1950, 5in (12.5cm) long.
£18–20 HAL

An SSS friction-drive tinplate police car, in black and white, Japan, c1950, 7in (18cm) long.
£45–50 HAL

A K friction-drive tinplate jeep, in khaki and cream, Japan, 1950s, 7in (18cm) long.
£35–40 HAL

▶ A Cragstan battery-operated musical chimp Hobo, in beige and wearing a green jacket, Japan, c1960, 10in (25.5cm) high, with original coloured box.
£120–150 BSA

TRAINS

A Bassett-Lowke 2in gauge 0-6-0 spirit-fired tank locomotive, in green and black, c1910, 14in (35.5cm) long.
£240–280 BKS

A Hornby 0 gauge No. 2 LMS green timber wagon, in original red box, 1928, 13in (33cm) long.
£60–70 HOB

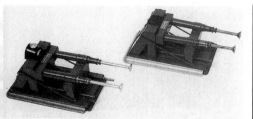

Two Hornby blue buffer stops, c1930, 6in (15cm) long.
l. No. 2E electric £20–40
r. No. 2 clockwork £10–20 HOB

A Hornby 0 gauge maroon locomotive, LMS electric 'Royal Scot', with shadow gold lettering 'RN6100' to cab sides, mid-1930s, 17in (43cm) long.
£250–300 WAL

▶ A Hornby No. 1 red, yellow and green water tank, in original red box, 1930, 6in (15cm) high.
£25–30 HOB

A Bassett-Lowke 0 gauge clockwork green tender locomotive, 'Duke of York', No. 1927, with original box postmarked December 1927, 14in (35.5cm) long, with additional track.
£300–330 DN

A Hornby clockwork 0 gauge 4-4-4 Great Western green and black locomotive, No. 2243, in original box, c1920s, 11in (28cm) long.
£400–450 HAL

A Hornby 0 gauge Cadbury's Chocolates blue private owner's wagon, c1936, 6in (15cm) long.
£200–240 HOB

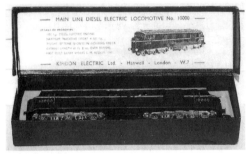

A Kirdon 00 gauge main line diesel electric engine, No. 10,000, in blue livery, 1950s, 9½in (24cm) long, with original red box.
£200–220 RAR

A Hornby 0 gauge 20v electric maroon engine and tender, 'Royal Scot', No. 6100, 1936, 17in (43cm) long.
£450–550 HOB

A Hornby 0 gauge No. 2 brown and cream Pullman coach, with detachable roof, gold lining to windows, in original matt paper-covered box, late 1930s, 15in (38cm) long.
£170–190 WAL

A Bassett-Lowke 0 gauge electric 4-6-2 LNER green locomotive and tender, 'Flying Scotsman', No. 4472, 1950s, 20in (51cm) long.
£800–900 WAL

A Hornby Dublo cream and red restaurant car, c1952, 9in (23cm) long, with original blue and white box.
£100–120 CWO

A Wrenn 00 gauge 0-6-0T green SE & CR diecast metal and plastic locomotive, No. W2201, 1970–80s, 5in (12.5cm) long, with original yellow, white and grey box.
£130–150 RAR

Treen

A piece of carved walnut, 17thC,
10in (25.5cm) long.
£75–85 OCH

A George III elm coaster,
7in (18cm) diam.
£200–240 AnSh

A Mauchline ware sycamore napkin
ring, depicting 'The Beach & Cliffs,
Cromer', 1880, 2in (5cm) diam.
£20–30 MB

A Victorian oak mouse
trap, 8in (20.5cm) high.
£150–165 BWA

◄ A boxwood
dice shaker,
19thC, 3in
(7.5cm) high.
£20–25 ALA

► A burrwood
chopping board,
1905, 10in
(25.5cm) diam.
£120–145 NEW

A Victorian boxwood bottle
case, 8½in (21.5cm) high.
£85–95 GLO

► A Tartan ware round
box, 1880, 1¼in (3cm) diam.
£70–80 BWA

A carved wood inkwell,
with original glass
container, 19thC,
3¼in (8.5cm) diam.
£150–170 SEA

Walking Sticks

A George III malacca walking stick, with cord hole and turned ivory knob handle, 33in (84cm) long.
£70–80 PFK

A malacca walking stick, with silver-plated handle in the shape of a lady's leg, c1890, 35in (89cm) long.
£140–160 HUM

An ebony walking stick, with inscribed silver top, c1850, 35in (89cm) long.
£120–140 HUM

A whalebone walking cane, with spiral-twist turning, the ivory handle with tortoiseshell and black-stained bands, 19thC, 36in (91.5cm) long.
£1,800–2,000 S(S)

A carved mahogany walking stick, the handle in the shape of a lady's leg, c1890, 35in (89cm) long.
£180–200 HUM

A malacca sword stick, with a silver knob, c1880, 35in (89cm) long.
£180–200 HUM

A brass triangular stick stand, 19thC, 30in (76cm) high.
£400–500 TWr

A cane sword stick, with hollow-ground triangular section blade, etched 'Bacon Brothers Cambridge', with leather-covered handle, c1900, blade 26½in (67.5cm) long.
£400–450 WAL

A walking stick, with horn dog's head handle and silver band, c1900, 29in (73.5cm) long.
£25–30 AL

◄ A walking cane, the silver dog's head handle with glass eyes, by Edward Lyon, marked London 1904, 35in (88.9cm) long.
£400–450 DN

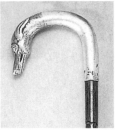

A walking stick, with a horn handle and silver band, c1900, 34in (86.5cm) long.
£25–30 AL

A farmer's hazel walking stick, with dog's head handle, c1900, 36in (91.5cm) long.
£30–40 AL

Watches & Clocks

An American carved oak mantel clock, Ansonia, c1880, 17½in (44.5cm) high.
£180–220 TO

An ebonized and inlaid portico clock, with ormolu foliate cast border between four barley-twist gilt-brass-capped columns, the eight-day drum movement striking on a bell, 19thC, 17½in (44.5cm) high.
£400–480 Hal

A Smith Electric black and white garage forecourt clock, advertising KLG Plugs, c1930s, 36in (91.5cm) high.
£600–700 JUN

A French eight-day brass carriage clock, c1900, 4¼in (11.5cm) high.
£150–175 TAC

A Ferranti brown Bakelite electric mantel clock, 1945, 6in (15cm) high.
£50–60 GAD

◄ A Japanese metal and chrome birdcage clock, with red clock face, and bird in red, yellow and green, c1960, 5in (12.5cm) high.
£80–90 FA

► A Smith clockwork Alarm clock, with green numerals and base, 1960, 5in (12.5cm) high.
£8–10 RTT

A French marble clock, by H. Marc, Paris, with brass inlay, the eight-day movement striking to a bell, signed, c1890, 19½in (49.5cm) high.
£500–600 PC

A French porcelain-mounted gilt-metal mantel clock, the white porcelain dial with Arabic numerals, surmounted by a maiden with a basket of flowers, on a porcelain inset rococo scroll base and separate plinth, early 20thC, 12in (30.5cm) high.
£150–180 Hal

A National Time Recorder Co wooden time recorder, inscribed 'St Mary Cray, Kent', c1895, 39in (99cm) high.
£200–240 WEL

A Hovis mahogany advertising clock, inscribed 'Hovis Bread Sold Here', early 20thC, 14in (35.5cm) diam.
£500–600 B&R

A Majak chrome and glass clock, with blue enamel face, USSR, c1970s, 8in (20.5cm) high.
£30–35 GIN

A Victorian carved wood watch stand, 4in (10cm) high.
£25–30 AOH

A Longines gun-metal pocket watch, signed, with original fitted box and stand, c1890, 40mm diam.
£250–300 HARP

An 18ct gold pocket watch, 1897, 40mm diam.
£200–220 AOH

A watch, barometer and thermometer, in a silver case by H. Matthews, Chester, 1907, 8in (20.5cm) high.
£1,550–1,750 THOM

A nurse's metal sand-timer, c1910, 3in (7.5cm) long.
£20–25 WAB
This was used to check a patient's pulse.

An H. Samuel 18ct gold watch, with rolled gold strap, in original case, 1913, 25mm diam.
£120–140 AOH

A Longines wristwatch, with leather strap, 1920s.
£150–175 JoV

A Goss watch stand, with City of Worcester crest in red, black and yellow, c1920, 6in (15cm) high.
£30–35 AOH

A Chevrolet Radiator Grill wristwatch, the case back inscribed 'For Making Quota 1927 Used Car Campaign'.
£1,000–1,200 HARP

An Omega steel cushion-cased wrist-watch, with manual wind, original shaded dial, triple signed, c1927.
£300–350 HARP

An Omega steel Art Deco-style wristwatch, with hand-wound formed movement with metal dust cover and two-tone redial, c1934.
£300–350 HARP

An International Watch Co two-colour gold wristwatch, c1930.
£1,000–1,250 JoV

A Rellum special pilot's watch, with turning inner bezel for time of flight, and extended crown for use with gloves, signed, slight damage to dial, pitted case, c1935.
£230–260 HARP

A Cartier-style gilt-metal and crystal wristwatch, 1940s, 22mm diam.
£165–195 LBe

An Ebel stainless steel moonphase calendar wristwatch, with manual wind, c1940.
£900–1,000 HARP

A Rolex Oyster Perpetual Datejust automatic wristwatch, with red and black calendar and original bracelet, 1950s.
£1,100–1,300 JoV

A Lemania 105 stainless steel chronograph, 1950s, 38mm diam.
£250–300 AOH

A Heuer Carrera chronograph wristwatch, with black dial and registers, c1970.
£1,600–1,800 S

A Longines Admiral HF steel wristwatch, with manual wind, special edition for Munich Olympic Games, 1972.
£245–265 HARP

A Heuer Silverstone automatic chronograph, c1973.
£1,300–1,500 HARP

A Heuer Jacky Ickx Easy-Rider steel chronograph, with registers and date, c1975.
£2,500–2,800 S
Heuer was founded in Switzerland in 1860 by Edouard Heuer. The company became a leader in sports watch technology. Heuer produced the first stop-watch accurate to 1/100th of a second in 1916, and in 1965 the microtimer was invented, permitting measurement to the nearest 1/1,000th of a second. Heuer became involved with motor-racing timekeeping, developing watches to meet the specific needs of Formula One drivers. Legendary figures from Jacky Ickx to Nicki Lauda to Steve McQueen in the film 'Le Mans', all sported Heuer watches.

▶ An Incabloc 17 jewels 9ct white gold wrist-watch, c1970s, 11mm diam.
£180–200 BWC

◀ An Old England 17 jewels chrome and Perspex wristwatch, with manual wind, 1970s, 32mm diam.
£65–75 LBe

◀ A Rolex Oyster Perpetual Datejust steel-cased wristwatch, with steel bracelet, signed, in original box with receipt and registration card, c1983.
£800–900 CGC

▶ A *Dick Tracy* Madonna promotion wristwatch, battery-operated, 1987, 32mm diam.
£40–45 TBoy

Welsh

Mona Antiqua Restaurata, by Henry Rowlands, an archaeological discourse on the antiquities, natural and historical, of the Isle of Anglesey, 2nd edition, with contemporary calf cover, 1766, 4to.
£150–175 DW

Cambria Depicta, A Series of Fifty Picturesque Views in Wales, by Edward Pugh, engraved in aquatinta, original half morocco cover, 1816, 4to.
£180–200 DW

Cross Reference
See Colour Review

A Welsh slate door stop, c1880, 8in (20.5cm) long.
£130–150 CoA

A Tour Through Monmouthshire and Wales, Made in the Months of June and July, 1774 and in the Months of June, July and August, 1777, by Henry Penruddocke Wyndham, 2nd edition, published Salisbury 1781, contemporary calf front cover with old reback, 4to.
£220–250 DW

A Swansea black and white pottery plate, depicting a sailing ship, c1840, 9in (23cm) diam.
£165–175 CoA

A Welsh sycamore dairy bowl, c1800, 16in (40.5cm) diam.
£300–330 MFB

This section is devoted to collectables connected with Wales, including books, ceramics, textiles and crafts.

A Welsh sycamore cawl spoon, 19thC, 9in (23cm) long.
£50–55 MFB

A Gaudy Welsh pottery cup and saucer, decorated with the Prince of Wales feathers in blue, orange and white, 1820-90, saucer 5¾in (14.5cm) diam.
£90–100 CoHA

◄ A stained pearwood love spoon, with chip-carved rectangular panel, with red paint spot decoration, 19thC, 8in (20.5cm) long.
£670–720 S(S)
Love spoons were given in the 18th and 19th centuries as a token of engagement or marriage. Wooden love spoons were a Welsh speciality and would be carved by the groom for his bride with a variety of symbols including hearts, and comma-shaped motifs, emblematic of the soul. Another popular form was two spoons carved from a single piece of wood and linked by a wooden chain. These examples of Welsh rural craftsmanship can fetch very high prices today.

A pine love spoon, with three panels inscribed 'A Present from Dyffryn, Febury 1894'; 'Ms La Davies, Cors-y-gedol, Farm, Dyffryn'; 'Maker Humphay Roberts', c1894, 14¾in (37.5cm) long.
£300–350 S(S)

◀ A Welsh folk art wooden wind whirligig, Sion & Sian, with original grey, white and red painted finish, c1890, 37in (94cm) wide.
£800–900 MFB

A Welsh pottery flagon, advertising KBC Flint Welsh Ales and Stout, c1900, 25in (63.5cm) high.
£75–95 HOP

A Goss Taper beaker, transfer-printed with Welsh antiquities, 1881–1934, 3in (7.5cm) high.
£100–120 CCC

A Goss model of a Welsh leek, with Carnarvon crest, 1900–25, 3½in (9cm) high.
£35–40 CCC
The leek became the national symbol of Wales when St David (d. c600 AD), patron saint of Wales, made his country-men wear leeks in their caps to distinguish them from their Saxon enemy. David or Daffydd was a popular name in Wales, leading to the corruption 'Taffy', the slang name for a Welshman.

A Buckley brown pottery jug, decorated with a brown boat on a green sea, inscribed in Welsh on reverse, translated 'There is no one more united than two Welshmen', 1910, 6in (15cm) high.
£60–70 IW

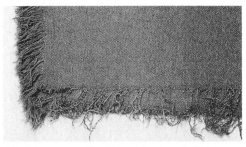

A Welsh green woollen fringed shawl, early 20thC, 72 x 70in (183 x 178cm).
£50–60 DE

A Welsh double-sided double weave red and pale green bed cover, fringed, 1910–20, 74 x 88in (188 x 223.5cm).
£110–120 JJ

A Welsh horse brass, Jenny Jones, c1920, 4in (10cm) high.
£8–10 PJo

A British Railways coloured advertising poster, PW46, 'Wales', by Frank Sherwin, printed by Waterlow, c1950, 40¼ x 50in (102 x 127cm).
£750–850 ONS

Whistles

A silver Patent whistle, c1900, 3½in (9cm) long.
£85–95 REG

A pottery whistle, modelled as a white bird on a green nest, 1910, 2¼in (5.5cm) high.
£40–45 BBR

▶ A tin whistle, c1910, 2in (5cm) long.
£8–10 FA

A silver whistle, complete with chain and holders, c1900, chain 22in (56cm) long.
£90–100 CoHA

A base-metal whistle, 1930s, 3in (7.5cm) long.
£10–12 AOH

A base-metal Boy Scout's whistle, with a compass on the side, 1930s, 3½in (9cm) long.
£28–32 AOH

The Acme Scout Master Patent whistle, 1930s, 4in (10cm) long.
£14–16 AOH

The Acme Scout Master Patent whistle, with a compass in the base, 1924, 4in (10cm) long.
£30–35 AOH

A Czechoslovakian ceramic egg cup whistle, shaped as a train, in red and blue with black wheels, 1930s, 4in (10cm) long.
£70–80 BEV

Condition

The condition is absolutely vital when assessing the value of a collectable. Damaged items on the whole appreciate much less than perfect examples. However, a rare desirable piece may command a high price even when damaged.

Writing

A fob seal, inscribed 'For Particulars Enquire Within', 1780–1820, 1in (2.5cm) long.
£45–50 WAC

A tortoiseshell *aide mémoire*, with gold inlay, 1840, 4in (10cm) long.
£70–80 MB

A cobalt blue fluted glass ink teakettle, with curved facets and upturned spout, 19thC, 2in (5cm) high
£200–220 BBR

A Mauchline ware sycamore paper knife, decorated with Melrose Abbey, 1880, 10in (25.5cm) long.
£45–50 MB

A seal, with bone-handle, inscribed 'B', c1840–60, 1½in (4cm) long.
£24–28 WAC

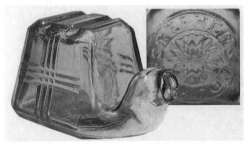

◄ A mid-blue glass ink teakettle, with two pen rests to top, upturned curved spout with sheared lip, embossed 'Stephens London' to base, 19thC, 2¼in (5.5cm) high.
£600–700 BBR
Sold ready filled with ink, disposable ink bottles were produced in large quantities in the Victorian and Edwardian period. Unusual examples, however, can fetch high prices, and values depend on shape and colour, since some shades are far rarer than others. A maker's mark can also add interest to an item.

An aqua glass inkwell, modelled as a cottage, with sheared lip, water butt to side and rear pen nib recess, embossed 'W. Chandler' to base, 19thC, 2¾in (7cm) high.
£90–100 BBR

A Wahl Eversharp gold-plated fountain pen, 1930, 4¾in (12cm) long.
£100–120 RUS

A Conway Stewart 851 marbled green and gold fountain pen, with lever filler, c1950, 6in (15cm) long.
£65–75 AOH

A tortoiseshell horse's hoof inkwell, with silver lid by Grey & Co, Chester, 1912, 2¼in (5.5cm) high.
£900–1,100 THOM

Record Breakers

This year we conclude *Miller's Collectables Price Guide* with a selection of objects that have achieved a world record price at auction. Though coming from many different fields, what all these works have in common is quality and above all rarity. What they also demonstrate is the passion of the collector. To the non-initiated, a loco name-plate is simply a piece of metal, unredeemed by any aesthetic merit. To the railwayana enthusiast it summons up all the glories of the age of steam, and the right example, as shown here, can be worth thousands of pounds. Passion is what collecting is all about and this page shows how far people will go to obtain the object of their dreams.

A Wemyss sleeping piglet, painted with pink cabbage roses, impressed 'WEMYSS', green script mark, early 20thC, 7in (18cm) long.
World Record Price £9,600 S

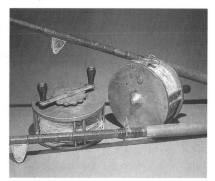

A pair of Hardy White-Wickham fishing reels, 1929, 8in (20.5cm) diam.
World Record Price £48,800 P(Ba)
Only one other Hardy White-Wickham reel is known to exist, in a museum in New Zealand.

A dark olive-green glass sealed shaft-and-globe bottle, with kick-up pontil base and applied string rim, seal reads 'E.B.', found in Shrewbury, c1660, 7½in (19cm) high.
World Record Price £19,800 BBR

The prices in this section include the auctioneers commission.

◄ A Wedgwood Festival of Britain 1951 commemorative mug, decorated in blue and red on a white ground, 4in (10cm) high.
World Record Price £317 FBS

An LMS cast-brass and black nameplate, 'Duchess of Devonshire', No. 6227, built at Crewe June 1938, it was scrapped in 1963, 85in (216cm) long.
World Record Price £37,500 SRA

A Carlton Ware ginger jar and cover, decorated with Jazz pattern on an orange lustre ground, Pattern No. 3258, script mark, 1930s, 11in (28cm) high.
World Record Price £9,690 PAC

▶ A *Daily Express* brown-faced *Rupert* Annual, 1973.
World Record Price £18,315 HTC
A. E. Bestall always drew Rupert with a brown face on the cover of the annual and a white face inside the book. In 1973 an executive at Express Newspapers decided to balance things up and blanked out the brown face on the cover. Bestall was not consulted and was furious, demanding that his name be removed from the back cover (it can still be seen on the common white-faced edition as a pink blur) and threatened legal action. To appease him, around a dozen copies were printed with a brown face and hurriedly bound. To date only six of them have been traced.

BACA

BRitish Antiques
And CoLLectaBLes
AwARDs

presented by

MILLER'S

In association with

Celebrating the Winners of the First Annual BACA

BACA was created to celebrate the outstanding qualities across the enormous range
of goods and services that make up the world of Antiques and Collectables.
The previous 12 months of planning for this event culminated in a wonderful evening
of champagne and applause on Tuesday 20th June 2000 at Grosvenor House, Park Lane, London.
Our second Awards will be held in June 2001 and will follow along the lines established this year.

Nominations – Who Can Vote? Who can be nominated?

Anybody from the leisure Collector to a member of the Trade itself can make a
nomination for any number of the Awards in any of the categories.

How to Vote for 2001

The voting process for the 2001 Awards begins now and will end in March 2001.
For a voting form, please apply to:

BACA/Miller's
2–4 Heron Quays
London E14 4JP
www.baca-awards.co.uk

The ideas, support and interest we have received for BACA have given these Awards
a fascinating start and we would be very interested to hear more from you
on the subject of new Categories and new Awards – but most importantly of course,
we want your vote!

PROUDLY SPONSORED BY

 MILLER'S CLUB Invaluable POWERED BY THESAURUS

The BACA *Winners...*

CATEGORY 1
General Antiques Dealer

LONDON *sponsored by*
Patricia Harvey
42 Church Street, Marylebone,
London NW8 8ED

ENGLAND *sponsored by* **invaluable**
Witney Antiques
96-100 Corn Street, Witney, Oxfordshire OX8 7BU

WALES
Country Antiques
Castle Mill, Kidwelly, Carmarthen,
Wales SA17 4UW

SCOTLAND
Georgian Antiques
Pattinson Street, Leith, Edinburgh EH6 7HF

NORTHERN IRELAND
MacHenry Antiques of Jordanstown
Newtown Abbey,
BT37 0RY

CATEGORY 2
Specialist Antiques Dealers

FURNITURE
Avon Antiques
25-27 Market Street, Bradford on Avon,
Wiltshire BA15 1LL

CERAMICS *sponsored by*
Jonathan Horne
66c Kensington Church Street,
London W8 4BY

CLOCKS, WATCHES & BAROMETERS
Derek Roberts
25 Shipbourne Road, Tonbridge,
Kent TN10 3DN

DECORATIVE ARTS
New Century
69 Kensington Church Street,
London W8 4BG

SILVER AND PLATE *sponsored by*
Marks Antiques
49 Curzon Street,
London W1Y 7RE

GLASS
Jeanette Hayhurst
32a Kensington Church Street,
London W8 4HA

COLLECTABLES
sponsored by **invaluable**
Cobwebs
78 Northam Road, Southhampton SO14 OPB

ORIENTAL
S. Marchant & Sons
120 Kensington Church Street
London W8

JEWELLERY
Wartski Ltd
14 Grafton Street, London W1X 4DE

CATEGORY 3
Auction Houses

LONDON *sponsored by* **invaluable**
Christie's South Kensington
85 Old Brompton Road, London SW7 3LD

ENGLAND *sponsored by* **invaluable**
Dreweatt Neate
Donnington Priory, Donnington, Newbury,
Berkshire RG13 2JE

WALES
Wingetts
29 Holt Street, Wrexham,
North Wales LL13 8DH

SCOTLAND
Lyon & Turnbull
33 Broughton Place, Edinburgh EH1 3RR

NORTHERN IRELAND
Temple Auctions
133 Carryduff Road, Temple,
Lisburn BT27 6YL

CATEGORY 4
Associated Awards

FAIR OF THE YEAR AWARD
sponsored by
BADA
British Antiques Dealers Association
20 Rutland Gate,
London SW7 1BD

**ANTIQUES PERSONALITY
OF THE YEAR** *sponsored by* **HOMES &ANTIQUES** MAGAZINE
Henry Sandon

**BEST ANTIQUES TOWN/
VILLAGE** *sponsored by* MILLER'S CLUB
Brighton – East Sussex

Directory of Specialists

If you require a valuation for an item it is advisable to check whether the dealer or specialist will carry out this service, and whether there is a charge. Please mention Miller's when making an enquiry. Having found a specialist who will carry out your valuation, it is best to send a description and photograph of the item to them, together with a stamped addressed envelope for the reply. A valuation by telephone is not possible. Most dealers are only too happy to help you with your enquiry, however, they are very busy people and consideration of the above points would be welcomed.

Bedfordshire
Paperchase, 77 Wingfield Road, Bromham, Bedford MK43 8JY
Tel: 01234 825942

Christopher Sykes,
The Old Parsonage, Woburn,
Milton Keynes MK17 9QM
Tel: 01525 290259
www.sykes-corkscrews.co.uk
Corkscrews and wine related items.

Berkshire
Collect It! Unit 11 Weller Drive, Hogwood Industrial Estate, Finchampstead RG40 4QZ
Tel: 0118 973 7888
sales@collectit.co.uk
www.collectit.co.uk
Magazine for collectors.

Mostly Boxes, 93 High Street, Eton, Windsor SL4 6AF
Tel: 01753 858470
Antique wooden boxes.

Special Auction Services,
The Coach House,
Midgham Park, Reading RG7 5UG
Tel: 0118 971 2949
www.invaluable.com/sas/
Commemoratives, pot lids, Prattware, fairings, Goss & Crested, Baxter and Le Blond prints.

Cambridgeshire
Antique Amusement Co, Mill Lane, Swaffham, Bulbeck CB5 0NF
Tel: 01223 813041
www.aamag.co.uk
Vintage amusement machines, also auctions of amusement machines, fairground art and other related collectables.

Cloister Antiques, 1a Lynn Road, Ely CB7 4EG Tel: 01353 668558
Sewing, writing, heavy horse and smoking.

James Fuller & Son,
51 Huntingdon Road, Chatteris
P16 6JE Tel: 01354 692740
Architectural antiques.

Warboys Antiques,
Old Church School,
High Street, Warboys,
Huntingdon PE17 2SX
Tel: 01487 823686
Sporting antiques and tins.

Cheshire
The Antique Garden,
Maria Hopwood, Grosvenor Garden Centre, Wrexham Road, Belgrave Chester CH4 9EB Tel: 01244 629191
info@antique-garden.co.uk

Collector's Corner, PO Box 8, Congleton CW12 4GD
Tel: 01260 270429
Rock and pop collectables, Sci-Fi, TV and Beatles memorabilia.

Dollectable, 53 Lower Bridge Street, Chester CH1 1RS
Tel: 01244 344888/679195
Antique dolls.

On The Air,
The Vintage Technology Centre,
The Highway, Hawarden,
Nr Chester CH5 3DX
Tel: 01244 530300
www.vintageradio.co.uk
Vintage radios.

Sweetbriar Gallery,
Robin Hood Lane, Helsby
WA6 9NH Tel: 01928 723851
sweetbr@globalnet.co.uk
www.sweetbriar.co.uk
Paperweights.

Charles Tomlinson, Chester
Tel: 01244 318395
Charles.Tomlinson@lineone.net
www.lineone.net/~Charles.Tomlinson

www.horsebrass.co.uk,
Diane Wilkinson, Cuddington Lane, Cuddington, Northwich CW8 2SY
Tel: 44 (0) 1606 882555
brasses@horsebrass.co.uk
www.horsebrass.co.uk/

Cornwall
British Watch & Clock Collectors Association, 5 Cathedral Lane, Truro TR1 2QS Tel: 01872 264010
tonybwcca@cs.comwww.timecap.co.uk
Membership by subscription to the bi-monthly newsletter 'Timepiece'. Regular features include 'For Sale & Wanted' section, trade articles, press releases, members letters and articles. Write, fax, phone or e-mail for application form.

Derbyshire
Goss Collectors' Club, Mrs Schofield
Tel: 0115 930 0441

Devon
Torquay Pottery Collectors' Society, Torre Abbey, Avenue Road, Torquay TQ2 5JX
tpcs@btinternet.com
www.scandyonline.com

Dorset
Chris Belton,
PO Box 356, Christchurch
BH23 1XQ Tel: 01202 478592
Antiquities.

Books Afloat,
66 Park Street, Weymouth
DT4 7DE Tel: 01305 779774
Books on all subjects, liner and naval memorabilia, old postcards, models and paintings.

The Crow's Nest, 3 Hope Square, opp. Brewers Quay,
Weymouth DT4 8TR
Tel: 01305 786930

Dalkeith Auctions Ltd,
Dalkeith Hall, Dalkeith Steps,
Rear of 81 Old Christchurch Road, Bournemouth BH1 1YL
Tel: 01202 292905
how@dalkeith-auctions.co.uk
www.dalkeith-auctions.co.uk
Auctions of postcards, cigarette cards, ephemera and collectors items.

Hardy's Collectables,
862 Christchurch Road,
Boscombe, Bournemouth
BH7 6DQ
Tel: 01202 422407/473744
Poole pottery,

Murrays' Antiques & Collectables
Tel: 01202 309094
Shipping, motoring, railway, cycling items always required. Also advertising related items, eg. showcards, enamel signs, tins and packaging and general quality collectables.

Old Button Shop Antiques,
Lytchett Minster,
Poole BH16 6JF
Tel: 01202 622169
Buttons and collectables

Poole Pottery, The Quay,
Poole BH15 1RF
Tel: 01202 666200
www.poolepottery.co.uk

Essex

Nick Garner Tel: 07970 206682
Nickgarner@btinternet.com
Dennis china, Dartington, Highland stoneware, Freshwell ceramics, John Hine pottery and Melting Pot glassware.

GKR Bonds Ltd, PO Box 1,
Kelvedon CO5 9EH
Tel: 01376 571711
Old bonds and share certificates.

Haddon Rocking Horses Ltd,
5 Telford Road, Clacton on Sea
CO15 4LP
Tel: 01255 424745
millers@rockinghorses.uk.com
www.rockinghorses.uk.com
www.haddonhorse.u-net.com
Rocking horses.

Megarry's and Forever Summer,
Jericho Cottage,
The Duckpond Green,
Blackmore CM4 0RR
Tel: 01277 821031/01277 822170
Antiques, Arts & Crafts. Summer 10am–6pm daily except Mon and Tues. Winter 11am–5pm daily except Mon and Tues. Member Essex Antiques Dealers Association.

The Old Telephone Company,
The Old Granary,
Battlesbridge Antiques Centre,
Nr Wickford SS11 7RF
Tel: 01245 400601
www.theoldtelephone.co.uk
Period telephones.

Gloucestershire

Bread & Roses, Durham House
Antique Centre, Sheep Street,
Stow on the Wold GL54 1AA
Tel: 01451 870404/01926 817342

Corner House Antiques and Ffoxe
Antiques, High Street,
Lechlade GL7 3AE
Tel: 01367 252007

Grimes House Antiques,
High Street, Moreton-in-Marsh
GL56 0AT Tel: 01608 651029
grimes_house@cix.co.uk
www.grimeshouse.co.uk
www.cranberryglass.co.uk
www.collectglass.com

Park House Antiques & Toy Museum,
Park Street, Stow-on-the-Wold
GL54 1AQ
Tel: 01451 830159
Come and see one of the best private collections of old toys in the country. Admission £2, OAPs £1.50. Summer 10am–1pm, 2–5pm. Winter 11am–1pm, 2–4pm. Closed Tues and all May. We buy old toys and teddy bears.

Q&C Militaria,
22 Suffolk Road, Cheltenham
GL50 2AQ
Tel: 01242 519815
John@qc-militaria.freeserve.co.uk
www.qcmilitaria.com
Orders, decorations, medals, uniforms, militaria and Trench Art.

Ruskin Decorative Arts,
5 Talbot Court, Stow-on-the-Wold,
Cheltenham GL54 1DP
Tel: 01451 832254

Specialised Postcard Auctions,
25 Gloucester Street,
Cirencester GL7 2DJ
Tel: 01285 659057

Telephone Lines Ltd,
304 High Street,
Cheltenham GL50 3JF
Tel: 01242 583699
Telephonelines.freeserve.co.uk
www.telephonelines.net

Hampshire

Bona Art Deco Store, The Hart
Shopping Centre, Fleet GU13 8AZ
Tel: 01252 372188/616666
www.bona.co.uk
claricecliff.co.uk
Art Deco, glass lighting, furniture, ceramics and Clarice Cliff.

Classic Amusements
Tel: 01425 472164
pennyslot@aol.com
www.classicamusements.net

Cobwebs, 78–80 Northam Road,
Southampton SO14 0PB
Tel: 023 8022 7458
www.cobwebs.uk.com
Ocean liner memorabilia. Also naval and aviation items.

Goss & Crested China Centre &
Museum, incorporating Milestone
Publications, 62 Murray Road,
Horndean PO8 9JL
Tel: 023 9259 7440
info@gosschinaclub.demon.co.uk
www.gosscrestedchina.co.uk

The Old Toy Shop, 7 Monmouth
Court, Ringwood BH24 1HE
Tel: 01425 476899
djwells@ntlworld.com
www.TheOldToyShop.com
Clockwork, steam and electric vintage toys and memorabilia and figures.

Romsey Medal Centre, PO Box 169,
Romsey SO51 6XU
Tel: 01794 324488
post@romseymedals.co.uk
www.romseymedals.co.uk
Orders, decorations and medals.

Solent Railwayana Auctions,
31 Newtown Road, Warsash SO31 9FY
Tel: 01489 578093/584633
Railway relics and model railway items. Railwayana auctions.

Hertfordshire

Brown & Merry, Tring Market
Auctions, Brook Street, Tring
HP23 5EF Tel: 01442 826446
sales@tringmarketauctions.co.uk
www.tringmarketauctions.co.uk

Forget-Me-Knot Antiques, Over the
Moon, 27 High Street, St Albans
AL3 4EH Tel: 01727 848907
Jewellery.

Isle of Wight

Nostalgia Toy Museum, High Street,
Godshill, Ventnor PO38 3HZ
Tel: 01983 730055
Diecast toys.

Kent

20th Century Marks,
12 Market Square,
Westerham TN16 1AW
Tel: 01959 562221
TCM@marks.plus.com
20thcenturymarks.co.uk

Beatcity, 331 High Street,
Rochester ME1 1DA
Tel: 01634 844525/077 70 65 08 90
www.beatcity.co.uk
Beatles and rock and roll memorabilia.

Candlestick & Bakelite,
PO Box 308,
Orpington BR5 1TB
Tel: 020 8467 3743/3799
candlestick.bakelite@tesco.net
Telephones.

Carlton Ware Collectors International,
PO Box 161, Sevenoaks
TN15 6GA Tel: 01474 853630
cwciclub@aol.com
www.stclere.co.uk
St Clere – Carltonware the UK's leading specialists in Carlton Ware. Selling and buying Carlton 1890–1992. Mail orders taken. Visa and Mastercard accepted. Contact Helen and Keith Martin.

Delf Stream Gallery,
14 New Street, Sandwich
CT13 9AB
Tel: 01304 617684
www.delfstreamgallery.com

Dragonlee Collectables
Tel: 01622 729502
Noritake.

Paul Haskell
Tel: 01634 669362
www.antiqueslotmachines.inuk.com

Stuart Heggie,
14 The Borough, Northgate,
Canterbury CT1 2DR
Tel: 01227 470422
Vintage cameras, optical toys and photographic images.

High Class Junk, 26 The Street,
Appledore TN26 2BX
Tel: 01233 758502
Old pine, china, old copper, brass, ironware and tools.

J & M Collectables
Tel: 01580 891657
jandmcollectables@tinyonline.co.uk
Postcards, Crested china, Osbourne (Ivorex) plaques and small collectables including Denton, Wade, etc.

Lambert & Foster, 102 High Street,
Tenterden TN30 6HT
Tel: 01580 762083/763233
lf@tenterden14.freeserve.co.uk
www.lambertandfoster.co.uk

Barbara Ann Newman,
London House Antiques,
4 Market Square, Westerham
TN16 1AW
Tel: 01959 564479
Antique dolls, teddy bears and collectables.

Old Tackle Box,
PO Box 55,
High Street, Cranbrook
TN17 3ZU
Tel: 01580 713979
Old fishing tackle.

Pretty Bizarre,
170 High Street,
Deal CT14 6BQ
Tel: 07973 794537

The Neville Pundole Gallery,
8A & 9 The Friars, Canterbury
CT1 2AS Tel: 01227 453471
www.pundole.co.uk
Moorcroft and Contemporary pottery and glass.

St Clere Carlton Ware, PO Box 161,
Sevenoaks TN15 6GA
Tel: 01474 853630
stclere@aol.com
www.stclere.co.uk

Stevenson Brothers, The Workshop,
Ashford Road, Bethersden, Ashford
TN26 3AP Tel: 01233 820363
sale@stevensonbros.com
www.stevensonbros.com
Rocking horses.

Variety Box, 16 Chapel Place,
Tunbridge Wells TN1 1YQ
Tel: 01892 531868
Tunbridge ware, Silver ware, glass, fans, hat pins, writing and sewing.

Wenderton Antiques
Tel: 01227 720295 (by appt only)
Kitchenware.

Woodville Antiques, The Street,
Hamstreet, Ashford TN26 2HG
Tel: 01233 732981
Tools.

Wot a Racket, 250 Shepherds Lane,
Dartford DA1 2PN
Tel: 01322 220619
wot-a-racket@talk21.com
Sporting.

Lancashire
Decades, 20 Lord St West,
Blackburn BB2 1JX
Tel: 01254 693320

Pendelfin Studio Ltd, Cameron Mill,
Housin Street, Burnley BB10 1PP
Tel: 01282 432301

Tracks, PO Box 117,
Chorley PR6 0UU Tel: 01257 269726
sales@tracks.co.uk
Beatles and rare pop memorabilia.

Leicestershire
House of Burleigh Tel: 01664 454570
HousBurl@aol.com

Pooks Motor Bookshop,
Fowke Street, Rothley LE7 7PJ
Tel: 0116 237 6222
Motoring books and automobilia.

Lincolnshire
Anthony Jackson,
Rocking Horse Maker & Restorer,
20 Westry Corner, Barrowby,
Grantham NG32 1DF
Tel: 01476 567477
sales@rockinghorsemaker.co.uk
www.rockinghorsemaker.co.uk

Junktion, The Old Railway Station,
New Bolingbroke,
Boston PE22 7LB
Tel: 01205 480068/480087
Advertising and packaging, automobilia.

Skip & Janie Smithson
Tel: 01754 810265
Kitchenware.

Stamp Unique, The Old Railway Yard,
Pinchbeck, Spalding PE11 3RF
Tel: 01775 723096

London
20th Century Glass,
Kensington Church Street Antique
Centre, 58–60 Kensington Church
Street W8 4DB
Tel: 020 7938 1137/020 7729 9875
Glass. Open Thurs, Fri and Sat 12–6pm or by appt.

Angling Auctions,
PO Box 2095 W12 8RU
Tel: 020 8749 4175
neil@anglingauctions.demon.co.uk

The Antique Dealer,
115 Shaftesbury Avenue WC2H 8AD
Tel: 020 7420 6684
info@theantiquedealer.co.uk

Beverley/Beth, 30 Church
Street/Alfie's Antique Market,
Marylebone NW8 8EP
Tel: 020 7262 1576
Art Deco furniture, glass, figures, metalware and pottery.

Bloomsbury Book Auctions,
3 & 4 Hardwick Street,
Off Rosebery Avenue EC1R 4RY
Tel: 020 7833 2636/7
info@bloomsbury-book-auct-.com
www.bloomsbury-book-auct.com

Christie's South Kensington Ltd,
85 Old Brompton Road SW7 3LD
Tel: 020 7581 7611
info@christies.com
christies.com
Auctioneers.

The Collector, Tom Power, 4 Queens
Parade Close, Friern Barnet N11 3FY
Tel: 020 8361 7787/020 8361 6111
collector@globalnet.co.uk
*Contemporary collectables; Royal
Doulton, Beswick, Pendelfin,
Worcester, Lladro, Border Fine Art,
Wade, Wedgwood, Coalport, Bossons,
Lilliput Lane, David Winter, etc.*

Collector's World London UK,
Units G143 & G101,
Alfies Antique Centre, 13/25 Church
Street, Marylebone NW8 8DT
Tel: 020 7724 1599
collectorsworld@btinternet.com
www.collectorsworld.net
www.collectorslondon.com
*19th and 20th century watches,
clocks, cameras. Toys, Dinky, Corgi
and diecast. TV/film related, tinplate
cars, boats, planes, robots, dolls and
teddy bears, Disneyana, memorabilia.*

Comic Book Postal Auctions Ltd,
40–42 Osnaburgh Street NW1 3ND
Tel: 020 7424 0007
comicbook@compuserve.com
www.compalcomics.com
www.compalcomics.com

Dix-Noonan-Webb,
1 Old Bond Street W1X 3TD
Tel: 020 7499 5022
auction@dnw.co.uk
www.dnw.co.uk

eBay International AG,
Bishop's Farm House,
25–29 Fulham High Street SW6 3JH
Tel: 020 7384 6717
ebay.co.uk

Gentry Antiques Tel: 020 7792 1402
info@cornishwarecollector.co.uk
www.cornishwarecollector.co.uk

Michael C. German,
38B Kensington Church Street
W8 4BX
Tel: 020 7937 2771
Walking canes.

Gooday Gallery, 14 Richmond Hill,
Richmond TW10 6QX
Tel: 020 8940 8652
*Arts & Crafts, Art Deco, Art Nouveau,
Tribal, 1950s and 60s.*

Harlequin House Puppets & Masks,
3 Kensington Mall W8 4EB
Tel: 020 7221 8629
*Best collection of Pelham puppets,
also antique rod puppets from Polka
Theatre Wimbledon, old ventriloquist
dummies, Czech puppets, Punch and
Judy. Open Tues, Fri and Sat
11am–5.30pm.*

Adrian Harrington, 64a Kensington
Church Street W8 4DB
Tel: 020 7937 1465
Antiquarian books, prints and maps.

Herzog, Hollender Phillips &
Company, The Scripophily Shop,
PO Box 14376 NW6 1ZD
Tel: 020 7433 3577
hollender@dial.pipex.com
www.Currency.dealers-on-
line.com/ScripophilyShop

David Huxtable, Stand S03/05
(Top Floor) Alfies Antique Market,
13–25 Church Street,
Marylebone NW8 8DT
Tel: 020 7724 2200
Old advertising collectables.

Charles Jeffreys Posters & Graphics,
12 Octavia Street SW11 3DN
Tel: 020 7978 7976
charlie@cjposters.com
www.cjposters.com
*Specializing in selling original, rare
and collectable posters from the birth
of modernism through bauhaus to
the 60s and 70s pop art and
psychedelic culture including
contemporary posters.*

Francis Joseph Publications,
5 Southbrook Mews
SE12 8LG Tel: 020 8318 9580
office@francisjoseph.com

Murray Cards (International) Ltd,
51 Watford Way,
Hendon Central NW4 3JH
Tel: 020 8202 5688
murraycards@ukbusiness.com
www.murraycards.com/
Cigarette and trade cards.

Colin Narbeth & Son Ltd,
20 Cecil Court, Leicester Square
WC2N 4HE
Tel: 020 7379 6975

Onslow's, The Depot,
2 Michael Road SW6 2AD
Tel: 020 7371 0505
*19th and 20th century posters,
railwayana, motoring, aviation, Titanic
and ocean liner collectors items.
Sales held twice a year, usually April
and October.*

Stevie Pearce, G144 Ground Floor,
Alfies Antique Market, 13–25 Church
Street, Marylebone NW8 8DT
Tel: 020 7723 2526
Stevie@steviepearce.co.uk
www.SteviePearce.co.uk
*Costume jewellery and fashion
accessories 1900–70.*

Phillips, Blenstock House,
101 New Bond Street W1Y 0AS
Tel: 020 7629 6602/7468 8233
www.phillips-auctions.com
Auctioneer.

Planet Bazaar,
149 Drummond Street NW1 2PB
Tel: 0207 387 8326
maureen@planetbazaar.demon.co.uk
www.planetbazaar.co.uk

Rumours, 4 The Mall, Upper Street,
Camden Passage, Islington N1 0PD
Tel: 020 7704 6549
Rumdec@aol.com
Moorcroft pottery.

Sparkle Moore, The Girl Can't Help
It!/Cad Van Swankster, G100 & G116
Ground Floor, Alfies Antique Market,
13–25 Church Street,
Marylebone NW8 8DT
Tel: 020 7724 8984/020 8809 3923
sparkle.moore@virgin.net
www.grays.clara.net
*Open 11am–5pm Tues–Sat, 20thC
Pin up and period clothing,
accessories and collectables for sale
or hire.*

Totem, 168 Stoke Newington,
Church Street N16 0JL
Tel: 020 7275 0234
*LPs, MCs, CDs bought, sold and
exchanged.*

Vintage Cameras Ltd,
256 Kirkdale, Sydenham SE26 4NL
Tel: 020 8778 5416
info@vintagecameras.co.uk
www.vintagecameras.co.uk
Antique and classic cameras.

Nigel Williams Rare Books,
22 & 25 Cecil Court
WC2N 4HE
Tel: 020 7836 7757
*Books – first editions, illustrated,
childrens and detective.*

Wimbledon Sewing Machine Co Ltd
and The London Sewing Machine
Museum, 292–312 Balham High
Road, Upper Tooting SW17 7AA
Tel: 020 8767 4724
wimbledonsewingmachinecoltd@btint
ernet.com
www.sewantique.com

Yesterday Child, Angel Arcade,
118 Islington High Street N1 8EG
Tel: 020 7354 1601
*Antique dolls and dolls' house
miniatures.*

Zoom, Arch 65 Cambridge Grove,
Hammersmith W6
Tel: 07000 9666 2001
eddiesandham@hotmail.com
www.retrozoom.com

Middlesex
Hobday Toys Tel: 01895 636737
wendyhobday@freenet.co.uk
Tinplate toys, trains and dolls houses.

John Ives, 5 Normanhurst Drive,
Twickenham TW1 1NA
Tel: 020 8892 6265
jives@btconnect.com
*Reference books on antiques and
collecting.*

When We were Young, The Old
Forge, High Street Harmondsworth
Village UB7 0AQ
Tel: 020 8897 3583
www.whenwewereyoung.co.uk
*Collectable items related to British
childhood characters and illustrators.*

Norfolk
Roger Bradbury Antiques,
Church Street, Coltishall
NR12 7DJ
Tel: 01603 737444
Oriental pottery.

Cat Pottery, 1 Grammar School
Road, North Walsham NR28 9JH
Tel: 01692 402962
Animal pottery.

Northamptonshire
The Old Brigade, 10A Harborough
Road, Kingsthorpe NN2 7AZ
Tel: 01604 719389
Militaria.

Nottinghamshire
Tramps, Tuxford Hall, Lincoln Road,
Tuxford, Newark NG22 0HR
Tel: 01777 872 543
info@trampsuk.com
www.trampsuk.com

T. Vennett-Smith,
11 Nottingham Road, Gotham
NG11 0HE
Tel: 0115 983 0541
info@vennett-smith.com
Ephemera and sporting auctions.

Oxfordshire
Dauphin Museum Services,
PO Box 602, Oxford OX44 9LU
Tel: 01865 343542
Display stands.

Michael Jackson Antiques,
The Quiet Woman Antiques Centre,
Southcombe, Chipping Norton
OX7 5QH
Tel: 01608 646262
mjcig@cards.fsnet.co.uk
www.our-web-site.com/cigarette-cards

Otter Antiques, 20 High Street,
Wallingford OX10 0BP
Tel: 01491 825544

Alvin Ross, Pelham Puppets
Tel: 01865 772409
hidden.valley@virgin.net
freespace.virgin.net/hidden.valley

Stone Gallery, 93 The High Street,
Burford OX18 4QA
Tel: 01993 823302
mail@stonegallery.co.uk
www.stonegallery.co.uk
*Specialist dealers in antique and
modern paperweights, gold and silver
designer jewellery and enamel boxes.*

Teddy Bears of Witney,
99 High Street,
Witney OX8 6LY
Tel: 01993 702616

Pembrokeshire
Arch House Collectables,
St George Street, Tenby
SA70 7JB
Tel: 01834 843246

Republic of Ireland
Michelina & George Stacpoole,
Main Street, Adare,
Co Limerick
Tel: 00 353 6139 6409
Pottery, ceramics, silver and prints.

Whyte's Auctioneers,
30 Marlborough St, Dublin 1
Tel: 00 353 1 874 6161

Scotland
Bow Well Antiques, 103 West Bow,
Edinburgh EH1 2JP
Tel: 0131 225 3335
Specialists in all things Scottish.

Courtyard Antiques,
108A Causewayside,
Edinburgh EH9 1PU
Tel: 0131 662 9008

Edinburgh Coin Shop,
11 West Crosscauseway,
Edinburgh EH8 9JW
Tel: 0131 668 2928/0131 667 9095
Coins, medals, militaria and stamps.

Rhod McEwan – Golf Books,
Glengarden, Ballater,
Aberdeenshire AB35 5UB
Tel: 013397 55429
rhodmcewan@easynet.co.uk
rhodmcewan.co.uk
Rare and out-of-print golfing books.

Shropshire
Decorative Antiques,
47 Church Street,
Bishop's Castle
SY9 5AD
Tel: 01588 638851
enquiries@decorative-antiques.co.uk
www.decorative-antiques.co.uk

Mullock & Madeley,
The Old Shippon, Wall-under-
Heywood, Nr Church Stretton
SY6 7DS
Tel: 01694 771771
auctions@mullockmadeley.co.uk
www.mullockmadeley.co.uk
Sporting auctions.

Ulric of England, PO Box 55,
Church Stretton SY6 6WR
Tel: 01694 781354

Somerset
Antiques & Collectables Magazine,
Western Publishing Ltd,
30a Monmouth Street,
Bath BA1 2AN
Tel: 01225 311077
antiques.collectables@btinternet.com

Bath Antiques Online, Bartlett Street
Antiques Centre, Bartlett Street,
Bath BA1 2QZ
Tel: 01225 311061
info@bathantiquesonline.com
www.BathAntiquesOnline.com

Bath Dolls' Hospital,
2 Grosvenor Place, London Road,
Bath BA1 6PT
Tel: 01225 319668
Doll restoration.

Bonapartes, 13 George Street,
Bath BA1 2EN
Tel: 01225 423873
Military figures.

Lynda Brine, Assembly Antique
Centre, 5–8 Saville Row,
Bath BA1 2QP
Tel: 01225 448488
Perfume bottles.

Julia Craig, Bartlett Street Antiques
Centre, 5–10 Bartlett Street,
Bath BA1 2QZ
Tel: 01225 448202/310457

Philip Knighton, 11 North Street,
Wellington TA21 8LX
Tel: 01823 661618
*Wireless, gramophones and all valve
equipment.*

Joanna Proops Antique Textiles
& Lighting, 34 Belvedere,
Lansdown Hill, Bath BA1 5HR
Tel: 01225 310795
Textiles and lighting.

Richard Twort Tel: 01934 641900
*Barographs and all types of
meteorological instruments.*

Staffordshire
Cottage Collectibles,
62 High Street,
Eccleshall ST21 6BZ
Tel: 01785 850210
sheila@cottagecollectibles.co.uk
www.cottagecollectibles.co.uk
*Showroom open by appointment
only. English and Continental country
antiques and kitchenalia.*

Peggy Davies Ceramics,
28 Liverpool Road,
Stoke-on-Trent ST4 1VJ
Tel: 01782 848002
rhys@kevinfrancis.co.uk
www.kevinfrancis.co.uk
*Ceramics, limited edition Toby jugs
and figures.*

Keystones, PO Box 387,
Stafford ST16 3FG
Tel: 01785 256648
gkey@keystones.demon.co.uk
www.denbymatch.com
Denby pottery.

Gordon Litherland, 25 Stapenhill
Road, Burton-on-Trent
DE15 9AE
Tel: 01283 567213
*Bottles, breweriana and pub Jug
commemoratives.*

The Potteries Antique Centre,
271 Waterloo Road, Cobridge,
Stoke-on-Trent ST6 3HR
Tel: 01782 201455
www@potteriesantiquecentre.com

Trevor Russell, PO Box 1258,
Uttoxeter ST14 8XL
Fountain pens and repairs.

Suffolk
Jamie Cross, PO Box 73,
Newmarket CB8 8RY
jamiecross@aol.com
www.thirdreichmedals.com
*We buy and sell, value for probate
and insurance British, German and
foreign war medals, badges and
decorations.*

W. L. Hoad, 9 St Peter's Road,
Kirkley, Lowestoft
NR33 0LH
Tel: 01502 587758
William@whoad.fsnet.co.uk
www.cigarettecardsplus.com
Cigarette cards.

Surrey
David Aldous-Cook, PO Box 413,
Sutton SM3 8SZ
Tel: 020 8642 4842
*Reference books on antiques and
collectables.*

British Notes, PO Box 257,
Sutton SM3 9WW
Tel: 020 8641 3224
pamwestbritnotes@compuserve.com
www.west-banknotes.co.uk
Banking collectables.

Iain Burn, 2 Compton Gardens,
53 Park Road, Camberley GU15 2SP
Tel: 01276 23304
iainburn@altavista.net

Childhood Memories,
57 Downing Street,
Farnham GU9 7PN
Tel: 01252 793704
maureen@childhood-memories.co.uk
www.childhood-memories.co.uk
Antique Teddies, dolls and miniatures.

Julian Eade
Tel: 020 8394 1515

Howard Hope, 21 Bridge Road,
East Molesey KT8 9EU
Tel: 020 8941 2472/020 8398 7130
Phonographs and gramophones.

Psychemania 67, PO Box 640,
Sutton SM1 4YL
Tel: 01953 602872
psyche67@popposter67.co.uk
www.popposter67.co.uk

East Sussex
Tony Horsley Tel: 01273 550770
*Candle extinguishers, Royal
Worcester and other porcelain.*

Ann Lingard,
Ropewalk Antiques,
Rye TN31 7NA
Tel: 01797 223486

Liz Seeber, Old Cookery,
Food & Wine Books,
Apple Tree Cottage,
High Street, Barcombe,
Nr Lewes BN8 5DH
Tel: 01273 401485
seeber.books@virgin.net
www.lizseeberbooks.co.uk

Wallis & Wallis,
West Street Auction Galleries,
Lewes BN7 2NJ
Tel: 01273 480208
auctions@wallisandwallis.co.uk
www.wallisandwallis.co.uk
*Specialist auctioneers of militaria,
arms, armour, coins and medals. Also
die-cast and tinplate toys, teddy
bears, dolls, model railways, toy
soldiers and models.*

Wales
A.P.E.S. Rocking Horses,
Ty Gwyn, Llannefydd,
Denbigh LL16 5HB
Tel: 01745 540365
macphersons@apes-rocking-
horses.co.uk

Corgi Collector Club,
Dept MP00,
PO Box 323,
Swansea SA1 1BJ
Tel: 0870 607 1204

The Emporium,
112 St Teilo St,
Pontarddulais,
Nr Swansea SA4 1QH
Tel: 01792 885185
Brass and cast iron.

Jen Jones, Pontbrendu,
LLanybydder,
Ceredigion
SA40 9UJ
Tel: 01570 480610
*Quilt expert dealing mainly in Welsh
quilts and blankets. Between 200 and
300 quilts in stock with a comparable
number of blankets. Looking to buy
as well as sell.*

Islwyn Watkins,
Offa's Dyke Antique Centre,
4 High Street, Knighton,
Powys LD7 1AT
Tel: 01547 520145
*18th and 19thC pottery, 20thC
country and Studio pottery, small
country furniture, treen and bygones.*

Warwickshire
A.M. & S.E.,
PO Box 194,
Warwick CV34 5ZG
Tel: 0115 9474137/01926 497340
www.medalsandmilitaria.co.uk
*British, German, Japanese and USSR
medals, swords, militaria and aviation
items for sale and purchased. 'The
International', The National Motorcycle
Museum, Birmingham, the UK's
largest militaria fair, 24th February 2002.*

The Antique Shop,
30 Henley Street,
Stratford upon Avon
CV37 6QW
Tel: 01789 292485
*Dolls, teddy bears, fishing tackle,
glass, porcelain, jewellery, oriental,
silver and collectables.*

Chinasearch, 9 Princes Drive,
Kenilworth CV8 2FD
Tel: 01926 512402
helen@chinasearch.uk.com
www.chinasearch.uk.com

Chris James Medals & Militaria,
Warwick Antiques Centre,
22–24 High Street,
Warwick CV34 4AP
Tel: 01926 495704
medalsandmilitaria.co.uk
*British, German, Japanese and USSR
medals, swords, militaria and aviation
items. For sale and purchased.
'The International', The National
Motorcycle Museum, Birmingham.
The U.K's largest militaria fair – 2001
dates (all Sundays) 10th June, 16th
Sept, 25th Nov and 24th Feb 2002.
10am–3.30pm. A.M. & S.E., PO Box
194, Warwick. Tel: 0115 947 4137.*

Sporting Memorabilia of Warwick,
13 Market Place,
Warwick CV34 4FS
Tel: 01926 410600
sales@sportantiques.com
sportsantiques.com

Tango Art Deco & Antiques,
46 Brook Street,
Warwick CV34 4BL
Tel: 01926 496999/0121 704 4969
info@tango-artdeco.co.uk
tango-artdeco.co.uk
*Large Art Deco specialist shop.
Open Thur–Sat 10am–5pm.*

West Midlands
Antiques Magazine,
H.P. Publishing,
2 Hampton Court Road, Harborne,
Birmingham B17 9AE
Tel: 0121 681 8000
subscriptions@antiquesbulletin.com
www.antiquesbulletin.com

Wiltshire
Dominic Winter Book Auctions,
The Old School, Maxwell Street,
Swindon SN1 5DR
Tel: 01793 611340
info@dominic-winter.co.uk
www.dominic-winter.co.uk
*Auctions of antiquarian and general
printed books and maps, sports
books and memorabilia, art reference
and pictures, photography and
ephemera (including toys, games
collectables).*

Worcestershire
Aladdin's Cave,
John Edwards, 35 Upper Tything,
Worcester WR1 1JZ
Tel: 01905 731737
John@RoyalWorcester.freeserve.co.uk
www.royalworcester.freeserve.co.uk

BBM Jewellery & Coins
(W. V. Crook), 8–9 Lion Street,
Kidderminster DY10 1PT
Tel: 01562 744118
Antique jewellery and coins.

John Neale,
11A Davenport Drive,
The Willows, Bromsgrove B60 2DW
Tel: 01527 871000
Vintage train and toy auctions.

Yorkshire
Antique & Collectors' Centre,
35 St Nicholas Cliff, Scarborough
YO11 2ES Tel: 01723 365221
sales@collectors.demon.co.uk
collectors.demon.co.uk
*International dealers in stamps,
postcards, silver, gold, medals,
cigarette cards and many more
collectables.*

BBR, Elsecar Heritage Centre,
Wath Road, Elsecar, Barnsley
S74 8HJ Tel: 01226 745156
sales@bbrauctions.co.uk
www.onlinebbr.com
*Advertising, breweriana, pot lids, bottles,
Doulton and Beswick.*

Briar's C20th Decorative Arts,
Skipton Antiques & Collectors Centre,
The Old Foundry, Cavendish Street,
Skipton BD23 2AB
Tel: 01756 798641
*Art Deco ceramics, furniture and
Charlotte Rhead pottery.*

The Camera House,
Oakworth Hall, Colne Road (B6143),
Oakworth, Keighley BD22 7HZ
Tel: 01535 642333
colin@the-camera-house.co.uk
www.the-camera-house.co.uk
*Cameras and photographic
equipment from 1850. Purchases,
sales, part exchange and repairs.
Valuations for probate and insurance.
Open Thurs, Fri 10am–5pm Sat
10am–3pm. Prop. C Cox*

Country Collector,
11–12 Birdgate,
Pickering YO18 7AL
Tel: 01751 477481
*Art Deco ceramics, blue and white,
pottery and porcelain.*

Crested China Co, The Station
House, Driffield YO25 7PY
Tel: 01377 257042

Echoes, 650a Halifax Road,
Eastwood, Todmorden OL14 6DW
Tel: 01706 817505
*Antique costume, textiles including
linen, lace and jewellery.*

Gerard Haley, Hippins Farm,
Black Shawhead,
Nr Hebden Bridge HX7 7JG
Tel: 01422 842484

John & Simon Haley,
89 Northgate, Halifax HX1 1XF
Tel: 01422 822148/360434
Old toys and money boxes.

Harpers Jewellers Ltd,
2/6 Minster Gates, York YO1 7HL
Tel: 01904 632634
harplist@aol.com
www.vintage-watches.co.uk
Sothebys.com associate dealer

Linen & Lace, Shirley Tomlinson,
Halifax Antiques Centre,
Queens Road/Gibbet Street,
Halifax HX1 4LR
Tel: 01422 366657
*Antique linen, textiles, period
costume and accessories.*

Sheffield Railwayana Auctions,
43 Little Norton Lane,
Sheffield S8 8GA
Tel: 0114 274 5085
ian@sheffrail.freeserve.co.uk
www.sheffieldrailwayana.co.uk
*Railwayana, posters and models
auctions.*

North Yorkshire
Botany Bay Antiques & Polly's Dolls
Hospital, 8 Grape Lane, Whitby
YO22 4BA Tel: 01947 602007
dollshospital@botanybay.madasafish.
com
www.botanbayantiques.co.uk
*Commemorative ware, collectable
dolls, doll and teddy repairs, curios
and collectables.*

Directory of Collectors' Clubs

This directory is in no way complete. If you wish to be included in next year's directory or if you have a change of address or telephone number, please inform us by 1 November 2001.

Age of Jazz Ceramic Circle Internet circle for collectors of twenties and thirties ceramics www.ageofjazz.com
American Business Card Club Robin Cleeter, 38 Abbotsbury Road, Morden, Surrey SM4 5LQ
The Antiquarian Horological Society New House, High Street, Ticehurst, East Sussex TN5 7AL Tel: 01580 200155 Fax: 01580 201323 secretary@ahsoc.demon.co.uk www.ahsoc.demon.co.uk
Antique Collectors' Club 5 Church Street, Woodbridge, Suffolk IP12 1DS Tel: 01394 385501
Association of Bottled Beer Collectors 127 Victoria Park Road, Tunstall, Stoke-on-Trent, Staffordshire ST6 6DY Tel: 01782 821459 www.abbc.org
Association of Comic Enthusiasts: (ACE)! l'Hopiteau, St Martin du Fouilloux 79420, France Tel: 00 33 549 702114 user218763@aol.com www.collectorfair.com/clubs/aca/index.html
Avon Magpies Club Mrs W. A. Fowler, 36 Castle View Road, Portchester, Fareham, Hampshire PO16 9LA Tel: 02392 642393 wendy@avonmagpies.fsnet.co.uk
Badge Collectors' Circle Frank Setchfield, 57 Middleton Place, Loughborough, Leicestershire LE11 2BY Tel: 01509 212897 frank@setchfield.freeserve.co.uk www.thebadge.co.uk
The James Bond Collectors' Club PO Box 1570, Christchurch, Dorset BH23 4XS Tel: 01425 276736 (Mon–Fri 9–6) Tel/Fax: 01425 271396 (24 hrs) Solo@enterprise.net
British Art Medal Society Dept of Coins and Medals, The British Museum, London WC1B 3DG Tel: 020 7323 8260 Fax: 020 7323 8171 pattwood@thebritishmuseum.ac.uk www.bams.org.uk/
British Association of Sound Collections Alan Ward, National Sound Archive, The British Library, 96 Euston Road, London NW1 2DB
The British Beermat Collectors' Society Honorary Secretary, 69 Dunnington Avenue, Kidderminster, Worcestershire DY10 2YT
The British Button Society Mr Roger Millward, 8 Hawksworth Drive, Weston-super-Mare, Somerset BS22 7YT
British Compact Collectors' Society SAE to: PO Box 131, Woking, Surrey GU21 9YR
British Matchbox Label and Booklet Society Honorary Secretary, Arthur Alderton, 122 High Street, Melbourn, Cambridgeshire SG8 6AL www.enterprise.shv.hb.se/~match/bml&bs
British Model Soldier Society Honorary Secretary, 44 Danemead, Hoddesdon, Hertfordshire EN11 9LU Tel: 01992 441078 www.model.soldiers.btinternet.co.uk
British Numismatic Society Warburg Institute, Woburn Square, London WC1H 0AB
British Stickmakers' Guild Brian Aries, 44a Eccles Road, Chapel-en-le-Frith, Derbyshire SK12 6RG
British Teddy Bear Association PO Box 290, Brighton, East Sussex BN2 1DR

British Watch & Clock Collectors' Association Tony Woolven, 5 Cathedral Lane, Truro, Cornwall TR1 2QS Tel: 01872 264010 Fax: 01872 241953 tonybwcca@cs.com www.timecap.co.uk
Bunnykins News 7 Spout Copse, Sheffield S6 6FB bunnykinsnews@talk21.com
The Burleigh Ware International Collectors' Circle Tel: 01664 454570
The Buttonhook Society Paul Moorehead, 2 Romney Place, Maidstone, Kent ME15 6LE
The Buttonhook Society (US contact) Priscilla Stoffel, White Marsh, Box 287, MD 21162–0287, USA Tel: 410 256 5541 info@thebuttonhooksociety.com www.thebuttonhooksociety.com
Byngo Collectors' Club 23 Longhedge, Caldecotte, Buckinghamshire MK7 8LA
Calculator Collectors' Club 77 Welland Road, Tonbridge, Kent TN10 3TA
Cambridge Paperweight Circle Mr T. Johnson, PO Box 941, Comberton, Cambridge PDO, CB3 7GQ Tel: +44 (0)20 8337 7077 www.adc-ltd.demon.co.uk/paperweights
Carlton Ware Collectors International PO Box 161, Sevenoaks, Kent TN15 6GA Tel: 01474 853630 Fax: 01474 854385 cwiclub@aol.com
The Carnival Glass Society (UK) Limited PO Box 14, Hayes, Middlesex UB3 5NU cgs.sec@btinternet.com
The Cartophilic Society of Great Britain Ltd Membership Secretary, Alan Stevens, 63 Ferndale Road, Church Crookham, Fleet, Hampshire GU13 0LN Tel: 01252 621586 www.cardclubs.ndirect.co.uk
Charlotte Rhead Newsletter 49 Honeybourne Road, Halesowen, West Midlands B63 3ET www.tubeliners.com
Chintzworld International Dancers End, Northall, Bedfordshire LU6 2EU www.chintzworld-intl.com
The City of London Photograph & Gramophone Society Ltd Membership Secretary, Suzanne Coleman, 51 Brockhurst Road, Chesham, Buckinghamshire HP5 3JB
Clarice Cliff Collectors' Club Fantasque House, Tennis Drive, The Park, Nottingham NG7 1AE www.claricecliff.com
The Comic Journal Bryon Whitworth, l'Hopiteau, St Martin du Fouilloux 79420, France Tel: 00 33 549 702114 user218763@aol.com www.collectorfair.com/clubs/ace/index.html
Commemorative Collectors' Society Steven Jackson, Lumless House, Gainsborough Road, Winthorpe, Newark, Nottinghamshire NG24 2NR Tel: 01636 671377
Susie Cooper Collectors' Club Fantasque House, Tennis Drive, The Park, Nottingham NG7 1AE www.susiecooper.co.uk
Corgi Collector Club Dept MP00, PO Box 323, Swansea, Wales SA1 1BJ Tel/Fax: 0870 607 1204
Cornish Collectors' Club PO Box 58, Buxton, Derbyshire SK17 0FH Tel: 01298 687070 Fax: 01298 687071 Cornish@btconnect.com

The Costume Society St Paul's House, Warwick Lane, London EC4P 4BN
www.costumesociety.org.uk

The Crested Circle 42 Douglas Road, Tolworth, Surbiton, Surrey KT6 7SA

Cricket Memorabilia Society Tony Sheldon, 29 Highclere Road, Crumpsall, Greater Manchester M8 4WH

The Crunch Club (Breakfast Cereal Collectables) John Cahill, 9 Weald Rise, Tilehurst, Reading, Berkshire RG30 6XB Tel: 0118 942 7291 Fax: 0118 941 5471 crunch@jcahill99.freeserve.co.uk

Danesby Collectors' Club (from April 2001) Fantasque House, Tennis Drive, The Park, Nottingham NG7 1AE
www.danesby.co.uk

Doll Club of Great Britain 16E Chalwyn Ind Est, St Clements Road, Parkstone, Poole, Dorset BH15 3PE

Egg Cup Collectors' Club of Great Britain Sue Wright suewright@sue.coll.freeserve.co.uk

Embroiderers' Guild Mrs F. Parsons, Apartment 41, Hampton Court Palace, East Molesey, Surrey KT8 9AU

The English Playing Card Society Major Donald Welsh, 11 Pierrepont Street, Bath, Somerset BA1 1LA

ETB Radford Collectors' Club 32 Westbourne Avenue, Clevedon, Somerset BS21 7UA
Tel: 01275 871359/02392 267483

The European Honeypot Collectors' Society John Doyle, The Honeypot, 18 Victoria Road, Chislehurst, Kent BR7 6DF
John@thehoneypot10.freeserve.co.uk

Fan Circle International Secretary, Mrs Joan Milligan, Cronk-y-Voddy, Rectory Road, Coltishall, Norwich NR12 7HF

Festival of Britain Society Martin Packer, 41 Lyall Gardens, Birmingham, West Midlands B45 9YW
Tel: 0121 453 8245
martin@packer34.freeserve.co.uk
www.packer34.freeserve.co.uk

Fieldings Crown Devon Collectors' Club PO Box 74, Corbridge, Northumberland NE45 5YP

The Flag Institute 9 Laurel Grove, Chester CH2 3HH

Friends of Blue Terry Sheppard, 45a Church Road, Bexley Heath, Kent DA7 4DD
www.fob.org.uk/bull02.htm

Friends of Broadfield House Glass Museum Compton Drive, Kingswinford, West Midlands DY6 9NS

Friends of Fred Homepride Flour Men Jennifer Woodward Tel: 01925 826158

The Furniture History Society Dr Brian Austen, 1 Mercedes Cottages, St John's Road, Haywards Heath, West Sussex RH16 4EH Tel: 01444 413845

Goss Collectors' Club Mrs Schofield
Tel: 0115 930 0441

Goss & Crested China Club & Museum incorporating Milestone Publications 62 Murray Road, Horndean, Hampshire PO8 9JL
Tel: 023 9259 7440 Fax: 023 9259 1975
info@gosschinaclub.demon.co.uk

Hagen Renaker Collectors' Club Chris & Derek Evans, 97 Campbell Road, Burton, Christchurch, Dorset BH23 7LY Tel: 01202 245076
Fax: 01202 471698
dwdevans@dwdevans.screaming.net
www.priorycollectables.co.uk

Robert Harrop Collectors' Club Robert Harrop Designs Ltd, Coalport House, Lamledge Lane, Shifnal, Shropshire TF11 8SD Tel: 01952 462721
www.robertharrop.com

The Hat Pin Society of Great Britain PO Box 110, Cheadle SK8 1GG

Historical Model Railway Society 59 Woodberry Way, London E4 7DY

Honiton Pottery Collectors' Society Robin Tinkler, 12 Beehive Lane, Gt Baddow, Chelmsford, Essex CM2 9SX

The Hornby Railway Collectors' Association 2 Ravensmore Road, Sherwood, Nottingham NG5 2AH

Hornsea Pottery Collectors' and Research Society Val and Terry Healey, 32 Hill View Road, Chelmsford, Essex CM1 7RX Terry@hornseacollector.co.uk
www.hornseacollector.co.k

Hurdy-Gurdy Society Doreen Muskett, The Old Mill, Duntish, Dorchester, Dorset DT2 7DR

Inn Sign Society Chairman, Mr R. P. Gatrell, 20 Rivington Road, Hale, Altrincham, Cheshire WA15 9PH

International Bank Note Society 36B Dartmouth Park Hill, London NW5 1HN

International Bond and Share Society Peter Duppa-Miller, Beechcroft, Combe Hay, Bath, Somerset BA2 7EG

International Collectors of Time Association 173 Coleherne Court, Redcliffe Gardens, London SW5 0DX

International Correspondence of Corkscrew Addicts Don MacLean, 4201 Sunflower Drive, Mississauga, Ontario L5L 2L4, Canada

International Perfume Bottle Association Lynda Brine, Assembly Antique Centre, 5–8 Saville Row, Bath, Somerset BA1 2QP
Tel: 01225 448482 Fax: 01225 429661
info@ukpbcc.co.uk www.ukpbcc.co.uk

King George VI Collectors' Society (Philately) 98 Albany, Manor Road, Bournemouth, Dorset BH1 3EW

The Knife Rest Collectors' Club Doreen Hornsblow, Braughingbury, Braughing, Hertfordshire SG11 2RD
Tel: 01920 822654

The Lace Guild The Hollies, 53 Audnam, Stourbridge, West Midlands DY8 4AE

Legend Lane Collector's Club Albion Mill, London Road, Macclesfield, Cheshire SK11 7SQ

Lock Collectors' Club Mr Richard Phillips, Merlewood, The Loan, West Linton, Peeblesshire EH46 7HE
Tel: 01968 661039 rphillips52@btinternet.com

The Maling Collectors' Society PO Box 1762, North Shields NE30 4YJ www.maling-pottery.org.uk

Manor Ware Club 66 Shirburn Road, Upton, Torquay, Devon TQ1 4HR

The Matchbox International Collectors' Association Stewart Orr, The Toy Museum, 13a Lower Bridge Street, Chester CH1 1RS

Mauchline Ware Collectors' Club Secretary, Mrs Christabelle Davey, Unit 37 Romsey Industrial Estate, Greatbridge Road, Romsey, Hampshire SO51 0HR
Tel: 0113 275 2730 www.mauchlineclub.org

Memories UK Mabel Lucie Attwell Club Abbey Antiques, 63 Great Whyte, Ramsey, Nr Huntingdon, Cambridgeshire PE26 1HL
Tel: 01487 814753

Merrythought International Collectors' Club Ironbridge, Telford, Shropshire TF8 7NJ

The Model Railway Club The Secretary, Keen House, 4 Calshot Street, London N1 9DA
www.themodelrailwayclub.org

Moorcroft Collectors' Club W. Moorcroft PLC, Sandbach Road, Burslem, Stoke-on-Trent, Staffordshire ST6 2DQ
Tel: 01782 820510 Fax: 01782 820501
cclub@moorcroft.com www.moorcroft.com

Muffin the Mule Collectors' Club 12 Woodland Close, Woodford Green, Essex IG8 0QH
Tel/Fax: 020 8504 4943
ra@hasler.fsnet.co.uk www.Muffin-the-Mule.com

Keith Murray Collectors' Club (Patron Constance Murray), Fantasue House, Tennis Drive, The Park, Nottingham NG7 1AE
www.keithmurray.co.uk

Musical Box Society of Great Britain PO Box 299, Waterbeach, Cambridgeshire CB4 8DT
mbsgb@kreedman.globalnet.co.uk
www.mbsgb.org.uk

National Horse Brass Society 12 Severndale, Droitwich Spa, Worcestershire WR9 8PD

New Baxter Society Membership Secretary, 205 Marshalswick Lane, St Albans, Hertfordshire AL1 4XA
www.rpsfamily.demon.co.uk

Observers Pocket Series Collectors' Society (OPSCS) Secretary, Alan Sledger, 10 Villiers Road, Kenilworth, Warwickshire CV8 2JB Tel: 01926 857047

The Official International Wade Collectors' Club Royal Works, Westport Road, Burslem, Stoke on Trent, Staffordshire ST6 4AP
club@wade.co.uk
www.wade.co.uk/wade

Old Bottle Club of Great Britain Alan Blakeman, c/o BBR, Elsecar Heritage Centre, Nr Barnsley, Yorkshire S74 8HJ Tel: 01226 745156
Fax: 01226 361561

The Old Hall Club Nigel Wiggin, Sandford House, Levedale, Stafford ST18 9AH Tel: 01785 780376
oht@gnwiggin.freeserve.co.uk
www.oldhallclub.co.uk

Ophthalmic Antiques International Collectors' Club 3 Moor Park Road, Northwood, Middlesex HA6 2DL

Orders and Medals Research Society 123 Turnpike Link, Croydon, Surrey CR0 5NU

The Oriental Ceramic Society The Secretary, 30b Torrington Square, London WC1E 7JL

Pendelfin Family Circle Collectors' Club Cameron Mill, Howsin Street, Burnley, Lancashire BB10 1PP Tel: 01282 432301
boswell@pendelfin.co.uk
www.pendelfin.co.uk

The Family Circle of Pendelfin Susan Beard, 230 Spring Street N.W., Suite 1238, Atlanta, Georgia 30303, USA

Pewter Society Llananant Farm, Penallt, Monmouth NP25 4AP Fax: 0870 167 4633
hayw@clara.net
www.members.aol.com/pewtrsocty/

Photographic Collectors' Club of Great Britain Membership Office P.C.C.G.B., 5 Buntingford Road, Puckeridge, Ware, Hertfordshire SG11 1RT
Tel: 01920 821611

Poole Pottery Collectors' Club Clive Bailey, The Quay, Poole, Dorset BH15 1RF
Tel: 01202 666200 Fax: 01202 676076
www.poolepottery.co.uk

The Postcard Club of Great Britain Mrs D. Brennan, 34 Harper House, St James's Crescent, London SW9 7LW Tel: 020 7771 9404

Potteries of Rye Society Membership Secretary, Barry Buckton, 2 Redyear Cottages, Kennington Road, Ashford, Kent TN24 0TF Tel: 01233 647898

Quimper Association Odin, Benbow Way, Cowley, Uxbridge, Middlesex UB8 2HD

Railwayana Collectors' Journal 7 Ascot Road, Moseley, Birmingham, West Midlands B13 9EN

Royal Doulton International Collectors' Club Minton House, London Road, Stoke-on-Trent, Staffordshire ST4 7QD Tel: 01782 292375
www.icc@royal-doulton.com

The Royal Numismatic Society Mr Joseph Cribb, Dept of Coins & Medals, The British Museum, London WC1B 3DG

The Russian Doll Collectors' Club Gardener's Cottage, Hatchlands, East Clandon, Surrey GU4 7RT
Tel: 01483 222789 Fax: 01483 211114
graham@ckazka.demon.co.uk
www.ckazka.demon.co.uk/russiandollclub

Scientific Instrument Society Wg Cdr G. Bennett, Executive Officer, 31 High Street, Stanford in the Vale, Faringdon, Oxfordshire SN7 8LH Tel: 01367 710223
www.sis.org.uk

Scottish Exhibitions Study Group S. K. Hunter, 34 Gray Street, Glasgow, Scotland G3 7TY

The Shelley Group 4 Fawley Road, Regents Park, Southampton, Hampshire SO2 1LL

Silhouette Collectors' Club Diana Joll, Flat 5, 13 Brunswick Sq, Hove, East Sussex BN3 1EH

The Silver Spoon Club of Great Britain Terry & Mary Haines, Glenleigh Park, Sticker, St Austell, Cornwall PL26 7JD Tel/Fax: 01726 65269
enquiries@silver-spoon.com

Snuff Bottle Society Michael Kaynes, 1 Tollard Court, West Hill Road, Bournemouth, Dorset BH2 5EH
Tel/Fax: 01202 292867
mikekaynes@snuffbottles.madasafish.com

The Soviet Collector's Club PO Box 56, Saltburn-by-the-Sea, Cleveland TS12 1YD
www.sovietclub.com

St Clere Carlton Ware PO Box 161, Sevenoaks, Kent TN15 6GA Tel: 01474 853630 Fax: 01474 854385
stclere@aol.com

The SylvaC Collectors' Circle SAE to 174 Portsmouth Road, Horndean, Waterlooville, Hampshire PO8 9HP
Tel: 023 9259 1725 Fax: 023 9278 8494
sylvac.club@cwc.net www.sylvac.cwc.net

Telecommunications Heritage Group PO Box 561, South Croydon, Surrey CR2 6YL
www.thg.org.uk

The Thimble Society of London Bridget McConnel, The Portobello Studios, 101 Portobello Road, London W11 2OB Open Sat only

Toby Fillpot Memorial Club Membership Secretary, Vadim Linetski, 609a High Road, Leyton, London E10 6RF

The Tool and Trades History Society Chris Hudson, 60 Swanley Lane, Swanley, Kent BR8 7JG

Torquay Pottery Collectors' Society Torre Abbey, Avenue Road, Torquay, Devon TQ2 5JX
tpcs@btinternet.com www.scandyonline.com

Totally Teapots The Novelty Teapot Collectors' Club Vince McDonald, Euxton, Chorley, Lancashire PR7 6EY
Tel/Fax: 01257 450366
vince@totallyteapots.com www.totallyteapots.com

Train Collectors' Society Joe Swain, Lock Cottage, Station Foot Path, Kings Langley, Hertfordshire WD4 8DZ

The Transport Ticket Society Membership Secretary, Courtney Haydon, 4 Gladridge Close, Earley, Reading, Berkshire RG6 7DL Tel: 0118 9264109
courtney@gladridgecl.demon.co.uk

Trix Twin Railway Collectors' Association Mr C. B. Arnold, 6 Ribble Avenue, Oadby, Leicester LE2 4NZ

The Victorian Military Society 20 Priory Road, Newbury, Berkshire RG14 7QN Tel: 01635 48628

The Vintage Model Yacht Group Trevor Smith, 1A Station Avenue, Epsom, Surrey KT19 9UD
Tel: 020 8393 1100

The Wedgwood Society of Great Britain PO Box 5921, Bishop's Stortford CM22 7FB

Kathie Winkle Collectors' Club SAE to Mrs Nadin-Leath, Greenacres, Calbourne Road, Carisbrooke, Isle of Wight PO30 5AP

The Writing Equipment Society Mr John Daniels, 33 Glanville Road, Hadleigh, Ipswich, Suffolk IP7 5SQ

Directory of Markets & Centres

Buckinghamshire

Jackdaw Antiques Centres Ltd, 25 West Street, Marlow SL7 2LS Tel: 01628 898285
sales@jackdaw-antiques.co.uk
www.jackdaw-antiques.co.uk
1,500 sq.ft. of furniture, collectables, silver, china, specialist areas, books, Victorian glass, Quimper, coins, fishing tackle.

Cheshire

Davenham Antique Centre, 461 London Road, Davenham, Northwich CW9 8NA
Shop Tel: 01606 44350 Fax: 01606 782317
maxwells@connectfree.co.uk
www.antiques-atlas.com/davenham.htm

Derbyshire

Alfreton Antique Centre, 11 King Street, Alfreton DE55 7AF Tel: 01773 520781
www.alfretonantiques.supanet.com
30 dealers on 2 floors. Antiques, collectables, furniture, books, militaria, postcards, silverware. Open 7 days Mon–Sat 10am–4.30pm, Sun 11am–4.30pm.

Chappells & The Antiques Centre – Bakewell, King Street, Bakewell DE45 1DZ
Tel: 01629 812496 bacc@chappells-antiques.co.uk
www.Chappells-antiques.co.uk
30 dealers inc. BADA & LAPADA members. Quality period furniture, ceramics, silver, plate, metals, treen, clocks, barometers, books, pictures, maps, prints, textiles, kitchenalia, lighting and furnishing accessories from the 17th–20thC, scientific, pharmaceutical and sporting antiques. Open Mon–Sat 10am–5pm, Sun 11am–5pm. Closed Christmas Day, Boxing Day & New Year's Day. Please ring for brochure.

Heanor Antiques Centre, Ilkeston Road, Heanor DE75 Tel: 01773 531181
Open 7 days 10.30am–4.30pm. 70+ dealers.

Matlock Antiques, Collectables & Riverside Café, 7 Dale Road, Matlock DE4 3LT
Tel: 01629 760808 Proprietor W. Shirley.
Over 70 dealers.

Devon

Quay Centre Topsham, Nr Exeter EX3 0JA
Tel: 01392 874006
80 dealers on 3 floors. Antiques, collectables and traditional furnishings. Ample parking. Open 7 days, 10am–5pm. All major cards accepted.

Essex

Gallerie Antiques, 62–70 Fowler Road, Hainault IG6 3XE Tel: 020 8501 2229
Over 80 dealers in 10,000 sq.ft. Furniture, porcelain, glass, pictures, militaria and much more. Mon–Sat 10am–5.30pm, Sun 10am–5pm.

Gloucestershire

Durham House Antiques Centre, Sheep Street, Stow-on-the-Wold GL54 1AA Tel: 01451 870404
30+ dealers. Town and country furniture, metalware, books, ceramics, kitchenalia, silver, jewellery, sewing ephemera and art. Mon–Sat 10am–5pm, Sun 11am–5pm. Stow-on-the-Wold, Cotswold home to over 40 antique shops, galleries and bookshops.

Hampshire

Dolphin Quay Antique Centre, Queen Street, Emsworth PO10 7BU Tel: 01243 379994
www.antiquesbulletin.com/dolphinquay
Open 7 days a week (inc. Bank Holidays) Mon–Sat 10am–5pm, Sun 10am–4pm. Marine, naval antiques, paintings, watercolours, prints, antique clocks, decorative arts, furniture, sporting apparel, luggage, specialist period lighting, conservatory, garden antiques, fine antique/country furniture, French/antique beds.

Lymington Antiques Centre, 76 High Street, Lymington SO41 9AL Tel: 01590 670934

Hereford

The Hay Antique Market, 6 Market Street, Hay-on-Wye HR3 5AF Tel: 01497 820175
Open 6 days 10am–5pm, Sun 11am–5pm. 17 separate units on 2 floors selling pine, country and period furniture. Rural and rustic items. China, glass, jewellery, linen and period clothes. Pictures, lighting, brass and collectables.

Mulberry's Antiques & Collectables, 30–32 St Owen Street, Hereford HR1 2PR
Tel: 01432 269925
A wide range of antiques and collectables on 2 floors – furniture, fine china, porcelain, silver, jewellery, textiles, pre-1930s clothing and accessories, objets d'art, prints, oils and watercolours. Trade welcome.

Humberside

Hull Antique Centre, Anderson Wharf, Wincolmlee, Hull HU2 8AH Tel: 01482 609958
www.@thehullantiquecentre.com
Open Mon–Fri 9am–5pm, Sat & Sun 10am–4pm.

Kent

Castle Antiques, 1 London Road (next to Post Office), Westerham TN16 1BB
Tel: 01959 562492
Open Mon–Sat 10am–5pm. Phone for Sun times. 4 rooms of antiques, small furniture, collectables, rural bygones, tools, costume, glass, books, linens, jewellery, kitsch, retro-clothing. Services: advice, valuations, theatre props, house clearance. Talks on antiques.

Malthouse Arcade, High Street,
Hythe CT21 5BW Tel: 01303 260103

Sidcup Antique & Craft Centre, Elm Parade, Main
Road, Sidcup DA14 6NF Tel: 020 8300 7387
*Over 100 dealers and crafts people. Open
7 days 10am–5pm.*

Lancashire

The Antique & Decorative Design Centre,
56 Garstang Road, Preston PR1 1NA
Tel: 01772 882078 Fax: 01772 252842
www.antiqueweb.co.uk-centre-
*Open 7 days a week 10am–5pm. 25,000 sq.ft.
of quality antiques, objets d'art, clocks, pine,
silverware, porcelain, upholstery, French
furniture for the home and garden.*

GB Antiques Centre, Lancaster Leisure Park,
(the former Hornsea Pottery), Wyresdale Road,
Lancaster LA1 3LA Tel: 01524 844734
*140 dealers in 40,000 sq.ft. of space.
Porcelain, pottery, Art Deco, glass, books,
linen, mahogany, oak and pine furniture. Open
7 days 10am–5pm.*

Kingsmill Antique Centre, Queen Street, Harle
Syke, Burnley BB10 2HX
Tel: 01282 431953

Leicestershire

Oxford Street Antiques Centre, 16–26 Oxford
Street, Leicester LE1 5XU Tel: 0116 255 3006
*30,000 sq.ft. on 4 floors. Extensive range of
Victorian, Edwardian and later furniture etc.
Open Mon–Fri 10am–5.30pm, Sat 10am–5pm,
Sun 2–5pm.*

Lincolnshire

St Martins Antiques Centre, 23a High Street,
St Martins, Stamford PE9 2LE Tel: 01780 481158
peter@st-martins-antiques.co.uk
www.st-martins-antiques.co.uk

London

Alfie's Antique Market, 13–25 Church Street,
Marylebone NW8 8DT Tel: 020 7723 6066
Fax: 020 7724 0999
post@ealfies.com www.ealfies.com

Grays Antique Market, 1–7 Davies Mews
W1K 5AB Tel: 020 7629 7034
Fax: 020 7493 9344 grays@clara.net
www.graysantiques.com

Northcote Road Antique Market,
155a Northcote Road, Battersea SW11 6QB
Tel: 020 7228 6850

Palmers Green Antiques Centre,
472 Green Lanes, Palmers Green N13 5PA
Tel: 020 8350 0878 Mobile: 0785 506 7544
*Over 40 dealers. Specializing in furniture,
jewellery, clocks, pictures, porcelain, china,
glass, silver and plate, metalware, kitchenalia
and lighting etc. Open 6 days a week, closed*

*Tues. Weekdays & Sats 10am–5.30pm, Sun
11am–5pm, open Bank Holidays. Removals and
house clearances, probate quality antiques and
collectables sold on commission basis.*

Norfolk

Tombland Antique Centre, Augustine Steward
House, 14 Tombland, Norwich
NR3 1HF Tel: 01603 619129

Northamptonshire

The Brackley Antique Cellar, Drayman's Walk,
Brackley NN13 6BE Tel: 01280 841841
*Situated under the Co-op supermarket. Open
7 days 10am–5pm. Very large range of antiques
and collectables. 30,000 sq.ft. of showroom
with up to 80 dealers. Disabled access.*

Nottinghamshire

Newark Antiques Centre, Regent House,
Lombard Street, Newark NG24 1XP
Tel: 01636 605504

Oxfordshire

Antiques on High, 85 High Street, Oxford
OX1 4BG Tel: 01865 251075
*Open 7 days a week 10am–5pm. Sun & Bank
Holidays 11am–5pm. 35 dealers with a wide
range of quality stock.*

Jackdaw Antiques Centres Ltd, 5 Reading
Road, Henley-on-Thames RG9 0AS
Tel: 01491 572289 sales@jackdaw-antiques.co.uk
www.jackdaw-antiques.co.uk
*Approx 1,000 sq.ft. of collectables (modern
& discontinued), furniture, books, specialist
areas, Carlton Ware, Doulton, Beswick.*

Lamb Arcade Antiques Centre, High Street,
Wallingford OX10 0BS Tel: 01491 835166
*Open 10am–5pm daily, Sat till 5.30pm, Bank
Holidays 11am–5pm. Furniture, silver, porcelain,
glass, books, boxes, crafts, rugs, jewellery,
lace and linens, pictures, tin toys, motoring
and aviation memorabilia, antique stringed
instruments, sports and fishing items,
decorative and ornamental items.*

Shropshire

Stretton Antiques Market, Sandford Avenue,
Church Stretton SY6 6BH Tel: 01694 723718

Somerset

Bartlett Street Antique Centre, 5–10 Bartlett
Street, Bath BA1 2QZ Tel: 01225 466689

Fountain Antiques Market, 6 Bladud Buildings,
The Paragon, Bath BA1 5LS
Tel: 01225 339104 Mobile: 07980 623926
*Open Mon–Sat 10am–5pm, Weds 7am–5pm.
BABADA members offering a selection of
antiques and collectables including glass and
china, silver plate, militaria, small furniture,
garden collectables, kitchenware, costume and
textiles, costume jewellery and beaded bags.*

Staffordshire

Rugeley Antique Centre, 161 Main Road, Brereton, Nr Rugeley WS15 1DX
Tel: 01889 577166
Open Mon–Sat 9am–5pm, Sun & Bank Holidays 12 noon–4.30pm. Find us: A51, 1 mile south of Rugeley.

Tutbury Mill Antiques Centre, Tutbury Mill Mews, Tutbury DE13 9LU Tel: 01283 520074
www.antiquesplus.co.uk
Open Mon–Sat 10.30am–5.30pm, Sun 12 noon–5pm

Surrey

Maltings Monthly Market, Bridge Square, Farnham GU9 7QR Tel: 01252 726234
FarnMalt@aol.com www.farnhammaltings.com

West Sussex

Roundabout Antiques Centre, 7 Commercial Square, Haywards Heath RH16 7DW
Tel: 01273 835926 roundabout@mistral.co.uk
Several specialist dealers with good quality extensive stock, including musical instruments. Open Mon–Sat 9.30am–5.30pm.

Tyne & Wear

The Antique Centre, 2nd floor, 142 Northumberland Street, Newcastle-upon-Tyne NE1 7DQ Tel: 0191 232 9832
Mon–Sat 10am–5pm

Wales

Afonwen Antiques & Craft Centre, Afonwen, Nr Caerwys, Mold CH7 5UB Tel: 01352 720965
The largest Antique and Craft Centre in North Wales and the Borders. 14,000 sq.ft. 40 dealers, antiques, china, silver, crystal, quality collectables. Fine furniture, oak, walnut, mahogany and pine from around the world. Open all year Tues–Sun, 9.30am–5.30pm. Closed Mon, except open all Bank Holiday Mon.

Offa's Dyke Antique Centre, 4 High Street, Knighton, Powys LD7 1AT
Tel: 01547 520145

Warwickshire

Barn Antiques Centre, Station Road, Long Marston, Nr Stratford-upon-Avon CV37 8RB
Tel: 01789 721399
One of the largest traditional Antique Centres in the Midlands. Now over 13,000 sq.ft. Open 7 days 10am–5pm. Antique furniture, antique pine, linen and lace, old fireplaces and surrounds, collectables, pictures and prints, silver, china, ceramics and objet d'art.

Dunchurch Antiques Centre, 16a Daventry Road, Dunchurch (Nr Rugby)
Tel: 01788 522450
Under new management.

The Stables Antique Centre, Hatton Country World, Dark Lane, Hatton, Warwick CV35 7LD
Tel: 01926 842405
25 independent dealers. Come and browse in friendly surroundings.

Stratford Antiques Centre, 59–60 Ely Street, Stratford-upon-Avon CV37 6LN Tel: 01789 204180

West Midlands

Birmingham Antique Centre, 1407 Pershore Road, Stirchley, Birmingham B30 2JR
Tel: 0121 459 4587 Fax: 0121 689 6566

Worcestershire

Worcester Antiques Centre, Unit 15, Reindeer Court, Mealcheapen Street, Worcester WR1 4DS
Tel: 01905 610680
Open Mon–Sun 10am–5pm, Mon–Sat 10am–5pm (Dec). Porcelain, silver, jewellery, Art Nouveau, Arts & Crafts, leather.

Yorkshire

Cavendish Antique & Collectors' Centre, 44 Stonegate, York YO1 8AS Tel: 01904 621666
Open 7 days a week 9am–6pm. Over 50 dealers on 3 floors.

Stonegate Antiques Centre, 41 Stonegate, York YO1 8AW Tel: 01904 613888
Open 9am–6pm 7 days a week. Over 110 dealers on 2 floors.

Key to Illustrations

Each illustration and descriptive caption is accompanied by a letter code. By referring to the following list of Auctioneers (denoted by *) and Dealers (•), the source of any item may be immediately determined. Inclusion in this edition in no way constitutes or implies a contract or binding offer on the part of any of our contributors to supply or sell the goods illustrated, or similar articles, at the prices stated. Advertisers in this year's directory are denoted by (†).

If you require a valuation for an item, it is advisable to check whether the dealer or specialist will carry out this service and if there is a charge. Please mention Miller's when making an enquiry. Having found a specialist who will carry out your valuation it is best to send a photograph and description of the item to the specialist together with a stamped addressed envelope for the reply. A valuation by telephone is not possible. Most dealers are only too happy to help you with your enquiry; however, they are very busy people and consideration of the above points would be welcomed.

A&H• Architectural & Historical Salvage, Spa Street, Ossett, Wakefield, Yorkshire WF5 0HJ Tel: 01924 262831

A&J• A & J Collectables, Bartlett Street Antique Centre, 10 Bartlett Street, Bath, Somerset BA1 2QZ Tel: 01225 466689

AAN No longer trading

ACO• Angela & Clive Oliver, 68 Watergate Street, Chester CH1 2LA Tel: 01244 312306/335157

ADE• Art Deco Etc, 73 Upper Gloucester Road, Brighton, East Sussex BN1 3LQ Tel: 01273 329268 poolepottery@artdeco.co.uk

AEF • A & E Foster Tel: 01494 562024

AEL • Argyll Etkin Ltd, 1–9 Hills Place, Oxford Circus, London W1R 1AG Tel: 020 7437 7800 argyll.etkin@btconnect.com

AG * Anderson & Garland (Auctioneers), Marlborough House, Marlborough Crescent, Newcastle-upon-Tyne, Tyne & Wear NE1 4EE Tel: 0191 232 6278

AH * Andrew Hartley, Victoria Hall Salerooms, Little Lane, Ilkley, Yorkshire LS29 8EA Tel: 01943 816363

AHa •† Adrian Harrington, 64a Kensington Church Street, London W8 4DB Tel: 020 7937 1465

AIL • Antique Irish Linen, Dublin, Republic of Ireland Tel: 00 353 1 451 2775

AL •† Ann Lingard, Ropewalk Antiques, Rye, East Sussex TN31 7NA Tel: 01797 223486

ALA • Alexander Antiques, Post House, Small Dole, Henfield, West Sussex BN5 9XE Tel: 01273 493121

ALiN • Andrew Lineham Fine Glass, The Mall, Camden Passage, London N1 8ED Tel: 020 7704 0195/01243 576241

AMc •† Antique Amusement Co, Mill Lane, Swaffham, Bulbeck, Cambridgeshire CB5 0NF Tel: 01223 813041 www.aamag.co.uk

AMH • Amherst Antiques, Monomark House, 27 Old Gloucester Street, London WC1N 3XX Tel: 01892 725552 amherstantiques@monomark.co.uk

AMR • Amron Antiques Tel: 01782 566895

AND • Joan & Bob Anderson Tel: 020 8572 4328

ANG •† Chris Belton, PO Box 356, Christchurch, Dorset BH23 1XQ Tel: 01202 478592

Ann • Annie's Dolls & Teddies Tel: 01424 882437 anniestoys@btinternet.com www.anniestoys.com

ANO • Art Nouveau Originals, Stamford Antiques Centre, The Exchange Hall, Broad Street, Stamford, Lincolnshire PE9 1PX Tel: 01780 762605

AnS •† The Antique Shop, 30 Henley Street, Stratford upon Avon, Warwickshire CV37 6QW Tel: 01789 292485

AnSh • Antique Shop, 136A High Street, Tenterden, Kent TN30 6HT Tel: 01580 764323

ANTH • Anthea, Grays Antique Market, South Molton Lane, London W1Y 2LP Tel: 020 7493 7564

AOH • Antiques on High, 85 High Street, Oxford OX1 4BG Tel: 01865 251075

AOT • Annie's Old Things, PO Box 6, Camphill, Queensland 4152, Australia Tel: 0061412353099 annie@fan.net.au

APC • Antique Photographic Company Ltd Tel: 01949 842192 alpaco@lineone.net www.thesaurus.co.uk/cook

ArA • Archers Addicts, The Village Voice Co Ltd, 1–117 The Custard Factory, Gibb Street, Birmingham, West Midlands B9 4AA Tel: 0121 683 1951

ArD • Art Deco Vintage Designer Tel: 01926 854745

ARo •† Alvin Ross, Pelham Puppets Tel: 01865 772409 hidden.valley@virgin.net freespace.virgin.net/hidden.valley

ASA • A. S. Antiques, 26 Broad Street, Pendleton, Salford, Greater Manchester M6 5BY Tel: 0161 737 5938

ASAA • ASA Antiques, 5–10 Bartlett Street, Bath, Somerset BA1 2QZ Tel: 01225 421037/312781

ASG • Asahi Gallery, 44A Kensington Church Street, London W8 4DB Tel: 020 8960 7299

ASH • Ashburton Marbles, Grate Hall, North Street, Ashburton, Devon TQ13 7QD Tel: 01364 653189

ATH • Apple Tree House Tel: 01694 722953

B&R •† Bread & Roses, Durham House Antique Centre, Sheep Street, Stow on the Wold, Gloucestershire GL54 1AA Tel: 01451 870404/01926 817342

BAf • Books Afloat, 66 Park Street, Weymouth, Dorset DT4 7DE Tel: 01305 779774

BAL • A.H. Baldwin & Sons Ltd, Numismatists, 11 Adelphi Terrace, London WC2N 6BJ Tel: 020 7930 6879

BaN •† Barbara Ann Newman, London House Antiques, 4 Market Square, Westerham, Kent TN16 1AW Tel: 01959 564479

BAO •† Bath Antiques Online, Bartlett Street Antiques Centre, Bartlett Street, Bath, Somerset BA1 2QZ Tel: 01225 311061 info@bathantiquesonline.com www.BathAntiquesOnline.com

BAY • George Bayntun, Manvers Street, Bath, Somerset BA1 1JW Tel: 01225 466000 EBayntun@aol.com

BBA *† Bloomsbury Book Auctions, 3 & 4 Hardwick Street, Off Rosebery Avenue, London EC1R 4RY Tel: 020 7833 2636/7 info@bloomsbury-book-auct-.com www.bloomsbury-book-auct.com

BBo • Bazaar Boxes Tel: 01992 504 454 bazaarboxes@hotmail.com commerce.icollector.com/BazaarBoxes/

BBR *† BBR, Elsecar Heritage Centre, Wath Road, Elsecar, Barnsley, Yorkshire S74 8HJ Tel: 01226 745156 sales@bbrauctions.co.uk www.onlinebbr.com

BDA • Briar's C20th Decorative Arts, Skipton Antiques & Collectors Centre, The Old Foundry, Cavendish Street, Skipton, Yorkshire BD23 2AB Tel: 01756 798641

Bea(E) * Bearnes, St Edmund's Court, Okehampton Street, Exeter, Devon EX4 1DU Tel: 01392 422800

BeG No longer trading

BEV •† Beverley, 30 Church Street/Alfie's Antique Market, Marylebone, London NW8 8EP Tel: 020 7262 1576

BEX • Daniel Bexfield Antiques, 26 Burlington Arcade, London W1V 9AD Tel: 020 7491 1720

BFR • Brian & Frances Rothery Tel: 020 8300 5410

BGC • Brenda Gerwat-Clark, Granny's Goodies, G3/4 Alfie's Antique Market, 13–25 Church Street, London NW8 8DT Tel: 020 7706 4699

BHa • Judy & Brian Harden Tel: 01451 810684

BHA • Bourbon-Hanby Antiques Centre, 151 Sydney Street, Chelsea, London SW3 6NT Tel: 020 7352 2106

BKS * Bonhams & Brooks, Montpelier Street, Knightsbridge, London SW7 1HH Tel: 020 7393 3900 www.bonhams.com

BLA • Blair Antiques, 14 Bonnethill Road, Pitlochry, Perthshire, Scotland PH16 5BS Tel: 01796 472624

BLH * BBG Ambrose, Ambrose House, Old Station Road, Loughton, Essex IG10 4PE Tel: 020 8502 3951

Bon * Bonhams & Brooks, Montpelier Street, Knightsbridge, London SW7 1HH Tel: 020 7393 3900 www.bonhams.com

Bon(C) * Bonhams & Brooks, 65–69 Lots Road, Chelsea, London SW10 0RN Tel: 020 7393 3900

Bon(W) * Bonhams & Brooks, Devon Fine Art Auction House, Dowell Street, Honiton, Devon EX14 8LX Tel: 01404 41872

BONA • Bonapartes, 13 George Street, Bath, Somerset BA1 2EN Tel: 01225 423873

BQ • The Button Queen, 19 Marylebone Lane, London W1M 5FE Tel: 020 7935 1505

BR * Bracketts, Auction Hall, Pantiles, Tunbridge Wells, Kent TN1 1UU Tel: 01892 544500

Bri * Bristol Auction Rooms, St John's Place, Apsley Road, Clifton, Bristol, Gloucestershire BS8 2ST Tel: 0117 973 7201

BRT • Britannia, Grays Antique Market, Stand 101, 58 Davies Street, London W1Y 1AR Tel: 020 7629 6772

BRU • Brunel Antiques, Bartlett Street Antiques Centre, Bath, Somerset BA1 2QZ Tel: 0117 968 1734

BrW • Brian Watson Antique Glass, Foxwarren Cottage, High Street, Marsham, Norwich NR10 5QA Tel: 01263 732519

BSA • Bartlett Street Antique Centre, 5/10 Bartlett Street, Bath, Somerset BA1 2QZ Tel: 01225 466689

BTB • Behind the Boxes, 98 Kirkdale, Sydenham, London SE26 4BG Tel: 020 8291 6116

BTC •† Beatcity, 331 High Street, Rochester, Kent ME1 1DA Tel: 01634 844525 www.beatcity.co.uk

BUR •† House of Burleigh Tel: 01664 454570 HousBurl@aol.com

BWA • Bow Well Antiques, 103 West Bow, Edinburgh, Scotland EH1 2JP Tel: 0131 225 3335

BWC British Watch & Clock Collectors Association, 5 Cathedral Lane, Truro, Cornwall TR1 2QS Tel: 01872 264010 tonybwcca@cs.com www.timecap.co.uk

BWe * Biddle and Webb Ltd, Ladywood, Middleway, Birmingham, West Midlands B16 0PP Tel: 0121 455 8042

BYG • Bygones Reclamation (Canterbury), Nackington Road, Canterbury, Kent Tel: 01227 767453

Byl • Bygones of Ireland Ltd, Lodge Road, Westport, County Mayo, Republic of Ireland Tel: 00 353 98 26132/25701

BZ Private Collection

C *† Christie, Manson & Woods Ltd, 8 King Street, St James's, London SW1Y 6QT Tel: 020 7839 9060

CAG * The Canterbury Auction Galleries, 40 Station Road West, Canterbury, Kent CT2 8AN Tel: 01227 763337

Cai • Caithness Glass Ltd, Inveralmond, Perth, Scotland PH1 3TZ Tel: 01738 637373 www.caithnessglass.co.uk

CAm •† Classic Amusements Tel: 01425 472164 pennyslot@aol.com www.classicamusements.net

CARS • C.A.R.S. (Classic Automobilia & Regalia Specialists), 4–4a Chapel Terrace Mews, Kemp Town, Brighton, East Sussex BN2 1HU Tel: 01273 60 1960

CAT • Lennox Cato, 1 The Square, Church Street, Edenbridge, Kent TN8 5BD Tel: 01732 865988

CATH • Cathac Books, 10 Duke Street, Dublin 2, Republic of Ireland Tel: 00 3531 6718676

CB • Christine Bridge Antiques, 78 Castelnau, London SW13 9EX Tel: 07000 445277

CBO • The Chaucer Bookshop, 6–7 Beer Cart Lane, Canterbury, Kent CT1 2NY Tel: 01227 453912 chaucerbooks@canterbury.dialnet.com www.chaucer-bookshop.co.uk/main.html

CBP *† Comic Book Postal Auctions Ltd, 40–42 Osnaburgh Street, London NW1 3ND Tel: 020 7424 0007 comicbook@compuserve.com www.compalcomics.com

CCB • Colin C. Bowdell, PO Box 65, Grantham, Lincolnshire NG31 6QR Tel: 01476 563206

CCC •† Crested China Co, The Station House, Driffield, Yorkshire YO25 7PY Tel: 01377 257042

CDC * Capes Dunn & Co, The Auction Galleries, 38 Charles Street, Off Princess Street, Greater Manchester M1 7DB Tel: 0161 273 6060/1911

CGC * Cheffins Grain & Comins, 2 Clifton Road, Cambridge CB2 4BW Tel: 01223 213343

CGX • Computer & Games Exchange, 65 Notting Hill Gate Road, London W11 3JS Tel: 020 7221 1123

ChA • The Chapel Antiques, The Chapel, Chapel Place, Tunbridge Wells, Kent TN1 1YR Tel: 01892 619921 chapelplace@hotmail.com

CHAP • Bill Chapman, Stand 11, Bourbon Hanby Antiques Centre, 151 Sydney Street, Chelsea, London SW3 6NT Tel: 020 7352 2106

CHU • Church Street Antiques, 2 Church Street, Wells Next the Sea, Norfolk NR23 1JA Tel: 01328 711698

CJP • Charles Jeffreys Posters & Graphics, 12 Octavia Street, London SW11 3DN Tel: 020 7978 7976 charlie@cjposters.com www.cjposters.com

CMF •† Childhood Memories, 57 Downing Street, Farnham, Surrey GU9 7PN Tel: 01252 793704 maureen@childhood-memories.co.uk www.childhood-memories.co.uk

CoA • Country Antiques (Wales), Castle Mill, Kidwelly, Carms, Wales SA17 4UU Tel: 01554 890534

COB •† Cobwebs, 78–80 Northam Road, Southampton, Hampshire SO14 0PB Tel: 023 8022 7458 www.cobwebs.uk.com

CoCo • Country Collector, 11–12 Birdgate, Pickering, Yorkshire YO18 7AL Tel: 01751 477481

CoHA •† Corner House Antiques and Ffoxe Antiques, High Street, Lechlade, Gloucestershire GL7 3AE Tel: 01367 252007

Cot • Cottage Collectibles, 62 High Street, Eccleshall, Staffordshire Tel: 01785 850210

CP •† Cat Pottery, 1 Grammar School Road, North Walsham, Norfolk NR28 9JH Tel: 01692 402962

CRN •† The Crow's Nest, 3 Hope Square, opp. Brewers Quay, Weymouth, Dorset DT4 8TR Tel: 01305 786930

CRU • Mary Cruz Antiques, 5 Broad Street, Bath, Somerset BA1 5LJ Tel: 01225 334174

CS •† Christopher Sykes, The Old Parsonage, Woburn, Milton Keynes, Bedfordshire MK17 9QM Tel: 01525 290259 www.sykes-corkscrews.co.uk

CSAC • Church Street Antiques Centre, 3–4 Church Street, Stow 0n the Wold, Gloucestershire GL54 1BB Tel: 01451 870186

CTO •† Collector's Corner, PO Box 8, Congleton, Cheshire CW12 4GD Tel: 01260 270429

CWO • Collectors World, Stand G101, G130/143 Alfies Antique Market, 13–25 Church Street, Marylebone, London NW8 8DT Tel: 020 7723 0564 collectorsworld@btinternet.com www.collectorsworld.net

CY • Carl & Yvonne Tel: 01785 606487

CYA • The Courtyard Antiques, 108A Causewayside, Edinburgh EH9 1PU Tel: 0131 662 9008

DA * Dee, Atkinson & Harrison, The Exchange Saleroom, Driffield, Yorkshire YO25 7LD Tel: 01377 253151

DAC • Didcot Antiques Centre now Trading as Yetta Decorative Arts, Oxfordshire

DAD • Decorative Arts @ Doune, Stand 26, Scottish Antique and Arts Centre, By Doune, Stirling, Scotland FK16 6HD Tel: 01786 461 439 gordonfoster@excite.co.uk fionamacsporran@btinternet.com

DAL *† Dalkeith Auctions Ltd, Dalkeith Hall, Dalkeith Steps, Rear of 81 Old Christchurch Road, Bournemouth, Dorset BH1 1YL Tel: 01202 292905 how@dalkeith-auctions.co.uk www.dalkeith-auctions.co.uk

DAN • Andrew Dando, 4 Wood Street, Queen Square, Bath, Somerset BA1 2JQ Tel: 01225 422702

DAn • Doll Antiques 0121 449 0637

DBo • Dorothy Bowler, Ely Street Antique Centre, Stratford-on-Avon, Warwickshire CV37 6LN Tel: 01789 204180

DBr • David Brown, 23 Claude Street, Larkhall, Lanarkshire, Scotland ML9 2BU Tel: 01555 880333

DD • David Duggleby, The Vine St Salerooms, Scarborough, Yorkshire YO11 1XN Tel: 01723 507111

DE •† Decades, 20 Lord St West, Blackburn, Lancashire BB2 1JX Tel: 01254 693320

DEC •† Decorative Antiques, 47 Church Street, Bishop's Castle, Shropshire SY9 5AD Tel: 01588 638851 enquiries@decorative-antiques.co.uk www.decorative-antiques.co.uk

Del • Delomosne & Son Ltd, Court Close, North Wraxall, Chippenham, Wiltshire SN14 7AD Tel: 01225 891505

DgC • Dragonlee Collectables Tel: 01622 729502

DHA • Durham House Antiques Centre, Sheep Street, Stow-on-the-Wold, Gloucestershire GL54 1AA Tel: 01451 870404

DHAR • Dave Hardman Antiques, The George Arcade, Broad Street, South Molton, Devon EX36 3AB Tel: 01769 574066

DHo • Paul Howard, Chelsea Antique Market, 245–253 King's Road, London SW3 5EL Tel: 020 7352 4113

DID • Didier Antiques, 58–60 Kensington Church Street, London W8 4DB Tel: 020 7938 2537

DN * Dreweatt Neate, Donnington Priory, Donnington, Newbury, Berkshire RG13 2JE Tel: 01635 553553

DNW *† Dix-Noonan-Webb, 1 Old Bond Street, London W1X 3TD Tel: 020 7499 5022 auction@dnw.co.uk www.dnw.co.uk

Do • Liz Farrow T/As Dodo, FO73/83 Alfie's Antique Market, Church Street, London NW8 8DT

DOL •† Dollectable, 53 Lower Bridge Street, Chester CH1 1RS Tel: 01244 344888/679195

DOR • Dorset Reclamation, Cow Drove, Bere Regis, Wareham, Dorset BH20 7JZ Tel: 01929 472200

DP • No 7 Antiques, 7 High Street, Dulverton, Somerset TA22 9HB Tel: 01398 324457

DPO • Doug Poultney, 219 Lynmouth Ave, Morden, Surrey SM4 4RX Tel: 020 8330 3472

DQ • Dolphin Quay Antique Centre, Queen Street, Emsworth, Hampshire PO10 7BU Tel: 01243 379994 www.antiquesbulletin.com/dolphinquay

DRJ • The Motorhouse, DS & RG Johnson, Thorton Hall, Thorton, Buckinghamshire MK17 0HB Tel: 01280 812280

DSG •† Delf Stream Gallery, 14 New Street, Sandwich, Kent CT13 9AB Tel: 01304 617684 www.delfstreamgallery.com

DT • David Thomas, 1 The Mews, Orchard Lane, Ledbury, Herefordshire HR8 1DX Tel: 01531 635114 www.allautobooks.com

DW *† Dominic Winter Book Auctions, The Old School, Maxwell Street, Swindon, Wiltshire SN1 5DR Tel: 01793 611340 info@dominic-winter.co.uk www.dominic-winter.co.uk

EAS • Eastgate Antiques, Stand 7/9 Alfies Antique Market, 13–25 Church Street, London NW8 8DT Tel: 077 74 206289

EDO • Evariste Doublet, 30 Rue de la Gare, 19100 Lisieux, Normandie, France Tel: 00 33 0231317979

EH * Edgar Horn Fine Art Auctioneers, 46–50 South Street, Eastbourne, East Sussex BN21 4XB Tel: 01323 410419

ERC • Zenith Antiques (Elizabeth Coupe), Hemswell Antiques Centre, Caenby Corner Estate, Hemswell Cliff, Gainsborough, Lincolnshire DN21 5TJ Tel: 01427 668389

ERCC ETB Radford Collectors' Club, 32 Westbourne Avenue, Clevedon, Somerset BS21 7UA Tel: 01371359/02392 267483

ES • Ernest R Sampson, 33 West End, Redruth, Cornwall TR15 2SA Tel: 01209 212536

ESA • East Street Antiques, 42 East Street, Crewkerne, Somerset TA18 7AG Tel: 01460 78600

ETO • Eric Tombs, 62a West Street, Dorking, Surrey RH4 1BS Tel: 01306 743661

EXC • Excalibur Antiques, Taunton Antique Centre, 27–29 Silver Street, Taunton, Somerset TA13DH Tel: 01823 289327

FA • No longer trading

Fai • Fair Finds Antiques, Rait Village Antiques Centre, Rait, Perthshire, Scotland PH2 7RT Tel: 01821 670379

FBG * Frank H Boos Gallery, 420 Enterprise Court, Bloomfield Hills, Michigan 48302 U.S.A. Tel: 001 248 332 1500

FBS Festival of Britain Society, c/o Martin Packer, 41 Lyall Gardens, Birmingham, West Midlands B45 9YW Tel: 0121 453 8245 martin@packer34.freeserve.co.uk www.packer34.freeserve.co.uk

FHF * Frank H Fellows & Sons, Augusta House, 19 Augusta Street, Hockley, Birmingham, West Midlands B18 6JA Tel: 0121 212 2131

FMa • Francesca Martire, Stand F131–137, Alfie's Antique Market, 13–25 Church Street, London NW8 0RH Tel: 020 7724 4802

FQA No longer trading

FRa • Frasers, 399 The Strand, London WC2 Tel: 020 7836 9325

FrG • The French Glasshouse, P14/16 Antiquarius, 135 King's Road, Chelsea, London SW3 4PW Tel: 020 7376 5394

G(T) * Gorringes, 15 The Pantiles, Tunbridge Wells, Kent TN2 5TD Tel: 01892 619670

G&CC † Goss & Crested China Club & Museum, incorporating Milestone Publications, 62 Murray Road, Horndean, Hampshire PO8 9JL Tel: (023) 9259 7440 info@gosschinaclub.demon.co.uk www.gosscrestedchina.co.uk

GAA • Gabrian Antiques Hertfordshire Tel: 01923 859675 gabrian.antiques@virgin.net

GaB • Garden Brocante Tel: 0118 9461905

GAD • Decodence, Gad Sassower, Shop 21 The Mall, Camden Passage, London N1 0PD Tel: 020 7354 4473/020 8458 4665 gad@decodence.demon.co.uk

GAK * Aylesham Salerooms, 8 Market Place, Aylsham, Norfolk NR11 6EH Tel: 01263 733195

GAZE * Thomas Wm Gaze & Son, Diss Auction Rooms, Roydon Road, Diss, Norfolk IP22 3LN Tel: 01379 650306

GeN •† Gentry Antiques Tel: 020 7792 1402 info@cornishwarecollector.co.uk www.cornishwarecollector.co.uk

GeW • Geoffrey Waters Ltd, F1 to F6 Antiquarius Antiques Centre, 135–141 King's Road, London SW3 4PW Tel: 020 7376 5467

GHC • Great Haul of China, PO Box 233, Sevenoaks, Kent TN13 3ZN Tel: 01732 741484

GIN • The Ginnell Gallery Antique Centre, 18–22 Lloyd Street, Greater Manchester M2 5WA Tel: 0161 833 9037

GKR •† GKR Bonds Ltd, PO Box 1, Kelvedon, Essex CO5 9EH Tel: 01376 571711

GLD • Glade Antiques, PO Box 939, Marlow, Buckinghamshire SL7 1SR Tel: 01628 487255

Gle * Glendinings & Co, 101 New Bond Street, London W1Y 9LG Tel: 020 7493 2445

GLO • Gordon Loraine Antiques, Rait Village Antiques Centre, Rait, Perthshire, Scotland PH2 7RT Tel: 01821 670760

GN • Gillian Neale Antiques, PO Box 247, Aylesbury, Buckinghamshire HP20 1JZ Tel: 01296 423754

GOH • Goya Hartogs, S001 Alfie's Antique Market, Church Street, London NW8 8DT Tel: 0788 7714477

GRa •† Grays Antique Market, 1–7 Davies Mews, London W1K 5AB Tel: 020 7629 7034 grays@clara.net www.graysantiques.com

GRI •† Grimes House Antiques, High Street, Moreton-in-Marsh, Gloucestershire GL56 0AT Tel: 01608 651029 grimes_house@cix.co.uk grimeshouse.co.uk www.cranberryglass.co.uk www.collectglass.com

GRo • Geoffrey Robinson, GO77–78 (Ground floor), Alfies Antique Market, 13–25 Church Street, Marylebone, London NW8 8DT Tel: 020 7723 0449

GTH * Greenslade Taylor Hunt Fine Art, Magdelene House, Church Square, Taunton, Somerset TA1 1SB Tel: 01823 332525

GWe • Graham Webb, 59 Ship Street, Brighton, East Sussex BN1 1AE Tel: 01273 321803

GWR • Gwen Riley, Stand 12 Bourbon Hanby Antique Centre, 151 Sydney Street, Chelsea, London SW3 6NT Tel: 020 7352 2106

HaG • Harington Glass, 2–3 Queen Street, Bath, Somerset BA1 1HE Tel: 01225 482179

HAL • John & Simon Haley, 89 Northgate, Halifax, Yorkshire HX1 1XF Tel: 01422 822148/360434

Hal * Halls Fine Art Auctions, Welsh Bridge, Shrewsbury, Shropshire SY3 8LA Tel: 01743 231212

Hal(C) * Halls Fine Art Auctions, Booth Mansion, 30 Watergate Street, Chester CH1 2LA Tel: 01244 312300/312112

HALB • Halbzwolf, Eschstrabe 21b, 32257 Bunde, Germany Tel: 00 49 05223 52 58

HALL • Hall's Nostalgia, 389 Chatham Street, Lynn, U.S.A. MA 01902 Tel: 001 781 595 7757 playball@hallsnostalgia.com www.hallsnostalgia.com

HAM * Hamptons International, 93 High Street, Godalming, Surrey GU7 1AL Tel: 01483 423567 fineart@hamptons-int.com

HaR • Mr A. Harris Tel: 020 8906 8151
HarC •† Hardy's Collectables, 862 Christchurch Road, Boscombe, Bournemouth, Dorset BH7 6DQ Tel: 01202 422407/473744
HARP •† Harpers Jewellers Ltd, 2/6 Minster Gates, York YO1 7HL Tel: 01904 632634 harplist@aol.com www.vintage-watches.co.uk
HBC * Heathcote Ball & Co, Castle Auction Rooms, 78 St Nicholas Circle, Leicester LE1 5NW Tel: 0116 253 6789 heathcote-ball@clara.co.uk www.heathcote-ball.clara.co.uk
HBo • Harrison's Books, Stand J20/21 Grays Mews Antiques Market, 1–7 Davies Street, London W1Y 2LP Tel: 020 7629 1374
HCJ • High Class Junk, 26 The Street, Appledore, Kent TN26 2BX Tel: 01233 758502
HEB • Hebeco, 47 West Street, Dorking, Surrey RH4 1BU Tel: 01306 875396
HEL • Helios Gallery, 292 Westbourne Grove, London W11 2PS Tel: 077 11 955 997 heliosgallery@btinternet.com
HGh • Hungry Ghost, 1 Brewery Yard, Sheep Street, Stow on the Wold, Gloucestershire GL54 1AA Tel: 01451 870101
HHO • Howard Hope, 21 Bridge Road, East Molesey, Surrey KT8 9EU Tel: 020 8941 2472/020 8398 7130
HOB •† Hobday Toys Tel: 01895 636737 wendyhobday@freenet.co.uk
HOP •† Maria Hopwood Antiques, Hulgrave Hall, Tiverton, Tarporley, Cheshire CW6 9UQ Tel: 01829 733313
HT • Heather's Treasures Tel: 01202 624018
HTC • Hamer 20th Century Books, 4 Springfield, Woodsetts, Worksop, Nottinghamshire S81 8QD Tel: 01909 569428 auctions@hamerbooks.co.uk
HUM • Humbleyard Fine Art, Unit 32 Admiral Vernon Arcade, Portobello Road, London W11 2DY Tel: 01362 637793
HUN • Huntercombe Manor Barn, Henley-on-Thames, Oxon RG9 5RY Tel: 01491 641349 wclegg@the countryseat.com www.thecountryseat.com
HUR • Hurst Gallery, 53 Mt. Auburn Street, Cambridge MA 02138, U.S.A. Tel: 617 491 6888 www.hurstgallery.com
HUX •† David Huxtable, Stand S03/05 (Top Floor) Alfies Antique Market, 13–25 Church Street, Marylebone, London NW8 8DT Tel: 020 7724 2200
HYD * Hy Duke & Son, Dorchester Fine Art Salerooms, Dorchester, Dorset DT1 1QS Tel: 01305 265080
ID • Identity, 100a Finsborough Road, London SW10 Tel: 020 7244 9509
IE • Imperial Echoes, The Antique Centre, 59–60 Ely Street, Stratford-upon-Avon, Warwickshire CV37 6LN Tel: 01789 204180
IM * Ibbett Mosely, 125 High Street, Sevenoaks, Kent TN13 1UT Tel: 01732 452246/456731
IQ • Ink Quest, GO58 (Ground floor) Alfies Antique Market, 13–25 Church Street, London NW8 8DT Tel: 07973 135 906 inkquest@dial.pipex.com www.inkquest.dial.pipex.com/
IS • Ian Sharp Antiques, 23 Front Street, Tynemouth, Tyne & Wear NE30 4DX Tel: 0191 296 0656

IW • Islwyn Watkins, Offa's Dyke Antique Centre, 4 High Street, Knighton, Powys, Wales LD7 1AT Tel: 01547 520145
J&J • J & J 's, Paragon Antiquities, Antiques & Collectors Market, 3 Bladud Buildings, The Paragon, Bath, Somerset BA1 5LS Tel: 01225 463715
JACK •† Michael Jackson Antiques, The Quiet Woman Antiques Centre, Southcombe, Chipping Norton, Oxfordshire OX7 5QH Tel: 01608 646262 mjcig@cards.fsnet.co.uk www.our-web-site.com/cigarette-cards
JaG • Japanese Gallery, 66d Kensington Church Street, London W8 4BY Tel: 020 7229 2034/020 7226 3347
JAK • Clive & Lynne Jackson Tel: 01242 254375
JBB • Jessie's Button Box, Bartlett Street Antique Centre, Bath, Somerset BA1 5DY Tel: 01225 310457
JBL • Judi Bland, Durham House Antique Centre, Sheep Street, Stow on the Wold, Gloucestershire GL54 1AA Tel: 01451 870404/01276 857576
JBy • Joanna Bygones, Grays Antique Market, 1–7 Davies Mews, London W1Y 2LP Tel: 020 7794 4603
JCa • J Cards, PO Box 12, Tetbury, Gloucestershire GL8 8WB Tel: 01454 238600
JE •† Julian Eade Tel: 020 8394 1515
JEA/ •† John Edwards Antiques, Aladdins Cave,
CAW 35 Upper Tything, Worcester, WR1 1JZ Tel: 01905 353840
JEB • Jenni Barke, Scottish Antique and Arts Centre, Carse of Cambus, Doune, Perthshire, Scotland FK16 6HD Tel: 01786 841203
JEZ • Jezebel, 14 Prince Albert Street, Brighton, East Sussex BN1 1HE Tel: 01273 206091
JHa • Jeanette Hayhurst Fine Glass, 32a Kensington Church Street, London W8 4HA Tel: 020 7938 1539
JHo • Jonathan Horne, 66 Kensington Church Street, London W8 4BY Tel: 020 7221 5658
JJ • Jen Jones, Pontbrendu, Llanybydder, Dyfed, Wales SA40 9UJ Tel: 01570 480610
JM * Maxwells of Wilmslow, 133A Woodford Road, Woodford, Cheshire SK7 1QD Tel: 0161 439 5182
JMC • J & M Collectables Tel: 01580 891657
JO • Jacqueline Oosthuizen, 23 Cale Street, Chelsea, London SW3 3QR Tel: 020 7352 6071
JOL • Kaizen International Ltd, 88 The High Street, Rochester, Kent ME1 1JT Tel: 01634 814132
JoV • Joe Vickers, Bartlett Street Antiques Market, Bath, Somerset BA1 2QZ
JP • Janice Paull, Beehive House, 125 Warwick Road, Kenilworth, Warwickshire CV8 1HY Tel: 01926 855253
JPr • Joanna Proops Antique Textiles & Lighting, 34 Belvedere, Lansdown Hill, Bath, Somerset BA1 5HR Tel: 01225 310795
JRe • John Read, 29 Lark Rise, Martlesham Heath, Ipswich, Suffolk IP5 7SA Tel: 01473 624897
JSM • J & S Millard Antiques, Assembly Antiques, 5–8 Saville Row, Bath, Somerset BA1 2QP Tel: 01225 469785
JU • Jukebox Showroom, 9 Park Parade, Gunnersbury Avenue, London W3 9BD Tel: 020 8992 8482/3

JuC •† Julia Craig, Bartlett Street Antiques Centre, 5–10 Bartlett Street, Bath, Somerset BA1 2QZ Tel: 01225 448202/310457

JUN •† Junktion, The Old Railway Station, New Bolingbroke, Boston, Lincolnshire PE22 7LB Tel: 01205 480068/480087

JW • Julian Wood, Exeter Antique Lighting, Cellar 15, The Quay, Exeter, Devon EX2 4AY Tel: 01392 490848

K • Kite, 15 Langton Street, Chelsea, London SW10 OJL Tel: 020 7351 2108

KEN • Alan Kenyon, PO Box 33, Port Talbot Tel: 01639 895359

KES •† Keystones, PO Box 387, Stafford ST16 3FG Tel: 01785 256648 gkey@keystones.demon.co.uk www.denbymatch.com

KIE • Netsuke, Bartlett Street Antique Centre, 5/10 Bartlett Street, Bath, Somerset BA1 2QZ Tel: 01225 464689

KJ • Katie Jones, 195 Westbourne Grove, London W11 2SB Tel: 020 7243 5600

KNI • Knight's, Cuckoo Cottage, Town Green, Alby, Norwich NR11 7HE Tel: 01263 768488

KOLN * Auction Team Koln, Postfach 50 11 19, 50971 Koln, Germany Tel: 00 49 0221 38 70 49 auction@breker.com

L * Lawrence Fine Art Auctioneers, South Street, Crewkerne, Somerset TA18 8AB Tel: 01460 73041

L(T) * Lawrence Fine Art Auctioneers, The Cornfield Hall, Magdalene Street, Taunton, Somerset TA1 1SG Tel: 01823 330567

L&L •† Linen & Lace, Shirley Tomlinson, Halifax Antiques Centre, Queens Road/Gibbet Street, Halifax, Yorkshire HX1 4LR Tel: 01422 366657

L&T * Lyon & Turnbull, 33 Broughton Place, Edinburgh, Scotland EH1 3RR Tel: 0131 557 8844

Law • Malcolm Law Collectables, Greenways Garden Centre, Bethersden, Kent Tel: 0777 3211603

LBe • Linda Bee Art Deco, Stand L18–21 Grays Antique Market, 1–7 Davies Mews, London W1Y 1AR Tel: 020 7629 5921

LeB • Le Boudoir Collectables, Bartlett Street Antique Centre, Bath, Somerset BA1 2QZ Tel: 01225 311061 www.bathantiquesonline.com

LEGE • Legend Tel: 0117 926 4637
LIB • Libra Antiques Tel: 01580 860569
LT * Louis Taylor Auctioneers & Valuers, Britannia House, 10 Town Road, Hanley Stoke on Trent, Staffordshire ST1 2QG Tel: 01782 214111

Ma • Marie Antiques, Stand G136–138 Alfie's Antique Market,13–25 Church Street, London NW8 8DT Tel: 020 7706 3727 marie136@globalnet.co.uk www.marieantiques.co.uk

MAr • Mint Arcade, 71 The Mint, Rye, East Sussex TN31 7EW Tel: 01797 225952

MARK •† 20th Century Marks, 12 Market Square, Westerham, Kent TN16 1AW Tel: 01959 562221 TCM@marks.plus.com 20thcenturymarks.co.uk

MAU • Sue Mautner, Stand P13 Antiquarius, 135 Kings Road, London SW3 4PW Tel: 020 7376 4419

MB •† Mostly Boxes, 93 High Street, Eton, Windsor, Berkshire SL4 6AF Tel: 01753 858470

MCN • MCN Antiques, 183 Westbourne Grove, London W11 2SB Tel: 020 7727 3796

MD • Much Ado About Deco, The Antiques Centre, 59–60 Ely Street, Stratford-upon- Avon, Warwickshire CV37 6LN Tel: 01789 204180

MED * Medway Auctions, Fagins, 23 High Street, Rochester, Kent ME1 1LN Tel: 01634 847444

MEM • Memories UK, Mabel Lucie Attwell Club, Abbey Antiques, 63 Great Whyte, Ramsey, Nr Huntingdon, Cambridgeshire PE26 1HL Tel: 01487 814753

MEx • Music Exchange, 21 Broad Street, Bath, Somerset BA1 5LN Music Tel: 01225 333963 Records Tel: 01225 339789

MFB • Manor Farm Barn Antiques Tel: 01296 658941 mfbn@btinternet.com btwebworld.com/mfbantiques

MG • Music Ground, 51 Hallgate, Doncaster, Yorkshire DN1 3PB Tel: 01302 320186

MGC • Midlands Goss & Commemoratives, The Old Cornmarket Antiques Centre, 70 Market Place, Warwick CV34 4SO Tel: 01926 419119

Mit * Mitchells, Fairfield House, Station Road, Cockermouth, Cumbria CA13 9PY Tel: 01900 827800

MLa • Marion Langham Tel: 020 7730 1002 mlangham@globalnet.co.uk ladymarion@btinternet.co.uk

MLL • Millers Antiques Ltd, Netherbrook House, 86 Christchurch Road, Ringwood, Hampshire BH24 1DR Tel: 01425 472062

MMa No longer trading
MRW • Malcolm Welch Antiques, Wild Jebbett, Pudding Bag Lane, Thurlaston, Nr. Rugby, Warwickshire CV23 9JZ Tel: 01788 810 616

MSB • Marilynn and Sheila Brass, PO Box 380503, Cambridge, U.S.A. MA 02238-0503 Tel: 617 491 6064

MTa • Maggie Tallentire, Mas De Pierrou, Saillagol 82160, St Projet, France Tel: 0033(0)5 63 24 05 27

MTM • More than Music, PO Box 68, Westerham, Kent TN16 1ZF Tel: +44 (0) 1959 56 55 14 morethnmus@aol.com www.mtmglobal.com

MUL *† Mullock & Madeley, The Old Shippon, Wall-under-Heywood, Nr Church Stretton, Shropshire SY6 7DS Tel: 01694 771771 auctions@mullockmadeley.co.uk www.mullockmadeley.co.uk

MUR •† Murray Cards (International) Ltd, 51 Watford Way, Hendon Central, London NW4 3JH Tel: 020 8202 5688 murraycards@ukbusiness.com www.murraycards.com/

MURR • Murrays' Antiques & Collectables Tel: 01202 309094

MVX • Music & Video Exchange, 1st Floor 38 Notting Hill Gate, London W11 3HX Tel: 020 7243 8574

NAR • Colin Narbeth & Son Ltd, 20 Cecil Court, Leicester Square, London WC2N 4HE Tel: 020 7379 6975

NC • The Nautical Centre, Harbour Passage, Hope Square, Weymouth, Dorset DT4 8TR Tel: 01305 777838

NCA • New Century, 69 Kensington Church Street, London W8 4DB Tel: 020 7937 2410/020 7376 2810

NDCR • North Devon China Restoration Tel: 01805 624936

NET • Nettlebed Antique Merchants, 1 High Street, Nettlebed, Henley on Thames, Oxfordshire RG9 5DA Tel: 07770 554559/01491 642062

NEW • Newsum Antiques, 2 High Street, Winchcombe, Gloucestershire GL54 5HT Tel: 01242 603446/07968 196668

NG Natalie Giltsoff

NOST • Nostalgia, Hollands Mill, 61 Shaw Heath, Stockport, Cheshire SK3 8BH Tel: 0161 477 7706

OCAC • Old Cornmarket Antiques Centre, 70 Market Place, Warwick CV34 4SO Tel: 01926 419119

OCB • The Old Children's Bookshelf, 175 Canongate, Edinburgh, Scotland EH8 8BN Tel: 0131 558 3411

OCH • Gillian Shepherd, Old Corner House Antiques, 6 Poplar Road, Wittersham, Tenterden, Kent TN30 7PG Tel: 01797 270236

OD • Offa's Dyke Antique Centre, 4 High Street, Knighton, Powys, Wales LD7 1AT Tel: 01547 520145

OE • Orient Expressions, Assembly Antiques Centre, 5–8 Saville Row, Bath, Somerset BA1 2QP Tel: 01225 313399

Oli * Olivers, Olivers Rooms, Burkitts Lane, Sudbury, Suffolk CO10 1HB Tel: 01787 880305

OLM • The Old Mill, High Street, Lamberhurst, Kent TN3 8EQ Tel: 01892 891196

ONS • Onslow's, The Depot, 2 Michael Road, London SW6 2AD Tel: 020 7371 0505

ONY • Onyx Music, 7 The Corridor, Bath, Somerset Tel: 01225 460945

OO • Pieter Oosthuizen, Unit 4 Bourbon Hanby Antiques Centre, 151 Sydney Street, London SW3 6NT Tel: 020 7460 3078

OPB • Olde Port Bookshop, 18 State Street, Newburyport, Massachusetts 01950, USA Tel: 001 978 462 0100 Oldeport@ttlc.net

OTB •† Old Tackle Box, PO Box 55, High Street, Cranbrook, Kent TN17 3ZU Tel: 01580 713979

OTC •† The Old Telephone Company, The Old Granary, Battlesbridge Antiques Centre, Nr Wickford, Essex SS11 7RF Tel: 01245 400601 www.theoldtelephone.co.uk

OTT • Otter Antiques, 20 High Street, Wallingford, Oxfordshire OX10 0BP Tel: 01491 825544

OVE • Chuck Overs

OW • Off World, Unit 20, Romford Shopping Halls, Market Place, Romford, Essex RM1 3AT Tel: 01708 765633/01908 240365

P *† Phillips, Blenstock House, 101 New Bond Street, London W1Y 0AS Tel: 020 7629 6602/7468 8233 www.phillips-auctions.com

P(B) * Phillips, 1 Old King Street, Bath, Somerset BA1 2JT Tel: 01225 310609

P(Ba) * Phillips Bayswater, 10 Salem Road, Bayswater, London W2 4DL Tel: 020 7229 9090

P(NW) * Phillips North West, New House, 150 Christleton Road, Chester CH3 5TD Tel: 01244 313936

P(Sc) * Phillips Scotland, The Beacon, 176 St Vincent Street, Glasgow, Scotland G2 5SG Tel: 0141 223 8866

P(WM) * Phillips, The Old House, Station Road, Knowle, Solihull, West Midlands B93 0HT Tel: 01564 776151

PAB • Paolo Bonino, Stand S001 Alfies Antique Market, 13–25 Church Street, London NW8 8DT Tel: 04674 98766/020 7624 2481

PAC •† The Potteries Antique Centre, 271 Waterloo Road, Cobridge, Stoke on Trent, Staffordshire ST6 3HR Tel: 01782 201455 www@potteriesantiquecentre.com www.potteriesantiquecentre.com

PBr • Pamela Brooks Tel: 0116 230 2625

PC Private Collection

PFK * Penrith Farmers' & Kidd's plc, Skirsgill Salerooms, Penrith, Cumbria CA11 0DN Tel: 01768 890781

PGA • Paul Gibbs Antiques, 25 Castle Street, Conway, Gwynedd, Wales LL32 8AY Tel: 01492 593429/596533

PIC • David & Susan Pickles Tel: 01282 707673

PIL • Pilgrim Antique Centre, 7 West Street, Dorking, Surrey RH4 Tel: 01306 875028

PJo • Paul Jones, The Quiet Woman Antiques Centre, Southcombe, Chipping Norton, Oxfordshire OX7 5QH Tel: 01608 646262

PLB •† Planet Bazaar, 149 Drummond Street, London NW1 2PB Tel: 020 7387 8326 maureen@planetbazaar.demon.co.uk www.planetbazaar.co.uk

POSH • Posh Tubs, Moriati's Workshop, High Halden, Ashford, Kent TN26 3LZ Tel: 01233 850155

PPH • Period Picnic Hampers Tel: 0115 937 2934

PrB •† Pretty Bizarre, 170 High Street, Deal, Kent CT14 6BQ Tel: 07973 794537

PSY •† Psychemania 67, PO Box 640, Sutton, Surrey SM1 4YL Tel: 01953 602872 psyche67@popposter67.co.uk www.popposter67.co.uk

PVD • Puritan Values at the Dome Art & Antiques Centre, St Edmunds Business Park, St Edmunds Road, Southwold, Suffolk IP18 6BZ Tel: 01502 722211 Puritanart@aol.com

Q&C • Q&C Militaria, 22 Suffolk Road, Cheltenham, Gloucestershire GL50 2AQ Tel: 01242 519815 john@qc-militaria.freeserve.co.uk www.qcmilitaria.com

Ram/ BTM • Rambo's Tattoo Studio, 42 Shudehill, Greater Manchester M4 1EY Tel: 0161 839 0090

RAR * Romsey Auction Rooms, 86 The Hundred, Romsey, Hampshire SO51 8BX Tel: 01794 513331

RAT • Room at the Topp, 1st Floor Antiques Warehouse, Glass Street, Hanley, Stoke on Trent, Staffordshire ST1 2ET Tel: 01782 752310

RBA •† Roger Bradbury Antiques, Church Street, Coltishall, Norfolk NR12 7DJ Tel: 01603 737444

RdeR • Rogers de Rin, 76 Royal Hospital Road, London SW3 4HN Tel: 020 7352 9007

RDG • Richard Dennis Gallery, 144 Kensington Church Street, London W8 4BN Tel: 020 7727 2061

RdV • Sudbury Antiques, Roger de Ville, Derbyshire Tel: 01889 564311

RECL • Reclamation Services Ltd, Cirencester Road, Aston Down, Minchinhampton, Stroud, Gloucestershire Tel: 01452 814064 rsltd@recserv.demon.co.uk www.recserv.demon.co.uk

REEL • The Reel Poster Gallery, 72 Westbourne Grove, London W2 5SH Tel: 020 7727 4488

REG • No longer trading

RIA • Riverside Antiques, 60 Ely Street, Stratford-upon-Avon, Warwickshire Tel: 01789 262090

RMC •† Romsey Medal Centre, PO Box 169, Romsey, Hampshire SO51 6XU Tel: 01794 324488 post@romseymedals.co.uk www.romseymedals.co.uk

ROU • Route One, Broad Street, Bath, Somerset BA1 5L2

RTo * Rupert Toovey & Co Ltd, Star Road, Partridge Green, West Sussex RH13 8RJ Tel: 01403 711744

RTT • Rin Tin Tin, 34 North Road, Brighton, East Sussex BN1 1YB Tel: 01273 672424/733689

RTW •† Richard Twort Tel: 01934 641900

RUL • Rules Antiques, 62 St Leonards Road, Windsor, Berkshire SL4 3BY Tel: 01753 833210/01491 642062

RUS • Trevor Russell, PO Box 1258, Uttoxeter, Staffordshire ST14 8XL

RUSK •† Ruskin Decorative Arts, 5 Talbot Court, Stow-on-the-Wold Cheltenham, Gloucestershire GL54 1DP Tel: 01451 832254

S * Sotheby's, 34–35 New Bond Street, London W1A 2AA Tel: 020 7293 5000

S(NY) * Sotheby's, 1334 York Avenue, New York, U.S.A. NY 10021 Tel: 00 1 212 606 7000

S(S) * Sotheby's Sussex, Summers Place, Billingshurst, West Sussex RH14 9AD Tel: 01403 833500

SAA/ SAAC • Scottish Antique and Arts Centre, Carse of Cambus, Doune, Perthshire, Scotland FK16 6HD Tel: 01786 841203

Sama • Samax, Bartlett Street Antiques Centre, 5–10 Bartlett Street, Bath, Somerset BA1 2QZ Tel: 01225 466689

SAN • Steven F. Anton Antiques & Collectables, Scottish Antique and Arts Centre, Carse of Cambus, Doune, Perthshire, Scotland FK16 6HD Tel: 01786 841203/01383 860520

SAS *† Special Auction Services, The Coach House, Midgham Park, Reading, Berkshire RG7 5UG Tel: 0118 971 2949 www.invaluable.com/sas/

Sck * Stockholms Auktionsverk, Jakobsgaten 10, PO Box 16256, S-103 25 Stockholm, Sweden Tel: 0046 8 453 67 00

SCM • Scarabond & The Moon, Scottish Antique and Arts Centre, Carse of Cambus, Doune, Perthshire, Scotland FK16 6HD Tel: 01786 841203

SCO • Peter Scott, Stand 39 Bartlett Street Antiques Centre, Bath, Somerset BA1 2QZ Tel: 01225 310457 or 0117 986 8468

SCP Scholastic Press, Commonwealth house, 1–19 Oxford Street, London WC11NU Tel: 020 7421 9000

SEA • Mark Seabrook Antiques, 9 West End, West Haddon, Northamptonshire NN6 7AY Tel: 01788 510772

SEE •† Liz Seeber, Old Cookery, Food & Wine Books, Apple Tree Cottage, High Street, Barcombe, Nr Lewes, East Sussex BN8 5DH Tel: 01273 401485 seeber.books@virgin.net www.lizseeberbooks.co.uk

SER • Serendipity, 125 High Street, Deal, Kent CT14 6BQ Tel: 01304 369165/366536

SEY • Mike Seymour, The Directors Cut, The Antiques Centre, Ely Street, Stratford-upon-Avon, Warwickshire CV37 6LN Tel: 07931 345784 mike@seymour.gsbusiness.co.uk

SK * Skinner Inc, The Heritage On The Garden, 63 Park Plaza, Boston, U.S.A. MA 02116 Tel: 001 617 350 5400

SK(B) * Skinner Inc, 357 Main Street, Bolton, U.S.A. MA 01740 Tel: 001 978 779 6241

SLL • Sylvanna LLewelyn Antiques, Unit 5 Bourbon-Hanby Antiques Centre, 151 Sydney Street, Chelsea, London SW3 6NT Tel: 020 7598 1278

SMI • Skip & Janie Smithson Tel: 01754 810265

SMW •† Sporting Memorabilia of Warwick, 13 Market Place, Warwick CV34 4FS Tel: 01926 410600 sales@sportantiques.com sportsantiques.com

SOL *† Solent Railwayana Auctions, 31 Newtown Road, Warsash, Hampshire SO31 9FY Tel: 01489 578093/584633

SOM • Somervale Antiques, 6 Radstock Road, Midsomer Norton, Bath, Somerset BA3 2AJ Tel: 01761 412686 ronthomas@somervaleantiquesglass.co.uk www.somervaleantiquesglass.co.uk

SOO • Soo San, 117 Stephendale Road, London SW6 2PS Tel: 020 7731 8989

SpM • Sparkle Moore, The Girl Can't Help It!/Cad Van Swankster, G100 & G116 Ground Floor Alfies Antique Market, 13–25 Church Street, Marylebone, London NW8 8DT Tel: 020 7724 8984/0208 809 3923 sparkle.moore@virgin.net www.grays.clara.net

SpP *† Specialised Postcard Auctions, 25 Gloucester Street, Cirencester, Gloucestershire GL7 2DJ Tel: 01285 659057

SPT • Sporting Times Gone By Tel: 01903 885656 www.sportingtimes.co.uk

SPU • Spurrier-Smith Antiques, 28, 30, 39 Church Street, Ashbourne, Derbyshire DE6 1AJ Tel: 01335 343669/342198

SQA • Squirrel Antiques, Scottish Antique and Arts Centre, Carse of Cambus, Doune, Perthshire, Scotland FK16 6HD Tel: 01786 841203

SRA *† Sheffield Railwayana Auctions, 43 Little Norton Lane, Sheffield, Yorkshire S8 8GA Tel: 0114 274 5085 ian@sheffrail.freeserve.co.uk www.sheffieldrailwayana.co.uk

StC •† St Clere Carlton Ware, PO Box 161, Sevenoaks, Kent TN15 6GA Tel: 01474 853630 stclere@aol.com www.stclere.co.uk

STE •† Stevenson Brothers, The Workshop, Ashford Road, Bethersden, Ashford, Kent TN26 3AP Tel: 01233 820363 sale@stevensonbros.com www.stevensonbros.com

STP •† Stevie Pearce, G144 Ground Floor Alfies Antique Market, 13–25 Church Street, Marylebone, London NW8 8DT Tel: 020 7723 2526 Stevie@steviepearce.co.uk www.SteviePearce.co.uk

STS • Shaw to Shore, Church Street Antiques Centre, Stow on the Wold, Gloucestershire GL54 1BB Tel: 01451 870186

SVB • Steve VeeBransgrove, 6 Catherine Hill, Frome, Somerset BA11 1BY Tel: 01373 453225

SWB •† Sweetbriar Gallery, Robin Road Lane, Helsby, Cheshire WA6 9NH Tel: 01928 723851 sweetbr@globalnet.co.uk www.sweetbriar.co.uk

SWO * G E Sworder & Sons, 14 Cambridge Road, Stansted Mountfitchet, Essex CM24 8BZ Tel: 01279 817778

TAC • Tenterden Antiques Centre, 66–66A High Street, Tenterden, Kent TN30 6AU Tel: 01580 765655/765885

TB • Millicent Safro, Tender Buttons, 143 E.62nd Street, New York NY10021, U.S.A. Tel: (212) 758 7004

TBoy • Toy Boy, G64–65 Alfies Antique Market, 13–25 Church Street, Marylebone, London NW8 8DT Tel: 020 7723 5613

TCG • 20th Century Glass, Kensington Church Street Antique Centre, 58–60 Kensington Church Street, London W8 4DB Tel: 020 7938 1137/020 7729 9875

TED •† Teddy Bears of Witney, 99 High Street, Witney, Oxfordshire OX8 6LY Tel: 01993 702616

TF * Tayler & Fletcher, London House, High Street, Bourton-on-the-Water, Cheltenham, Gloucestershire GL54 2AP Tel: 01451 821666

TH •† Tony Horsley Tel: 01273 550770

THOM • S & A Thompson Tel: 01306 711970

TMA *† Brown & Merry, Tring Market Auctions, Brook Street, Tring, Hertfordshire HP23 5EF Tel: 01442 826446

TMi • T. J. Millard Antiques, Assembly Antiques, 5–8 Saville Row, Bath, Somerset BA1 2QP Tel: 01225 448488

TO •† Tombland Antique Centre, Augustine Steward House, 14 Tombland, Norwich NR3 1HF Tel: 01603 619129

TOM •† Charles Tomlinson Tel: 01244 318395 Charles.Tomlinson@lineone.net lineone.net/-Charles.Tomlinson

TOT •† Totem, 168 Stoke Newington, Church Street, London N16 0JL Tel: 020 7275 0234

TOY No longer trading

TPCS † Torquay Pottery Collectors' Society, Torre Abbey, Avenue Road, Torquay, Devon TQ2 5JX tpcs@btinternet.com www.scandyonline.com

TRA •† Tramps, Tuxford Hall, Lincoln Road, Tuxford, Newark, Nottinghamshire NG22 0HR Tel: 01777 872 543 info@trampsuk.com www.trampsuk.com

TRL/ * Thomson, Roddick & Metcalf, 60 Whitesands,
TRM Dumfries, Scotland DG1 2RS Tel: 01387 255586

TT • Treasures in Textiles Tel: 01244 328968

TWa • Time Warp, c/o Curioser & Curioser, Sydney Street, Brighton, East Sussex BN1 Tel: 01273 821243

TWr • Tim Wright Antiques, Richmond Chambers, 147 Bath Street, Glasgow, Scotland G2 4SQ Tel: 0141 221 0364

UNI • Unicorn Antique Centre, 2 Romney Enterprise Centre, North Street, New Romney, Kent TN28 8DW Tel: 01797 361940

V&S No longer trading

VB •† Variety Box, 16 Chapel Place, Tunbridge Wells, Kent TN1 1YQ Tel: 01892 531868

VCL •† Vintage Cameras Ltd, 256 Kirkdale, Sydenham, London SE26 4NL Tel: 020 8778 5416 info@vintagecameras.co.uk www.vintagecameras.co.uk

VEY • Paul Veysey Tel: 01452 790672 www.drivepast.com

VH • Valerie Howard, 4 Campden Street, Off Kensington Church Street, London W8 7EP Tel: 020 7792 9702

VINE • Vine Antiques Tel: 01235 812708

VS *† T. Vennett-Smith, 11 Nottingham Road, Gotham, Nottinghamshire NG11 0HE Tel: 0115 983 0541 info@vennett-smith.com

WAB •† Warboys Antiques, Old Church School, High Street, Warboys, Huntingdon, Cambridgeshire PE17 2SX Tel: 01487 823686

WAC • Worcester Antiques Centre, Reindeer Court, Mealcheapen Street, Worcester WR1 4DF Tel: 01905 610680

Wai • Peter Wain, Glynde Cottage, Longford, Market Drayton, Shropshire TF9 3PW Tel: 01630 639613

WAL *† Wallis & Wallis, West Street Auction Galleries, Lewes, East Sussex BN7 2NJ Tel: 01273 480208 auctions@wallisandwallis.co.uk www.wallisandwallis.co.uk

WBH * Walker, Barnett & Hill, Waterloo Road Salerooms, Clarence Street, Wolverhampton, West Midlands WV1 4JE Tel: 01902 773531

WD * Weller & Dufty Ltd, 141 Bromsgrove Street, Birmingham, West Midlands B5 6RQ Tel: 0121 692 1414 wellerdufty@freewire.co.uk www.welleranddufty.co.uk

WeA • Wenderton Antiques Tel: 01227 720295

WEL • Wells Reclamation & Co, Coxley, Nr Wells, Somerset BA5 1RQ Tel: 01749 677087/677484

WilP * BBG Wilson Peacock, 26 Newnham Street, Bedford MK40 3JR Tel: 01234 266366

WIM • Wimpole Antiques, Stand 349 Grays Antique Market, South Molton Lane, London W1Y 2LP Tel: 020 7499 2889

WO • Woodville Antiques, The Street, Hamstreet, Ashford, Kent TN26 2HG Tel: 01233 732981

Woo Woolworths

WP •† British Notes, PO Box 257, Sutton, Surrey SM3 9WW Tel: 020 8641 3224 pamwestbritnotes@compuserve.com www.west-banknotes.co.uk

WRe • Walcot Reclamations, 108 Walcot Street, Bath, Somerset BA1 5BG Tel: 01225 444404

WSM •† Wimbledon Sewing Machine Co Ltd and The London Sewing Machine Museum, 292–312 Balham High Road, Upper Tooting, London SW17 7AA Tel: 020 8767 4724 wimbledonsewingmachinecoltd@btinternet.com www.sewantique.com

WW * Woolley & Wallis, 51–61 Castle Street, Salisbury, Wiltshire SP1 3SU Tel: 01722 424500/01722 411854

WWY •† When We were Young, The Old Forge, High Street, Harmondsworth Village, Middlesex UB7 0AQ Tel: 020 8897 3583 www.whenwewereyoung.co.uk

YC •† Yesterday Child, Angel Arcade, 118 Islington High Street, London N1 8EG Tel: 020 7354 1601

YEST • Yesterday's, V.O.F. Yesterday's, Maaseikerweg 202, 6006 AD Weert, The Netherlands Tel: 0475 531207

YO • Martin Burton, 201 Hull Road, York YO10 3JY Tel: 01904 415347 yoyomonster@jugglers.net

YR • Yorkshire Relics of Haworth, 11 Main Street, Haworth, Yorkshire BD22 8DA Tel: 01535 642218

ZOOM •† Zoom, Arch 65 Cambridge Grove, Hammersmith, London W6 Tel: 07000 9666 2001 eddiesandham@hotmail.com www.retrozoom.com

Index to Advertisers

Index

Italic page numbers denote colour pages; **bold** numbers refer to information and pointer boxes

Collect it!